LIGHTNING STRIKING

TEN TRANSFORMATIVE MOMENTS IN ROCK AND ROLL

LENNY KAYE

ecco

An Imprint of HarperCollins*Publishers*

HarperCollins books may be purchased for educational, business, or sales
promotional use. For information, please email the Special Markets Department at SPsales@harpercollins.com.

Ecco® and HarperCollins® are trademarks of HarperCollins Publishers.

A continuation of this page, with credits and permissions, appears on
page 449.

FIRST EDITION

Library of Congress Cataloging-in-Publication Data has been applied for.

ISBN 978–0–06–244920–7

22 23 24 25 26 LSC 10 9 8 7 6 5 4 3 2 1

LIGHTNING STRIKING

For Rylan and Emmet
My Rock and My Roll

Lightning is striking
Again and again and again and again

—LOU CHRISTIE

CONTENTS

INTRODUCTION

I WAS BORN WITH ROCK AND ROLL.

One of my earliest memories is hearing Little Richard's "Tutti Frutti" over the radio in our Brooklyn apartment, rolling on the floor in uncontrollable laughter and joy in its infectious, unbridled release and madness.

I grew up with rock and roll.

The music marks each stage of my awareness, a life lived in parallel with its intimations of immortality. It has charged and challenged the way I perceive and understand the world about me, continuously renewing vows taken at the junction where the spark of a vibrating guitar string jumps the gap to a magnetic pickup and becomes electricity.

I grow old with rock and roll, traversing its leap to faith over a lifetime spent in quest of *Spinal Tap's* mystical 11, turning it uppermost.

The odds of being struck by lightning are 300,000 to 1. I think that's an underestimate. I've been struck by lightning many a time, many a place.

||||||

EVERYWHERE MAKES MUSIC. Everywhen makes music. But where and when space and time align, undercurrents spinning into whirlpools, stars binarying, trends signifying and amplifying, a mile marker notches the road map of musical cartography. An energy locus. In these key moments, each with its inner dynamics and outer radiances, flashpoints irradiate station and crossroad, border and bridge, the beginning of again.

Lightning Striking traces rock and roll's geographic and temporal journey, its *kulturati* impact and shifts in style and identity, as it moves from epicenter to epicenter, the stopovers where music evolves and renews, distinct with elements of chance, cunning, inspired personalities, major players, hustlers, and bystanders.

The impulse to convert sound waves and microtones into repeatable scales, a heartbeat into recognizable rhythms, at times adding word-based lyrics or "singing" beyond lyrics, defines cities of ethni- and filters emotions. Music accompanies, commemorates, backtracks, and soundtracks, fills silence in the air, and moves us consciously or unconsciously whether we're listening or not. Shapes of sounds, how they're made, their tonal quality, the instruments chosen to express, the blend of different sources and the way an octave splits its defining notes; this belongs to the moment. As Lerner and Lowe put it in their ode to dimensional mating, *Who Knows Where or When.*

Each time and place, no matter how unique, offers a similar narrative of invention and diaspora on the way to mutation. There is an onrush of accidental-on-purpose discovery, of insular triumph, and then archetype, after which decadence. Like the moral fable of empires, this ebb and flow spirals a staircase ascending or descending, depending on taste and circumstance. Musical generations usually have a life span of half a decade, with most of the action happening in the terrible two's. *Catch 'em while you can.*

These conflagrations usually begin as a consequence from what came before; reactively predicated. Old guard, new guard, each feeling they're the guard dogs of future past. Nineteen seventies Nashville countrypolitan, with its sleek strings and carefully contained contraries, schisms into outlaw country; the pole-dance of 1980s hair metal gives way to shambolic grunge in the 1990s. Does rock and roll even exist anymore or is it a continuum of revival?

Within each scenario, musically inclined characters intermingle, form alliances, give each other encouragement and head, dream up a mood and performance that reflects cultish identifiers, garb and gadget, guitar tone and preferred aphrodisiac; and gathers a like-minded audience. Those onstage mirror those off, evening the odds. The moment calls forth a mood-swing pendulum hardening into definable style, eventually becoming the cliché that will mark it in the future, even though it's still a-borning. Outlanders and immigrants infiltrate hit charts as they step into the spotlight, planting seeds of demise in their ascendance.

Change never arrives unbidden. Mainstream and substrata inextricably mix, helped along by wild-card prophets and profiteers, who sometimes can't stop long enough to realize what they're doing, or realize it all too well, understanding after the fact.

Most social histories, this one included, usually work from the top down, the visionary artists who embody transformation. Brian Eno, speaking at the Sydney Luminous Festival in 2009, upends this concept with what he calls *scenius*, ". . . the intelligence and the intuition of a whole cultural scene. It is the communal form of the concept of genius." He adds, "Let's forget the idea of 'genius' . . . let's think about the whole ecology of ideas that give rise to good new thoughts and good new work." Not only epic characters, but those hovering off-frame, there for the instamatic and then gone.

||||||

WISHING I COULD BE THERE.

I've always been drawn to a scene, its shared togetherness, its come-hither weave, its stars, its character actors and bit players. To feel the adrenaline rush of excitement and possibility as convergence coalesces into where-it's-at. What was it like on Fifty-Second Street in Manhattan, when jazz clubs lined the block in the late 1940s, and the high-flying sounds of bebop came out of the Onyx and the Three Deuces; or when, after hours, the goateed gang would gather at the Baroness Nica de Koenigswarter's suite at the Stanhope Hotel and she would ask them their three wishes. How did it feel carrying an acoustic guitar along that much hitchhiked song-and-cinema intersection of Bleecker and MacDougal in the folk sixties? The something's happening here that Buffalo Springfield caught in the air when Los Angeles rioted on the Sunset Strip? Or more revealing to my own lifeline, what was it like tripping in San Francisco on that New Year's Eve ushering in 1967, when the Grateful Dead, the Jefferson Airplane, and Quicksilver Messenger Service headlined the Fillmore. The poster on my New Jersey wall from that show, bought at an East Village psychedelic shop, made me want to journey there, to see its beacon firsthand.

Then, as luck and the alignment of the stars would have it, I entered my own scene, which centered on CBGB, a small Bowery bar in Manhattan in the mid-seventies, and became the place I'd always wished I'd be.

What was it like? The had-to-be of there. To play your part. Going somewhere as it meets arrival, crossing the porous border between past and future when music is remade in its own image.

||||||

BY THEN, EVERYONE IS BEMOANING *shoulda-been-here-when.* When it was only spending the night at the local, cold beer, importuning, watching who cavorts in front of you. At the Cavern, the Grande, CBGB, the Roxy, other stations of my particular cross to bear. My route chosen; or did my route choose me, from the music I learned to play, the space-time crossroads where I grew up, when I came of age, race-religion-gender, my fault lines and high times, the reveal of who I'd be. "Definitions define limit," Mayo of the Red Krayola taught me on *The Parable of Arable Land* in 1967, all my yet ahead. I identify *rock and roll* when asked, but that's just ancestry. *I sing all kinds,* as Elvis will say in a couple of pages.

You can't be everywhere at once. Sometimes it doesn't matter if you're there or not. Kool Herc on a Bronx playground, Fugazi at D.C.'s 9:30 Club, Green Day at Gilman Street, that Happy Mondays all-nighter at the Hacienda in Manchester; Lagos, Kingston, Koln. Maybe next pilgrimage. There is always refraction, heard and misheard from afar.

You, making a loud noise in the night.

A strobe of incandescent bolt.

Count the seconds from flash to thunder. That's how long it lasts. And then the storm.

Lightning. To be filled with light.

CLEVELAND
1952

START A RIOT.

The Arena on Euclid, March 21, spring's first full day. The Moondog Coronation Ball, hosted by WJW disc jockey Alan Freed (*"He spins 'em keed / He's HEP that Freed"*) has brought Paul Williams and the Hucklebuckers, Tiny Grimes and His Rockin' Highlanders, Billy Ward's Dominoes, Varetta Dillard, and Danny Cobb to town. The highlight will be the crowning of a teenage king and queen chosen from the audience, and a chance for Freed to connect with his Moondoggers, the increasingly biracial tune-ins to 850 AM for his late-night slot starting at 11:15.

The bill promises a raucous time, but except for the Dominoes, who have the coital "Sixty Minute Man" topping the r&b charts the year before, most are between or awaiting hits, another night on the endless road, Flexible bus by the backstage door on the way to the next stop. Three nights ago they were an hour outside of Cleveland in Meyers Lake; tomorrow they head up to Detroit, where Williams was discovered. Paul provides the house band, named after his 1949 dance hit, "The Hucklebuck," based on a riff by Charlie Parker from Bird's 1945 session for Savoy, "Now's The Time." Tiny Grimes, a four-string tenor guitarist, has Parker solo over his 1944 "Romance Without Finance," also on Savoy: the bebop roots of rock and roll. What Freed—*Blues, Rhythm, Jazz*—spins has bebop's frantic energy, but it never leaves the dance floor.

Freed plays records supplied to him by Leo Mintz, whose Record Rendezvous on Prospect Avenue has been recycling used jukebox 78s since 1939. He specializes in releases of the many independent labels fanned out across the country, musics not fit for the pop charts: blues, country and western, salvation, crackpots. In 1951 Mintz sponsors Freed on WJW's 50,000 clear channel watts, covering most of the upper Midwest, starting from the premise that you play the records, I sell 'em. Alan insists on featuring original r&b hits before they are made over by white artists, pumping up the show's frenzy with howls and hollers, keeping time on a phone book, and finds a crossover audience of white listeners who want the real thing. Shared publishing royalties and promotional payments might be involved, along with other tempting inducements, but that's the music business as usual. Who knows where a hit begins?

The broadened appeal requires a signifier to set it apart, to reflect newness and novelty. Rock and Roll: fraternal syllables made for each other, twin *r*'s, the first clipped, the second a sigh of breath. Countless are the sightings: a Male Quartette at "The Camp Meeting Jubilee" in 1910 (*rock and roll me in your arms*); Trixie Smith in 1922 with "My Man Rocks Me (with One Steady Roll)"; the Boswell Sisters' "Rock and Roll" in the 1934 movie *Transatlantic Merry-Go-Round*; Buddy Jones's 1939 "Rockin' Rollin' Mama"; Wild Bill Moore's 1948 "We're Gonna Rock, We're Gonna Roll." Freed and Mintz take the mate and give it a married name.

It would've been a memorable show. Varetta Dillard, on crutches, undeterred by a childhood congenital bone illness, sassing it up, her next year's hit of "Mercy Mr. Percy" in the wings.

Danny Cobb, born in Greensboro, North Carolina, winner of a talent contest at the Baby Grand in New York in 1950 when he was nineteen. He's the "boy singer" in Williams's band, a shouter in the Wynonie Harris tradition, and he's already cut a record, also on Savoy, with Williams: "I'm So Happy." He has a Latin tinge, the mambo-phonic of "Hey Isabella" coming in 1955 and burlesque humor with his 1957 "Hey Mr. Warden," where he requests dinosaur eggs for his last meal. Search and ye shall find.

Clyde McPhatter is the voice of the Dominoes, though bassist Bill Brown takes the lead on "Sixty Minute Man"—*I rock 'em roll 'em all night long*—and takes leave of the group after it's a hit when Ward's penny-pinching discipline proves unbearable. Billy handpicked the group, played piano and arranged, but he had been in the military and ran *his* Dominoes like a drill sergeant. Members were confined to their hotel rooms after a show, chronically underpaid, required to drink a glass of milk each night. In the wake of their un-appearance at the Cleveland Arena, they release "Have Mercy Baby" in April, a secular conversion from the gospel "Have Mercy Jesus." A year later Clyde will quit the Dominoes to lead the Drifters; his replacement is an ex-boxer named Jackie Wilson.

Grimes is an interesting anomaly, a tenor electric guitar player—four strings, "'cause I couldn't afford the other two"—amid all the honking saxophones, a progeny of Charlie Christian who doesn't adhere to the roughened guttural amplification of Chicago blues when he goes r&b. He has a 1949 hit with the Scottish chestnut "Loch Lomond"—*You take the high road, I'll take the low road*—and it's a choice many jazz musicians have to make postwar, to go for the hit parade or explore the new innovations coming out of West Fifty-Second Street. Grimes has a deft and dexterous touch on the guitar, easily able to keep pace with Art Tatum's keyboard flourishes in the early forties, but r&b wants it simple, subtracting notes where bebop multiplies the harmonies.

Tiny burlesques his presentation by having his Highlanders wear kilts, prompting tenor saxophonist Red Prysock to quit in protest.

The saxophone's insistent bleat holds sway in these post-swing dance bands. Illinois Jacquet's "Flying Home" stokes the frenzy of Arnett Cobb, Big Jay McNeely, Sam "the Man" Taylor, Willis "Gatortail" Jackson, and Prysock, an animal wail that will find purity of expression in free jazz. Freed uses Freddie Mitchell's growling "Moon Dog Boogie" as his theme. Williams's baritone showstopper is "The Twister," where he plays one note over and over as the microphone lowers, he bending down, down, until he's writhing on the floor, one continuous squeal, biting the reed, crowd eating it up. He is barely through his first number when the fire marshals arrive with the police in tow.

"Suddenly I looked up," Williams remembered to the *Plain Dealer* twenty years later. "The doors seemed to be moving. Just like they were breathing." A newborn's first cry. The Arena has a 10,000-person capacity, but Record Rendezvous keeps printing tickets, until twice that number are impatiently jostling for entrance. Glass shatters as the crowd pushes its way into the arena. Fistfights break out, knives brandished, arrests made. It takes three hours for the Arena to clear.

MOON DOG MADNESS is the next day's headline, along with threatening legal action, but when Freed goes on the air that evening, apology quickly dispensed with ("I was hired, just as the bands were hired . . . to allow the Moondog name to be used in connection with the dance"), he asks his listeners to telegram or call the station to support the music he champions, adding that WJW's management has just added a *Moondog Matinee*, five to six each afternoon, and extended the evening show. "So you see, Moondoggers," he proudly says; "it all goes to show ya, that you can't push people around."

Two months later the Moondog Maytime Ball returns for three nights at the Arena, accompanied by fifty extra police officers, with the Dominoes headlining along with H-Bomb Ferguson and the orchestras of Todd Rhodes and Freddie Mitchell. Two years later, Freed is on his way to New York City, WINS, television, movies, holidays at the Paramount. Seven years later he'll pay the price for having a ball, the mortal sin of crowning rock and roll.

MEMPHIS
1954

LEVI. THAT'S WHAT THEY NICKNAME HIM—HIS REAL name unusual, not a Johnny or an Eddie—inside the covenant ark that is Sun Studio. The Levites are the tribe of Aaron, overlooking the Promised Land, poised to enter. Can he?

"We were hittin' it that time, Levi," the stocky, jocular stand-up bass player encourages, flashing a grin at the jumped-up teenager barely able to contain himself. "That's just fine, Levi," the engineer-producer-studio-owner adds from the control room. Levi nervously strums at his acoustic guitar while the electric guitarist on the other wing of their arrayed isosceles fiddles with his amplifier.

He's chosen, in this birth moment before choice is made. His twin brother, stillborn; he knows it could have been the other way around. It makes him want to honor his mother twofold, to be both himself and sibling for her. When he drives past the neon reds and blues of a record-yourself facility on Union Avenue in his truck, delivering for Crown Electric, Levi thinks that he would like to make a disc of himself singing for her, perhaps one of her favorite songs, "My Happiness." It's from the late forties, and hard to say where he learned it, from the Steeles (Jon and

Sondra), the Marlin Sisters, the Pied Pipers, or Ella Fitzgerald. He accompanies himself on guitar.

Or maybe he just wants to hear how he looks in the mirror of a microphone. He's heard Johnny Bragg of the Prisonaires this summer of 1953, the group brought to 706 Union from the Tennessee State Penitentiary in Nashville under armed guard to record. As "Just Walkin' in the Rain" gathers airplay around Memphis on the black-slanted radio stations, on the jukeboxes and off the porches of shotgun houses, he can sense the exalt and release of the song, its quality of mercy. Like Bragg, like the Ink Spots' high tenor Bill Kenny, Levi's voice floats along the upper registers. He sticks close to the Spots' "That's When the Heartaches Begin" until he twists the melody aloft in the last chorus. He will use this beguile to his advantage.

The woman at the front desk of the Memphis Recording Service is impressed when he walks in. Thinks he's cute. His mix of bravado and uncertainty, his shy demeanor. His sideburns. The studio owner is out in the back, or maybe on an errand; the story gets murky after so many years. She thinks he's cute as well, heartbreakingly so, because he's a married man, and not to her, even if she's more partner and helpmeet than he cares to admit.

"I sing all kinds," the boy says when asked what type of song he likes, as much bravura as prophecy. *I don't sing like nobody.* She watches over him in the studio. There's a hint of sneer when he sings *share* mid-song; then, much as Hoppy Jones did in the original version, he sidles into the talking part of "That's When the Heartaches Begin": *That love is a thing that never can share / And when you bring a friend into your love affair . . .* , and she feels his persuasion even behind the glass partition. *That's the end*, he says, as the acetate runs out of cutting room. She hears *begin*.

Good ballad singer, she notes. *Hold.* She doesn't know why, but when she writes that word, she gets a thrill.

||||||

LEVI STOPS BY THE STUDIO as the fall wears on, perhaps wondering if they might invite him inside to do more, striking up a conversation with the secretary, coyly turning on the charm, peeking around the corner to see if the man in the control room might come out and notice him. But the engineer-producer-studio owner has his hands full, his mind on other things, bills piling up and even glimmerings of hits revealing the dog-eat-cat nature of the record business at his level. His Sun label has scored with "Bear Cat" by Rufus Thomas, a local radio personality, and now he's being sued by the publishing company of Big Mama Thornton's "Hound Dog." He's not going to win in court.

She brings the boy's name up every once in a while, and the studio owner only half-listens, because his ears are somewhere else. He's trying to tune his sound, like he would dial the frequency of a radio signal to broadcast to another galaxy. Or at least another kind of music.

In the first month of 1954 the boy comes back to cut another acetate. He's more plaintive-country on "I'll Never Stand in Your Way," a pop hit for Joni James, his guitar jangling slightly out of tune. He's trying to impress. The second song is another wistful number, Jimmy Wakely's "It Wouldn't Be the Same Without You," and by the *callous romance* of the bridge, he has entered the song's seduction, letting it tell his voice where to go. Chords to follow.

||||||

THEY'RE CUTTING UP. Letting off steam. Playing the fool. It's Memphis hot outside, even at night, and there's no air-conditioning inside the studio and they've been here for a few hours and they have no other place to go. They've run out of ideas.

The engineer-producer-studio owner had been given a demo by a song plugger in Nashville, where he'd been recording the Prisonaires in their home jail. The tune was a country-ish weeper called "Without You," not really his meat-and-taters, but he couldn't get it out of his head. The secretary brought up the name of the boy again. Well, why not?

He calls him into Sun on June 26 and sits around with him, just the boy and his guitar, not even bothering to record him. Levi doesn't seem to bring anything to "Without You." Over the course of the afternoon he sings everything he knows and it's still not enough. The engineer-producer-studio-owner listens with an intimation of probability yet to be realized. But there's something plaintive there. He can sense the boy's eagerness to please, and to displease.

A week later the studio owner is sitting around at Taylor's, the corner luncheonette, with a guitar player from a cowboy-country band he'd recorded a month earlier. He admires the guitarist for his serious demeanor; his professionalism, the way he runs the Starlight Wranglers, even though the lead singer sounds like every lead singer in a country band: two parts Hank Williams, one part Red Foley, a dash of Ernest Tubb bitters.

The engineer-producer-studio-owner thinks a full band might overwhelm the kid. Maybe try him with just a guitar and dog-house bass. He's not ready to commit to a full session. Maybe, he says to the guitarist, go see what he's about? Invite him over to your house. Take him away from the studio, somewhere he might be more at ease.

Levi comes over to the guitarist's apartment on July 4. It's a Sunday, a day off from their day jobs, and because of the Sabbath, there'll be no fireworks till tomorrow. He's dressed in pink pants with a black stripe along the leg, white bucks, hair slicked into a ducktail. Whether the boy turns out promising or not, the guitar-ist knows an opportunity when he sees it, a chance to get on the engineer-producer-studio owner's go-to list. He's a married man, with responsibilities, and his attention to detail extends to meticulously learning his instrument, borrowing equally from Chet Atkins and Merle Travis on the country side, and Tal Farlow on the jazz, applying his technique to a pick-and-fingers that double-stops and inverts chords. Derived from country, with this hint of jazz, he's enjoying the propulsion of an amplifier. He's ready to turn up. The bass player, who is uncharacteristically noncommittal as the kid runs through his repertoire, has his own get-up-and-go, slapping at his instrument as if he's behind a trap set.

They go into Sun's studio the next day, July 5. They start with ballads, which is how they perceive him, a "Harbor Lights" to the lilt of Bing Crosby; and Leon Payne's "I Love You Because." Levi leans toward "Because" songs—the guitarist's wife, Bobbie, remembered he also tried "Because of You" and "Because You Think You're So Pretty" when he visited—but he's yet to understand the more complex reasons of *why*; the how-to of his own need. And he knows that if he doesn't do something soon, shows what he's come to feel is his calling, he'll be back driving his truck, and the studio-owner-producer-engineer will turn his attention to someone else, and he will be the road not taken. This might be his last chance. The tape is rewound after each attempt, erasing history being made, until it meets its maker.

The tension is too much. Levi starts scrubbing at his acoustic guitar, a song coming into his line of hearing, making fun of himself and the expectant air. The bass player picks up on it, slapping his bull fiddle, the electric guitarist decorating and counterpointing and underlining. It's "That's Alright Mama," an old Arthur "Big Boy" Crudup r&b stomper kicking around since the mid-forties. They're banging away, enough rhythm to go around even without drums, when the engineer-producer-studio owner sticks his head out of the control room and tells them to keep going.

Going, going. Then gone.

Now he's really making a record for his mother.

||||||

THEY WORK ON IT ANOTHER few times, trying to keep the sudden inspiration intact and aim it with intent. A delicate matter. A record can be a live performance, but it also has a focal point when it becomes something to be listened to over and again, often in far-removed circumstances. The Take. When it becomes a record. An early attempt has guitarist Scotty Moore moving downward on his answering phrases; he's learning his part before forgetting it and letting himself fly free. The bassist—Bill Black—allows the smack of the bass strings to ricochet off the neck, matching the thrum of Levi's guitar, which is driving the tune, and which will be the first heard sound of this new whatever-it-is. In the control room, where he's raised his console so he can sit and look his musicians in the eye and ear, Sam C. Phillips checks his input levels, adjusts his rheostats, finding the exact tonal placement to bottle the urgency he's hearing.

Lightning in a bottle. Phillips knew what it was like. In both 1944, and then a couple of years back, he had undergone electroshock therapy. In each instance he had overstressed himself, driven himself into exhaustion and a frenzy that looped back on his ability to keep ahead of his rampant ambitions. It's no wonder Sam likes his new Echosonic slap-back unit, the repeat like the jolts to the cranium he'd experienced when he pushed himself into his personal red zone, wondering about committing full-time to running a record label called Sun in the face of practical responsibilities. After a few more volts, he had made his decision.

It's the sound of electricity as much as the singer, he realizes. He's studied how Les Paul achieved his sonic breakthroughs, the space-age ping-pong that will send the electric guitar into interstellar orbit, though Sam hasn't got the patience to meticulously overdub and manipulate the speeds of his tape machine. Where Les is precise, pinpointed, Sam wants it pinwheeled; a blurrier sound, live and spontaneous as if it's being made up on the spot right in front of the speaker. With this Levi, he thinks he's come upon the preternatural voice that will make his sound work.

Elvis Aron Presley, out in the studio trying to come to terms with this sudden revelation, this acknowledgment of who he will be, doesn't know what to think. But then he doesn't have to. His voice has come easy to him, sometimes too easily; and he can feel the music shiver up and down within him, jiggling his leg, rippling his shoulders, causing his head to snap on his vertebrae. He likes the feeling.

He's been making the rounds of amateur nights at Memphis clubs while hoping for an opportunity to sing with a newly formed gospel quartet, the Strongfellows, from the family tree of the Blackwood Brothers Quartet, though until a member leaves, he's the fifth wheel. The Blackwoods, one of the premier gospel groups in the region, are based in the local Assembly of God church. In attendance, Elvis witnesses firsthand the slow burn of a congregation on the way to deliverance, the preacher's ability to raise the holy spirit, one parable at a time.

And he sharpens his look, bold enough to wear forbidden colors for boys, to deploy the come-ons of girls, his lips pouty, his dark eyes shadowed in invitation, enhancing the importune of his voice.

They finish the song in time for Sam to take it over to his disc jockey pal at 560 WHBQ, "Daddy-O" Dewey Phillips (*no relation*, in the disclaimer forever attached to Dewey's name). They're of like minds, Sam and Dewey, to the point of starting a record label—*It's the Phillips* "HOTTEST THING IN THE COUNTRY"—in 1950 to put out one of Sam's first discoveries,

Joe Hill Louis. That naïve venture may have come undone in a matter of weeks, but Sam liked to stop by Dewey's broadcasts from the "magazine floor of the Hotel Chisca" at the corner of Linden and Main in the wee hours, where they'd wind each other up while Dewey motor-mouthed and slapped on the r&b discs for his mixed-race audience, shouting out choruses and sponsors. *Tell 'em Phillips sent ya!* is Dewey's catchphrase, but he needs something to send. Sam uses him as a bellwether. "That's All Right Mama" rings Dewey's bell; he plays it over and over as the phones start pealing. Dewey invites a nervous Elvis—who has taken refuge in a nearby movie theater—down to the station and asks what high school he's from. "Hume," he replies, race revealing. Dewey and Sam have long straddled the color line, but it is less than two months after the Supreme Court has decided the merits of *Brown v. Board of Education.* The South and its adjacent compass points are getting used to its implications. *Red Hot and Blue* is Dewey's show, integration as a given-and-take. Substitute "white" for "hot" and his American flag unfurls, just like the music on this hybrid acetate.

||||||

"HELL, THAT'S DIFFERENT," Sam Phillips drawls with some satisfaction over the intercom at Sun Studio. "That's a pop song now, nearly 'bout."

It makes all the difference. *Nearly 'bout.* What does Phillips mean by that, in the first month he's done gone deduced what rock and roll could be, what it sounds like if he flicks *record* on the tape machine at just the right moment? His apocryphal wish fulfillment—"If I could find a white man with the Negro sound, and the Negro feel"—is too reductive, too easy. For Sam, the music's *sui generis* starts with what is called rhythm and blues.

And what is called country and western. Big-band orchestras and Appalachian balladry and show tune standards and gospels of all persuasions.

The entanglements resist ancestral genealogy. Song form and performance have been intermingling for decades now, the brazen masks of minstrelsy giving way to Bing Crosby insinuating black rhythms and Charley Patton repertoiring vaudeville favorites and Charlie Christian plugging in with Benny Goodman and be-bop borrowing from Broadway and radio waves intersecting at the twist of a dial. It's too late to turn back the clock.

It's a pop song now. It has to cross genres, appeal to suspiciously segregated self-identifications and situations, divine universal truth and lure appreciation even before realization is made aware. Not as easy as it sounds, or will as Sam finally hears what he's been looking for, listening for, whenever someone comes knocking on the door. You never know. "Anything, Anywhere, Anytime," it says on Sam's business card. Anything goes.

The tunes are around, and have been for a while, pretty much ripe for the plucking. Best-selling vocalists rule the pop charts, graduated from swing orchestralia and ballrooms, known to snag catchy hits from the underclass of the music business, removing offensive elements of arrangement and suggestiveness and discordance, and covering—in the truest sense of the word, as in to overlay, to conceal, to render invisible—the original inspiration, hits once removed. Patti Page's "Tennessee Waltz" (Pee Wee King), Georgia Gibbs's "Dance with Me Henry" (Etta James's "Roll With Me Henry"), the Crewcuts' "Sh-Boom" (the Chords). Mostly, though, the renegade genres are ignored, left to their own roadhouse devices. This allows each music to push its eccentricities to the fore, since it doesn't need to attract outside listeners. It's preaching to those already inside the church, holding their own rituals and hollers and transcendental experiences. The chitlin' circuit keeps swallowing its own tail. R&b, c&w: they have their separate-but-equal itineraries, parallel one-nighters that add up to all-nighters.

Sam's not content with that, and he's not alone in seeing how the winds drift. Everyone wants to cross over to the pop charts, though there's a worry that the indie business is still too small time, nickels and dimes, table scraps and leftovers from the major labels' myopia and red ink in the ledger. You have to be one hit ahead with the distributors, to have the ready cash to let a disc jockey know you appreciate their efforts on behalf of your coin-flip into the marketplace. Modern, of Los Angeles, and Chess out of Chicago have their way of doing things. Atlantic—operating out of New York—is even more connected to the main stem of the music business. But Atlantic's Jerry Wexler was looking for a black man that might translate to a white audience, and in hindsight realizes Sam had a more expansive vision: Elvis, a white man, as "conduit." In a 1993 interview with WGBH in Boston, Wexler calls Presley "the greatest cultural boon. . . . He gave [the American People] the great present of black music transmitted through his own sensitivity." (Wexler and Atlantic's Ahmet Ertegun will acknowledge this when Sam eventually opens the bidding for Elvis's sale to a larger label. Atlantic offers thirty thousand dollars, which they don't have, soon to be topped by RCA Victor's deeper pockets.) Either way, both he and Phillips were hoping for a two-way street that crossed the color line.

It wasn't always like that at Sun, at the triangulate of Union Avenue as it intersects with Marshall. When he opened his door in January during the first month of the new half century, putting in the neon tubing that advertised Memphis Recording Service in each window, infrared to ultraviolet to catch the passing eye, he drew from the other side of the Illinois Central tracks. It made a break from mixing genteel orchestras downtown at the Starlight Ballroom atop the Peabody Hotel, pushing the drums

as much as he dared, or recording commercials, overseeing remote broadcasts, or setting up his equipment discreetly at funeral
parlors to capture the last rites of the bereaved. He was reminded
of his initial thrill, the hustle and frantic bustle of Beale Street,
where he'd stopped as a sixteen-year-old on his way to a religious
revival in Dallas, his first time out of Alabama. He found a curious
salvation, like he had felt standing outside Silas Payne's Method-
ist church in Florence when he was a little boy, hearing the black
redemption within, an offering of hope even to the hopeless.

Sam loved sound. He was a listener, first and foremost, hoping
to hear something he'd never heard before. He'd built the future
home of Sun himself, putting up the acoustic tiles and the angular
ceiling, bouncing and damping reflections off the walls and floor,
wanting it to be just live enough, with a clarity and harmonic
resonance so he could manipulate the balance and the attack. He
didn't watch the clock. He believed you make your best records
when people feel at home, when they were just themselves, possessed. Usually it happens when you least expect. Here comes Joe
Hill Louis, a one-man band ambling into Sun in the summer of
1950. He's more street singer than measured performer, one step
up from the jug bands that used to gather in Handy Park. He
evokes in Sam the same fascination as W. C. Handy "discovering"
the blues on a lonesome railroad platform in the slide of a knife
along a guitar string. There's nary a street corner on Beale that
doesn't have its sidewalk sideshow. Sam only has to unlock his
door.

Joe Hill Louis is knocking even before Phillips is open for
business. "That's just what we need here in Memphis," says Louis,
who plays guitar and drums and a harmonica, looking around
the half-finished recording room where Sam is sheetrocking and
clapping his hands to see how the sound reverberates. Despite (or
perhaps because of) his three-instruments-for-the-price-of-one,
Louis has already recorded for Columbia, and has a show on

WDIA, Memphis's leading black station, where he's known as "Be Bop Boy" though he's yet to flat a fifth. He usually sets up outside the ballpark of the Memphis Red Sox—the black baseball team—and "Boogie in the Park," recorded in mid-1950, is like a spikes-high hard slide into second, his harmonica solo riding a choppy electric guitar rhythm; flip it over and "Gotta Let You Go" works a single chord until Joe feels like changing it, beyond bars. Released on Sam and Dewey's shot-in-the-dark It's The Phillips label in a pressing of perhaps three hundred, "The resulting 78 RPM disc," relates primitivo fan Jim "The Hound" Marshall, "is so rare today you would need to trade a kidney, two Russian sex slaves and a kilo of real Chandu opium for a copy, if one ever came up for sale." Sam Phillips never lost faith in Joe Hill Louis, however, recording and leasing his songs to Modern, Chess (on their Checker subsidiary), and finally, when he took the plunge and opened Sun, bringing him back to his auspices with the double-sided some-time of "We All Gotta Go Sometime" / "She May Be Yours (But She Comes to See Me Sometime)," adding a piano and drummer to Joe's solitaire.

Another performer not far from the streets to sit before Sam's microphones in the first months of the Memphis Recording Service is Charlie Bourse, whose tenor guitar in the Memphis Jug Band was accompanied by a foot-tapping so insistent that they had to put a pillow under his foot when the group cut records for Victor in the late 1920s and into the 1930s. His unissued and ribald "Shorty the Barber" may have to wait thirty-five years to be released, but it shows Sam's instincts on overload: the spontaneity and quick release of emotion preceding expression.

"Memphis was the inducement," he tells Peter Guralnick in *The Man Who Invented Rock 'n' Roll*, describing the ultimate simplicity of "hearing a black man pick a guitar and pat his foot and put a wood box under his foot to pat as he sings." Or, as Guralnick will distill from Phillips's "original dream . . . the sense that there were all these people of little education and even less social standing, both black and white, who had so much to say but were prohibited from saying it; the belief that somehow it had been given to him, in a manner that he had yet to determine, to bring it out of them, to coax out of them the inarticulate speech of the human heart." The less preconceived the better. "The perfect imperfection," as Sam will define it in years to come, after he has perfected his creation tale.

He's drawn to oddball characters: Harmonica Frank, who blows his harp out the side of his mouth or his nose, Doctor Isaiah Ross with a boogie vengeance. In fact, Sun in its first years is all about the boogie. Sam's taste shoves at the beat, slightly faster and on the verge of recklessness. One of his first masters to find a home is from the blind pianist Lost John Hunter (and his Blind Bats), who hyperdrives "Boogie for Me Baby" ("Not Recommended for Radio Broadcast" it says on the 4-Star label, which picks up Sam's recording), crow-flying a Memphis street grid back to Handy Park. There's Willie Nix's "Baker Shop Boogie," Hot Shot Love's "Wolf Call Boogie," Earl (Michigan's Singing Cowboy) Peterson's "Boogie Blues," the last fiddle-borne, steel strings, and yodeling. It's as close to straight country as Sam comes, flirting with operating in a new market, even if it resembles the confined stockade he's been operating in over the past couple of years. There has to be something more.

||||||

AT FIRST PHILLIPS TRIES TO play by the rules. He'll make records and sell them to the independent labels that have set up shop in the underbelly of the music business; but by 1952, tired of being caught in the crossfire of the Hatfield-McCoy family feud that is the brothers Chess and Bihari, Sam is forced to take his masters and matters in hand. It's nothing personal, just the way business is wagered when everyone's looking for an edge, on the edge, where the minorities cluster.

The major companies—RCA Victor, Columbia, Capitol, Decca, maybe MGM—have sway over popular tastes, but a network of mostly Jewish schemers and dreamers have furrowed deep into ethnic neighborhoods, working from the jukebox up: Jules and Saul Bihari of Modern and Lew Chudd of Imperial from Los Angeles; Leonard and Phil Chess in Chicago; Herman Lubinski of Savoy spreading out from Newark; Syd Nathan of King castled in Cincinnati. Sam feels like a gentile when he deals with these *finaglers*; but he respects the drive of their ethnicity, the same qualities that attract him to the blues and its dogged need to make itself heard. He'd make Yiddish records if there was a market. But there's not, especially in Memphis, so he's recording race records, rebranded rhythm and blues by Jerry Wexler in 1948 when he is a cub reporter at *Billboard* before becoming Atlantic's resident philosopher-executive. R&b is now a sales hierarchy with its own star system, rewarding the ability to get a record on the streets as soon as possible, before the next disc ships and the returns start to come in. No room for error, it's cash in motion, like the title of that other music trade magazine, *Cash Box*, which gets the flow of capital right. Nickel and dimes into the slot. You have to make them want what you're hawking before the next record plays.

The Biharis are first to come calling at Phillips's studio, on a field trip to Memphis in mid-1950, arranging with Sam to record a local disc jockey. Riley "B.B." King comes by his signature initials in stages, from Singing Black Boy to Beale St. Boy to Blues Boy to Bee Bee, until he's a grown man and assured performer who needs no explication. He's on WDIA, sponsored by Lucky Strike cigarettes, and has been playing around town since he arrived from Indianola, Mississippi, in the late forties. B.B. is the last in a long line of medicine show attractions—WDIA has its own Pep-Ti-Kon patent elixir—as well as a harbinger of streamlined urban blues. Phillips shakes hands with Saul and Joe, cuts four songs in the summer of 1950, and sends them to Modern for their blues-slanted RPM label, expecting to get his promised share of royalties. Even at this early stage, "B.B. Boogie" is a deft display of King's command of the guitar, and demonstrates that Phillips knows how to forefront a straining guitar amplifier. King is perfecting the tight-throated impassioned vocal delivery that will carry him to the Regal Theater in Chicago for a classic concert on November 21, 1964, and then enshrine him as the leading ambassador of the blues through a long and storied career that lasts into the next century.

But Jules and Saul know a handshake isn't legal tender, and Sam has neglected to do the paperwork. What deal? they respond. It's at this time, feeling betrayed, that Phillips partners with Phillips and puts out Joe Hill Louis's record, though it's immediately apparent that neither Sam nor Dewey is equipped to oversee a record company, not helped by Dewey's car accident in September under questionable and compromising circumstances (he's critically injured, and a nineteen-year-old not-his-wife in the front seat with him is killed). Sam has to swallow his pride and make amends with the Biharis, continuing to record B.B. in a series of formative releases while nurturing his own dreams of independent production. He's learning his studio. By King's "She's Dynamite," recorded in May 1951, he's figured out his sonic reflections, and has a room that sounds like he means it to, plenty of low end, mid-highs emphasizing guitar and voice, maximum drive.

Fit for an automobile, and Jackie Brenston's "Rocket 88" is the Oldsmobile awaiting. The song's image heralds a dawning era of space exploration, the decade that will orbit the first satellite around the earth, when automobile styling reaches for the futuristic, the tail-fin sci-fi scenarios of atomic power and alien invaders. Bandleader Ike Turner has traveled with his Kings of Rhythm up from Clarksdale, Mississippi, to the Memphis Recording Service on a tip from B. B. King, driving all night to make his session on March 5, 1951. Guitarist Willie Kizart's amp falls off the roof mid-journey, and its raspy cracked speaker underpins "Rocket 88." Ike is set to sing it, but Phillips feels Brenston, the writer, is better suited; he sounds like Joe Liggins, or maybe his brother Jimmy. Grudgingly, Ike takes his seat behind the piano, which despite his later reputation as a guitarist, is his main instrument, and assumes the role he will grow into as a talent scout and record producer. "Rocket 88" is released under the name of Jackie Brenston and his Delta Cats, much to Ike's displeasure, especially when it becomes a runaway hit in May 1951 and takes the top spot in *Billboard*'s r&b charts the next month. Ike's vocal on the formulaic blues "Heartbroken and Worried," cut at the same session, shows Turner is perhaps better suited to masterminding than stepping out front. The Ikettes and marriage to Tina awaits.

Perennially in the running for the coveted title of first rock and roll record, "Rocket 88" is still within the jump-blues tradition, however accelerated it may be (it's lasciviously followed by Connee Allen's "Rocket 69" for King). And though it's Sam's first bona fide hit, it creates a further schism between him and the Bihari brothers. Leonard Chess has been courting Sam as Memphis increasingly becomes a hotbed of blues artists, and snatches it for his label. This time it's the Biharis who walk out in a huff.

Phillips had been recording the pianist Rosco(e) Gordon with an eye toward placing him with RPM. He thought he had an ongoing deal with the Biharis, but they'd only begrudgingly released a Joe Hill Louis disc, and were sticking his other discoveries in the waiting room. Sam was getting impatient, still disgruntled at the way he'd been treated. When Leonard showed an interest in what Sam had going on, Phillips gave him "Rocket 88." The Chess label was just getting off the ground, hitting with Muddy Waters, and Leonard made a deal to go 50–50 on anything Chess picked up. Sam couldn't afford to remain exclusive; along with respect, it came down to cash flow. He hoped to supply records to both companies, but the V-8 success of "Rocket 88" prompted the Biharis to sever ties with Phillips. Gordon wound up on Chess with "Booted," a slurred and sleazy threat of retribution disguised as a twelve-barroom blues, with Roscoe's stride-back piano and a greasy saxophone solo, and the Biharis called in their bets. Gordon had signed contracts with anyone who fronted him an advance, knowing royalties only meant a new car every so often, and that came with white-wall tires. Take what you get might be all you get. Gordon took from Chess, and Modern, until Houston-based Don Robey's Duke strong-armed his contract, especially attracted by a member of Gordon's band, Bobby "Blue" Bland, who would become one of the most assured singers to stand "Two Steps from the Blues." Adding insult to injury, Jackie Brenston moved over to the Biharis, joined by Ike Turner as talent scout and producer.

Losing Howlin' Wolf was the final blow. Later, when he looked back over the many artists he had found, or found him, those hours spent in the control room waiting until the musicians locked into the sweet spot within the space he had fashioned to accommodate their out-of-body experience, snatching emanation from the air, Phillips would have an especial affection for Chester Burnette. Wolf was an older man, in his early forties when he came to Sam, growing into the title character of his "Getting Old and Grey." In grit voice, he is The Howling Wolf, stalking the stage, head pivoting in conqueroo frenzy, overcome with the music coursing through him. The records he makes with Sam are a reading of the blues backward to before the blues began, when it was just a lament set to music, even as it points forward to the crackling electric pulsation of Chicago's south side. Chester had sat at the feet of Charley Patton on his way to lycanthropy, learning his howl from the blue yodel of Jimmie Rodgers, and made the transition from solo country blues to a full city band after he moved to West Memphis in 1948. Phillips heard him on Wolf's weekly Saturday broadcast over KWEM, and from their first single, the ghostly "Moanin' at Midnight," with Wolf's gruff harmonica set against guitarist Buddy Johnson's distorted outbursts, Sam knew he was in the presence of something supernatural in its feral intensity. The flip side of Chess 1479, Wolf's debut released in September 1951, is "How Many More Years," featuring Bill "D'Struction" Johnson's shortcut-through-the-graveyard piano, Wolf baying this most definitive of blues that will count down each of his many subsequent years.

But Sam is once again caught short. The Biharis, claiming Wolf's signature on a piece of paper, have come to town with Ike Turner to competitively record him. In early 1952, they barter with the Chess brothers, Roscoe Gordon going to RPM and Wolf traded (along with a future draft choice) to Chess. Any hopes Sam might be able to continue recording Wolf are dashed when Leonard and Phil give Howlin' a new car and three thousand dollars in cash and convince him to move north, Sam receding in the distance.

Not that he doesn't have a lot going on. Even if the history of Sun cuts off at 1954, the range of incantatory artists that walk through the doors of 706 Union, and that Phillips will then begin to release on his Sun label in 1952, would suffice to mark him as a worthy conduit of classic blues. Sleepy John Estes connects the prewar with postwar by strapping on an electric guitar for the first time; Sam discovers James Cotton playing with Howlin' Wolf, before recording him solo with "Cotton Crop Blues" for Sun, after which Cotton takes his harmonica to Muddy Waters's band in Chicago; another harpist, "Little" Walter Horton, presages Little Walter (Jacobs), though loses his diminutive when Jacobs's "Juke" hits the r&b charts for Chess. Phillips has another "Little" up his sleeve in Little Junior Parker's Blue Flames, as well as Little Milton, who has been brought to Sam by Ike Turner, and has a knack for replicating blues styles from Fats Domino to Elmore James.

Style is one thing; copyright is another. Big Mama Thornton's "Hound Dog" is barely a hit in January 1953 when Phillips releases "Bear Cat (The Answer to Hound Dog)," yowled by Rufus Thomas and given a raunchy extended guitar solo by Joe Hill Louis. As soon as it enters the charts Don Robey unsurprisingly claims the lion's share of the profits for his Lion Music publishing company, making Phillips once again aware of his vulnerability, the scissoring he faces as an independent label owner. In the ensuing cat fight, Rufus scratches back with "Tiger Man (King of the Jungle)" but despite its tribal drumming (a rhythmic feel picked up when Elvis covers Little Junior Parker's "Mystery Train") and chest-thumping vocal, the record falters.

Two recordings from these Old Testament years, B.E. one might calendar them, are the heaven and hell of Sun. The Prisonaires were doing hard time—their collective crimes ranged from murder and larceny to involuntary manslaughter—but the cell tier lament of "Just Walking in the Rain" finds leader Johnny Bragg gazing past penitentiary bars to the repentance of clouds shedding tears. Pat Hare isn't sorry at all. "Cheating and Lying Blues" (aka "I'm Gonna Murder My Baby") is a malevolent threat made good a decade hence in Minneapolis when, in a drunken frenzy, he kills his girlfriend and a police officer. "I just thought you'd like to know, Jury," Pat shrugs before a vindictive burst of guitar tells you he wasn't sorry he did what he had to do. Recorded May 14, 1954, Sam dares not put it out. He has gone as far as he can with the blues.

||||||

HARMONICA FRANK FLOYD'S "Rockin' Chair Daddy" is as much a throwback in time as it is clairvoyant. Phillips had nurtured a soft spot for Frank, a white one-man stomper like John Lee Hooker, since 1951 when he'd sold some masters to Chess— "Swamp Root" and "Howlin' Tomcat" sound like they could have been recorded anytime in the previous three decades, drawled talking hokum and feline yowls. Three years later, on his only Sun single, "The Great Medical Menagerist," Floyd puts it in the past: *Step right around closely / I'll tell you all about a wonderful medicine show I used to work with*, selling soap and *ladies a wonderful tonic you give to husbands* and then moving sleight-of-hand to the next come-on. Now he's a "Rockin' Chair Daddy," *Oh shove, boot it now . . . Rock to Memphis on Vance and Main!* It's released the same month as Elvis's debut.

Rock is all the rage; everyone wants a piece. It's been a by-word in r&b since the 1940s, and now it's a handy signifier for anything up-tempo, perfectly angled toward country music's roadhouse wing. Country boogie has been around since 1945, when Arthur "Guitar Boogie" Smith transcribes the piano's left hand over to guitar, and it's driven home with the Delmore Brothers' succession of "Freight Train Boogie," "Hillbilly Boogie," "Barnyard Boogie," and finally "Stop That Boogie" in the late forties. Hank Williams will not live to see the onset of rock and roll, but his spirit pervades the music's emergence, its backseat-of-a-Cadillac on the way to eternity, the clean slate of a new year and a roughshod resolution. There's a lot of song-swapping between the country and r&b charts, despite segregation's resolute divide; both drink from the same fountain. Rockin' is something they can agree on, each to their own. Everyone's getting a band together to hop on the wagon.

One of the first is Bill Haley, a disc jockey from Chester, Pennsylvania, who, beginning in 1951, starts cherry-picking r&b hits like "Rocket 88" and country-frying them. With his fabricated spit-curl and overeagerness to please, Haley is an inelegant pioneer, but his Comets—whose guitars fill in for horn stabs and whose drums are the focal point—bear down on the rhythmic backbone of their versions. If he fails to override Big Joe Turner's "Shake, Rattle and Roll," his 1953 "Crazy Man Crazy" cracks like a whip. It's got two guitar breaks, one played by steel guitarist Billy Williamson that underlines Haley's country roots (his band started out as the Saddlemen). In early 1954, Decca producer Milt Gabler channels his experience recording Louis Jordan into Haley's "Rock Around the Clock," with its nod to Hank's "Move It on Over" and a flurrying guitar break by session player Danny Cedrone, who dies from a fall before the record is released, having devised one of rock and roll's most essential solos. The courtship between country and r&b is well on the way to consummation.

If there's a matchmaker, it's the electric guitar. It's already allowed the blues to transition from rural jukes to the booming clubs of Chicago's South Side. Now it's time for country music to plug in. When Sam McGee attempted to bring an electric guitar to the Grand Ole Opry in 1940 with Uncle Dave Macon, he was told it was too "modern" by Opry head George Hay. But in wartime you need to get louder to be heard. A year later Ernest Tubb liked the pierce of Fay "Smitty" Smith's electric enough to let him solo on "Walking the Floor Over You." Arthur Smith's acoustic version of "Guitar Boogie" was followed with a more popular electric interpolation. Western swing bands started featuring the instrument, following the Dust Bowl migration to California and the defense plants, where they found savvy guitar makers to further its technical capabilities. In 1932, Adolph Rickenbacker had converted George Beauchamp's idea of a vibrating string amplified by a magnetic pickup into the Frying Pan, a Hawaiian-style lap guitar. Following the evolutionary solid-body path, Paul Bigsby, a motorcycle tinkerer, takes up the challenge of building a guitar for Merle Travis; Leo Fender, a radio repairman, debuts a solid-body Esquire with one pickup in 1948, and tops it with the two-pickup Broadcaster in 1950. AM to UHF, in 1952, the model changes its name to the Telecaster.

All are taking a cue from Les Paul's railroad tie, a "log" that Gibson has now metamorphosed into a gold-topped signature model.

There are now a school of players to show off its potential: Paul himself, Travis, Joe Maphis, the tag team of Jimmy Bryant and bar-swooping steel guitarist Speedy West. Amps to match. The guitar's volume makes drums essential; soon the stand-up bass will need its own magnetic field, taking on the shape and swiveling ease of a guitar (Fender is prescient with the Precision in 1951).

The classic lineup of a rock and roll band. Keyboard optional.

|||||

THEY NEED A B-SIDE. Flip the coin. If "That's All Right" draws from the Tigris of rhythm and blues, they'll salute country music's Euphrates. After all, Scotty and Bill are first and foremost a cowboy band, though apart from the trappings of brocaded gunslinger wear, they're more country than western. The Starlight Ramblers, with Scotty on guitar and Bill on bass fiddle, don't usually stray far from country familiars and their regular Saturday night gig at the Bon Air Club on the corner of Summer Avenue and Mendenhall Road. Their sole Sun single, recorded June 1, 1954, is credited to leader Doug Poindexter, who deadpans his way through "Now She Cares No More for Me" and "My Kind of Carryin' On," and is none too happy when Scotty and Bill bring Elvis onstage with them at the Bon Air to play both sides of his new single.

"Blue Moon of Kentucky" started out as a waltz, *one-two-three* with a swirl and lilt to the dance step. Elvis and Scotty and Bill divide the moon in quarters, emphasizing the crescent and the full, and the melancholia of Bill Monroe's original begins to lift. Sam turns up the echo on Elvis, filling the *and*s of each 4/4, adding urgency in place of an accenting high-hat. "Blue Moon" has been getting faster the whole session, and now they're in full gallop across the Cumberland Gap. On the way to rock and roll.

When the record is released two weeks later, on July 19, Sam takes out a half-page *Cash Box* ad, lauding the ménage à trois he foresees with Elvis: *Pop, Hillbilly, R&B. A Hit! All Three Ways*, he enthuses, and heads out in his car to work the record throughout the Southeast, throwing all of Sun's spare resources into promotion, one disc jockey and distributor at a time. His efforts, and Elvis's surprising agility as a live performer, apparent from his first formal appearance on a show headlined by Slim Whitman at Memphis's Overton Park on July 30, rise both sides of Sun 209 to regional commotion, breaking out of Memphis to Nashville and heading south, making a joyful noise on the charts as September enters its equinox.

The records that follow—the Sun Singles, as they are gathered in folkloric myth, much as the opening five books of the Pentateuch Bible—still sound alive with the wonder of discovery. Phillips resists the temptation to expand the band—Elvis is comfortable with Scotty and Bill, and each musician has more than enough room to play their part. In the control room, Phillips makes sure the sound fills all frequencies. With both Elvis and Bill holding down the rhythmic pulse, Scotty's guitar embellishes gaps and emphases with arpeggios, counterpoint runs and slides, quick interjections, and on the ballads, languorous melodic duets with Elvis's vocal. He is accomplished and sensitive, aware Phillips wants him to keep it frugal, yet his solos and riffs will accessorize the licks of rockabilly as it becomes a formalized style. Scotty and Bill breathe with Elvis, wherever he adjusts the beat, keeping up with his nervous strumming and bursts of self-discovery.

They succeed "That's All Right" with another forties r&b

shouter, "Good Rockin' Tonight." The song has come a long way since Roy Brown wrote it on a grocery bag and tried to sell it to Wynonie Harris, a tale better related over a shot-and-beer at the Circle Bar on Lee Circle in New Orleans. It's a telling choice: the phrase-of-the-hour in its title, the *heard-the-news* invitation of *c'mon and rock*; the repeating *rock!* in the coda like the whack of a drum. The b-side, as expected, is country-inflected, though "I Don't Care If the Sun Don't Shine" is from the Disney soundtrack of *Cinderella*, bongo clip-clops and Dean Martin nonchalance, a singer who influences Elvis as much as Bing Crosby. There's a developing prototype even this early in the game. By the time of "Milkcow Blues Boogie," the third single and released on Elvis's twentieth birthday, with its staged slowpoke beginning and *Hold it fellers, that don't move me, let's get real real gone for a change*, the awareness of what they're doing has been cast into a working mold. It's a change, all right. They've figured it out. These are not cover versions, despite their crossover. They sound like nothing heard before, a mutation, a cross-breeding that splits off its own taxonomic line. *Let's milk it!*

The new music needs an Elvis: *I don't sound like nobody*, a double-negative underlining his across-the-board appeal. He hiccups his way through "Baby Let's Play House," a minor hit for Arthur Gunter earlier in the year, and even chuckles at his presumption when he *baby-baby-baybee*s toward the end. It's his most mannered vocal yet, down to the *pink Cadillac* he throws in. A local drummer, James Lott, fills out the sound, and it makes the national c&w charts, proving Sam is onto something with staying power.

Scotty gets a lot of room to stretch in these early Sun singles, and his tempered playing isn't confined to his instrument. He is savvy enough to sign a "complete" management contract with Elvis on July 9, 1954, stipulating his duties are to "book him professionally for all appearances that can be secured for him, and to promote him, generally, in his professional endeavors." But he'll never receive his promised 10 percent. Elvis's rapid rise, and Moore's musical responsibilities within the Blue Moon Boys, mean he has no choice but to cede control. Phillips approaches booker Bob Neal, a local promoter who uses his radio outlet on WMPS to advance shows, hoping to extend Elvis's range of motion, especially with his recent success on the KWKH *Louisiana Hayride*. Elvis appears in Shreveport on October 16 after driving all night from his regular appearance at the Eagle's Nest off Lamar Avenue in Memphis. Announcer Frank Page makes mention of his "new distinctive style." There's already screams of delight from the audience. How'd he derive that "rhythm 'n' blues style, that's all it is?" "Well, sir," Elvis demurs, "to be honest with you, we just stumbled upon it." "Well you're mighty lucky," says Page. "They've been looking for something new in the folk music field." Behind Elvis, there's an ad for cigarettes: *Be Happy Go Lucky!* The bull's-eye of *Lucky Strike*. And he is.

By the time they finish at the *Hayride* in December, Neal is prepared to take over full management, but he too will be left in the dust. Elvis has come to the attention of one Dries van Kuijk, a Dutch immigrant who has entered the country under shady circumstances and has reinvented himself as Colonel Tom Parker. After a long career as a carny and a shyster, he has parlayed management of Eddy Arnold, who fires him in 1953, into a similar position with Hank Snow, overseeing the package shows on which Elvis appears and taking note of the fact that Elvis is creating more of a stir than the headliner. The Colonel has an in with Snow's label, RCA Victor, and as Presley's star novas over 1955, he takes over as Elvis's intermediary. Soon Sam can ignore no longer the rumors that Parker is negotiating with other companies. Though initially resistant, Phillips needs operating capital; if he's going to give up his sensational discovery, he wants over-the-top dollar. Sun asks for the moon, and RCA Victor gives him the green cheese.

Elvis's final single for Sun is "Mystery Train," originally re-corded for the label by Little Junior's Blue Flames in 1953, and one of the songs that first points Elvis in the direction of the Memphis Recording Service. Herman "Junior" Parker's original (if it can be called that, rewriting the Carter Family's "Worried Man Blues" in another example of black-and-white back-and-forth) has a lope that emphasizes the off-beat, as if the train is putting on the brakes approaching the station. Elvis and Scotty and Bill up the chug, borrowing the rhythmic feel of Parker's "Mystery Train" flip, "Love My Baby," and its guitar pattern by the redoubtable Pat Hare. Sam is perfectly poised between his past and future. Presley and Phillips's collaborative sensibilities are so in tune that it's realized in one take. The train arrives, picks up its passenger, and leaves the station, bound for who knows where?

Sam looks out his door, at the hillbillies encamping, wanting him to give a listen, gift them the same chance he offered Elvis, and thinks that if he did it once, he can do it again.

||||||

AMERICA AWAITS, standing on a corner, impatiently looking at its watch. Elvis washes in with the cultural tide of a national craze for Davy Crockett, his frontier buckskin and coonskin, a teenage soundtrack spread by the shiny new medium of the 45 record and television's hypnotic beamed cathode across the nation. He is pre-figured by movie heroes rebellious and yearning, trying to articu-late their own smoldering screen presence: James Dean, Marlon Brando, Montgomery Clift. In 1955 Bill Haley's "Rock Around the Clock" high-noons at number one for eight weeks, western swing honky-tonk as r&b, courtesy of the movie *Blackboard Jun-gle* and its rebellious juvenile delinquents smashing big-band 78s. By 1956 the pop charts are porous, blues and country crossing over, the occasional pop hit returning home with them. Now that the major labels have taken notice, bringing their resources and monopolies, the stakes are immeasurably higher. RCA has paid an unprecedented $35 million for Elvis, plus $5 million for the rights to his Sun output, and they want to make sure they recoup their investment.

They send him to Nashville, to record under the supervision of Steve Sholes, the head of RCA's country music division, who has been with Victor Talking Machines since the age of eighteen when he began as a messenger in the Camden factory. Sholes adds master guitarist Chet Atkins and pianist Floyd Cramer to the Blue Moon Boys core of Scotty and Bill and D.J., hoping to keep the mystery train of Elvis's sound intact while expanding its parameters, but he's clearly feeling his way. RCA's studio is larger and less compacted than Sun, and the engineers have to jerry-rig a slap-back that adds more distance than Sam's tight manipulation of echo. The song Elvis wants to record is "Heartbreak Hotel," written by Tommy Durden and Mae Boren Axton, derived from a syndicated story in the newspapers about a small-time crook killed in an El Paso liquor store robbery named Aaron Krolik, who had written in his unpublished memoirs that he'd *walked a lonely street*. Like playing *Monopoly*, Durden and Axton put a hotel at the end of it, and present it to Elvis, along with a third of the publishing. RCA doesn't have much faith in its doom-laden atmosphere, the minimal walking bass and Cramer's tinkling piano making it an odd choice for a lead-off single. It's a sleeper, and takes some getting used to after all the ruckus Presley has been causing, but its controlled smolder speaks to Elvis's confidence. He's relying on his own instincts, at least in the studio. The rest of it, the outside clamor, is best left to others.

In an irony not lost on Phillips, "Hound Dog" puts Elvis over the top, a genuine phenomenon bordering on fad. Elvis twice removes it from Big Mama Thornton, referencing a version by Freddie Bell and the Bell Boys he had seen in Las Vegas, more novelty than curt dismissal, giving him plenty of wiggle room. He's the Pelvis: a rhyme scheme boon to headline writers everywhere. D.J.'s *rat-a-tat-a-tat-a-tat-a-tat-a-tat-a-tat*, the clattering hand claps, and Scotty's punchy breaks (there's an out-of-nowhere phrase opening the second that jolts his solo into overdrive) are abetted by the double-A side, Otis Blackwell's "Don't Be Cruel." Both go to number one in the summer of 1956. The echo is gone, as are any doubts about his omnipresence. As Elvis says about fifty-two seconds into "Don't Be Cruel": *Mmmmmm. . . .*

Up north, in an outer borough of New York City, I'm just starting to become aware of the radiophonic static emanating from a friend's older brother's room, the transistor blare from the corner candy store where the teenagers cluster. I'm cresting nine years old, learning (and eventually abandoning) the accordion, "Lady of Spain" to "Mattinata," and getting my worldview from *Mad* magazine. I only experience Elvis when he appears in full figurehead, as a phenomenon and changeling; as the face— the poster boy, the cover girl—of this new music called rock and roll.

Removed from his home swath of Southeast, the Texarkana backtrack he traverses with Scotty and Bill and D.J., making regional inroads and leaving western-and-bop nascent rockers in his wake (in Texas, the Buddys Holly and Knox; in Virginia, Gene Vincent; in Detroit, Skeets MacDonald), Elvis ignites in a hallelujah frenzy, his canon of song barely keeping up with his sudden ascent. He is both missionary and celebrant, caught onstage in dot-matrix photos, suspended stop-time before pandemonium breaks loose, clutching the microphone, guitar slung to one side, knees knocking inward, on tiptoes, drawing out the held breath of expectation. Girls scream; boys ape mannerisms. He invites controversy, a presumption of guilt or innocence that forces everyone to take sides. Colonel Tom prints up buttons that say "I Love Elvis" and "I Hate Elvis" and knows it doesn't matter. Either way, it's Elvis. He only needs one name. He is the music come into being.

Television's network outreach, still a novelty, allows his hip-shake instant access into the American living room, especially on the vaudeville-like network variety shows that partner Elvis's savant stage presence with a skeptical and soon-won-over host. No matter how they patronize him—Milton Berle ruffling his coiffure, Steve Allen dressing him in tux-and-tails and making him croon to an actual hound dog, Ed Sullivan swording him at the waist—he good-humoredly goes along, knowing that as soon as he counts off the future can begin.

Tommy and Jimmy Dorsey are first to welcome him to the new medium, introducing him on their Saturday night *Stage Show* on January 28, 1956. The oft-contentious brothers have seen it all before with Frank Sinatra, the swagger of youth and the hysteria that follows, this brash arc of a rising star; it's too early to tell how long the new kid will be around, but they bring him back week after week, six times in all, as Presley adapts to the confines of stage and camera. He debuts with an unexpected "Shake Rattle and Roll," not his first RCA single, ducking back into the circle of the group for Scotty's solos, his legs twitching. Moore takes two: for the first break it's Elvis who pulls the band along, for the second they push back and he's assailed by the music, shaking in frenzy. He may look convulsive, but he's learning his moves, and how far to take them. By the time he plays "Hound Dog" for Steve Allen on June 5, just over four months later, he's dispensed with his guitar altogether, now a confident dancer with a microphone stand for a partner, on his way to being an all-around entertainer. He sets the microphone low so he has to lean into it, legs spread or bent at the knee, hands flailing and flopping, exuding command. It's only been two years since he was invited into Sun's inner sanctum. When he performs "Hound Dog," complete with bump-and-grind coda, he knows what squeal each move will encourage, what ripple of excitement ensues. He also does "I Want You I Need You I Love You," a song that could have been a hit in any era before him, *doo-wah* vocals from the Jordanaires and an air of propriety. As threatening as he might seem, he's also family-friendly.

He grooms himself for the movies almost immediately. His first film is *Love Me Tender*, a western vehicle in which his character doesn't survive, though the title song, with its elegiac strummed acoustic guitar—*all my dreams fulfill*, even this early in his career—will live forever. The follow-up *Jailhouse Rock* profiles his bad boy persona—"I guess that's just the beast in me," he admits to Judy Tyler—set to choreography inspired by his stage tableaux. Lieber-Stoller's witty libretto—*You're the cutest jailbird I ever did see*—allows Elvis to pole-dance within the first twenty seconds of the title song. He is a helluva dancer.

And rock and roll's graven image. There is a candid photo by Alfred Wertheimer of twenty-one-year-old Elvis in full, playful seduction, touching tongues backstage with a comely beauty, turning on the charm in the same way he can look at his pubescent audience and make them feel they're also alone with him in a dark stairwell, on the verge of surrender. He's not on his own in his subversion of the adolescent pop parade. The We Three Kings of Chuck Berry, Bo Diddley, and Little Richard teenage accordingly, without losing their leer. Elvis's original sin is that he creates his own birthright. *I don't sing like nobody.* He doesn't write songs; he doesn't need to. Early on his mannerisms, his vocal depths, his immediately recognizable voice, and his looming animal presence overwhelm his choice of material. He doesn't have to do more than be Elvis, "Jailhouse Rock" or "Viva Las Vegas," translating *O Solo Mio* with "It's Now or Never" (his own favorite recording), letting loose with "Hard Hearted Woman" and "Burnin' Love," or wandering the proscenium handing out sweat-soaked scarves to eager supplicants, supremely himself without hardly trying.

He realizes he need only let adulation have its way with him; the battle is won over. The only difference is in how much he cares, or cares to care. During the televised *Singer Special* in 1968, known henceforth as the Comeback, garbed in black leather (anticipating Robert Mapplethorpe), his radiant charisma once again compressed into the atomic nucleus of the small screen, he takes Scotty's guitar and throws himself into "Guitar Man" to prove he doesn't need to prove anything, even as he must. His contemporaries have long been rendered golden oldies, trapped on the revival circuit. He might have joined them, indifferent to his movies after *Kid Creole* in 1958, content to be a caricature in whatever setting they care to overlay him—the hot rods and hot bods of *Roustabout* and *Spinout*, *Blue Hawaii* and *Fun in Acapulco*. He plays the same part, bad boy gone good, the girl got. To always know triumph, that conquest is never in doubt, no matter what you do, is to know ennui.

It's why, in the end, he only has to uncloak himself to his congregation, to spread his cape and accept his diadem, and then return to a castle keep in which whims are anticipated, indulged, confined within a protective entourage and his long-shadowed legend.

In 1972, I see him at a press conference, paving the way for his first true appearance—outside of a television studio—in New York City at Madison Square Garden. As Colonel Tom hands out souvenir pens to the assembled, Elvis politely answers stock questions with answers that reporters have already filled-in-the-blanks. He shows off his "championship belt" from the Hotel International, claims his fitness derives from "vitamin E," and he's "only an entertainer," as if that "only" allows him to sidestep artistic responsibility, an aw-shucks downplaying the concentrated projection his charismatic stagecraft requires.

"It's very hard to live up to an image," he says at one point. Yet when he enters to the heraldry of *Thus Spake Zarathustra* (the cinematic "Theme from Space Odyssey 2001"; Elvis as alien monolith), sparkle-toned by the flash of thousands of Instamatics, there is little doubt he only need manifest presence to provoke salutation. He rushes through the early rock and roll hits to get to what he cares most about—the anthems of Mickey Newbury's "American Trilogy" climaxing with the "Battle Hymn of the Republic," Paul Simon's "Bridge Over Troubled Water"—and leaves the audience with a heartfelt "Can't Help Falling in Love," the last *youuu* embracing the mirror that he holds up to the faithful, fairest of them all, before "Elvis has left the building," as he does for the last time on August 16, 1977.

Two score years later, once and future divinity assured, at each anniversary of his death the Elvists, as John Strausbaugh dubs them in *Reflections on the Birth of the Elvis Faith*, gather outside the gates of his Memphis estate, Graceland (*thank you for the food on our table*), arrayed in their own station of the Elvis crossing: the hillbilly cat, the gold-lamé *50,000,000 Elvis Fans Can't Be Wrong* superstar, the caped-and-spangled Las Vegas showstopper, offering ritual sacrifice. As He did, or is assumed, given the hagiohomage that encloses and shadows his afterlife.

He loved to sing, with a magnificent instrument of a voice, and it's fitting that his last recordings return him to a single room in Memphis removed from the outside world, surrounded by empathetic musicians, where he might reconnect with why he drove past Sam Phillips's studio in the first place, to uplift that which was his alone. In 1976, a year before he dies, a remote recording truck parks outside the Jungle Room of Graceland and brings-back-alive his leonine way with a stirring chorus, the ripples of vibrato rounding each phrase. "The Last Farewell" sums his gift of song: *For you are beautiful / I have loved you dearly / More dearly than the spoken word can tell.*

Home at last.

IIIIII

ON DECEMBER 4, 1956, AN impromptu quartet gathers around a piano in Sun's studio. Given their collective belief in the hereafter and the answered prayers that have risen them to the top of their calling, they stick close to gospel go-to's: "Down by the Riverside," haphazardly remembering words to "Blessed Jesus (Hold My Hand)," fragmenting "As We Travel on the Jericho Road" and "Little Cabin Home on the Hill," a tent revival of "I Shall Not Be Moved," picking vocal spots when they close-harmony "Peace in the Valley" ("In D," Elvis calls over to Carl Perkins), hootin' and hollerin' along, clapping and applauding themselves when they make it to the end of each song.

Slowly they gravitate toward the secular, as they themselves have: from Chuck Berry's "Brown Eyed Handsome Man" to an affectionate stab at "Don't Be Cruel," Elvis joining in to poke fun at his renown, telling a story of how he'd seen the singer from Billy Ward and the Dominoes (Jackie Wilson) mimic him in Las Vegas—"I was under the table when he got through singing"—and yet proud of how he's the center of attention here among his peers.

The harmonic convergence is not lost on Sam. All four are comfortably at ease within the familiar confines of Union Avenue. The holidays are approaching. It's Carl's session with his brothers—Elvis had noticed the Cadillacs parked outside the studio when he drove past, deciding on a whim to stop by. A relatively new Sun artist, Jerry Lee Lewis, is playing piano on the session. When Elvis shows up, Phillips places a call to Johnny Cash to come on down, join the party, get his picture taken with the gang for the *Press-Scimitar*. And puts on a fresh reel of tape.

In Sun's New Testament, this will become the Gospel according to Carl, Johnny, Jerry Lee. All will be no strangers to sin and its come-round-the-bend salvation, each outsize bio-discography overflowing with defiance, blasphemy, contrition and atonement, reinvention and ultimate sainthood. Perkins is no stranger to "the Devil's playground," mixing whiskey and beer. Johnny comes to Sun wanting to cut gospel records. Jerry Lee has done time in the Assembly of God's Southwestern Bible Institute. They know how to implore the Lord, and then ask for living proof.

In Elvis's wake the hillbillies have started showing up at Sam's door, asking for a few precious moments to show what they can do, even if they're not sure what is being asked of them. The "country" music that has given Presley his renown sounds nothing like what is happening on the other side of the state in Nashville. There's nary a fiddle or pedal steel to be heard, at a time when the country charts are piling on arrangements, veering toward sweeteners, corn sugar instead of corn likker. Sam is more than willing to give the most talented a shot in the dark, but he wants to get to the core, subtracting, down to as few instruments as possible.

He makes the most of their shortcomings, as do the bands. Luther Perkins may play an elementary guitar, and you have to watch him during takes in case he wanders off the mark, but John R. Cash (Sam makes him less foreboding by adding –ny to his first name) stays down in the baritone with him. Their metered resonance, Johnny's strummed acoustic guitar, and Marshall Grant's bass pretty much doing what Luther does, bare-bones Cash's dry, laconic delivery. He writes his songs out of snippets of conversation he hears, even if it's the cross-talk between his selves. There is threat—*for every lie you're gonna* "Cry Cry Cry"—as well as avowal. In "I Walk the Line," paper weaved between the strings of Johnny's guitar mutes the sound, more snare brush than pick, like a scratch that needs to be itched. The song keeps changing keys in unsettling directions: up a pair of fourths, down two fifths, back where you started and not sure how you got there. The verse enters on the V chord, Johnny humming, Luther moon-walking the line.

The directness of Cash's plainspoke, more talk than sing, moved with him to Memphis in the summer of 1954 after his discharge from a four-year "miserable" stint with the air force. A chance meeting with Gus Cannon (of Cannon's Jug Stompers and "Walk Right In" fame) while selling appliances door-to-door introduced him to the blues, though his own music was resolutely in the country tradition. He sat outside the Memphis Recording Service until Phillips took notice of him. Sam wasn't interested in Cash's religious bent, but was intrigued with "Hey Porter," a homesick poem written for the military newspaper *Stars and Stripes*, as well as the couple of musicians from the local Chrysler plant that Johnny brought with him, soon to be the Tennessee Two. They clip along at a fast clickety-clack, railroad rhythms. Coupled with "Cry Cry, Cry," which Johnny obligingly pens when Phillips asks for an "up-tempo weeper" for the b-side, it climbs the country charts over the summer of 1955. It's the same instrumental configuration as Elvis. At this point, Phillips is still wary of adding drums, and with his ricocheting slap-back echo, he doesn't need to. There is enough sound bouncing around to keep up the tension.

In "Luther Played the Boogie," recorded in 1958 at the tail of Cash's career with Sun, Johnny looks fondly back to when *We were just a plain ol' hillbilly band / with a plain ol' country sound.* . . . But he knows the secret of his success. Perkins twins Cash's vocal range, his cadence, even his taciturn man-in-black persona, which Johnny begins to fashion with "Folsom Prison Blues," his second single. More Pat Hare than the Prisonaires, he wants—he deserves to be—behind bars. *I killed a man in Reno / Just to watch him die.* "Play it strange," Cash tells Luther. Perkins likes the key of F; he doesn't have to worry about open strings, and when you're in the guitar's lower register, it all licks the same.

The introductory phrase of "Folsom Prison Blues" is one of the classic guitar openers of all time; please learn should you be in the vicinity of a C chord.

He's a volatile man. Johnny takes his first two Sun singles to the Grand Ole Opry in early 1956. With only the four songs, he encores seven times, repeating them over and over. He'd like to join the Opry, but he has to be on the road most Saturday nights. They'll give him an ultimatum to show up or not if he wants to be part of the WSM broadcast. He answers by dragging his microphone stand along the footlights at the edge of the stage: "I was just having fun, watching them pop," even as he goes pop, on his own terms, the satisfaction of a network television show that will broadcast weekly from the Ryman Auditorium starting in 1969.

He tells this tale on a break from recording a Highwaymen record in 1994, in Los Angeles's Ocean Way Studios along with the other members of the Mount Rushmore of country music: Waylon Jennings, Willie Nelson, Kris Kristofferson. Outlaws all. It's there I get a glimpse into the coiled spring that is John Cash, no -*ny*. I've set up a table with a microcassette recorder in between two chairs. He sits in one and it's broken; we put it to the side and bring over another. We speak for a while, and then he's called in to do a take. When he returns, he sits down, only to find it's the broken chair again. He gets up, flings it across the room where it splinters against a wall, and calmly retrieves a replacement. *Now where were we?* My Johnny Cash story.

||||||

CARL PERKINS HAS TO AWAIT his just reward. When recognition comes, nearly a decade after his initial success, he finds himself far more influential than he might've dreamed at the disappointing moment he lay in a hospital bed after an auto accident that severely injured his brother, and prevented Perkins from making his first television network appearance following the runaway success of "Blue Suede Shoes," his second single for Sun, and truthfully, a bigger hit than anything Phillips has put out before. Sam hardly has a chance to miss Elvis, seeing in Carl the same claim to fame; perhaps more so, given that he doesn't really like "Heartbreak Hotel," that it's too sepulchral of a song. By the time Carl makes up his date on the Perry Como show in late May 1956, he's got a million seller in hand, and at least during the first part of the year, has the RCA executives worried that they've signed the wrong Sun star.

Perkins comes to Union Avenue after hearing Elvis sing "Blue Moon of Kentucky," recognizing in it "a country man's song with a black man's rhythm," the same blend he intuited when he'd grown up as the son of a poor sharecropper in the Lake County cotton district of northwest Tennessee, learning his first chords from "an old black man that lived right down this little dirt road from me on the same plantation." As a teenager he played along with the single-string picking of Tommy "Butterball" Paige from Ernest Tubb's band, listened to Arthur "Guitar Boogie" Smith and the Delmore Brothers, and especially liked Bill Monroe. "His kind of country music was uptempo, and you could lay that boogie lick in there."

Forming a band with his brothers, Jay on rhythm guitar and Clayton on bass, he was making the rounds of roadhouses and honky-tonks when he went to see Presley at a high school gymnasium in Bethal Springs, Tennessee, about fifteen miles from his hometown of Jackson. Perkins was surprised at the carryings-on of the many teenagers in attendance, and resolved to seek out Elvis's record company, arriving in Memphis in October 1954. Unlike Presley, he had a drummer, probably to cut through the noise of a bar in full clamor, using his guitar lines to punctuate his vocal, though you can hardly hear W. S. Holland on "Movie Magg," which Phillips releases on his Flip subsidiary in February

1955, about as country as can be; the b-side, "Turn Around," is replete with mournful fiddle and caterwaul vocal. It's only after Elvis is on his way to RCA that Perkins has a chance to go into the studio with Phillips's full attention.

They cut "Blue Suede Shoes"—a title suggested to Carl by Johnny Cash when they're on tour together, a favor returned when Perkins picks "I walk the line" out of a Cash conversation about being married—on December 19, 1955. *Cash Box* calls it "a lively reading on a gay rhythm ditty with a strong r&b styled backing." It hits *Billboard*'s Hot 100 the same week as Elvis's RCA debut, "Heartbreak Hotel." By March, Carl is riding high on all three— country, r&b, and pop—countdowns, but the first day of spring finds him recovering from a broken shoulder and head injuries in a Delaware hospital, unable to capitalize on his big break. Though many see it as a critical loss of momentum, Carl's failure to take advantage of his breakthrough, to challenge Elvis in his first glow of ascendance, has more to do with Perkins's amiable maturity. He's not really teenage, despite his attempts to attract a younger crowd as rock and roll locks into its chosen audience. He tries to skew more youthful, with Sam even speeding up Carl's vocal on "Your True Love" to configure him as a pop adolescent. Yet he doesn't have Cash's sonority, or the new boy Jerry Lee Lewis's manic energy, and he slides down the hierarchy of Sun until, in desperation, he signs with Columbia in 1958. By the early 1960s he's considering dropping out of music entirely.

But across the ocean, it's Carl the new beat groups of England want to hear, his guitar stylings encouraging emulation. Of all the Sun artists, he is an instrumentalist first, a raconteur second, a singer by default. The songs that make him famous— "Matchbox," "Honey Don't," "Boppin' the Blues"—feature economical fills and decorations, hardly showy—"If you listen to the guitar break on 'Blue Suede Shoes' I just speeded up some of the slow blues licks"—but they are the vocabulary of rockabilly at its most distilled. He is, as will be demonstrated when he meets the starstruck Beatles, on a 1964 tour of Britain that brings him back from the brink of alcoholism and relative obscurity, a guitarist's guitarist, and a gentleman.

|||||||

HIS FIRST PIANO SITS IN an anteroom off the kitchen, at rest now, bearing the scars and bruisings of a long apprenticeship teaching Jerry Lee Lewis to play. Most of the keys have their ivory chipped to the sharps and flats, pummeled until they can no longer rise again. He says the first song he picked out by ear was "Silent Night," but if that's the case, it was the last time quietude was upon him.

He gives ground to no performer, then or now, sure in the knowledge that he took rock and roll as far as it could go, even in its callow youth, and somehow—miraculously—has lived to tell the tale, or have it told for him. "I was born to be on a stage" he says to his most recent biographer, Rick Bragg, who has made it as far as Jerry Lee's bedroom in his northern Mississippi refuge, with its private lake behind a wrought-iron gate embossed with piano and musical notes, where he spends secluded days in zebra-striped pajamas watching cowboy movies until it's time for him to go out on the road again. He might not be able to leap atop the piano or kick his stool a dozen yards away, but he can take his cane and hammer the keys into submission, shake an audience out of their skins, leaving them . . . well, breath*lessss* . . . !

He courts the hot coals of Hell—did he really set his piano afire to prove to Chuck Berry that only Jerry Lee could close an Alan Freed show?—even as he wonders if rock and roll opens the doors to damnation. There is a famous converse and chorus with Sam when he's recording "Great Balls of Fire" in 1957, a few months before his career will be truly rocked and holy-rolled by the tabloid sensation of his marriage to his thirteen-year-old third cousin. Lewis may worry about earthly transgressions—"How can the Devil save souls? Man, I've got the Devil in me." You could make a song out of that. Sam takes the high road: "Hallelujah!" he proclaims, getting on Jerry Lee's wavelength. "*You* can save souls." And then after all the metaphysical wrangling, ol' Jerry Lee-uciver proves it by making a pact with the demon in all of us, down to the last *goodness gracious.*

As Lewis topples from sanctity, revelations about his marriage baiting an English press looking to scandalize rock and roll, following him back to America, he refuses to bend, to plead nolo contendere, even after his star has imploded to where he's reduced to playing bars where drunks insult him and he has to wade off the stage swinging a microphone stand to let them know he'll take no hypocritical sass from anyone.

It's Jack Clement, a local bluegrass and steel player newly installed as Sam's assistant to listen to audition tapes and sort through incoming talent and take care of the studio while Phillips is on the road, who originally spots Lewis when he travels up from Louisiana in late 1956. After all the guitar players, Sam is on the lookout for a singing pianist. Jerry Lee and his "Pumping Piano," as Sun dubs Lewis's two-fisted accompaniment, can take just about any extant music and render it unto Caesar, a stylist with no remorse. When Clement gets him with drummer Jimmy Van Eaton and guitarist Roland Janes, Lewis runs the gamut from Al Jolson and Gene Autry to Ray Price's current country hit, "Crazy Arms," which Sun releases as Lewis's first single. But it's "Whole Lotta Shakin' Going On," Jerry Lee raking his fingers up the keyboard in his soon-trademark *gliss*, circling his index finger when he brings it real low and then lower and *wiggle around just a little bit*, almost giddy on the *Steve Allen Show* in July 1957, grabbing the *bull by the horn*, peroxide hair and piano stool flying, that explodes him, makes him a star. And a target.

The song that keeps "Whole Lotta Shakin'" out of the number one spot is Debbie Reynolds's "Tammy," a courtly, hymnlike evocation of *in-love*. They look good atop the charts together, Isolde and Tristan. Reckoning awaits. Rock and roll, now that it's been let loose, needs to learn its place, respect its elders. The major labels want in, and they don't like things too risky, too risqué.

Clement intuited this. Even before Lewis incurred the ire of moral backlash, Jack had convinced Johnny Cash to record the mawkish "Ballad of a Teenage Queen," with its overdubbed barbershop quartet and deliberately virginal slant. Cash, already dissatisfied with Sun's concentration on Jerry Lee (who also skews younger with "High School Confidential"), had one foot out the door, secretly signing a contract with Columbia Records that would take effect as soon as his agreement with Sam ran out. They promised him a gospel album, which he'd always wanted to do, and two more percentage points of royalty. And he was sure to get paid.

He wasn't the only one who felt left out at Sun. In the shoulda-woulda are billy-boppers like Billy Lee Riley ("Flying Saucers Rock and Roll," "Red Hot,") Warren Smith ("Ubangi Stomp," "Rock and Roll Ruby"), and Roy Orbison ("Ooby-Dooby"). Their hindsight hits have a long lifeline, despite their inability to chart at the time, crowd-pleasers whenever the tropes of rockabilly are trotted out in a sharp-dressed revival that keeps replicating every few years, with its tattooed look and attitude repeating like its emblematic echo. Only Orbison is able to evolve from his Sun persona, and then because his bel canto is more suited to aria than the ready-mades of rockabilly. He brings his quaver to the magnificat of "Only the Lonely" and "Crying" when he jumps ship to Monument Records.

Sam is beginning to lose interest as well, now that he's seeing the tide recede. He diversifies, building an advanced studio (four-track!) a few blocks away, which makes his records sound like everyone else's, as well as a Nashville branch, starting the Phillips International label with his brother Jud to broaden their offerings. There might still be artists-in-the-making, such as Charlie Rich, whose "Lonely Weekend" will be Sun's twilight-last-gleaming, but he's increasingly involved in his outside investments, a zinc mine or the Memphis-based Holiday Inn chain. Closer to his heart is WHER, an all-female radio station. He'd originally wanted to set his thousand watts on the dial to Memphis's black population, nearly half the city, but turned down by the FCC, he shifted to the next available underrepresented demographic that needed radio presence, in the same way he changed course from the blues to concentrate on white rock and rollers. In 1959 he'll announce that he's a millionaire. By then dusk is coming on.

Elvis's entrance into the military, though he's long outgrown Sun, is a turning point for the music he embodies. Where better to learn to march in lockstep than the army? He has to serve his country, caught in a concentric trap of courting respectability, on his way to the innocuous films, akin to home movies, that will be waiting for him when he returns from Germany with his child bride in tow. He gets away with it. Jerry Lee has already paid the price. Lewis may have to bide his "Another Place, Another Time" until 1968, when he moves his career to Nashville, but the retribution and absolution of country music will be his.

||||||

TO SEE MEMPHIS THROUGH THE refracted lens of Sun is blinding, like staring into the corona of an eclipse, an afterimage seared on your cornea, dazzling all else. If we arrived in town a few years later, in the mid-sixties, we could peer into the repurposed movie theater at 926 East McLemore Avenue, where Stax-Volt in-houses a production style that matches Motown groove for groove; or backward to W. C. Handy scraping together his memory of a train platform in Tutwiler, Mississippi, and transmuting it to the twelve bars of Jim Turner's "Joe Turney's Been Here and Gone," in the process, as Preston Lauterbach notes, crossing "the music over from Beale Street to Main Street, from colored honky-tonks to mainstream America"; or, for me, sideways to Meteor Records, run by a Bihari brother, which follows in Sun's shadow with artists like Charlie Feathers ("Tongue Tied Jill"), Little Milton, Smokey Hogg, and worthy wildsters like Brad Suggs with his Swingsters ("Bop, Baby, Bop") and Elmore James's Broomdusters ("Sax Symphonic Boogie").

One Sun. One star system out of many.

NEW ORLEANS
1957

OOOH-WEE!

It's the squeal of New Orleans. That first rush of pleasure realized, and then Mississlipping and Misssssliding off the rim of the soup bowl that contains this swampy city, plunging into the alluvial okra of its musical mélange.

In spring of 1957, Professor Longhair cuts "Look What You're Doing to Me," subtitled *"Oooh-wee* Baby!"* He's kicking the piano in time with his right foot, so much so that they've had to nail a board over the pedals so he doesn't punch through to the other side. His foot lands on the afterbeat, where the *and* would be, between the numbers. It's the way they like to count in New Orleans, side by side as well as up and down, sway as well as insouciance.

The phrase is in the air. "I'm in Love Again," Fats Domino chortles a year earlier, in mid-1956, enjoying the again of his second entry onto *Billboard*'s pop charts. His oooh-wee is leavened by the twice-shy of *baby don't let your dog bite me.* He's been hurt by cover versions—"Ain't That a Shame," his first entry to break pop, wages a summer's-long battle with Pat Boone in 1955—and now there's no arguing with his undeniable crossover. He'll enter the new year of 1957 with "Blueberry Hill" atop *Billboard*'s Hot 100.

In the same January, a young Art Neville, under the direction of an equally youthful Harold Battiste, records "Oooh-Wee Baby" for Art Rupe's Specialty label, which has discovered its own 1956 pop breakthroughs with the fiery intemperance of Little Richard, "Tutti Frutti" to "Long Tall Sally." Mr./Mme. Penniman will continue hollering gals' names into 1957: "Jenny, Jenny" and "Lucille," delighting in dueling with Jerry Lee Lewis for the title of rock's most outrageous pianist. In some ways, Jerry Lee can't top him, because New Orleans is a piano town. Even Lewis came there to record his first attempt to hear what he sounded like, in 1952, at Cosimo Matassa's studio on North Rampart on the edge of the French Quarter, where Little Richard found his voice as well. Where Fats recorded his first hit, "The Fat Man." Where Lloyd Price recorded "Lawdy Miss Clawdy." Where Smiley Lewis recorded "I Hear You Knocking." Where they all record, because it's the only place in town.

The Professor will etch a total of nine songs today for Ebb Records, run by Leonora "Lee" Rupe, who uses the divorce settlement from her once-husband Art to found the Ebb label, of which Longhair is one of her first signings. 'Fess is used to working fast in the studio, it's just like another gig to him, in a peripatetic existence that has seen him stay resolutely in New Orleans while the winds of opportunity swirl about him, never really changing his fate. He's been up, he's been down. He works anywhere that wants to hire him, in whatever band configuration he's offered, sweeping floors at a record shop when he's "between engagements" as the vaudevillians liked to say, or gambling, because it has a greater return than the music business. Or he can do it himself, his own drum, left jab holding down the bottom, while he peppers the melody with his right; or he can do it with a band.

He records his classic "Mardi Gras in New Orleans" (also known as "Go to the Mardi Gras") at least four times, not to mention countless live renditions as it becomes an anthem for the Crescent City's annual Lent-inspired bacchanalia. Each version features him whistling his way into the song, ticket in hand, approaching the home of the Mardi Gras as if he didn't live there already. He's anxious to see the Zulu King and hopefully catch a glimpse of his Queen. There's a spare version with insistent horns doubling his left hand, and little else, from his debut sessions in mid-1949 for the Dallas-based Star Talent label; another from November later that year for Atlantic Records where the horns answer his vocal in tandem, where his whistle is like a saxophone solo as he places himself at the corner of North Rampart and Dumaine, inside Cosimo's. There's one with an insistent clave underlining the song's blue-rumba rhythm that Atlantic releases as a single in 1950; in later years label founder Ahmet Ertegun will delight in telling how he took a ferry across the river to Algiers, walking through an overgrown moonlit field to a shack where Longhair was holding forth all on his own, mesmerized by his "weird, wide harmonies." The best known from 1959 is on the local Ron label, where drummer John Bodreaux makes like a train clattering down the tracks and Longhair cake-walks along Dumaine up to St. Claude, a long-vanished corner now within a park where stands a statue of the patron saint of New Orleans, Louis Armstrong.

The Professor was born Henry Roeland "Roy" Byrd on December 18, 1918, in Bogalusa, Louisiana, a stronghold of the Ku Klux Klan, a year after the red light district of Storyville was forcibly closed. He grew up in New Orleans, tap dancing in the Vieux Carré—the French Quarter, which by then had been colorized and colonized by Creoles and Italians—and acting as a pie-in-the-face foil for a snake-oil salesman peddling a concoction of alcohol and B vitamins called Hadacol, which he would later immortalize in "Hadacol Bounce." More bounce to the ounce: *keeps a young man from feelin' old . . .*

By 1949 he had gained enough bravado on the piano to walk up to bandleader Dave Bartholomew at the Caldonia Inn and ask if he could sit in. The element of ribaldry in Byrd's music caught on and soon Professor Longhair and His Four Hairs Combo were given an in-house residency and new haircuts: Short Hair, Need Some Hair, and Ain't Got No Hair. This emphasis on the hirsute resulted in Longhair's most prominent r&b hit, "Baldhead," which shimmied up the barber pole of the r&b charts in August 1950 for Mercury Records. Byrd had signed with two companies at the same time, using Roy Byrd for his Mercury sides and having Atlantic record him as Professor Longhair. To confuse matters further, "Baldhead" was a remake of "She Ain't Got No Hair," which he'd recorded for Star Talent; the company had gone out of business shortly after releasing Longhair's debut recording. Longhair was not averse to keep recycling his songs until one might get lucky: "Hey Now Baby," from an all-night session in February 1952 in National Recorders on Canal Street (Mercury A&R producer Murray Nash couldn't afford Cosimo's studio, and for Longhair it was a step up from the Hi-Hat Club, where he'd cut his session for Star Talent), is an early glimpse of "Look What You're Doing to Me," complete with *Oooh-wee!*

He's not just a novelty singer, despite his madcap humor. He can boogie with the best, left hand propulsing the beat, right hand romping. He calls his approach "cross-chording," a result of having learned to play on pianos with broken keys, leapfrogging the bad ones, creating new intervals as he vaults from note to note. His party piece, "Longhair Stomp," captures his deftness on the keyboard; he introduces "Between the Night and the Day" with a cascading overture and the sonorities of "Rhapsody in Blue" before he starts chugging with the band.

Atlantic gives him another shot in 1953 and in November Ahmet and Jerry Wexler go to New Orleans to record him at J&M. In "Tipitina," his hoarse voice shards into baby talk—*little mama wants a dollar* becomes *oola malla walla dalla*—as the parade rhythms bob and sashay. He's got the cream of New Orleans session musicians with him—drummer Earl Palmer, tenor sax Lee Allen, baritone sax Red Tyler, Edgar Blanchard on the bass—and yet he sounds like no one else, sitting back on the piano stool, his long arms outstretched to the keyboard, where he ripples and tipples the keys. Sometimes, when the work slows, Roy Byrd can't even be Professor Longhair, and he spends most of the 1960s in obscurity, doing odd jobs between stints as a card shark, before a belated rediscovery in 1970 brings him recognition and even a home of his own, on Terpsichore Street, in what was once New Orleans's Jewish district. In 1977, the former 501 Club on Napoleon Avenue changes its name to Tipitina's. He plays regularly there before his unexpected passing in January 1980, just enough time for New Orleans to show its appreciation for him. *Tra la la la!*

||||||

THE PRIMACY OF THE PIANO. It sets New Orleans apart in the early years of rock and roll, with a beat all its own.

As early as the mid-nineteenth century, pianists in New Orleans were attempting to translate the rhythms they heard in the air. Louis Moreau Gottschalk, referred to as the Chopin of the Creoles, born and raised in New Orleans, was a world away in Paris when he wrote *Bamboula*—a "Danse des Nègres" transposed from a Creole song—in 1848 at the age of nineteen, which builds on a *habanera* rhythm that crosses the Gulf of Mexico to find a responsive echo in New Orleans. Growing up on the edge of the French Quarter, Gottschalk's mother, Aimee, was a child of refugees fleeing the slave revolt in the French colony of Saint-Domingue (modern-day Haiti). It is likely he heard French-inflected Creole melodies through her, and the business acumen of his London-born father sends the child prodigy to Europe at the age of thirteen to complete his education and perhaps be accepted within more classically appropriate circles.

As a pianist, Louis has undeniable gifts, though sometimes his virtuosity overcomes his sense of composition. Still, he draws from sources exotic to European classical models in a romantic age that venerated the pianoforte and its players. The "Fantaisie Grotesque" of *Le Banjo*, from 1855, takes an African-derived stringed instrument thought primitive by cultured society and replicates a hypnotic figure as much four-string banjo finger roll as keyboard flourish, a familiar and hummable air that sounds like something Aaron Copland may have heard in the back of his mind when he captures the flings of rural courtship a century hence in *Appalachian Spring*.

Louis travels incessantly, throughout France and into Spain, within the United States from New York City (Richard Grant White, reviewing his debut in the February 12, 1853 *Courier and Enquirer*, notes "His command of the instrument is so vast, so unerring, that it seems as if it must have been born with him; as if it were impossible that mere practice and mere will could enable a man to do all that he does with his fingers") to California, and to Latin America. He has a memorable year's stopover in Havana in 1854, where the *habanera* will transfer from his right hand, where it expresses itself in *Bamboula*, to his left, as it will take root in New Orleans. The "Danse Cubaine" of his *Ojo Criollos (Les Yeux Créoles)*, or *Souvenir de la Havane* or *Souvenir de Porto Rico* are as much wish-you-were-here postcards to future pianists as his Opus 50 *Réponds-moi*, which anticipates ragtime and makes him seem prescient, were it not for the imminent interruption of Civil War, New Orleans on the side of the Confederates. Even such as Hector Berlioz approves of his "ingenious fantasies," in which the "tropical melody assuages so agreeably our restless and insatiable passion for novelty" (a good description of pop music, and indeed, Gottschalk was regarded as somewhat of a swoon-worthy ladies' man, making a dramatic entrance and taking off his gloves one finger at a time before placing his fingers on the keyboard). Berlioz influences him to start thinking ever larger. The resulting "monster" performances, such as one in Havana in which forty pianos clash with seventy massed violins, eleven cellos, and an equal number of contrabasses, joined by "all the amateur vocalists of the city," create a wall of sound a Phil Spector could only envy.

||||||

OFTEN CHARACTERIZED AS a Caribbean city, distinct from its Anglo-Protestant neighbors to the north, New Orleans has more in common with its Catholic Latin neighbors across the Gulf of Mexico; none are more important than Havana, which, according to cowboy-rumba enthusiast Ned Sublette, is the most important musical place marker of a transitional century on its way to pop music.

Gottschalk's 1859 *Souvenir de la Havane* provides a genealogical chromosome to Jelly Roll Morton's characteristic "Spanish tinge." Morton had been toying with these rhythms since 1923 and his first known recording sessions as a bandleader, heard most clearly in his composition "New Orleans Joys." In "The Crave," recorded on December 14, 1938, what is subliminal within his music becomes overt. He skips the two in the bar, a slight hop between the three and four, giving the music a hesitating sidestep, enhancing the music's strut and preen. That he is performing this composition for a 78 album (five discs) called *New Orleans Memories* shows him consciously burnishing his roots. Scattered among the straight ragtime remakes are trips down memory lane

like "Buddy Bolden's Blues" and "Mister Joe (for King Oliver),"
a retrospective elegiac mood made poignant by the fact that these
will be among Morton's final recordings.

Tellingly Morton referred to the dark-skinned Oliver as
"Blondie," not only a rare acknowledgment for Jelly Roll of a fellow pioneer in jazz, but an ironic sign of respect in New Orleans's
ongoing antebellum color wars. Jelly Roll himself downplayed
having any African blood, despite evidence to the contrary. "My
folks were in the city of New Orleans long before the Louisiana Purchase," he tells folklorist Alan Lomax at the Library
of Congress, "and all my folks came directly from the shores of
France." The city's acute ethnic segregation met with an urban
compression that invited cross-pollination, each tribe looking at
each other across the great divide of Canal Street, neighborhoods
separated by inviolable yet porous borders complicated by a racial
mix that blurred the races. Occupying the middle ground between black and white were the Creoles, Francophone people of
color whose mixed bloodline—*gens de couleur libres*—put them
on the far side of the *Plessy v. Ferguson* Supreme Court decision
in 1896 that institutionalized Jim Crow segregation, unable to
qualify for "whites only" status in the rigorous caste divisions of
New Orleans.

No matter how much the races kept to their own side of the
fence, the appeal to miscegenate was powerful. Black uptown was
"ratty," in the parlance of the day, infused with the blues and
jass just starting to shape its rhythms and chants and bent notes,
arriving from rural parishes and the dispersal of the plantations,
fueled by a surfeit of US army band instruments left over from the
Spanish-American War. The downtown "dicty" Creoles prided
themselves on European forebears, learning *solfège* and to read
music, aspiring to be proper musicians whose pitch and intonation
were impeccable, whose precision and adherence to form was to
be admired. Each had something to learn from the other.

The Spanish influence in New Orleans never really lost its hold on the city, even as it was overlaid by the French, and then sold into indentured statehood when Jefferson bought the Louisiana Territory in 1803 from a Napoleon looking to downsize his unmanageable territory, especially after the bloody loss of Haiti. The early 1800s Sunday gatherings at *Place des Nègres*, known as Congo Square, where the drums and dances of African culture could take haven from the violent dislocations of slavery, couldn't survive the loss of French inclusiveness, the *mais oui* acceptance of tangled cross-bred roots, and were gone by the 1850s. The spirit of *Moulin Rouge* would remain, however, finding its way into the thirty-eight blocks of Storyville, a sporting district of opulent to seedy vice whose wide-open reputation would continue to infuse the Isle of Orleans as a mythical party destination; the contemporary theme park that is the French Quarter.

In the brothels of Storyville, a strong left hand on the piano helped keep customers moving in and out and back again for another round. When the red lights were extinguished in a World War I wave of decency, aligning prohibitionists, moral reformers, a flu epidemic, and the US Department of War, New Orleans musicians migrated northward, finding fame and an open-arms welcome in Chicago, Kansas City, New York, even Europe as jazz spilled out into the world like a flood, as if New Orleans was on the other side of its levees and the dam had broken. The name of this mongrel music (among many, to be sure)—*Dixieland*—represents the color line as it crosses back over itself, where the proclamate emancipates, when jazz is born, and borne aloft.

The Depression hit New Orleans hard. For musicians who remained, Samuel Charters noted, "The thirties were empty. No one had money to listen to music." When better times returned, "there had been an eleven-year break in the continuity of New Orleans music," and as a result, the jazz that was played looked over its shoulder, mostly performed for tourists on Bourbon

Street. In its stead, the inherent blues that had shadowed New Orleans jazz, a rougher style encapsulated by the word "gutbucket" (which means exactly what it implies), took precedence in clubs that sprang up along an alternative chitlin' (another intestinal by-product) circuit, serving black communities throughout the North and Southeast, providing a chain of showcases for black artists and fertile ground for the music that would soon be known as rhythm and blues.

In New Orleans, this meant uptown venues like Club Desire, Club Ti(a)juana, nightspots on the "stroll" along South Rampart like the Tick Tock and the Downbeat, and most especially, the Dew Drop Inn, the last located just far enough "back-of-town" at 2836 LaSalle to be in its own world. The Dew Drop had opened in 1939 when a barber named Frank Painia bought a two-story building down the street from his shop, and converted it over the war years into a nightclub, with adjoining restaurant and hotel, allowing it to stay open all night. "The Groove Room" featured some of the best post-swing performers working the circuit, most of whom were circling around from Houston through San Antonio, on their way to Atlanta and Macon, or upriver to Memphis and St. Louis, with many whistle stops in between. Through its vaguely Moorish-shaped front entrance passed those who were making the new small combo "jump" blues into a phenomenon: Amos Milburn, T-Bone Walker, Charles Brown, Wynonie Harris, Gatemouth Brown, Joe Turner.

"The South's Swankiest Night Spot" not only featured musicians but a floor show with "exotic dancers," novelty acts like Iron Jaw Harris "dancing with three tables in his mouth," amateur contests and jam sessions, emceed by mistresses-of-ceremony like Patsy Valdalia, a female impersonator before the descriptive transitioned to drag queen. Like New Orleans's famed annual Gay Halloween Ball, it was easier for genders to mix than the races. In 1952, the white actor Zachary Scott stopped at the Dew

Drop to see Papa Lightfoot partake of his Imperial hit, "Wine, Women, Whiskey," and was arrested along with Painia for disturbing the peace and "congregating in a Negro saloon." Charges were dropped the next day.

|||||

WHEN TWENTY-ONE-YEAR-OLD ROY BROWN shyly approached Wynonie Harris at the bar of Foster's Rainbow Room on LaSalle in April 1947 to show him the words he had written on a brown paper grocery bag, Wynonie shrugged him off. "Don't bother me, son," he said, walking away. Disheartened, Roy wandered down the street to the Dew Drop Inn, where pianist Cecil Gant was holding forth. Gant asked Roy to sing the lyrics to him, and though it was two thirty in the morning, immediately put him on the phone with Jules Braun, owner (with his brother David) of DeLuxe Records, based in Linden, New Jersey. There was something in Roy's voice, a flutter in the high register, straining as if it was trapped behind his collarbone, that caught Braun's ear, and he told Roy to write three more songs and he would record him.

It was a fateful and fortuitous homecoming for Brown, who had been born in New Orleans, worked the sugarcane fields on the western flank of Louisiana as it edges its way along the Gulf toward Texas, and had migrated to Los Angeles, where he tried his hand at being a welterweight boxer. Roy had better luck winning talent contests with his voice, specializing in Bing Crosby impressions that came to him by way of Billy Eckstine. Circling back through Galveston, Texas, Brown took up residence at the Club Granada, run by a local brothel madame, fronting a band called the Melodeers. He composed a song for her establishment and sang it on the radio, sloganeering "Good Rockin' Tonight," one of the many sexual slangs that seemed to go well with a foursquare beat. When his luck ran out in Galveston, he headed back to where he'd begun, with little else than one suit, his shoes soled with cardboard, and the lyrics to his whorehouse advertisement on offer to any taker.

DeLuxe was one of the first independent record companies to come to New Orleans and swim in its talent pool, signing Annie Laurie, Paul Gayten, Smiley Lewis, a nascent Dave Bartholemew, as well as the *voodoo down* of Papa Celestin's "Marie Le Veau," a living link to Buddy Bolden's time. The Brauns made good on their word, and later that spring Roy found himself in Cosimo's J&M studio cutting his songs directly to acetate disc. The room was cramped, and there were only two microphones, one for the piano, the other on the horns. Backed by drummer Bob Ogden's band, who had been accompanying him at nightspots in the Treme, Roy had to stoop over and sing into the pianist's microphone. The songs were expectedly salacious—"Lolly Pop Mama" keeps pleading for her *Daddy, daddy, daddydaddydaddy* as *she shakes like jelly*—even while their buoyant delivery was enough to remove them from the mattress and place them feet first on the dance floor. Jazz might have sacrificed its relentless beat in the flurry of notes and staggered phrasings of bebop; rhythm and blues was bringing it back to the jitterbugs.

The headlong motion of "Good Rockin' Tonight" in Roy's original version, a jukebox favorite that ultimately had Wynonie Harris eating fried crow when he covered it for King (though Wynonie, being the bigger name, would also have the bigger hit in 1948. . . . *mmm, that crow sure taste mighty good!*), represented a watershed that hindsight treats with a great deal of reverence. Whether it was the first rock and roll record is a moot point; certainly it was an elevation of a phrase that seemed to capture this new music brewing, in the same way jazz won out over its competitors, in the same way bop would mark a divergence in jazz, words chosen for visceral sound and impact, Roy Brown verb to

Elvis noun (with many whistle stops in between). So too is the way Roy sings, which informs Elvis's version, the chosen a-side for Presley's all-important second Sun release. Roy is all gospel wails as he steps up to each line—he stretches *wellllll, yeaahhhh, ooooh*, before he spreads his news—and if there's any doubt where he stomps his foot, DeLuxe adds "Rocking Blues with instrumental Accompaniment" on the label.

Like Elvis, Roy never forgets his debt to Bing. "A Fool in Love," a 1953 ballad on King, sounds pretty much like early Crosby as he emerges from the Gus Arnheim Orchestra, unaffected as yet by his approaching iconic fame. In 1947, perhaps seeing that the Braun brothers are onto something, King purchases DeLuxe so they can have Roy Brown to themselves; even Wynonie can't keep up with his driving abandon, as the pace quickens and the instrumental breaks get more frantic. The flurry of "Hurry Hurry Baby" and the floogie of "Roy Brown's Boogie" is emotively nuanced by the blueswailing "Lonesome Lover" and the melodramatic sobs of "Laughing but Crying." There are his many Midnights: the 1948 "Long About Midnight," "Boogie at Midnight," which captures his road band at their frenetic peak in 1949, and "Rockin' After Midnight," his first hit sideways.

Unfortunately for Roy, he wouldn't be "Rockin' After Midnight" when rock and roll dawned. In 1953 he chose to sue King for unpaid royalties, and report his booking agency to the musicians' union for fraudulent contracts. While you can't blame him—he eventually won—King's benevolent despot Syd Nathan never let him forget his betrayal. Even as rhythm and blues entered the mainstream, Brown's own songs seemed trapped in a previous era. Despite a brief resurface in 1957 on Imperial, his "Let the Four Winds Blow" did little to stop his downward slide. In that same year he was audited by the IRS, facing prison time, Roy went to Elvis for financial assistance. Presley wrote him a check on a brown paper bag, like the one Roy held out when he first approached Wynonie, back in the days when race records had yet to become rock and roll.

||||||

IF THE WALLS HAVE EARS, they're hearing the hum of whirling dryers. The back door is open, as it must have been sometimes between takes, to let the oversaturated air release, filled with cigarette smoke and electrons still colliding in tempodromic motion, letting in the wet New Orleans air. The musicians stretch, perhaps take a swallow of Jax beer or a passed-around pint, ready to talk about what they might do better, or whether they can move on to the next song.

It's not easy to imagine this as a recording studio, even with the dryers spinning like a big ten-inch shellac disc. Sun Records is preserved in amber, complete to the soundproofing on the walls and a working control booth that still overlooks the room where Elvis, Scotty, and Bill gathered. But here, in a scrub-a-dub laundromat, the last in a succession of mundane businesses that have occupied this North Rampart storefront for some sixty years, the only clue that here was once a place that changed rock and roll history is the stone tile inlay at the front entrance proclaiming J&M Music Shop.

There's just enough 15x16 in the back room to cram a drum set and a piano and hang a few microphones. There's photographs over the folding tables where socks are paired—of Little Richard, Professor Longhair, Lloyd Price, Fats Domino, Sam Phillips putting his arm around Cosimo, the two polar opposites of rock and roll's breech birth. I try to frame each instrument where they might have been placed, the Baldwin 6465 Style R piano in one corner with the lid propped up that Fats pummeled, horns led by Lee Allen semicircled in the middle, drums against the back brick with Earl Palmer about to click his sticks, stop-time before the band counts in. The control room must be where they have a tiny office now. "It wasn't bigger than a closet," and I see Cosimo behind his board with hardly enough room to twist a dial.

Matassa hadn't thought to be a recording engineer, growing up in the family grocery store on the corner of Dauphine and St. Philip (where it still stands) in "Little Palermo," the downriver end of the Vieux Carré. Italian immigration had swelled in New Orleans at the turn of the twentieth century, bringing with it the clan wars of the Old Country as well as its ornate musical traditions. The Matassas stayed out of both, peripherally branching into servicing jukeboxes and pinball machines from their appliance store a couple of blocks away. Along with his father, Joe, a partnership with the similarly initialed Joe Mancuso gave their business a name.

It was Cosimo who would make it into New Orleans's premier recording studio. In 1945, the nineteen-year-old Matassa dropped out of Tulane, where he had been studying chemistry, and started working at the appliance store. He would sell used records from the jukeboxes and began getting requests for other titles. It soon gave him an idea to convert the back room into a place to make those records, and he bought a Presto disc cutter that came with a three-input mixer and started slicing recordings direct into acetate. He learned from scratch, though he was an inveterate tinkerer—as a child he had built his own crystal set out of an oatmeal box to listen to the Max Schmeling–Joe Louis fight. If Cosimo found that being a chemist was too confining, "highly routine, where you did the same thing five times with slight changes" he told *Goldmine*'s Emily Gaul, he enjoyed applying the same exactitudes to the recording process, where the results could be divined immediately, to hear firsthand how the process of combining elements—each musician's place within the periodic chart of frequency range—resulted in mnemonic breakthrough. "If you had a bass and guitar line and a gap in the middle," he explained to Gianluca Tramonta, "you needed to get an instrument in there."

As opposed to Sam Phillips's approach, he considered himself a transparent part of the recording process, not advising on arrangements, instead going out into the room to listen to how it sounded to the musicians, trying to capture a performance with "the least interference and the least resistance." He schooled himself, and tried to keep the musicians in a good mood. When he heard them laughing, he knew it was time to record. Cosimo made the best out of a no-frills setup, charging fifteen dollars an hour plus supplies, though he hardly ever had state-of-the-art equipment, working his way up to one of the new Ampex magnetic tape recorders so he might have editing possibilities. He had only a few microphones for his placements, but they were good ones, buying his Telefunken (Neumann) U-47 from a Jewish congregation who thought it wasn't right to be using German microphones, having an assistant swing his Altec M11 on a boom stand from the drums to the saxophone when it came time for the solo.

He recorded locally until the Brauns came to town hoping to stockpile enough product to see DeLuxe through the anticipated musicians' strike coming in 1948. Lasting throughout the year, the recording ban would surprisingly work to the advantage of the independent labels serving the niche markets of rhythm and blues, Latin, country, gospel, and small combo jazz. Operating under cloud cover of the majors, Deluxe was seeing significant sales for its blues-oriented artists, notably Annie Laurie, whose gently swinging version of "Since I Fell for You," backed by Paul Gayten and His Trio, would be the Brauns' biggest hit from their New Orleans hunting-and-gathering expedition, aside from "Good Rockin' Tonight."

Gayten, a pianist whose band held forth at the Robin Hood Club, and who would later serve as a go-between for New Orleans talent and Chess, was the de facto musical director for DeLuxe's sessions at J&M. It's probable that Dave Bartholomew observed him closely. Bartholomew was used to being a bandleader, a trumpet player and arranger who worked his way up through the house band at the Dew Drop Inn, backing anyone who came through town, specializing in music of all styles, before forming his own group in March 1946. He had separate chart books for jazz, dance, and popular standards, and was conversant in all of them, his debut single for DeLuxe a smooth "Stardust." Bartholomew, according to Matassa, was "a strict taskmaster" who instilled in his players a sense of responsibility, and ran his band with a "very firm hand," so gathering about him a clutch of musicians who would become the go-to session musicians in New Orleans: drummer Earl Palmer, tenor saxman Red Tyler, guitarist Ernest McLean, bassist Frank Fields. He also began radio remotes once a week from J&M over the local WJMR, aimed at the city's black population, though the station's most visible disc jockey, Duke "Poppa Stoppa" Thiele, was a white man being coached by a black scriptwriter, even as the music broadcast was the new sound of "Good Rockin'" rhythm and blues.

Dave was more raconteur than a singer with an emotional connection, more at home in the broad stroke of rhyme, especially his 1952 "My Ding-A-Ling" (which became an unlikely pop number one for Chuck Berry twenty years later), "Who Drank My Beer When I Was in the Rear" and the signifying chimpin' of "The Monkey (Speaks His Mind)."

Shortly after he first recorded for DeLuxe, in mid-1947, Bartholomew was playing the Club Rocket when Don Robey, a promoter-entrepreneur who had the r&b circuit tied up in southeastern Texas, visited the nightspot and hired the band for a five-week booking at his Bronze Peacock Club in Houston. There, Dave's path intersected with Lew Chudd, chieftain of Imperial Records, who was passing through selling Mexican records from the trunk of his car. Imperial, founded a year earlier in Los

Angeles, specialized in international fare, grouped under "Folk Dance Parade" (along with the expected sambas and rumbas he ranged as far afield as the Philippines and Russia), and "Latin American Stars," where Eduardo "Lalo" Guerrero had found favor with "La Mula Branca" (a cover of Frankie Laine's "Mule Train"). Chudd loved Louis Jordan, and was drawn to r&b, even going so far as to offer Bartholomew a job as talent scout; his burst of enthusiasm turned out to be premature. It would take Imperial another year before they inaugurated their 5000 series of "Boogie Woogie Stars" with Dick Lewis and His Harlem Rhythm Boys, and a year after that when Lew Chudd came to New Orleans to knock, along with opportunity, on Dave's door.

In the intervening time, Bartholomew had worked his way to the top of the local music scene, especially when his "Country Boy" broke out of New Orleans and into a Southeast hit for DeLuxe. New Orleans was fast becoming recognized for its musical synergies, galvanized by Sticks McGee's "Drinking Wine Spo-Dee-O-Dee" that Atlantic rushed to rerecord in the new uptempo style, Professor Longhair's paean to his native city, and Roy Brown's continued ascendance. For his first Imperial session as musical director, on November 29, 1949, Bartholomew took his band vocalist, Tommy Ridgley, into J&M studio, where he combined the session with Creole chanteuse Jewel King, whose coming-of-age "3 x 7 = 21" scored the bigger hit.

But a landmark recording less than two weeks later put Imperial on the New Orleans street map to stay. On December 10, Antoine "Fats" Domino pound-for-pounded "The Fat Man." He drowns out and overpowers Bartholomew's band, pushes Cosimo's cutting lathe into red zone distortion, and finds in his refingering of Champion Jack Dupree's "Junker's Blues" a blood rush more powerful than any *reefers in my hand* and *sniffed cocaine* and *loaded all the time*, as Dupree sang it. Fats made it personal, embracing the nickname he had once looked askance at when he was given it by bandleader Billy Diamond at the Robin Hood when he was just starting out; Antoine did like his rice and red beans. Domino takes the relentless fours of Champion Jack and stakes his claim on the corner of "Rampart and Canal," at the compass pivot where all shades of New Orleans's races cross paths, a short prophetic walk west from Cosimo's studio past where Congo Square once held Sunday soirées. When the instrumental break comes around, Fats wordlessly mimics a mouth harp solo, riffing to the point of glee, *whaa whaa*. Domino is one of the architects of rock and roll, his amiable and self-effacing manner often causing his contributions to be taken for granted, just as his huggable onstage personality will mask his concentration and virtuosity, and the sixty million records he will sell over the next decade sublimate the rhythms he and Bartholomew expand upon in their work together, making them an essential part of rock and roll's percussions and repercussions.

||||||

SHRIMP AND GUMBO!! **HOLLERS DAVE** Bartholomew at Al's Starlight Inn, ladling *okra* and *craaab* into the stew pot while his band bangs on anything at hand, a cowbell, castanets, even beer bottles, as Rick Coleman evokes in *Blue Monday*, his definitive biography of Fats. The syncopations are Latino, especially the skipped two and the lilt as three dances with four. When the one comes down hard, as it will in the next song, the snare drum answers emphatically, heavy on the upbeat. Interlocking rhythms, emphasized by simple framing lines doubled by bass and guitar, the horns short and pungent, letting the saxophone solo breathe.

You can hear Bartholomew's feel for the Latinate in "Country Boy," his DeLuxe hit before he steps behind Fats to create music *au pair*. The bass walks straight-legged while horns conjure rhythmic sway, capped by a sweat-drenched trumpet solo from Bartholomew himself that shows how steeped he is in New Orleans's wailing cornet traditions. It's Latin music's time, when Dizzy Gillespie imports conga player Chano Pozo into his orchestra to see how Afro-Cuban polyrhythms skew his bopmatism, when the Cha-cha-cha (always three, despite its shortened moniker) makes inroads into the popular music of midcentury, with crossovers like Perez Prado and Xaviar Cugat sounding familiar and accommodating to American ears, when Havana has the widest-open reputation in the Western Hemisphere. Professor Longhair frolics over a clattering clave in November 1949 with "Longhair's Blues-Rhumba." By 1953, country artist Jodie Levens records "Mardi Gras Mambo," though technically it's a rumba, or at least how North American listeners hear it, with a bass bump on the two-*and* and the 4. The Hawketts, with Art Neville taking the lead for his first recording, cover it a year later. A sixteen-year-old Earl Palmer visits Havana as a stowaway on a United Fruit Company boat. Richard Berry hears "El Loco Cha Cha" by René Touzet and converts it into "Louie Louie" in 1956, the same year Chuck Berry is 'neath the "Havana Moon." There is an extra wood block overdub on Ritchie Valens's 1958 recording of "La Bamba" just in case the point hasn't been made, with drumming by Palmer. The "tinge of Spanish" is there in Bo Diddley's famous beat, these days named after him, and in Buddy Holly's "Not Fade Away." There are mambo rock records: "Tequila" by the Champs, the Beatles' "Daytripper," the Doors' "Break on Through (to the Other Side)." "Once you start hearing it," says Ned Sublette, "it's everywhere."

Where it most assuredly could be found—and despite Fats's r&b chart preeminence, Bartholomew's biggest early 1950s hit—is Lloyd Price's "Lawdy Miss Clawdy," recorded for Specialty on March 13, 1952, though in feel and approach it might easily be a Fats vehicle with a different vocalist. Pianist Salvador

Doucette, a mainstay of Bartholomew's house band, had started the session, but when Domino walked into J&M, Dave put him on the keyboard, resulting in the trilling intro and hypnotic triplets aligned against Palmer's shuffling ride-cymbal and two-four snare cracks. The teenage Price had originally written it as a radio jingle, a catchphrase of local WBOK disc jockey James "Okey Dokey" Smith, and its consequent success—the song was in the r&b charts for half a year—meant it wouldn't be the last time Specialty's Rupe would visit J&M. Art was aware of how well Imperial was doing with the city's homegrown talent, and by his own admission, to New Orleans r&b scholar John Broven, "the only reason I went south was because I really dug Fats Domino. Our musicians (in Los Angeles) were getting a little bit glib, doing the same thing. I didn't feel the spontaneity that I felt originally."

It did seem as if New Orleans had found its métier, as well as its unique sense of rhythm, and Bartholomew was there to translate and shape it. He's on the Imperial session in March 1950 when the uni-named pianist Archibald (real name: Leon T. Gross) turns the murder ballad of "Stack-A-Lee" into a precursor of Jamaican ska, a wrist flick of banjo upstrokes on the *and*s. That fatal argument on Christmas Day, 1895, of Lee Shelton and Billy Lyons, grows with each retelling, as it transmutes into fable, complete with Stetson hat (which makes its first appearance in Mississippi John Hurt's 1928 version), even time-traveling into the future when Lloyd Price—who is surely aware of Archibald's rendition—will take it to a pop number one in 1959.

Perhaps Jerry Lee Lewis also saw into the future when he came to Cosimo's studio in the summer of 1952, fresh out of Southwestern Bible Institute, to attempt his first recording, inspired by the piano-centric sounds he'd heard emanating from within. He's sixteen years old and has enough money for two songs, two dollars and twenty-five cents supplied by his friend Cecil; and Cosimo gives him the acetate when the session is over.

Lewis does a country song by Lefty Frizell, "Don't Stay Away (Till Love Grows Cold)," with an emphasis on the falsetto, and "Jerry's Boogie," which has all the hammers and smears he would later display when he begins with Sun.

Archibald has a song called "Shake Baby Shake." For Jerry Lee, that's a *whole lotta*, and then some *goin' on* . . .

|||||

DOMINO'S PORTLY SHADOW MIGHT ECLIPSE Dave's contributions to Fats's success, but their long-lasting partnership, even after a year and a half apart when Bartholomew quit Imperial, feeling like he was not given the credit or the cash deserved (or a seat at the table when executives of WJMR lunched with Lew at the Jung Hotel, which didn't admit blacks), is one of mutual beneficence. In the beginning Chudd relied more on the advice and connections of Al Young, who owned Bop Shop Records on South Rampart, and recommended artists (like Archibald) and musicians to record companies on the prowl in New Orleans, making sure everyone knew he was the one who was firmly planted as middleman. But Bartholomew had the musical vision, and the leadership skills to hone a band, and knew how to make records that were irresistible. He kept them short and uncomplicated, and in Domino he had a singer with a gift for making the most prosaic couplets into sung poetry.

They worked well in the studio, each offsetting the other. The businesslike Bartholomew would arrive shortly before Fats, going over the arrangement, tightening the unison horns so they aligned along the bass and guitar line. His frontline musicians—Palmer and Fields in the rhythm section, Lee Allen or fellow tenor Herbert Hardesty taking the solos—were accomplished jazzers, but they were not above downplaying their chops into the repetitious riffs and simplistic scales of blues. In lyric writing Dave and Fats took different tacks: Bartholomew's "Blue Monday" is a narrative tale that unfolds in verité, a character study, Fats's "Ain't That a Shame" a minimalist text that could be any character.

When Domino arrived, he would let Fats wander his fingers over the piano until they found the sweet spot of the rhythm. "Dave kept him focused and working," said Cosimo. "Fats liked to dawdle and noodle; that was his style. He'd get a tune and deal with it a while and there'd be a place all of a sudden where you'd hear it's now Fats Domino's tune." Against the piano's insistent rhythm, his singing would laze behind the phrase, drawling out words in a way that had more of the swamp than the Mississippi. Bartholomew thought he had a country-western quality, "not the gutbucket sound." Domino, somewhat Creole (as shown by his first name) and "I think Mama might have had a little Indian in her," was born and raised in the lower Ninth Ward, a part of New Orleans reclaimed from wetlands that were always on the verge of inundation. Cutting his teeth on "Pine Top's Boogie Woogie," as did just about any barrelhouse player in those days, Fats began showing up at clubs, often playing without a bass or drummer, strengthening his left hand, his nickname evoking a pianistic lineage of Waller and Pinchon. He was playing the Hideaway when Lew Chudd first came to town, and went to hear him with Bartholomew and Poppa Stoppa, the influential white disc jockey from WJMR, the voice of New Orleans's black-oriented radio station with all implicit minstrelsies intact.

After the success of "Lawdy Miss Clawdy," Chudd made peace with Bartholomew, and Fats and Dave resumed their collaboration. Lew was a savvy businessman, and relied on his own instincts for what made a hit, aware of the breakthrough of r&b to the pop charts, which was quickening in the same way Imperial liked to speed up records in mastering so they came off that much more urgent. When Bartholomew brought him "Blueberry Hill" in June 1956—Dave's mind on the troubles he'd had recording it,

especially since it was in the unfamiliar climes of Master Recorders in Hollywood, and they'd never gotten a proper take, and he'd
had to edit Fats's first chorus onto the second chorus—Chudd immediately heard its pop potential, following on the heels of "My
Blue Heaven," which Fats had spun into a gold standard. Or was
it standards into gold? "My Blue Heaven" dated back to 1927 and
pre-crooner Gene Austin. As for "Blueberry Hill," it had been
around since 1940, and everyone from Glenn Miller to Sammy
Kaye to Gene Autry had fetched its pail of water. Fats's version
has become definitive, a warm and comforting vocal navigating
a childlike allegory of Jack and Jill's upward climb and their fall
from grace, its nursery rhyme recitative like the first rhymes we
learn, as language becomes distinct from sound.

Domino's run in 1957 is remarkable. He follows "Blueberry
Hill" with "Blue Monday," no mistaking what shade of the spectrum his music is filtering, and yet his music seems part of the
new rock and roll world, which has become the musical craze of
1956. He starts out 1957 moving more than a million and a half
records a month, and has the wardrobe, the sparkling jewelry, and
the Cadillacs to show for it. In "I'm Walking," Palmer steps out
with a second-line parade rhythm that moves the song through
the neighborhoods of Domino's home city, even as the loping
underlay that Bartholomew and Domino invent becomes part of
the fabric of rock and roll, which artists as diverse as the Platters
("Only You"), Nappy Brown ("Open Up That Door"), Eddie Cochran ("Twenty Flight Rock"), Bobby Darin ("Splish Splash"),
and Elvis Presley ("Don't Be Cruel") build their hits upon.

Fats's last single of 1957 is "The Big Beat," and he is. When
last seen, as I see him in January 1970 opening for Ike and Tina
Turner and Mongo Santamaria at the Fillmore East, a skillfully
curated bill given the seasonings of New Orleans, he medleys his
many hits, listing to the right as he leans toward the microphone,
bumping his grand piano across the stage with his considerable

girth, all the weight of his contributions to rock and roll's formulation pushing behind him.

|||||

IT'S BUSY AT COSIMO'S. For $42.50 apiece for a three-hour session that usually throws in overtime at no extra charge, a core of local musicians known as the Clique—grandfathered by Dave Bartholomew—will come up with an arrangement on the spot. That's Palmer on the drums, at least until he's lured to more lucrative recording work out in Los Angeles, ably replaced by Charles "Hungry" Williams or Frank Butler. Frank Fields or Clemont Tervalon on the bass. Keyboard players like Huey "Piano" Smith or Edward Frank. The sax players especially like to step out on their own, improvising off-the-cuff solos to shake up the action. Red Tyler and Lee Allen's honk and growl raise the roof on Roy Montrell's ironically titled 1956 "(Every Time I Hear) That Mellow Saxophone," one of the most frantic records to come out of J&M; and Allen will have his own solo hit in 1958, "Walkin' with Mr. Lee," a riff he comes up with while playing "When the Saints Go Marching In" with Fats on tour that lands him, much to his surprise, on *American Bandstand*, where white high school students—guys dancing with girls, girls dancing with girls—show how far the sound of New Orleans has penetrated the new pop charts.

A few years earlier that was hardly possible. Smiley Lewis, produced by Bartholomew with a 12/8 shuffle beat to the fore and cadenced by Huey Smith's undulating piano, finds his 1955 "I Hear You Knockin'" whitewashed by Gail Storm of *My Little Margie* television fame, a knock-knock joke if there ever was one. It's as close as he'll get to a hit, watching his songs ascend in the hands of others—Elvis covers "One Night (of Sin)," changing its rueful paying-for to the more praying-for "One Night (of Love)."

Even Fats gets in on the act; Smiley's version of "Blue Monday" is from 1953, four years before Domino makes it his.

Shirley Goodman and Leonard Lee will have better luck. They're teenagers themselves when they walk into J&M with a group of kids from Joseph Clark High School in 1950 and persuade Cosimo to record them. More to get them out of his hair, he tapes a song called "I'm Gone," allowing each to sing a verse, and sends them on their way with an acetate. Two years later, Eddie Messner of Aladdin Records stops by. Cosimo is about to erase the tape when Shirley's voice attracts Messner's interest. Paired with Lee, the disparity between his low and her high pitch gives the duo a style that separates them, trading verses rather than harmonizing, a screenplay to dramatize their romantic ups-and-downs as "Sweethearts of the Blues": "Shirley, Marry Me," "Lee Goofed," "Shirley, Come Back to Me," "Shirley's Back." By 1956 and "Let the Good Times Roll," they are certifiable teen stars, even if they're just nudging twenty, even if the suggestive words—*rock all night long*—raise parental concerns. A year earlier they "Feel So Good," Shirley's shrill spine-tingling delivery offset by the harmonies of one of New Orleans's finest vocal groups, the Spiders.

Compared with other cities, New Orleans's harmonizers are often overlooked, despite the superior quality of their recordings. The Spiders' finger-poppin' "I Didn't Want to Do It" is spun from the same web as Hank Ballard's Annie trilogy, recorded a month before Ballard worked his Annie in the studio with the Midnighters. On "The Real Thing," brotherly lead singers Chuck and Chick Carbo show they can innuendo with the best: *She says hold me Daddy please don't stop / 'cause I'm crazy about my lollipop*, recanting their gospel beginnings as the Zion City Harmonizers, further braving the flames of damnation with "Witchcraft."

Guitar players were similarly underplayed in New Orleans, tucked in the rhythm section, where they provide headstrong encouragement for the horns, as in the Mellow Drops' 1954 "I Want Your Love." Pee Wee Crayton comes by to bend a string ("Runnin Wild"); it's either guitar stalwarts Ernest McLean or Justin Adams taking a rare solo on the Spiders' "That's Enough," or Edgar Blanchard ("Mr. Bumps") and Earl King ("Don't Take It So Hard") trading turns in the spotlight, take after take. I would love to know who the unknown fretster is on the Kidds' "Drunk, Drunk, Drunk," a *nom de groupe* of the Pelicans, who have answered the Spiders with "Ain't Gonna Do It."

But Guitar Slim knows you don't get noticed sticking close to the rhythm section. He's going to steal the show, with a guitar cord three hundred feet long and suits in all rainbow shades, infrareds and ultraviolets. He rides through the Dew Drop atop the crowd's shoulders, blaring his guitar, his amplifier straining to keep up with him, through the throng and spilling out to LaSalle, where Johnny Vincent, the promotion man for Specialty in New Orleans, watches him. Slim had already been to J&M for Imperial in 1951, but Vincent brings him back to the studio in the fall of 1953 knowing he has to make the guitar louder. Ray Charles is on piano, just come to town, bailed out of jail for the occasion, arranging and producing. On "The Things I Used to Do," Slim's big hit in 1954, you can hear Charles holler *yeah!* to signal climax, just like he would throughout his life, bridging genres, being Ray. When Guitar Slim records his follow-up, "Story of My Life," Eddie Lee Jones of Greenwood, Mississippi, digs deep into what made him so anguished as to become Guitar Slim. The song says he's born in Alabama, raised up in Tennessee, place-names changed to protect the guilt-ridden. "The Things I Used to Do" is a penitential moan, the guitar as confessor; but the *alone* can never be absolved. Guitarists from Jimi Hendrix to Stevie Ray Vaughn understand that, playing Slim's blues.

When the lights turn down low, as they will in the Marigny when even the bars have gone home, walking toward Esplanade, the Bees' "I Want to Be Loved," the Barons' "Eternally Yours," and the Dukes' "Precious Moments" carry you down Elysian Fields and across Rampart so you can pass the corner of Dumaine just one more time.

IIIIII

AND THEN THERE'S the Georgia Peach.

Little Richard finds his force-of-nature at J&M in September 1955. Two days of sessions, the 13th and 14th, have proved disappointing, and Robert "Bumps" Blackwell, sent here by Specialty to record Richard, feels he doesn't have much to bring back to the home office at 8508 Sunset Boulevard. Blackwell—a thirty-seven-year-old classically trained musician whose lineage is a lot like New Orleans, with French, Negro, and Indian bloodlines intermingled—is Art Rupe's filter in Los Angeles, listening to tapes sent in by hopefuls across the country. Rupe wants him to unearth "the next B. B. King," which means that two songs by a piano-playing singer from Macon, Georgia, are in the pile to be returned. But the sender—*she's a solid sender, you know you'd better surrender!*—seems a little "nutty," in Art's word, calling every day, wondering "when you going to listen to my tapes?" It was Lloyd Price who recommended that Little Richard approach Specialty, and to this end, Richard Penniman goes into his hometown WBML on February 9, 1955, to record two blues-ish songs, "Wonderin'" and "He's My Star," which he hopes will provide the dialogue he'll have with Art when Specialty listens to his tape. His sheer persistence finally persuades Rupe and Blackwell to dig out his demo. Bumps hears "a gospel singer who could sing the blues," in the mold of Ray Charles, as he tells authoritative Little Richard biographer Charles White. Art thinks "This guy has got something," and sends Bumps to New Orleans to see if he can find that some and make it a thing.

There are problems. Richard is under contract to Don Robey of Peacock Records in Houston. They're not having much success with him, though they've teamed him with Johnny Otis, which is why—especially since Richard can be a royal pain in the ass—Robey agrees to release Richard's contract to Specialty for $600. A few years earlier, in 1951, Little Richard had spent time on RCA-Victor, making records as serviceable and sentimental ("Thinkin' 'bout My Mother") as they were anonymous; they could've been sung by any honey-toned sepia singer of the era. All this as his live show becomes more outrageous, lascivious, and daring, leading a two-saxophone hard-charging band called the Upsetters, carving a swath from Florida to Tennessee ladling out that "Tutti Frutti": *If it don't fit, don't force it* . . . He is flamboyant, flaunting, and seems to embrace all genders and proclivities. He calls himself the "King of the Blues . . . and the Queen too!" His hair rises straight up from his head in a processed do he's appropriated—as well as a frontal piano style—from the equally exhibitionistic Esquerita. He's no angel. On the eve of his discovery, Richard is watching a girlfriend have sex with strangers—"She'd be in the back of the car, her legs open and no panties on . . ."—when he's busted for "lewd conduct," and has to leave Macon. Fortunately, New Orleans is just down the road.

Something happens to Richard when he gets in a recording studio. He holds himself in reserve, wanting to make a good impression, aware that he's within music's sacramental church, where gospel and secular hymns are woven into raiment. He surrenders the reprobate within him, one of nine siblings, his father shot to death in the family bar. Yet in live performance he can hardly contain his pansexualities, the satyr with the beguiling flute. His madcap exuberance—all those falsetto *whooos!*—unleashes mayhem as he excites the crowd, sometimes scaring himself with how far he'll go in his lustful indulgence, his quest for the purity of sensation. He thinks of sin, and redemption, and wonders about the distance between his conflicting selves, the A and B sides of his own record.

He and Bumps hope to find four usable titles; of eight recorded, none seem any more than filler. They take a break, head over to the Dew Drop Inn (or, in Earl Palmer's remembrance, Buster's next door), fry some food, have a drink. Richard goes to the piano, banging on the keys, launching into his last-call crowd pleaser. *Tutti Frutti! Big booty! Awopbopaloomopagoodgoddamn!* Nothing more need be said.

There's just enough time to rewrite the salacious rhyme scheme, a task given to Dorothea LaBostrie, a local girl who has been hanging around Cosimo's studio watching how her lyrics to "I'm Just a Lonely Guy" turn out when Richard records it. She scribbles some alternate verses—where it's *greasy*, to *make it easy*, she *aw rootys*—and now it's time to light a fire under the band. Bumps puts Richard on piano, where he can't second-guess himself. Rupe had wanted him to use Bartholomew's regulars instead of Richard's Upsetters, but Blackwell needs Richard to take command. There's three quick takes—*wham, bam, thank you ma'am!*—and in his demonic hammer of the keys Richard pushes the studio band over-the-top, to a place they've never gone before, counting off the song with his own scatted drum fill. Even Palmer is taken by surprise, realizing after the fact that he should've been laying into a backbeat rather than a shuffle. Not that it matters.

As Little Richard lets loose, he loosens the bounds of rock and roll. Letmehearyousay *Awopbopaloomopalopbombom! Amen!*

||||||

COSIMO MOVES HIS STUDIO AT the beginning of 1956, when rock and roll is beginning to incite mass hysteria. Spurred by Little Richard's and Fats's catalytic success, he needs larger quarters. He's gotten a good offer on the Rampart building, and found an old warehouse at 523 Governor Nichols, a few blocks away, still within walking distance of the family grocery store.

Matassa isn't the only one moving on. Johnny Vincent had kept his ears open during his time at Specialty. "I studied records, listened to records," he told Donald Mabry in the late 1980s. "Anytime a record was a hit I'd study it . . . was it the beat, the voice, was it the song?" He'd gotten his homeschooled education through the jukebox trade in his native Jackson, Mississippi, starting his own Champion label, and then shifting his allegiance to Specialty in 1950 when Art Rupe offered him six hundred dollars a month, plus an "unlimited" expense account, to watch over distribution and promotion. But Rupe, according to Vincent, hadn't paid him a promised royalty for Guitar Slim's hit, and in 1955, Vincent returned to Jackson to found Ace Records, taking some of Specialty's roster (and business practices) with him. Earl King's "Those Lonely, Lonely Nights," with Huey "Piano" Smith playing the triplets, King fast-fingering a slightly out-of-pitch solo, and Huey rolling a riposte of his own, gave him his first taste of success, as well as a reputation for fast-and-loosing the truth to attract attention. The record label said "Featuring Fats on piano," a blatant misprint, though the arrangement did owe much to Domino's style.

Huey was used to being secondhanded. When he did his debut record for Ace in 1956, "We Like Mambo," Vincent credited it to Eddie Bo, a jazz-oriented pianist then garnering some renown with "I'm Wise," a song later to resurface as Little Richard's "Slippin' and Slidin'" (Smith himself would resurrect his "Mambo" riff with "We Like Birdland"). He was Guitar Slim's piano player when "The Things I Used to Do" was recorded, only to be replaced by Ray Charles; and the pianist on the "Tutti Frutti" session before Little Richard took over. But he had ideas for his own band, a zany crew more circus than serious. With the Clowns, he would make some of New Orleans's most infectious and rollicking records, beginning with 1957's pandemic "Rocking Pneumonia and the Boogie Woogie Flu."

They're a bawdy bunch, trading off vocals, cutting up, each a character in their own right. None is more provocative than Bobby Marchan, a "female impersonator" who makes no bones of his predilections, starring in Club Tiajuana's Powder Box Revue before recording for Ace. His 1956 "Chickee Wah-Wah," written by Huey, sealed their partnership and brought him into the Clowns, where he was joined by singer "Scarface" John Williams, chanteuse Gerri Hall, and on "Rocking Pneumonia" some of J&M's top-shelf studio musicians, who made the three-hour trek up to Jackson to record. Huey didn't see himself as a singer, more a bandleader like Johnny Otis, and the group played catch with the vocals, tossing lines back and forth, a call-and-response that would find an echo with Sly and the Family Stone. The Clowns' unison chanting, as on the schoolyard sing-a-long "Liza Jane," and the whoop-it-up when "Don't You Just Know It" became a national smash in 1958, seeming to affirm New Orleans rhythm and blues preeminence in the rock and roll pantheon.

But the awakening pop charts and the emergent teen idol pop sweepstakes would prove too alluring for New Orleans's music makers. In early 1958, Jimmy Clanton, a white nineteen-year-old from Baton Rouge, brought his high school band the Rockets into Cosimo's to record a demo. Matassa signed him to a management contract, remade "Just a Dream" with Allen Toussaint on piano and guitarist Mac Rebennack (then just beginning the infusion of Cajun mumbo-jumbo-gumbo that will become his future Dr. John persona), and made a deal with Vincent. By the summer, Clanton's teen-a-genic features and plaintive *why why do I love you* had made "Just a Dream" come true, leading him to receive his gold record from Dick Clark on *American Bandstand*.

Huey, who had headlined on *Bandstand* with the Clowns only a few months previously, now found himself devalued. He records "Sea Cruise" with the idea that Bobby Marchan will be featured, but Vincent takes the advice of his business partner, Joe Caronna, who is managing an Italian youngster from Gretna named Frank Guzzo, and replaces the vocal note for note, *oooh-wee* for *oooh-wee*. "Frankie Ford" not only scores the national hit, but appropriates the flip side as well, name-changing "Loberta" to "Roberta," shifting the song's ethnic identity. You can still hear the Clowns chanting *Loberta!* in the background.

The assimilation outward from an insular New Orleans is under way. The independent labels that have been favoring the city aren't coming around as much. Imperial has Ricky Nelson, who in June 1957 covers Fats's "I'm Walkin'" with Lew Chudd's blessing and Earl Palmer on drums. Specialty has their hands full with Little Richard and his sound-alike, Larry Williams, whose "Short Fat Fannie," "Bony Maronie," and "Dizzy, Miss Lizzy" are all produced by Bumps. Bobby Marchan hitches his tight skirt up north to Bobby Robinson's Fire imprint and in 1960 records "There Is Something on Your Mind" with a long recitative about finding his girl with his best friend. He shoots him, then when another best friend comes around, he shoots her. Marchan will access this trigger-finger imagery when he takes an interest in New Orleans's hip-hop scene in the early 1990s, encouraging brothers Bryan and Ronald Williams to form Cash Money Records, soon to feature the telling Storyville of Li'l Wayne, Pimp Daddy, and Juvenile.

As the city's metric influence absorbs into the lingua franca of pop, making way for the Meters, it manages to retain its traditional crawfish boil. New Orleans's next generation will be led by the songwriter and producer Allen Toussaint, sung by the Neville Brothers, captured in daft prosody by Ernie K. Doe ("Mother-In-Law"), caught on the fly by Lee Dorsey ("Ya Ya") and Chris Kenner ("I Like It Like That"). Even the "Spanish tinge" travels well when Kenner's 1963 "Land of a Thousand Dances" becomes a favorite at *un millar de bailes* in East Los Angeles, with competing versions two years later by Thee Midnighters and Cannibal and the Headhunters.

It's not easy in the outside world. Johnny Vincent tries to align Ace with the Chicago independent Vee-Jay, and now finds he's the one not being paid, nor for that matter is Vee-Jay, though they have the Four Seasons and will sign the Beatles (to little avail) on the eve of the British Invasion. Cosimo starts a record company, Nola, and has a hit out of the box with Robert Parker's 1966 "Barefootin'," but can't turn up the cash flow like he could boost the bottom end at his studio, unable to press enough records to meet demand. Maybe it's too much of a good thing, which is sometimes how you feel on a Crescent City morning after the night before.

"It Will Stand," the Showmen declare in their 1961 hosanna on Allen Toussaint's Minit label, acknowledging the resilience of New Orleans, its omnipresent music: *Hear those sax blowin' / Sharp as lightnin' / Hear those drums beatin' / Loud as thunder . . .* Storms may come, and they will, as Fats's home is washed away in the flood that is Katrina.

But. *Rock and roll forever will stand.*

||||||

HE SEES ANGELS ON AIRPLANE wings afire. He witnesses Sputnik orbiting, a man-made object invading the heavens, the arrogance of looking God in the eye. He knows he has given in to weaknesses of the flesh. He, the Girl, can't help it, even as he ogles Jayne Mansfield in the movie of the same name, also starring Fats Domino, the Platters, Gene Vincent and His Blue Caps, Eddie Cochran.

Both Gene and Eddie, as well as Jimmy Clanton, are on the Australian package tour that Little Richard begins in October

1957. It has been an incandescent year for him, ascending the heights of pop stardom, riding a string of hit singles—his version of "Keep A Knockin'" is cresting the charts as he leaves for the other side of the world—and a reputation that has made him the wild child of rock and roll. If Elvis is the so-called King, Richard's stage antics make him seem the power behind the throne, pushing the music into the flagrant and transgressive. By the end of a performance he has usually stripped off his clothes, his jeweled turban, his canary yellow suit and scarlet cape, his belt and two-tone shoes, down to his underpants, and tossed them to a screaming mob. At the opening show, in New Castle, the stage is swarmed by teenagers as Richard lies prone, enjoying the trample. The tour moves to Sydney, Adelaide, Melbourne, back to Sydney, accompanied by all-night orgiastic parties.

But he's troubled. He has lately taken to talking with Joe Lutcher, the onetime King of Mambo (there are many kingdoms), a late-forties bandleader—"Rockin' Boogie," "Mardi Gras"—who had undergone religious awakening and left secular music. Richard wonders if his success is worth his salvation, experiencing full-frontal racism—"The screaming idiotic words and savage music of these records are undermining the morals of our white youth of America," reads one screed from the White Citizens Council of New Orleans under the heading "Don't Buy Negro Records,"—and financial pressures and a sense of sin he can't seem to shake. He reads the Bible between shows, repenting even as he knows he cannot resist temptation.

It's October 12, ten days left on the tour, but Richard believes it's now or never if he is to save his mortal soul. On the ferry in Sydney Harbour, he tells his band he's canceling the remaining dates, leaving half a million contracted dollars behind, not to mention a career that seemed stratospheric. They look at him in disbelief. To show them he's serious, he takes off his trinkets, his diamond ring and encrusted bracelet, and throws them into the waters, baptism by jewelry. He returns home to enter the Oak-wood Seminary in Huntsville, Alabama, to be ordained as a minister in the Seventh Day Adventist Church. He will not return to the secular stage until five years later, when he goes to England, a second coming upstaged by the second-billed Beatles.

PHILADELPHIA
1959

IT'S AFTER SCHOOL, IN THAT LATE AFTERNOON GLOW
when you're released from the confines of class and before the
family starts up its clamor again. Just you and the television.
Bandstand, after school gone national, teens united.

What is this *twixt twelve and twenty*? It's been around forever,
but before the 1950s it never had its own music. Like a hand-me-
down from a big sister or brother, it was the adult hit parade that
crossed over to youth. Grown-ups. Sometimes the young singer
fronting the band would create frenzy, but that wasn't the intended audience. Now adolescence has its own channel, on television, on radio, on a 45 single that is the approved disseminator of
social grace.

Chuck Berry's "Sweet Little Sixteen" is attuned to the grainy
black-and-white images, caught by air currents and the vagaries
of antenna: *They're really rockin' on Bandstand* . . . Bobby Darin's
Queen of the Hop *tunes into Bandstand every day / To watch the
kids a-dancing 'cross the USA.*

"It's all about the kids," Tony Mammarella says when tele-
prompted, the show's first producer when it goes on-air in 1952

over WFIL-TV in Philadelphia, so seemingly simple, radio come to life before your eyes. But *Bandstand*'s trick photography reverses the viewpoint, turns the cameras about face, a lens on the audience, how they move, dress, mingle, interact. Stars might come and go—"Come Go with Me" as the Del-Vikings suggest—offering their latest hit and a bit of glitz, and the host might read off the day's chart-toppers and intro the commercials, but at least in the beginning, the dancers—culled from local high schools—both secular and parochial—are the main attraction. Dancing with the stars, before the all-too-real of reality television.

Bandstand started as a radio show on WFIL-AM. *Six Ten: First on Your Dial.* Its announcer was Bob Horn, holding down an afternoon drive-time slot, playing a mixture of milder rhythm and blues and popular hits, and as a sideline, promoting jazz concerts with the likes of Oscar Pettiford and sidemen from the Dizzy Gillespie Orchestra. Mid-thirtyish, round-faced and stocky, his discophonic model was Martin Block's popular *Make Believe Ballroom*. Block's audience was adult, holdovers from the swing generation, Horn's target younger listeners. He understood that this new crop of ripening teenagers wanted their own sound; Cleveland, where Alan Freed was based, was not that far from Philadelphia. He could feel change in the musical winds, and he had a taste for rhythm and blues. Nor was he alone in sensing a converging adolescent audience in Philadelphia. Over on WPEN, Joe Grady and Ed Hurst's *950 Club* often invited local teenagers to sit in on their afternoon mixture of interviews and back-and-forth patter interspersed with records and commerce. They would sometimes ask the kids where they were from, which high school they attended, reinforcing the local flavor of the show. The children of the immigrant neighborhoods were growing up, American even as they retained the dash of their forebears. Especially Italian-Americans, as would later prove in Philadelphia's musical geography, when such artists as Frankie Avalon, Bobby Rydell, and Fabian found a national stage.

WFIL's broadcast outlets, as well as the new publication *TV Guide*, *The Daily Racing Form*, and the city's leading newspaper, the *Philadelphia Inquirer*, were all owned by Walter Annenberg's Triangle Publications, which included radio and television ventures. One of the reasons Annenberg bought the WFIL radio stations (AM and FM) in 1945 for $190,000 was that he also had the right to secure a license to be one of Philadelphia's three television outlets, which he did in 1948. "It didn't cost me much," he was fond of saying. "Only a three-cent stamp." Annenberg was surely ahead of the media curve—WFIL was the thirteenth station licensed in the United States, and he now had the octipoidal arms to take advantage of his broadcast empire. With WFIL-TV's afternoon slot the lowest rated of Philadelphia's three television stations (soap operas had yet to make the leap from theatrical radio), general manager George Koehler and Roger Clipp, who was in charge of all WFILs, thought to make use of a collection of short films Triangle had bought, five- and six-minute musical vignettes produced by Louis D. Snader and featuring the likes of Nat King Cole, George Shearing, and Teresa Brewer. *Telescriptions*, as Snader dubbed them, were 16mm versions of the sixteen-inch recorded transcriptions that provided canned live entertainment to radio. The strangest character in Snader's celluloid assemblage was Koral Pandit, a Los Angeles quasi-mystic who wore a swami's turban and played the Hammond B-3 organ in a manner that would later be known as "exotica," bringing new meaning to television as a medium. When the two fell out of favor, Snader turned his attention to another keyboardist with a predilection for the otherworldly: Liberace.

In 1952, the Snader shorts were not yet the historical oddities they would become. Though arguably they might be considered the first music videos, a format formally acknowledged thirty years later with MTV's airing of the Buggles' "Video Killed the Radio Star," they were also behind the fast-moving times, unable to catch up with the blossoming teenage hit parade.

Bob Horn had been interested in television since dabbling in a game show called *Laugh, Grin and Giggle* that had failed to find guffaws. But he'd also hosted a late-night radio program called *C'mon and Dance*, an idea that had been around since 1934, and the nationwide *Let's Dance*, featuring Benny Goodman's Orchestra, broadcast on Saturday nights starting at midnight over the NBC network and doing much to popularize swing across the country. When he moved to WFIL-AM at the invitation of program director Jack Steck, he'd worked both afternoons and late nights, with his early show aimed at teenagers. His experience as an emcee at local events gave him a ready-made persona and bonhomie ease in front of a live audience, and despite misgivings by Clipp (who had initially tried to hire Grady and Hurst), Bob seemed a natural fit to be straight man. And he would only have to move from one WFIL to another. As a foil, Lee Stewart was paired as his gag partner, his main qualification being that he was the local pitchman for Muntz televisions ("Make Mine Muntz!" and therefore ensuring Muntz as *Bandstand*'s first sponsor). But when *Bandstand* went on the air in late September, the show was already past its prime. Even the presence of Dizzy Gillespie as the first interviewee wasn't enough to attract viewers. The give-and-take between Stewart and Horn was forced, stilted, and would get worse over time. Picking up on Grady and Hurst's idea of an inbuilt audience, and with four high schools in the immediate vicinity of WFIL's studios at Forty-Sixth and Walnut, right by the elevated tracks, Koehler and Clipp thought to invite local teenagers to give the camera something to look at while Horn spun records and Stewart Muntzed.

At 2:45 on Tuesday, October 7, producer Mammarella—

newly promoted from being a WFIL cameraman—peered out the back studio door to see if the hoopla surrounding the new *Bandstand* would drum up a studio audience. "You Can't Beat the Beat on Bob Horn's Bandstand," capital-lettered the *Philadelphia Inquirer*. No one had yet arrived, not even from nearby West Catholic High School for Girls, which let out at 2:30. When the show's theme song, Bob Crosby's "High Society," started up, there were only a handful of onlookers. But more trickled in as the show's clock ticked to five, and by the end there were fifty teenagers on the floor, some dancing, some curious and shy, girls outnumbering boys four to one. Horn walked over to one, asked her name and school, and so Blanche McCleary "became one of the first dancers on Bandstand . . . by the end of the third day we were trying to find a way to get 1,000 kids into a studio that could only hold 250." Mammarella knew they were on to a winner.

To be on television. Seen by your aunts, uncles, other kids in the neighborhood. Everybody wanted to be on *Bandstand*. Horn and WFIL—Stewart was eased out by 1955—had a hit on their hands, and over the next two years, they formulated the template of what would become the television teenage dance party, though Clay Cole—himself a television dance party host in the 1960s—claims that Soupy Sales's *Soda Shop* was an early entrant, in Cincinnati in 1950. Still, Horn's *Bandstand* was the first to rate a record, to point the camera at the dancer's feet so that others in their audience could keep up on the new dance steps, and to pocket the ready cash and favors bestowed by promotion men intent on using the new program as a way to showcase their new releases. There were regulars, guaranteeing an inbuilt audience, and a committee to help choose songs, and specialty dances. The twenties had their Charleston; thirties swing had its Lindy Hop; forties jump-flipped the Jitterbug. Horn popularized Ray Anthony's "Bunny Hop," and though he was advised to keep his playlist more pop and Caucasian—early guests were Joni James,

Frankie Laine, Georgia Gibbs—rhythm and blues did sneak in, as did the new hopped-up country music, exemplified by Bill Haley's Saddlemen from nearby Chester, making their transition to the Comets on the local Essex label before decamping to Decca Records, New York's Pythian Temple, and 1954's "Rock Around the Clock."

But even as *Bandstand*'s success prompted thoughts of going national by the mid-fifties, Horn self-destructed. He began to think he was the reason the show was successful, buoyed by the large green Cadillac El Dorado parked in his coveted employee space, the cabin cruiser docked in the Chesapeake Bay, the attention lavished on him by record promoters. Clipp and Koehler were not as sure of his viability on a national stage, feeling that he didn't have the right look for a teenage show; and Horn didn't make matters better by being unwilling to see eye to eye with them. After Stewart's forced exit, he had the show to himself, and wanted to keep it that way. After all, he had invented *Bandstand*, hadn't he?

Philadelphia was known as a breakout market, a stepping-stone to possible national success for any record that might make its mark as a regional hit. The city's ethnic makeup allowed for almost any type of music to find favor, the proximity of neighborhoods blurring genre borders, and with a larger population than both St. Louis and Boston combined, it was close enough to New York that it could be regarded as a test market. It was an easy ride down the New Jersey Turnpike.

The Brown Jug, an Irish bar with a back room that had a large oval table where much of Philadelphia's record business convened and conversed, was around the corner from WFIL's studios. Distributors, promotion men, and disc jockeys all gathered there to make deals, and be dealt the rewards of a hit: booze, broads, and dollar bills. Horn liked to drink, with a taste for Old Grandad and imported beer, and one night, on the first day of summer in 1956, he might've slipped over the line. Arrested for drunken driving at the corner of Erie and Rising Sun, he was promptly suspended from the show, a ready-made excuse for Koehler and Clipp to ease him out of his *Bandstand* position. That the resulting scandal was enhanced by trumped-up vice charges of consorting with an underage dancer on his show, and tax problems with the IRS, who liened on him for not reporting nearly $400,000 of under-the-table income, only accelerated his downfall. Horn was later found innocent on the morals charge, but too late to regain his standing on *Bandstand*. A serious car accident on January 22, 1957, driving the wrong direction down a one-way street into another car and injuring five people, including a five-year-old girl, sealed his inebriated fate. He would later move to Houston, change his last name to Adams, and always feel that his removal was a conspiracy orchestrated by the owners of WFIL. The jukebox jury remains deadlocked.

His sudden fall from grace was convenient. Three weeks after Horn's arrest on June 21, a twenty-six-year-old disc jockey working at WFIL-AM, Dick Clark, was named the host of *Bandstand*. Bestowed this holiest of communions by the Annenberg empire, so he would be canonized forevermore.

||||||

HOW TO SING TO A GIRL. In the voice of a girl. That is Philadelphia's tradition.

The feminine register can be heard throughout this city of Brotherly Love, in the high tenor sounds of the great early Philadelphia r&b labels, captured most magnificently by fourteen-year-old Renee Hinton of "God Only Knows" by the Capris on Gotham. Or, singing from the other side of the sexual divide, George Grant, scaling the upper peaks of the human voice, and his Castelles, with "My Girl Awaits Me" and "Marcella" on Grand

Records, operating from Treegoob's appliance store at Forty-First Street on Lancaster Avenue in West Philadelphia.

Herb Slotkin, the owner, was behind the counter of Tree-goob's in the summer of 1953 when the Castelles walked in with an acetate they'd just recorded for a quarter at a nearby penny arcade. "My Girl Awaits Me" was written by Frank Vance, their second tenor and guitarist, very much in the style of Edna McGriff's "Heavenly Father." It opens with his gentle chording, and then the group chimes a major arpeggio, spanning two octaves with a falsetto trill on the tail. *The clouds seem to smile as they roll by overhead / The birds are singing / I have nothing to dread* . . . "How could I go about writing something like this?" Vance remembered to group harmony aficionado Marv Goldberg. "I listened to her voice and her words and I imagined myself as a soldier in a foxhole. The shelling has stopped and I'm thinking about the happy things like the sun, the sky, the birds, the trees, and my girl." Life itself renewed.

The core of the group—lead singer George Grant, Octavius Anthony, and Billy Taylor—had been singing together since they were eleven, when they met in Miss Joy Goings's junior high school choir, very much in thrall to the harmonies of Sonny Til and the Orioles and the Flamingos. Now, four years later, with Vance rounding out their ethereal and eerie blend, with two and sometimes three tenor harmonies ongoing, the Castelles were about to have a regional hit within a northeast region that stretched up the east coast to Newark and back down toward Baltimore, one-stopping all the way.

Slotkin had only a peripheral interest in record distribution before then, but was not unaware that records were a primary sales item in his store. He partnered with Jerry Ragovoy, the twenty-three-year-old son of a local optometrist who worked for him at the appliance store. Ragovoy, then just starting out upon a long career as a songwriter, was fascinated by rhythm and blues and gospel; "My Girl Awaits Me" by the Castelles would be his first production. By the 1960s he would have taken what he learned to New York, hoping to break into Broadway, but instead producing the theatrical and vulnerable soul stylings of Garnett Mimms's "Cry Baby" and Howard Tate's "Get It While You Can." Janis Joplin would make those her own, as well as Erma Franklin's "Piece of My Heart," which Ragovoy cowrote with Bert Berns. His sensibility combined the intensity of gospel with an innate sense of the pop phrase, as in "Time Is on My Side," originally by Irma Thomas, covered by the Rolling Stones, not far in feel and tremulous emotion from what he learned in his time at Grand Records.

George Grant takes the lead on "Marcella," fragile as a windblown twig; the delicate stir of "Over a Cup of Coffee"; and the most heartbroken Yuletide song ever, "It's Christmas Time." Others in Grand's high-pitched roster include the Angels ("Wedding Bells Are Ringing in My Ears"), who were gathered from nearby Overbrook High School, signed by Slotkin and Ragovoy in August 1954, taking their place alongside the similarly tintinnabulated Marquees ("The Bells"), the Carter Rays ("Take Everything but You"), the Dreamers ("Tears in My Eyes"), the Cherokees ("Brenda"), and the Belltones ("Estelle"). A strange anomaly buried deep within Grand's vaults is an unreleased early version of Screamin' Jay Hawkins's "I Put a Spell on You" that Slotkin declined to release, an off-kilter experiment sounding more like a slow blues than the sheets-to-the-wind scary-monster hit recorded in October 1956 for Okeh, even though Herb did secure his name on the writer credits.

The only singing group to nationally break out from the West Philadelphia school of pleading was Lee Andrews and the Hearts, sitting in their room *looking out at the rain*, watching the tears *like crystals they cover my windowpane*. The heartbreak in "Teardrops" is palpable, as is their initial success, "Long Lonely Nights"—the hit they sing on *Bandstand* on August 9, 1957, during the first week of Clark's national broadcast, immediately entering the *Billboard* charts.

||||||

"I'LL GIVE IT A 90 cause it's got a good beat and you can dance to it." It's how they rate a record on *Bandstand*, the benchmark, fittingly, a grade. These kids are not far from the schoolyard. The girls wear bobby sox, skirts covering the tops of their shins, party dresses. The boys are in sport coat and tie, hair slicked. There's no dungarees allowed, no gum-chewing. Except, when the show goes national, and Beechnut Gum is clamoring to get aboard, they'll be masticating in rhythm, clapping along, keeping time with their lower jaw.

There's a Top 10 pretty much like the Top 10 on a transistor radio, bleachers to perch on like a gym, dress codes and decorum. The kids on-screen aren't so different than the ones clustered at the Friday night hop at St. Augustine, or outside Vinnie's, wherever Vinnie's might be on your particular block. Dick Clark says things like "By Jiminy," a genial host with the air of a one-of-the-kids teacher, chaperoning a dance, which he actually is. The couples cluster, sing along, join the queue at the autograph table, dance among themselves, look alternately self-conscious and poised. There is no elaborate choreography, unless they're doing the Stroll, down the aisle, running a gauntlet of their peers.

On August 5, 1957, *Bandstand* goes national on the ABC network. It's scheduled as a summer replacement show, but after a trial run proves successful, it's five days a week, an hour and a half of watching kids dance to records on the hit parade. "Kids love to watch kids," reasons Tony Mammarella, and after nearly five years, the show has been honed to a slick formula. All it needs is someone to personify it to America's nascent youth.

Richard Wagstaff Clark Jr. was not as young as "the kids,"

but he was youthful. Twenty-six years old, hair smoothed with lanolin, his manner friendly, involving, and never condescending to his adolescent charges, he had a wholesome air, soothing as he entertained. Like his predecessor, he was drawn into radio by Martin Block's *Make Believe Ballroom* and Art Ford's *Milkman's Matinee*, imagining himself as a midnight disc jockey over the airwaves. His father and uncle were in radio in Utica, New York, and Clark quickly moved into the family business, though he took pains to distance himself, transferring to Philadelphia when an opening for an announcer came up at WFIL. He seemed eager to play by the rules. When Koehler gave him Horn's old radio slot in the afternoon, at first called *Dick Clark's Caravan of Stars*, and then *Bandstand* with Bob coming in to announce a couple of records before and aft to promote the television show, an arrangement that probably annoyed them both, he kept his opinions to himself. Clark chose not to rock the boat, though he did put his finger to the wind. One day in the fall of 1955 he substituted for Horn on television, enjoying the experience so much he pitched the *Bandstand* idea to WEWS-TV in Cleveland. They weren't interested.

But Koehler and Clipp were. They'd always seen *Bandstand* as more than a Bob Horn vehicle; early on they'd removed his possessive (when it was *Bob Horn's Bandstand*) from the show's branding. Clark's boyish collegiate looks and casual delivery, a folksy patter learned from Arthur Godfrey, and generational fit (the dozen years separating Clark from Horn were an eternity in teen time) made him an obvious successor. For a while, Mammarella was in the running, but even he, not much over thirty, seemed too old. Maybe it was the bow ties he always wore, or the no mean feat of directing when the audience is overflowing with teenage synapses.

Clark made the switchover on July 9, 1956, taking his place behind a podium that now had *his* picture inside the emblazoned record. The set hadn't changed much since 1952, still a canvas-painted record department within a music store with its shelved rows of 78 albums, already obsolete. In the time it took from Carl Perkins's "Blue Suede Shoes" to Elvis Presley's "Hound Dog" to trade places atop *Bandstand*'s chart of Top Tunes, the torch—well, a Zippo anyway—was passed. Dick Clark was on his way to becoming his later subtitle, "America's oldest living teenager."

The age bracket to be on *Bandstand* was the sweet spot of adolescence, fourteen to eighteen, high school years when the voice changes and love's ideal is yet to be tested. As vicarious dating, *Bandstand* regulars played up the going-steady aspect, the slam-book pairing of Bob (Clayton) and Justine (Carelli), Kenny (Rossi) and Arlene (Sullivan), surrogate couples who knew how to woo and dance, along with Bunny and Eddie and Carmen and Frank and Frani and Billy. Some of them even had their own profiles in the teen magazines, their own fan clubs and sacks of fan mail. All of them would remember it as the best time of their lives, when they were the most popular kids in class, a clique to aspire to. Even the *Bandstand* official yearbook seems more like a high school annual, centered on rock and roll instead of football, with candid close-ups and backstaging at the senior play, girls in crinoline, guys with jackets they're outgrowing. No class clowns allowed. This was teenagers as their parents idealized them to be, teens as they aspired to be.

It was also how white America pictured their young, a racially filtered view of high school society that *Bandstand* chose to portray, despite the prominence of black performers as guests on the show. The show was de facto segregated in Philadelphia, and though Clark would claim that he crossed the color line in 1957, a hindsight embellished over the years ("We were truly going where no television show had gone before," he proclaimed in 2003), the evidence—as scrupulously gathered in Matthew Delmont's *The Nicest Kids in Town*—shows that *Bandstand* was behind the eight-ball throughout most of the 1950s and even into the 1960s. Blacks were an invisible presence on *Bandstand*, except for guest stars, despite Clark's conflated remembrance that "[b]lack and white kids would not only be sitting together in the bleachers, but out on the same floor *dancing*."

Even when black teenagers gained limited entrance, usually in single figures, they were not granted camera angles or publicity. While they waited in line outside the stage door, or requested tickets in advance, black students could only watch as their white schoolmates were ushered inside. A station map in the *American Bandstand Yearbook* for 1958 features a dozen teenage head shots, as far-flung from WFIL's home base as Salt Lake City, Utah; Lawton, Oklahoma; and Clatskanie, Oregon. All are white. The controversy that accompanied Frankie Lyman dancing with a white girl on Alan Freed's television show, *The Big Beat*, in 1957, and its consequent cancellation two weeks before Clark went on the air nationally, allows that *Bandstand* had little choice than to play it safe. In the quest for national affiliates, the ABC network wanted to offend few sensibilities; but long before it beaconed across the country, *Bandstand* was exclusionary, and known to be so.

In October 1957, a demonstration took place outside *Bandstand*'s studios, organized by a South Philadelphian named Vivian Brooker, who was inspired by the school demonstrations in Little Rock, Arkansas, seeing its parallels in her hometown. Through concentrated pressure, she and her fellow protesters were eventually able to integrate the show, but it was a short-lived triumph. There seemed more urgent battles to fight on the path to full citizenship, and Clark proved too passive-aggressive a personality to confront, amiable even as *Bandstand* provided only token assimilation. After a while, it was useless to try, or pretend interest in the pale shadow of the dances and rhythmic blues that *Bandstand* was appropriating. Besides, black teenagers could watch themselves on the *Mitch Thomas Show*, its signal beaming from Wilmington, Delaware, into the valley surrounding, which included Philadelphia, or as Clark's station attempted to lay claim to their viewing area, *WFIL-adelphia*.

Thomas grew up in New Brunswick, New Jersey, halfway between New York and Philadelphia, which paralleled his journey along a Northeast black radio station circuit, moving from New York's WADO to a spot on Philadelphia's WDAS, which featured larger-than-life disc jockeys like Doug "Jocko" Henderson (*First on the scene with the record machine!*) and Georgie Woods (*The Guy with the Goods!*). Woods, especially, had no problem blending social activism with rock and roll, and his promoted concerts throughout the Philadelphia region, beginning in April 1955, did much to spread the music across racial lines, as did his later support of the NAACP, Martin Luther King Jr., and outreach into the black community. In fact, Woods felt the term "rock and roll" was more about an expansive audience than a type of music; in his ears, it all came from rhythm and blues.

Later that year, on August 13, WPFH, an independent television station from Wilmington, Delaware, unaffiliated with the three major networks, decided to put on a Saturday afternoon version of *Bandstand* aimed at a black audience, hosted by a black disc jockey. Thomas was chosen, and for the next three years, his show provided an alternative to Clark's, though Mitch could not hope to compete when *Bandstand* went national. That would have to wait another fifteen years, until 1970, when Don Cornelius begat *Soul Train* in Chicago, syndicating nationally the next year and continuing for the next three and a half decades.

The tacit acceptance of *Bandstand*'s status quo was compromised by how important the show was in crossing over black rock and roll to the pop charts. *Bandstand* did much to provide a national audience for records and artists who might have found themselves on the far side of a racial chasm, and no one wanted to rock the boat by politicizing the show. In an example of this re-verse exploitation, Chuck Berry's first appearance, in 1957, gamed the system by turning *Bandstand*'s teen appeal into a roll call of affiliated cities—Boston, Pittsburgh, the Frisco Bay—where his Sweet L'il Sixteen might be found dancing to the television, guaranteeing him continual exposure and a hit record; though his prominence as a black performer wouldn't stop him from spend-ing twenty months in prison for violating the Mann Act, trans-porting a minor across state lines in December 1959. His teenager with the grown-up blues, high heels, and lipstick looked older than she was.

||||||

THE TOP TEN NEEDED CONSTANT replenishment; even a ma-jor hit could not count on much more than a month or two of longevity, with radio charts vying to get the drop on each other, and independent labels rife with producers and songwriters look-ing to jump on the teen *bandstand*-wagon. It was almost too easy. The kids were singing on the corner, getting together in corridors and stairwells and underneath the elevated tracks, pleading in four-part harmony to be discovered. Sometimes they even had their own songs. If not, the new teen pan alley, located in New York's Brill Building and staffed with aspiring youngsters from the outer boroughs, was more than happy to supply a con-stant stream of rhyme-friendly sing-a-longs.

The world of Philly's record men was small, entangled, and insular, gathering in the back room of the Brown Jug, entertained by visiting promotion and label representatives. There was Harry Finfer and lawyer Frank Lipsius, of Jamie Records, who through their contacts on *Bandstand* would use the show as a springboard for their new guitar instrumentalist, Duane Eddy, complete with whoops and a low-stringed sound hollowed out by the reverb of a grain tank in Arizona, courtesy of producer Lee Hazlewood. There was Bernie Binnick of Swan, by all accounts a nice guy who tried to remain friends with his artists, which meant he didn't take them for all they were worth, who had partnered with Tony Mammarella of that selfsame *Bandstand*, and had found success in the onomatopoeic nonsense syllables of Dickie Doo and the Donts' "Click Clack" and "Nee Nee Na Na Na Na Nu Nu." Swan shared offices at 1405 Locust Street and was distributed by Cameo-Parkway Records, founded in 1956 by songwriter Bernie Lowe, who, with lyricist Kal Mann, would strike teen gold the following year with Elvis Presley's "Let Me Be Your Teddy Bear." While waiting for that to be released, Mann joined Lowe in his label venture, along with Dave Appell, an instrumentalist who led Cameo's house band, the Applejacks. Cameo's first hit was Charlie Gracie's "Butterfly" in March 1957, and over the next eight years it became one of Philadelphia's most successful imprints. These three labels would, along with Bob Marcucci and Peter DeAngelis's Chancellor Records, soon define how the world would hear the sounds bartered within the Brown Jug.

With Horn's example as warning, Clark stayed away from overt monetary payoffs, though the practice was widespread among those seeking airplay favor. That wasn't to say conflict of interest couldn't be camouflaged by a well-placed writer's credit, or publishing royalties routed through one's own company. The stakes rose when *Bandstand* was given a weekly prime-time slot every Saturday night. The audience was seated—a high school assembly instead of a dance in the gym—in the Little Theater on West Forty-Fourth Street in New York. The show's parade of acts gave it the feel of a fast-paced revue. The first guests, braving a snowstorm on February 15, 1958, were Pat Boone, Johnnie Ray, the Royal Teens, Chuck Willis, and Connie Francis. Jerry Lee Lewis sang both "Breathless" and "Great Balls of Fire." Regardless of where their records stood in the charts, this was the countdown that mattered in terms of being *seen.*

Playing favorites didn't necessarily make hitting the hit parade any easier if the hit wasn't there. Intense competition meant that once a record came out of the gate, it had to make its own way, as quickly and indelibly as possible, a survival of the catchiest. The scat-like harmonies of group rhythm and blues began to staccato, clipping the consonants and drawing out vowels behind the lead singer, who was more inclined to shout.

But it had to be heard first, and *Bandstand* provided a showcase like no other. On Clark's January 9, 1958, Top Ten survey, "Get a Job" by the Silhouettes is at number 9. A silhouette of a silhouette, the group took their name from another hit that came out of Philadelphia in 1957, the Rays' "Silhouettes." It was written by Bob Crewe, who would later guide that fullest flowering of Philadelphia's falsetto sound, the tenor heights ascended by the Four Seasons, as Philadelphia's sons and daughters dispersed to the suburbs (Franki Valli, from north Jersey, might have recorded for Grand, but he would've had to soften his vibrato), and his partner Frank Slay. "Silhouettes" had been played on *Bandstand* for the first time on September 26, 1957. Three days later it entered *Billboard's* Hot 100; three weeks later it stood at number three, an equilateral triangle.

"Get a Job" was originally released on the Junior label, owned by Kae Williams, a WHAT disc jockey who guaranteed his own airplay. Half the publishing rights were assigned to Wildcat Music, in which Mammarella had an interest, and on March 8, 1958, the Silhouettes appeared on Clark's Saturday night edition of *Bandstand.* "Get a Job"'s *Sha Na Na Na* chant has since become a signature logo for 1950s doo-wop music, even to the point of birthing its own eponymous revival band in time for Woodstock. In 1962 the Silhouettes, now on the other side of the shade, recorded for Grand, "I Wish I Could Be There," bringing the prodigal sound of Philadelphia back home.

"We sat in the office, and figured out our own hits. We had no formal yardstick, only what we heard through the mail, on the phone, at the Jug, from gut reaction and from the kids," Clark said in his 1976 autobiography. *Bandstand* had "Get a Job" on the board for six weeks before it made the national charts. Persistence pays.

But you had to be clever. Even inspired. One word could change everything. One of Clark's most intuitive pop decisions might have been with a local Philadelphia singing group called Danny and the Juniors. The Bop was a new dance step imported from Los Angeles, based on Gene Vincent's "Be-Bop-A-Lula," with Cliff Gallup's ricochet guitar and Vincent's heavy breathing. Dave White and John Madara had written a song called "Do the Bop," and Artie Singer of Singular Records took an interest in the group, then called the Juvenaires. Singer had begun as a vocal coach, as befits the son of a cantor, and had composed "Be My Girl," with which Madara grazed the underside of the charts in mid-1957. But when Singer brought "Do the Bop" to Clark, the dance was already past its prime. The demo was undeniably infectious, though, opening with a jackhammer piano derived from Jerry Lee Lewis and "Whole Lotta Shakin' Goin' On" and a vocal G major arpeggio, each member climbing the chordal staircase to introduce themselves in order: Joe Terranova, Danny Rapp, Frank Maffei, and Dave White. Even in its nascent state, "Do the Bop" had possibilities, driven by its keyboard pummeling sixteenths to the bar that will be echoed in the rock revivalism of the Ramones and the relentless downstrokes of "Beat on the Brat."

"Why don't you change it to 'At the Hop'?" suggested Clark, who, after all, is running not much more than a televised version of the quintessential teen mixer, and who otherwise had little interest in writing music, except to stomp his foot over the phone (as he does with Freddie Cannon's "Tallahassee Lassie"), showing where the dance step should land. White and Madara rewrote the lyrics to fit the new theme, *bop* softened to *bahhh* like so many black sheep in the opening harmonies. *Hear the dance sensations that are sweepin' the nation / At the Hop.* They name-check as many gyrations as possible, even sending out a hoped-for mating—the *chalypso*, combining the cha-cha with the calypso in a dance that never gets off the ground, the recorded pronunciation of which I wondered about for many years until I found Clark's quote—"I noticed there wasn't a record to go with the dance, so I told two independent songwriters and producers I knew, Bob Crewe and Frank Slay, they could fill a need for a record."

Records are all about need. That you're not yet aware of. Heartbreak, heart back together, some dance floor somewhere. A favorite song for you to play along.

Danny and the Juniors are more than novelty merchants, teen-mongering as their hits might suggest. The b-side of "At the Hop" is a fervent classic of doo-wop existentialism, "Sometimes (When I'm All Alone)," tinged with *bel* and *bella* canto, like the wrought pleadings of Mario Lanza these singers hear growing up within the neighborhood. They follow it with the lightweight juvenile delinquency of "Rock and Roll Is Here to Stay." *We don't care what people say.* Though perhaps a Senate subcommittee, then in the process of preparing its response to this purported subversive threat to national morals, would soon have their own say.

Clark was on the ABC network. ABC-Paramount picked up the master from Singular and made it a nationwide hit, the Juniors alphabetically pyramiding in the same way the harmonies stack at the beginning of "At the Hop." (In later years Clark would host a game show called *The $10,000 Pyramid*, the prize money continually increasing to keep pace with inflation.) Dick was a savvy and at times blunt businessman, despite his casual demeanor. Along with his suggestion to slant "At the Hop," he not-so-subtly demanded that the song be administered by his publishing company, in effect gaining half the writers' royalties. Singer knew he had no choice, and though he thought this "bittersweet" in later years (a fact ironically seconded by Madara, who felt it was Singer who had unfairly taken more than his share of credit for writing and producing), Artie recognized Clark's seal of approval was an open-door opportunity to break his biggest hit. "Without him, there would've been no 'At the Hop,' no Danny and the Juniors."

By that same January 9 countdown, Danny and the Juniors' "At the Hop" is at number one. Bop hop pop.

|||||

NO MATTER HOW HE SPUN IT, Clark was in the record business, and *Bandstand*'s coast-to-coast exposure was an incalculable boon. The chalypso beat would be the underpinning to Billie and Lillie's "Lucky Ladybug," on the same Swan label that will find its most reliable hitmaker in the carnival-barker thump of Freddie "Boom Boom" Cannon, given liberal exposure on *Bandstand*.

Dick Clark, it was later revealed, owned a quarter of Swan, along with Binnick and *Bandstand*'s producer, Tony Mammarella; not to mention a share of Jamie Records. He was the head of Sea-Lark Music Publishing, a clever play on his name, as well as January Music, christened after the month his son was born, controlling publishing rights to more than one hundred and fifty songs; he owned a record manufacturing plant, Mallard Pressing Corporation; a record distributorship, Chips, that he managed with Lowe and Harry Chipetz; and a management company, SRO Artists. While his audience members showed off the latest steps, Clark was toe-tapping his own unique song-and-dance: the vertical integration. In all, he had financial interests in thirty-three companies, including expanding ventures in television and film production (*Because They're Young*), and ancillary novelty licensings of the *Bandstand* brand that included a stuffed kitten, the Platter-Puss.

For example, Clark would pay guest performers union scale for appearing on his show. Clark's production company, Click Corporation, wrote a check to the artist, the local distributor doing the promotion would reimburse Click for the performance, and the group would endorse their checks to the distributor. No cash changed hands, everyone profited, an invisible carousel of remuneration going round and round. Just like a record.

He saw nothing wrong in this. "It was the way things were done," he said later, insisting he never accepted the type of up-front bribes that the press was increasingly referring to as "payola," the practice of paying disc jockeys to play records. Clark might've looked down his nose at "the crassest form of promotion," but he wasn't above using *Bandstand*'s considerable reach to enrich himself. Far from impropriety, Dick said he simply "followed normal business practices under the ground rules that then existed," a narrowcasting definition of payola that was well within the blurred definitions of illegality. His share of Jamie initially cost him $125, and within two years had brought in $31,700 in salary and stock profits. "This happens in the nature of the business," he dissembles in his 1976 autobiography, *Rock, Roll and Remember*, "where on small investments you can reap large returns."

He had backed into this sleight-of-hand way of doing business as early as the success of Philadelphia's own Charlie Gracie singing "Butterfly," when Lowe came to him in hopes of fending off cover versions that were threatening to undercut Cameo's chance for a debut hit. Clark agreed to help, bringing two dozen copies of the song to a disc jockey convention in New York, his level of naiveté later compounding when, after the song spent seventeen weeks on the charts in March 1957, Bernie came to him with a check for $7,000 in appreciation for his kindness. Though he would "live to regret my decision to take the money," Dick understood that exposure on the scale of *Bandstand* was unprecedented. For performers and their promoters to reach a nationwide audience immediately, without having to do endless one-nighters and personal appearances, to target a specific teen demographic eager to pick up on the latest hit, to utilize television's direct umbilical connection to the living room—there was no reason for regretful living. Clark would prove a survivor, especially when his interlocking business interests came under scrutiny.

In November 1959, having revealed the seamy truths of the television quiz-show scandal to a horrified and rapt America, the House Subcommittee on Legislative Oversight, headed by Representative Emanuel Celler (D-NY), turned its aggrieved attention to the music business. The public hearings that centered on Charles Van Doren's rigged appearances on *Twenty-One* (that his answers had been provided beforehand) generated their own political quiz show, the investigators of the committee scripting their answers even before the questions were asked. The rampant conflict of interest within the world of rock and roll song plugging promised an even more flagellating public spectacle.

And make no mistake, this vendetta was about rock and roll, not the money behind it. The showdown was prompted by a long-term war between two songwriter performing rights associations: ASCAP (American Society of Composers, Authors and Publishers) and BMI (Broadcast Music Incorporated). The former represented "good music," the Broadway tunesmiths and those who had provided the mainstay of the American Songbook, and who looked down their noses at BMI, founded in 1941 to represent the renegade genres: country, blues, and all forms in between. That rock and roll was regarded as the devil's music, *jungle music,* immoral, appealing to baser instincts and resulting in youth-gone-wild, only proved that these records would not have been bought unless there was an insidious plot to corrupt America's teenagers. In a decade that banned comics, feared racial

miscegenation, and imagined communist conspiracies in every corner, rock and roll was an easy target. The major labels, suddenly
aware that independent labels were growing competitive, even
shutting them out from the changed marketplace, were more than
happy to join in the shaming—why were these kids not listening
to Sinatra, Bing Crosby, Les Paul and Mary Ford, Perry Como?
What about Chopin? *kvetched* comedian Sam Levenson, though it
is amusing to think of Frederic appearing on *Bandstand*, the gals
swooning at his rippling piano swirls and wan, effeminate profile.
The inference was that the only reason disc jockeys would play
such obvious trash is that they were being paid.

Clark proved a slippery witness. In front of the subcommittee looking into "Payola and Other Deceptive Practices in the
Broadcasting Fields," beginning in May 1960, Dick held his own,
refusing to budge from his protestations of innocence, despite the
fur stole given his wife by Lou Bedel of Era/Dore records; despite
the copyrights of the Dubs' "Could This Be Magic" from George
Goldner of End Records; or the outright gift of Huey Smith and
the Clowns' "Don't You Just Know It" from Johnny Vincent of
Ace Records, soon to show up on *All-Time Hits Vol. II*, a Clark
anthologized EP available by mail order. In response he submit-
ted an analysis by an "electronic data" firm called Computech
(an early demonstration of the binary future) that created enough
slanted number-crunching between his programming and the
number of hits resulting that showed how easy it was to manipulate data streams. Representative Steve Derounian, a Republican
from Long Island, chased him doggedly. "You didn't get payola,
but you got a lot of royola." The *Washington Post* dubbed it Clark-
ola, pointing their finger at the escalating *o-la-la* (perhaps Clark
thought that Billie and Lillie could use that phrase for their next
hit), overlooking the entrenched payola of politics driving this
inquisition.

Even as his fellow disc jockeys revealed culpability, telling tales of car payments and bribes proffered, Clark stayed calm and forth-right. He gave a good performance, his clean-cut image and air of innocence honed in his *Bandstand* persona, and he was used to being in front of the cameras. ABC, who recognized that Clark was one of their most valuable assets, made sure he stayed that way. Under pressure, Dick divested himself of his conflicting mu-sical interests ("I estimate I lost more than $8 million"), espe-cially when it came to Mammarella, who admitted to having taken cash payments. ("I was staggered," said Clark disingenuously. "I couldn't look Tony in the eye.") Tony had never shared in the largesse as much as Clark, and knowing he would never be the face of *Bandstand*, he resigned, preferring to take his chances with the music business and Swan. Alan Freed refused to sign a state-ment saying he had never accepted gifts or money in exchange for playing records, fearing a charge of perjury, and this act of defiance would ultimately sink his career, leaving him penniless and a broken man, dying in 1964 forgotten by the music he had championed. Clark, of course, had recognized that the future was in television.

Already *Bandstand* was a bigger juggernaut than anyone could have imagined, tapping into a consumer base that seemed to be gathering strength as the postwar baby boom generation came of teen-age and exerted its considerable buying power. ABC, seek-ing to differentiate itself from its rivals, had scored considerably with the youth market. In 1954, Walt Disney's weekly prime-time hour, the self-promoting *Disneyland*, had shown that an 1800s frontier woodsman named Davy Crockett could become a na-tional icon; following *Bandstand* each afternoon at five was the *Mickey Mouse Club*, whose Annette Funicello was a heartthrob phenomenon, mine included. On the *Ozzie and Harriet* show, a family comedy migrated from radio, it was their seventeen-year-old son Ricky and his 1957 hit records ("A Teenager's Romance," "Be-Bop Baby") that were stimulating viewership, and he would only get bigger in 1958 with "Poor Little Fool" and "Lonesome Town."

The sense of a national youth culture was reinforced by *Bandstand*, quickly transmitting fashion and visual stimuli and all manner of consumable products. The advertising emphasis was on sugar—soft drinks, candy, and snacks—and medicine for adolescent ailments, especially acne, which Clearasil promised to magically cure, paving the way to popularity and inclusion. The idea of a teenage market had been expanding since bobby-soxers danced in the aisle of the New York Paramount to Benny Goodman, finally able to see their idol outside of establishments that served liquor; and Frank Sinatra had coalesced this ready audience, always outgrowing itself, and thus ripe for renewal. A virtual community, hormones on carbonated overload, teenagers were amped and ready to rock.

On air. The camera dollies through a blue-sparkle cutout map of the continental United States. Les Elgart's "Bandstand Boogie" plays as theme song, a 1954 release that nonetheless harks back to the Big Band era, a comforting reminder of *Bandstand*'s respect for their elders. The kids cavort, the host looks out sincerely to those tuned in, and announces the first record.

The audience starts to dance.

||||||

THERE ARE TWO TYPES OF SONG—fast or slow, each with its own heartbeat. One for each side. Of the 45.

Everything else is just steps in between. *Bandstand* alternated one after another. With its emphasis on dancing, at a time when dancing had yet to go freestyle, *Bandstand* was in the unique position of both fostering dances and rendering them obsolete in a matter of weeks, a dizzying array of styles that would be replicated in teen gatherings across the nation. Each new style seemed to move the participants closer in physical proximity, as had the Volta in the Renaissance 1500s, breaching levels of immodest touch and similarly decried. Charleston, the animal dances of Bunny Hug and Pigeon Walk and Angle Worm Wiggle and especially the Fox Trot, Lindy Hop, Jitterbug, all seemed an escalation, and so would in future decades the disco Hustle, the Slam Dance moshing the pit, the jiggles-and-wiggles of the Humpty and the Lambada and the Macarena closing out the twentieth century, making way for Twerking.

In no decade has there been such a proliferation and sheer number of formal ways to move the human body as these later years of fifties-into-sixties, each with its crafted, even manufactured soundtrack. *Bandstand*'s first realized craze was the Stroll, when Clark took note of its sashay on his dance floor, pointing out to the manager of the Diamonds that the group might want to create a record crystallizing it. Songwriter Clyde Otis obliged, and the Diamonds soon had a top-five hit, seconded only by their sprightly appropriation of the Gladiolas' original "Little Darlin'." Dick was reluctant to admit that the step's laid-back glide was originated by black youth dancing to Chuck Willis's "C. C. Rider" on the Mitch Thomas show. It was a classic line dance, two parallel rows of boys and girls, partnering and walking down the aisle, a wedding march allowing each couple room to strut their stuff. When Thomas called to complain that Clark claimed the Stroll as his own, Dick was his amiable self, and took the time to mention the Stroll's lineage on the show the next day, quickly returning to business as usual. Any recognition accorded Thomas was small acknowledgment compared to Clark's national pulpit.

The dances came and went with astonishing frequency, but when Chubby Checker did the twist on *Bandstand* in April 1960, the floodgates opened. A pun on the name of Fats Domino, thought up by Clark's first wife, Barbara, Ernest Evans had been discovered working at Sonny's Cut Up Chickens at Ninth and

Washington, and had lately taken to hanging around the Cameo-Parkway offices. One of his party tricks was to imitate other singers, and in the summer of 1959, he had scored a midsized hit with "The Class" on Parkway, where he instructed his rowdy pupils to pay attention and listen to him interpret "Mary Had a Little Lamb" in the style of Fats, the Coasters, Elvis, and the Chipmunks, with a Cozy Cole–ish drum solo thrown in for good measure. The crispness of the arrangement presaged the pop emphases propelling Chubby's "The Twist," frontal drums and background chorus trading percussions, with a saxophone underlining each phrase. The song had evolved Checker's way through the sly entendres of Hank Ballard and the Midnighters, in a version Ballard himself transmuted from the Sensational Nightingales. King Records, Ballard's label, had released it as the b-side of "Teardrops on Your Letter" in the beginning of 1959, but it was increasingly flipped at black teen parties. Clark was aware of Ballard's record, seeing the twist migrate to his own audience, but thought the record too suggestive, except the suggestion that another version of "The Twist" was called for. Though they didn't own the publishing, Kal Mann urged Cameo-Parkway to go ahead with a cover version. More important, a dance was formalized to go with the upcoming appearance on *American Bandstand*, and Chubby, with a cuddly and nonthreatening air in the midst of the twist's sexual intimations, was a good spokesman. His description of putting out a cigarette with a toe and drying off his butt with a towel is more post-sexual, rather than the act itself; which was hardly Ballard's approach.

The twist would go on to have a long afterlife of its own when it was adopted by the fashionable celebrity set. A signifier of early-sixties swinging epicentered in New York's Peppermint Lounge, the dance made teenagers out of an adult generation that had the money and the privilege to make the society pages. And in its wake would come the Pony, the Fly, the Slop, the Watusi, the

Hully-Gully, the Mashed Potatoes, the Bristol Stomp; many of these pas de deux would bear a Cameo or Parkway label, as *Bandstand* found in Cameo a more-than-willing choreographer.

The abstract interpretative movements of music's motion. The rituals of attraction in the mating dance. Who then will embody why these youngsters dance?

IIIIII

BANDSTAND HAD PROVED IT COULD make hits; now could it create its own star map? The apparent answer, to Bob Marcucci and Peter DeAngelis of Chancellor Records, was as clear as giving Dick Clark a first come, first served, and then finding the faces to fill it.

On March 7, 1959, Frankie Avalon's "Venus" ascends to the top of the charts in *Cash Box*, an aptly titled trade magazine whose focus has shifted from coin-operated jukeboxes and pinball machines to the tilts and flippers of rock's flashing lights, the high score and free game of this week's Top 100. A Saturday later, with "Venus" still at number one, Avalon appears on *Bandstand* to sing his hit and receive his gold record. As he pleads for *a little girl for me to thrill* he clasps his hands in prayer, in gratitude, accepting a solid gold watch to commemorate this achievement, and then he's off to Australia for a headlining tour. Only six months before, Frankie was holding his nose as an adenoidal joke recording "DeDe Dinah," which proved his breakthrough hit, following it with the sound-alike "Gingerbread." Now he has a ballad that allows him full voice. Impeccably groomed, the shoulders of his suit squared off, curly hair waved, he is able to work the adulation of an adoring throng like the valves of the trumpet that was his first instrument. An assured gentleman, like the overall gentling of rock and roll on the charts.

Following "Venus," the Fleetwoods' "Come Softly to Me"

soft-focuses its way to the top position. In the last year, the Poni-Tails' "Born Too Late," the Teddybears' (featuring a nascent Phil Spector) "To Know Him Is to Love Him," and the Everly Brothers' "All I Have to Do Is Dream" have trilled adolescent hearts. "Young Love," Sonny James avers in 1957, the delicate naiveté of "First Date, First Kiss, First Love" (his follow-up), with the simplistic chords to match. Tommy Sands has a "Teenage Crush." Orchestral flourishes wait in the wings, the raw sound of early rock and roll smoothed into place, no more an unruly lock of duck tail. "Venus" may rise in the east a month after Buddy Holly's fateful plane crash, but even Holly intuited the sweetening to come, adding pizzicato violins to his final hit, "I Guess It Doesn't Matter Anymore."

On the pop charts, Italian-Americans seem a negotiated compromise. They split the difference between the bland—Pat Boone's "April Love" springs into summer of 1958—and the blacker, those crossovers from the r&b charts that, even if teen-age, are hardly homogenized. Italians are no stranger to marginalization and discrimination, almost but not quite assimilated into the American norm, even exotic outside of northeastern urban clusters, but it gives these once-*dagos* or *wops* (a syllable that will characterize the rise of Italian-inflected group harmony) just enough third-generation ethnicity to be clandestinely appealing. To their *buona fortuna*, Italians are able to align on the white side of racial divide, and conveniently enough for *Bandstand*, their neighborhood is just a few blocks away, not only in locale, but within handy grasp of Philadelphia's music moguls.

As all Italian mamas know, they're good boys. They respect where they came from. Frankie lives on South 13. Bobby Rydell is from 2423 South 11, Fabian from the 2500 block. "It was a water trough on 12th and Dickinson," Bobby tells Paul Perrello on *Philly Factor*, a TV show with the same local appeal as the original *Bandstand*, only in 2013. "If you drank from it you became a singer, if you put your feet in it you became a dancer." It may be a well-practiced line, but it resonates, not only from those who remember the Old Country, but those making their way in the new country of teen.

South Philadelphia had always been fertile ground for Italian musicians. Russ Columbo, one of the first crooners, grew up around South Seventh, in the early years of the century, as did Eddie Lang (birthname Salvatore Massaro), who practically invents the possibilities of the guitar. Only this wasn't the older guys clustered around the fruit and vegetable stands on Ninth Street, sipping shot cups of expresso and water glasses of chianti, the wise guys who styled themselves after the Lanzettis or their archrival crime family, the Brunos. There is the Hoboken-bred example of Frank Sinatra, one of the first teen idols when he breaks from Tommy Dorsey's band, and those in his wake: Tony Bennett (Benedetto), Vic Damone (Vito Rocco Farinola), Frankie Laine (Francesco LoVecchio), Jimmy Roselli. *Goombahs* all.

This new breed of Italian teen aspires to be an all-around-entertainer, more at home in a nightclub than a roadhouse, dressed in tux and cravat, or in Fabian's case, perhaps a collar carelessly pulled open at the neck, as if pre-rock pop had survived Elvis's onslaught. Their appeal is the innocence and ingratiation, especially when measured against the more threatening idolatry of rock and roll's first generation. There was always an undercurrent of out-of-control in Elvis, Little Richard, Chuck Berry; subsurface menace was part of their allure. But the idols of Philadelphia were boys next door who would show up a-courting on the doorstep bearing flowers, a well-cuffed suit, a winning smile, and a *please thank you*. For girls, they were made to be pinned on bedroom walls, or star in deflowering fantasies. For guys, they were the ultimate pals, to meet on the street corner, shoot the breeze, get some kicks and look for chicks, to put the top down and ride around in circles. They are resolutely teenage, and their songs reflect the rites of adolescent passage. Bobby goes to a "Swinging School," Frankie sings to a femme on the 'twixt-teens border of "Bobby Sox to Stockings." Fabian imagines himself a "Hound Dog Man," though compared to Presley, he's still a boy.

Francis Thomas Avallone had taken up the trumpet after seeing Kirk Douglas in *Young Man with a Horn.* At nine he won a talent contest at the President Theatre on South Twenty-Third, around the corner from the Italo-American Bocce Club, and in 1951 he was awarded a refrigerator and console record player from Paul Whiteman's *TV Teen Club*, a local show for which Bernie Lowe was musical director. When he was eleven, Frankie crashed a party for the singer Al Martino (also *paisan* from Philadelphia) showing off his Younger Man with a Horn skills, and Martino was sufficiently impressed to take him to New York to meet Jackie Gleason. Two weeks later he was playing "Tenderly" on Gleason's network television show. Frankie reached diminutive television heights as "The Boy with the Magic Trumpet" on Pinky Lee's afternoon show, and then, as child prodigality faded, found a place in a local band called Rocco and His Saints, which is where Bob Marcucci came upon him one night. He could see the incipient possibilities for a good-looking wholesome teen who could sing. Chancellor Records, founded in the dining room of the Chancellor Hotel, had gotten a toehold in the music business with Jodie Sands's "With All My Heart," using it as entrée to a distribution alliance with Am-Par, one of ABC's subsidiaries, with a direct line to Clark and *Bandstand.* The new teen stars emphasized sensitivity—Ricky Nelson was the archetype, though it helped his credibility that he did have James Burton as a guitar player—and visual appeal.

Marcucci's in with *Bandstand* provided opportunity as he developed Avalon. Bob did everything to make the most of it, as he'd always done with Clark. When he and Clark first became friendly, Bob had sent him a diamond ring to celebrate the birth of Dick's son, which Clark judiciously returned. Their ties had been brokered with the 1957 movie *(Disc Jockey) Jamboree*, interspersing musical appearances by Charlie Gracie (Binnick had an interest), Jodie Sands (which brought Marcucci into the picture), Jerry Lee Lewis, Fats Domino, Slim Whitman, and even the Count Basie Orchestra, introduced by various record spinners from across the country, including Clark himself. A callow Avalon, barely beyond sixteen and still backed by Rocco and His Saints, sings "Teacher's Pet," and though the movie didn't break the song, which shows Frankie gamely trying to get comfortable with his frontman status and turn on the charm, it did introduce Frankie to the *Bandstand* regulars, many of whom knew him from the neighborhood.

For Avalon's eighteenth birthday, Bob wangled an invitation for the singer to appear on the show, wheeling in a cake and unfurling a congratulatory scroll presented by the president of his fan club. While Marcucci worked the stunts, Peter DeAngelis, classically trained, tried to lower his musical expectations—he didn't particularly care for rock and roll. It might explain "DeDe Dinah," when, attempting to project a dumbed-down song, Avalon got some studio laughs holding his nose and singing (less comedic is that he just had a cold that day). It went top ten in the beginning of 1958, Chancellor was in the teen idol sweepstakes, and *Bandstand* had a homegrown star.

Avalon was soft-spoken, and DeAngelis played up his dreaminess. "A Boy Without a Girl" has a lullaby rhyme scheme—*tune/ June, night/light, shine/mine*—and a sincerity far beyond the schoolyard pleadings of a stolen kiss. *Swingin' on a Rainbow*, his third album, along with a tear-out poster and almost as many head shots as there are songs, finds him taking on standards like "Secret Love" and "Try a Little Tenderness." Guitarist Al Caiola tickles the jazz chords behind him. There is no hint of impropriety.

Flipping the coin, Marcucci didn't have to range far to find his next creation. Fabiano Forte was sitting on a stoop near Thirteenth and Rittner when Bob drove by. Though the youth was distraught because his father had just suffered a heart attack, Marcucci's first reaction was "He had the look, he had the face," and wondered if the soon uni-named Fabian could sing. Not that it would matter, if he could get on television. The songs would come. What was most important was Fabian's feral visage. As Avalon's hits softened in 1958 on the way to "Venus"—"I'll Wait for You" was a plaintive ballad—Marcucci wanted to craft another singer, this time emphasizing animal passion. Fabian would be the one to deliver "I'm Your Tiger," or "Turn Me Loose," his voice husky with desire à la Presley, though there was trepidation as he approached the undercut of the note. Luckily, the screams that greeted his appearance at local record shops, and then on *Bandstand*, overshadowed pitch; and he had a genuine winning humility in the face of his physical appeal—he repeatedly turned down Marcucci's initial inquiries because he'd never thought of himself as a performer. His father's worsening condition and inability to work pressured him to take a financial chance.

Despite immediate pandemonium even before he sang, Fabian's first two records, the DeAngelis-Marcucci penned "Shivers" and "Lilly Lou," failed to generate a reciprocal hit. Clark told them, like the "chalypso," they needed a song to go with their phenomenon. Chancellor imported Doc Pomus and Mort Shuman from New York to shape the teen bravado of "I'm a Man," following it with the barely contained smolder of "Turn Me Loose." Like they had for Avalon, Chancellor put pinup posters inside his albums and even referred to him as Tiger. Marcucci coached him to pick one girl in the audience and sing to her, and so sing to all. By mid-1959, Fabian was the teen ideal, an idea gone idol.

In *The Idolmaker*, a 1980 movie loosely roman-à-clef'd on Marcucci and Fabian's dynamic, the maker (Ray Sharkey) tells the made (Peter Gallagher, playing Caesare), "You know something? With the right handling you could go all the way." This loss of virginity, with its "*National Bandstand*" appearances and betrayals and exaltations, has inevitable consequences. In the same year it was released, an ambivalent Fabian sued the co-conspirators of the film (which included Marcucci) and said, "Sometimes I wish I could wake up and be an unknown. . . . The public is so wonderful, and so cruel. . . . Why me?" As wounding was the harsh criticism Fabian faced for being a pretty boy embodying the supposed sins of rock and roll, especially in the press. Harriet Van Horne, a Scripps-Howard columnist, dismissed him as "a depraved cub scout . . . ," and was "repelled" by the "strange, off-key wails of the strange, off-keyed lad." But Fabian didn't pretend to be anything other than he was. "I don't think my voice alone has brought me success," he told his fans on the back of number 20 of his own bubble-gum card series. "I try to put to music what we teenagers feel in our hearts." And it's Fabian's heart that comes through on his records, as it does in his wedding video from September 19, 1998, where he dances with his bride Amanda to "Can You Feel the Love Tonight" in the reflected gleam of her tiara.

Over at Cameo, Bernie Lowe wanted his own idol. His relationship with Charlie Gracie had terminated when Gracie wondered why his royalties were half what they should be, resulting in an acrimonious but eventually settled lawsuit. Gracie would never grace *Bandstand* again. Lowe watched in envy as Chancellor seemed to have a lock on *Bandstand*, though he always ran his records by Clark to see if they would get on the show, and canned them if they didn't. The success of John Zacherle's "Dinner with Drac," a spookified monster takeoff that had the same novelty appeal as *I Was A Teenage Werewolf*, wasn't enough to keep the lights on at the office he shared with Swan. So when Frankie Day, the bass player for the Applejacks, came into Bernie Binnick's side of Locust Avenue to play him a demo from one Bobby Rydell, a drummer with Rocco and His Saints among other local bands, Bernie turned to Bernie and asked what he thought. Lowe didn't think much, or so he said. As soon as Binnick left the room, he promptly signed Rydell. Besides, Swan had their hands full with Freddie Cannon, though his raspy voice could never provoke a romantic teen crush.

Another veteran of *Paul Whiteman's TV Teen Club*, Robert Ridarelli was an inveterate entertainer, specializing in comedy routines imitating the Reds Skelton and Buttons, Frank Fontaine's Crazy Guggenheim and James Cagney and Johnnie Ray, drumming in the style of Gene Krupa. His father showed him off at local nightspots, Palumbo's and Sciolli's and the Erie Social, though Bobby—now Rydell—seemed to get no further than the clubs surrounding Atlantic City, which is where Frankie Day saw him in Somers Point when both were working in Billy Duke's Dukes. Even as Avalon and Fabian ascended the heights, Bobby could only sit on the sidelines as his first two releases on Cameo, "Please Don't Be Mad" and "All I Want Is You," fizzled, despite proximity to *Bandstand*. Clark liked to get behind songs that had a hit potential, and he hadn't heard it yet. But "Tallahassee Lassie" had a punctuated drum break to punch home the title. When Mann and Appell inserted a similar semicolon and exclamation point to "Kissin' Time" in June 1959, as well as a roll call of cities that mimicked "Sweet Little Sixteen," Cameo gave Dick something to work with. Bobby's narrow chin, wide smile, and upper row of perfect pearlies added to his telegenic looks. He moved easily, a natural dancer, balancing a pompadour on his forehead more ship's prow than stylized wave.

Bobby had the most pizzazz (I'll take a slice) of Philadelphia's teen idols, with the provolone hits to prove it. The arrangements of "Wild One," "We Got Love," the vow of "I'll Never Dance Again" broken by "The Cha Cha Cha" and "The Fish" (this was Cameo-Parkway's dance floor after all), even an English-language version of "Volare" that returned the song to the top of the charts just two years after Domenico Modugno had the original hit version of Italy's also-ran in the 1958 Eurovision song competition, are consistently sprightly, background vocals providing a Greek chorus to Bobby's grin. It was his winning ways that paired him with Ann-Margret in the 1962 film version of *Bye Bye Birdie*, an honorific to go with Rydell High School, named after him in the 1978 movie *Grease*, and Bobby Rydell Boulevard, which runs past the row house where he grew up.

It was the growing that would prove the problem. There was a built-in obsolescence in being a teen idol. Almost immediately thoughts turned to what might happen after one reached drinking age. They all aspire to the career path of a Bobby Darin, another Italo-American (Robert Rissotto) who will move from the teen sploosh of "Splish Splash" to reimagining "Mack the Knife" with big-band panache, arriving at the Copa in June 1960 brandishing a swagger that owes more to Frank Sinatra than Elvis.

The vacuum created by Presley's army induction, rapidly filled by Tommys and Johnnys and even more Bobbys, was a foreshortened career path encapsulated by "Bill Parsons" (actually country singer Bobby Bare) in "All American Boy," whose manager promises to *get ya on Bandstand* before Uncle Sam comes a-knocking. Rydell always doffed his hat to pre–rock and roll; one of his favored recalls is the first time he appears in Las Vegas, singing "Some of These Days" with George Burns at the Sahara Hotel, brandishing a derby and cane and soft-shoeing in tandem. He watches and learns from Burns's timing, Red Skeleton's comic *cadiddle*-hopping, Perry Como's sway with a song. "People would go crazy," he says, "seeing the young and the old." Or the young becoming old.

||||||

A LOVER'S ISLAND. The Sheppards are warming up the radio on Jerry Blavat's show. The *Geator with the Heater*, the *Boss with the Hot Sauce*, is broadcasting at the high end of Philly's dial, actually from across the river in Camden, but he takes to heart his *yon* teenagers, the lorn and the lost, the dreamers and the merely adolescent, longing for pop fealty.

Blavat's show begins in September 1960, moving station to station in the Delaware Valley, spinning oldies sometimes no more than a year or two from memory, keeping their flame alive: the Paragons meet the Jesters, the Five Satins casting "Shadows" over the Dubs, the Click-ettes, the Students, the Chantels. His clipped accent slaps you on the back, calls you *mah man*, pours you a glass of *vino* and glad-hands you into being his best friend. His specialty is group harmony, the fast and the slow, one made for swaggering, the other for late nights by candlelight, his *coyotes* romancing *foxes* as he introduces each record and then talks over the fade: *"Young love . . . teenage love . . . it's timeless . . . it has no beginning no end . . . it will never end as long as there are teenagers. . . ."*

Blavat got his start as a dancer on Bob Horn's *Bandstand*, a Jewish-Italian kid whose father ran a gambling operation. When Horn was fired, Jerry was arrested for picketing the arrival of Dick Clark, though both soon became fast friends. He was the road manager for Danny and the Juniors, made the rounds of late-night hangouts befriending and advising and promoting Philadelphia's movers and shakers, touting songs to disc jockeys and running dances. In 1964, he is approached to do his own television show, *The Discophonic Scene*. The reason: *Bandstand* is moving to Los Angeles.

With his interest in television, Clark's relocation makes sense. ABC has intimated it wants to switch *Bandstand* to a once-a-week slot, and he senses change in the wind. When Bernie Binnick brings over a bunch of masters he has licensed from EMI in

England in the fall of 1963, he asks Dick to listen to one. "She Loves You" by the Beatles reminds him of Bobby Rydell's "We Got Love," with its *yeah-yeah-yeah* chorus hook, and sounds "old-fashioned, real mid-fifties." He puts it on the Record Revue and it gets a 73, with references made to Chuck Berry and the Everly Brothers. Dick shows them a picture of the group and it's laughed at by the kids on the show. "I left the station that afternoon," he tells autobiographer Richard Robinson, "without the faintest idea that the days of good ol' rock 'n' roll were about to become a few scratched film clips, a list of golden oldies, and some cherished memories of growing up in the fifties." Which he will make good use of in the future, as *Bandstand*'s characterization of the decade becomes the lineage of *Happy Days* and the Fonz.

They're all heading to California. Frankie and Fabian have Hollywood experience, requisite screen test roles (*Guns of the Timberland* for Avalon, "Fabe" with his own vehicle, *Hound Dog Man*) as the young buck, settings distinctly rural for these distinctly urban kids. True to type, Avalon will pair with Annette Funicello to provide striking brunette contrast to the beach blanket bingo of bleach blond bikinis. They bring a touch of Mediterranean to the Pacific, setting them apart from the sun-baked teens that are invited to the parties of these American-International drive-in specials, a Fred Astaire and Ginger Rogers for the surf set.

Fabian takes a more cliff-diving chance. In "The Lion Walks Among Us," an episode directed by Robert Altman from a 1961 television series, *Bus Stop*, he walks into a club, picks up the singer's guitar, plays an E chord. *Now I see a pretty girl*, he sings to the blonde on the owner's arm. "I'm everyman and any man, one man and all man," he adds before pulling a switchblade, a thrill killer on the turn-me-loose. He will rob and humiliate, set fire to his own hands to implicate police brutality, and finally murder his lawyer. To see Fabian shift almost too easily into the psychotic role made the harrow of the tale even more chilling, and the network backpedaled as sponsors bailed and television affiliates chose not to run the sequence. It was broadcast on December 3 before being buried, like a good corpse. Fabian hoped it might counter his teen image, but his name and his looks worked against him, unable to disappear into the performance he played.

Bobby Rydell had the most prestigious cinematic outing come his way, a starring role opposite Ann-Margret in 1963's *Bye Bye Birdie* as Hugo Peabody, the "One Boy" who stands up to uncivilized Conrad Birdie, a Presleyesque rocker on the verge of being drafted. The era that *Birdie* heralds is already bygone, framed within a traditional boy-wins-girl-wins-boy musical restoring a sense of winsome tradition, much like *Fiddler on the Roof.* Rydell's on-screen chemistry with Ann-Margret is such that the producers of the film expand his part from the original Broadway production, where Hugo was played rather differently by Michael Pollard. When Conrad finally sings "One Last Kiss" on Ed Sullivan's show, it might well be *Bandstand* saying farewell to Philadelphia.

The confluence of events couldn't be more synchronous. Clark would leave town, moving his production company to Hollywood in February 1964 even as the impact of the Beatles' appearance on Ed Sullivan's Sunday night variety show heralded a new hierarchy of idol. *Bikini Beach*, released in the summer of 1964, has Frankie trading barbs with the Potato Bug, a visiting English interloper who seems to be stealing his thunder, dual-roled by Avalon in a shaggy mop-top and *jolly good* Terry-Thomas inflection. Actually, when the Bug picks up an electric double-neck (guitar top, bass bottom) Danelectro to sing "Gimme Your Love," with *ooh-yeah-yeah* and falsetto swoops, it gives an alternate career path of how Avalon might have progressed had he not gone to the beach. The shopworn plot tries to contain the "wild perversions" of rock and roll, boiled down to "surfing, speed, and sex," within the basic chastity of Annette and Frankie, the real generational schism

replaying the Revolutionary War, an English counteroffensive re-
conquering the colonies. Avalon takes strategic leave from the city
of the Liberty Bell and the Declaration of Independence just as
the British arrive. Candy Johnson shimmies her fringed-dress a-
go-go into a frenzy and the surf-rock Pyramids jump onstage,
heads shaved in retaliation to the Brits' long hair. *Bandstand* is
readying to morph into *Where the Action Is*. South Philadelphia is
becoming the Old Country.

The Hollywood life is not for Rydell, a family man, and he
returns home though his prospects are waning. Also left behind
by Clark's California relocation are Chancellor and Cameo and
Swan. They are lost without *Bandstand*'s ready access. Dance
crazes are on the way out, except for the Freddie, an ungainly
flapping of arms promoted by Freddie and the Dreamers from
Manchester in the midlands of England. Girls are screaming for
some other ethnicity, which isn't Italian from Philadelphia.

Even Clark finds his influence diminished in California. Other
televised music outlets, like *Shindig* and *Hullabaloo*, seem more
with-it, their kaleidoscopic stage sets and Carnaby costuming and
less decorous artists making *Bandstand* seem like kid stuff.

The steep decline and consequent upheaval in Philadelphia's
old guard allows new players to enter the city's mainline. Kenny
Gamble and Leon Huff meet at Cameo working together on
Candy and the Kisses' "The 81," counting down yet another
dance. Though there were black artists at the company, they
soon realized any management positions were closed to African-
Americans and set out on their own. The result would be the lush
soul fantasias of Philadelphia International, whose hi-hat rhythms
usher in the arrival of disco, and whose groups—the O'Jays,
Harold Melvin and the Bluenotes, and especially the Intruders
("Cowboys to Girls")—will come to represent the soundscape of
the city. Producer Thom Bell, originally partnered with Gamble,
continues Philadelphia's high-tenor tradition with his production

of the Delfonics (the ineffable "Didn't I Blow Your Mind This Time") on his Philly Groove label, and the Stylistics ("You Make Me Feel Brand New"). And in a twist of fate that should give Mitch Thomas a measure of satisfaction, Gamble and Huff's plush, string-driven "TSOP" becomes the theme song of *Soul Train*.

The sound of Philadelphia dancing anew.

|||||

AND ME. MY SLEEVES ARE rolled up on my short-sleeved shirt. My hair is parted on the left side, combed to the right, held in slope by Wildroot Cream Oil. I'm wearing a pair of ripple-soled shoes. There's a key chain looped along my right leg, into my front pocket, a stylistic remnant from the zoot suit era. Or maybe it's just on the verge of going out of fashion after twenty-five years. I'm clearly catching up with the times, standing outside my apartment building in Brooklyn in the last year of the fifties, the moment before I enter my teens. Someday I will discover that Bobby Fischer walked this stretch of Lenox Road playing oral chess games with his teacher, on his way to the Silver Moon Chinese Restaurant, a neon fluorescent shining on nearby Flatbush Avenue that we also frequent on Sunday nights for chow mein and egg drop soup, next to the shop where I'll buy my first records at the end of 1958, when I get a record player in the shape of a conga drum for my twelfth birthday, and purchase four 45s, three of which are on the MGM label: Sheb Wooley's "Purple People Eater," Tommy Edwards's "It's All in the Game," and Conway Twitty's "It's Only Make Believe." Novelty and romance, that's what I'm about.

Upstairs from my prideful pose, on the fifth floor, there's a television set that hasn't gone color yet. I watch the wrestling matches from Madison Square Garden, Antonino Rocca versus

Argentine Zuma, Haystacks Calhoun and the Graham Brothers and Killer Kowalski; *Million Dollar Movie*, with its *Gone with the Wind* theme music; I dial channel 7 for *Bandstand* in the afternoons, and especially on Saturday night at eight, when it's really like a concert come to life in your living room. It's a world away from the condescension that accompanies these stars' appearances on other variety shows, those of Ed Sullivan or Steve Allen, poking bemused fun at this goofy teen claptrap.

One after another, it's all the records you've been hearing on the radio come to life. Eddie Cochran thrumming his guitar to "Summertime Blues"; Sandy Nelson on the traps for "Teen Beat." Jan and Dean gurgling "Baby Talk." The Cadillacs "Peek-a-Boo" and the Olympics' shoot-'em-up "Western Movies." There's Fats Domino and the Coasters, Little Anthony and the Imperials, the Isley Brothers. The Big Bopper and Ritchie Valens. Frankie Ford with his triangular face, Jimmie Rodgers and "Honeycomb," my fave song of 1957; Tommy Sands, Jack Scott, James Darren, Sal Mineo. Connie Francis, Dodie Stevens, and Brenda Lee, girls in crinolined skirts and high collars. All lip-synching, which adds to the illusion of a record come alive. When Connie does "Lipstick on Your Collar," herself Italian (Conchetta Rosa Maria Franconero) with a *mama mia* determination, the camera pans the kids in the audience as George Barnes magic-fingers his inimitable solo, wearing IFIC buttons (standing for flavor-*ific*, Beechnut's slogan) like name tags, brand loyalty to the acts mouthing their hits onstage.

I try to imagine myself among them, but I'm still learning how to be a teen, not quite ready to fit in, lost in the realms of science fiction. I haven't yet danced at the Teen Canteen, as the local rendezvous is called on Caton Avenue. Teen can Teen. The song that continually goes through my head is Dion and the Belmonts' yearnful "A Teenager in Love." I don't yet know the writers, Doc

Pomus and Mort Shuman, but Dion comes from the Bronx. So close and yet so far.

Across the street is the Parade Grounds, where soldiers once drilled. One time I see a football game between rival Flatbush street gangs there, the Erasmus Hall Bishops against the Royal Jokers from over in Midwood. It's beyond touch, clenched fists and no attention to the referee's whistle. If they were singing groups, they'd be on the corner, rising up the scale in a manner that Leonard Bernstein will capture in *West Side Story*, the dance step of the streets, the harmonizing that forms impromptu. Soon to become the Mystics, the Passions, the Excellents, all within subway reach, except for the Elegants, who hail from Staten Island. Hitting notes, but it might as well be each other. The echo they find is not in a stairwell but throughout the boroughs, and then throughout the nation.

All you need is a song and a voice, and a streetlamp.

LIVERPOOL
1962

YEAH TIMES THREE. THE MATHEMATICS OF DREAM.
John Lennon, Paul McCartney, and George Harrison swear allegiance in a seaport town; learn their craft in another sailor's port of call. The songs are carried over waves, oceanic or radio. They have to search them out, traveling across town to find a jukebox with the latest American import, tuning through the static to pull in Radio Luxembourg. America is on the other side of the world, especially in British pop music.

The Isles miss out on the first frenetic explosives of rock and roll, left with hearsay and pop idolatry at its most efficient, not without charm. Names are altered to project danger or fealty— Marty Wilde, Billy Fury, Vince Eager, Adam Faith—though Cliff Richard, the British Elvis (there is also a French Elvis, Johnny Hallyday, cut from a rougher cloth), has little of Presley's dark undercurrents. Of more interest, especially to those fancying a guitar, is Richard's backing band, the Shadows, curvaceous electric stringed instruments lined up with amps to match. How can you resist? Especially if there isn't much more life awaiting than the same pub, the same pulled pint, the same same of Everton versus Liverpool.

Scouse, the local lingo, has its own melody, its lilt a split "t" that softens and *s*'s it, rising at the end of a sentence. It gets its name from *lobscouse*, a stew served with hardtack biscuit, chanty on the side. Liverpool opens out through the Mersey into the Celtic Sea, and from there the vast Atlantic, the music smuggled in on passenger and cargo ships like a stowaway. Two centuries before, the British Isles had migrated their songs to the American southern highlands in a similar seafaring voyage, offshored in an exchange of balladry documented on its native soil by Francis James Child, collected by folklorist Cecil Sharp in their new Appalachia homestead, spread by oral tradition and keened whenever "Barbara Allen" or "The Cuckoo" is raised. Now the descendants of these songs—"Rock Island Line," "Freight Train," "Frankie and Johnny"—return the favor.

Skiffle is all the rage in 1956, more jug than professional band. Dominant instruments are washboards, tea-chest bass, harmonica, or kazoo, driven by guitars, the people's instrument: easy to learn three chords and play most songs, intricate enough to spend a life restringing it. It makes for homemade music, portable and frugal, fit for postwar austerity and a prelapsarian longing for a world already at the vanishing point. In America, in the early 1950s, Harry Smith's *Anthology of American Folk Music* becomes an eighty-two-song canon of folk archeology that will fuel its own revival as it travels overland to the crossing of Bleecker and MacDougal. In Britain, trad jazz dresses the Dixieland part, down to banjo and bowler hat; a retrenchment back to when jazz was supposedly jazz, before the be and the bop met.

Lonnie Donegan emerges from Chris Barber's Jazz Band, where he plays banjo and, during intermission, takes a barking vocal turn on Leadbelly's "Rock Island Line." His staccato rhythm on the banjo translates well to his guitar's chordal accelerant. Credited to Lonnie Donegan and his Skiffle Band, it even makes the American charts. He won't be back on US soil again until he's in full novelty mode with "Does Your Chewing Gum Lose Its Flavor" in 1961; by then he's given in to the broad-beamed humor of the English music hall. His biggest hit in England, "My Old Man's a Dustman," is another bit o' jollity, but his mid-fifties output—"Cumberland Gap," highlighted by Les Bennett's zippity solo, veers dangerously close to high-octane rockabilly, as does the bluer-grass of "My Dixie Darling" and "Jack of Diamonds"—finds willing ears and devotees.

On June 6, 1957, at St. Peter's Church Field in Liverpool, on a blurry tape recording that has miraculously survived through the years, can be heard the harmonies and flailing rhythm of Lonnie's "Putting on the Style," part of the repertoire of a ramshackle group of teenagers at an outdoor fête celebrating the Crowning of the Rose Queen. They're a newly formed skiffle band, the Quarry Men, named after the grammar school that the leader attends. He's dressed in a checked shirt with his hair swept back in a teddy-boy quiff.

Paul watches John onstage for the first time, and so they are conjoined.

||||||

THERE ARE RULES TO FOLLOW in the English music business. Ways things are done. Even with an upstart rock and roll, stoked by the clamor surrounding Bill Haley's rallying "Rock Around the Clock" storming the *Melody Maker* charts in 1955 and an abiding fascination with Eddie Cochran and Gene Vincent, record companies and managers and even their young hopefuls strive to be elder-respectful. Talents are groomed, stylized, placed within studio proprieties and musicianly mores.

For the most part, the star-begotten, drawn from England's working class, are happy to take any direction. The records are generally covers of American hits, made in studios with the air of a laboratory. The "balance engineers," as they're referred to, try to keep within the midrange, no unsightly peaks or valleys on their frequency chart. There are only major record companies, controlling the few outlets available in a world the BBC created. Unlike the United States, there is no network of independent record promoters looking to try the new before it's known. You play the game, or you don't play at all.

Larry Parnes was a gambler, by way of the rag trade, and he parlayed. He made "fifteen shillings profit" in a play he'd invested in, *Women of the Streets*, in which publicist John Kennedy had hired actresses to play prostitutes in front of the theater. When Kennedy told Parnes about something called "rock and roll," and there was a singer he thought he should see, the two went off to discover the youth who would become Britain's first homebred star. He was Tommy Hicks when Parnes walked into the 2 I's coffee bar in Soho, adjacent to Denmark Street, where the music publishers and instrument dealers encamped, and Tommy Steele when Parnes walked out.

"Rock Like a Caveman" was a hit in November 1956, serviceable rock-a-wannabe that gained Tommy notoriety. Handsome, with an elfin demeanor and sporting a wide grin, he looked good with a guitar and a cooing female chorus. Yet it was as if he was playing the part of a rock and roller, comfortable on a stage set, less so in the heart of a song. His cover of a cover of a cover—Guy Mitchell's US hit version of "Singing the Blues" from Marty Robbins's original—is winning; he turns up the heat on the slow-fuse "Shiralee" but he's more interested in the remove that pantomime and film give him. In *Kill Me Tomorrow* (1957), he lip-synchs in character to "Rebel Rock," while dancers hip-toss as oldsters look on disapprovingly. Tommy has similar reservations, presaged by his dystopian "Doomsday Rock" in 1956, where *sinners rock*, and *the three-point prong* awaits; by 1959 he has forsaken rock and roll for the variety show, trading hooves with the likes of Gene Kelly and Fred Astaire.

Parnes rechristened his discoveries with missionary zeal. He flipped a coin with Reg Smith on his resemblance to Ernest Borgnine in *Marty*, name change on the line. "I was a shocking gambler," once-Reg said later. "I'd gamble on two flies crawling up a wall." With his dimpled chin and burly voice, "Marty Wilde" was Parnes's roll of the dice, seven come eleven, especially when television producer Jack Good spotted Wilde for his new teen-slanted *Oh Boy!*. Every camera angle was choreographed in advance, accompanied by squeals of adolescent glee. Wilde would be on every Friday, a regular at least until Cliff Richard came along to learn from and ultimately dethrone him. Though Marty's records shade next to their American originals—his "Endless Sleep" is hardly as ominous as Jody Reynolds's; his best, "Bad Boy," has a husky air of mystery—he was a rousing live performer, with a band, the Wildcats, featuring the guitar of Big Jim Sullivan, one of the mainstays of the up-and-coming British guitar generation. The Wildcats weren't allowed in the studio with Wilde, and the difference shows.

Parnes kept gaming names with Billy Fury, who preceded Mersey Beat in Liverpool, earning Parnes's divided attention at a Birkenhead theater in 1959. A fatalist—"Just forget about tomorrow," he once told an interviewer, beset by an ill health that began when he was a child with rheumatic fever. It gave him an undercurrent of foreboding, when you hear the clock ticking, a record spinning toward its run-out groove. Like Bobby Darin, whom he resembles in more than just onrushing mortality, there is the feeling they're both caught between here and hereafter, and need to sing all they know before they're pulled offstage. Though he could display a rougher edge than any of his contemporaries, his innate shyness leaned his chart entries toward the softer side. In

May 1962, he is flown over to Hollywood to meet and exchange silver discs with Elvis on the set of *Girls Girls Girls*: one "Halfway to Paradise" for Billy, "It's Now or Never" and "Rock-A-Hula Baby" for Presley. But Fury can hardly muster up the confidence to speak to Elvis. He shrugs off his own movie, the twist-heavy *Play It Cool*. It's in black and white and Elvis is already in Technicolor.

Parnes also took 50 percent of Dickie Pride (many cite him as the most talented of Larry's "Stable of Stars," and the most troubled, dying of a drug overdose after a mid-sixties lobotomy), Duffy Power, and Johnny Gentle. The only woman was Dubliner Sally Kelly, bannered as "Miss Rock 'n' Roll" despite a surfeit of orchestral flourishes and having to answer Jim Reeves with "He'll Have to Stay." Parnes found something more than a malleable pop star in spiky-haired-and-mannered Joe Brown. Jack Good had spotted Joe as a background band member at an audition for his televised follow-up to *Oh Boy!*, the crossed heart of *Boy Meets Girl*. Parnes declared himself manager even before he met Joe. As a guitarist Brown played in the house band behind visiting Americans who couldn't bring their own musicians to Britain, even to going on the road with them, as he did with Eddie Cochran, to witness the furor firsthand. Despite Parnes's entreaties, he refused to change his name, and insisted on bringing along the skiffle group he fronted, the Spacemen, to be his backing band, changing their name to the more down-to-earth Bruvvers. Joe's *dahn-the-boozer* Cockney demeanor (his parents had run the Sultan, in East London) was offset by his futuristic porcupine hair, which would reappear virtually unchanged twenty years later atop the head of another *x* of generation, bearing a name of which Larry Parnes would be proud: Billy Idol. Brown's takeoff on "Darktown Strutter's Ball" was heavy on the bottom strings, in the manner of Cochran's "C'mon Everybody," debuting Joe on the British charts in March 1960, a short month before Eddie was killed in a car accident in England. Its flip, "Swagger," shows Brown's guitar acumen, and while most of his records lean toward the snuggly, like his touching number one "A Picture of You," one of the highlights of 1962, he was clearly his own man.

That didn't stop Brown from being a weekly salaried and overworked cog in Parnes's traveling package-extravaganzas—*Joe Brown with Lance Fortune and Tommy Bruce at the Victoria! Meet the Beat with Billy Fury, Vince Eager, Johnny Gentle, and Dickie "The Sheik of Shake" Pride at the Brittania!*—tramping up and down England with nary a night off. Though it provided pocket money, especially for Parnes, increasingly, as in America, it was television that was the motorway to exposure. *Juke Box Jury* allowed celebrities like Diana Dors and a pre–*Man from U.N.C.L.E.* David McCallum to rate-a-hit, though Jack Good thought hits were made to be seen. He had just witnessed Cliff Richard performing "Move It," and immediately put him in regular rotation on *Oh Boy!*

There was no more photogenic pop star in Britain than Cliff. Not managed by Parnes (who was jealous enough to pull Marty Wilde off *Oh Boy!* for perceived slights to *his* star), Richard was the face of rock and roll in Britain in pre-Mersey years. He was too good to be true, piled hair and cherub-faced, with something of the naïf about him, eagerly initialing the dotted line, eager to please. Born in British-colonized India, he was eight-year-old Harry Webb when his family left after independence in 1948 to return to the setting sun of empire. Ten years later, Norrie Paramor, the recording manager of Columbia Records, was casting about for an entrant in the teen idol sweepstakes. Paramor had taken the long way around to rock and roll; his first written hit was the 1952 "Cornflakes" for Sidney Torch's light orchestra, and he arranged mood music for, among others, Mantovani. He preferred the easiest of listenings—*In London in Love* would gain favor with space-pop fans of a later generation for its wordless female vocal, more Theremin than human—but he'd tried to figure out how to orchestrate this new teenage craze as early as 1956 with Tony Crombie and His Rockets' "Teach You to Rock," which actually fulfilled its scholastic promise; though like Bill Haley, Crombie, a jazz drummer nudging past thirty, was short on teen appeal.

Norrie first saw Cliff audition at the Gaumont Cinema in Shepherd's Bush in the summer of 1958, and thought to pair him with "Schoolboy Crush," a song Paramor had in hand awaiting the right matriculant, which had been a non-hit for Bobby Helms in America. He played Cliff's version, complete with whistling and treacly chorus for his fourteen-year-old daughter, Carolyn. She preferred the b-side, an upthrust rocker called "Move It," written by Ian Samwell, a guitarist in Richard's backing band, then called the Drifters. The stinging leads that answered Cliff's huffing *Let me tell you baby it's called rock and roll* were spurred by session guitarist Ernie Shear, whose skill on the banjo (he was a mainstay of Norrie's Big Ben Banjo Band) added a knife-sharp percussive attack, and did much to toughen the more uncertain phrases of Cliff's delivery.

Paramor might not have had a natural affinity for the new music, but with Cliff's instrumental foils, now called the Shadows, he didn't need to. He had played safe at Richard's first session, using session musicians on bass and guitar, but by Richard's third single, founding members Hank Marvin and Bruce Welch had taken their rightful places, and from then on, the band was an integral part of Richard's presentation. Marvin's wobble of sway bar and precise solos, clean and melodic and seldom showy, and the band's momentum—Jet Harris on bass, Welch on rhythm, Tony Meehan on the drums—encouraged a string of hit instrumentals: "Apache," "F.B.I.," "Kon-Tiki." Though they never made much of an impact in the United States, the Shadows prefigured other guitar-centric musicians like Duane Eddy, the Ventures, and even

Sweden's Spotnicks, and their sound would become a harbinger of what would be surf music: heavy strings, a twist of reverb and clattery 4/4 beat. Perhaps the Shadows' greatest impact for the Isles' impressionable musicians-in-the-making would be archetyping the classic rock and roll band format of two guitars, bass, and drums.

As for their singer, Richard's star ascended with the movies. He had a supporting role in 1959's *Serious Charge*, a down-tempo account of a vicar's ("a square with a round collar" one proto-hoodlum sneers) tribulations set in a teen-noir world where swirling skirts and petticoats signify perdition, and sings an up-tempo version of "Living Doll." Later slowed, it became Cliff's first number one in England, the roman à clef inescapable.

In the film *Expresso Bongo*, directed by Val Guest, he is Bongo Herbert with Laurence Harvey playing his manipulative Parnes-like manager. Based on a short story by Wolf Mankowitz, and adapted from a satirical West End stage play that beat out *My Fair Lady* as Best British Musical in 1958 (the notion of uplifting young innocents to be conversant in proper society was in the air), Bongo changes from guileless to beguiled, when guile appears in the persona of over-the-hill songstress Dixie, who convinces him to sign her contract and leave Harvey. His taming is measured from the raucous "Bongo Beat" by which we're first introduced to his untrammeled youth in a Soho coffee bar, to the sob-soppy "Voice in the Wilderness" that he sings at his record company audition as the Shadows oscillate behind him, to the duplicity of "The Shrine on the Second Floor" ("It's not generally known that I'm a deeply religious boy," he intones, as a choir in white robes is revealed as the curtain parts behind him). But it wasn't far from his own career arc, a disavowal of rock and roll that, much like Little Richard, placed him on the wrong side of religious fervor. Even the screams that accompanied his frequent television appearances seemed overly enthusiastic, orchestrated much as Norrie

Paramor might add a flurry of screeching violins. He was already left behind.

|||||

THERE WAS NO LOOKING BACKWARD for Joe Meek, architect of sound. He believed in the future. In *I Hear a New World*, a 1960 concept album subtitled "An Outer Space Music Fantasy," he hoped to not only demonstrate the possibilities of stereo equipment (at a time when people did listen and marvel at a train traveling from one speaker to another) but explore the outré limits of what could be molecularly captured within the relatively primitive audio recording techniques he bent to his will. He wanted to conceive the "impression of space," and admitted that "Yes! This is a strange record. I meant it to be. I wanted to create a picture of what could be up there in outer space." What he found were alien creatures like the merry Globbots and the melancholy Saroos cavorting on the moon, complete with speeded-up vocals (a popular alien signifier, as in Sheb Wooley's "The Purple People Eater" and Jesse Lee Turner's "Little Space Girl"), exotic-sounding instruments like the Hawaiian steel guitar, and a variety of sound effects made by anything at hand—bubbles blowing, scraping teeth combs, rattling steel washers. More than anything, he was exploring the inner space of his own sonic mission, which was to manipulate the recording studio as its own instrument.

Meek was Britain's first independent producer, an obsessive maverick who rebelled against the staid environment of three-hour sessions with a fifteen-minute break for tea, engineers in white surgical coats, and listening to so-called producers drone on when *he knew how to do it better* and *they were stealing his ideas* and *if the bloody landlady came up to tell him one more time that she wanted him out . . .*

His biggest hit was the Tornados' "Telstar" in 1962, inspired by the first communications satellite to receive and send a live television transmission from America. It was a debt repaid: Meek had started out repairing televisions, even building them in his provincial hometown of Newent, Gloucestershire, which had yet to receive signal. Fascinated by electronics and sound, he went to London and got a job at IBC Studios, working his way up from junior to senior balance engineer, an apprenticeship that he turned to his advantage when jazz trumpeter Humphrey Lyttelton came into the studio in April 1956 to cut "Bad Penny Blues." In the control room Joe close-miked the brushes on the snare drum and the bottom end of the piano, compressing the sound so it pushed against the speakers. Before Lyttelton could have a chance to complain, the record sat at number 19 in the charts, the first jazz record to make the pop grade, two places behind Bill Haley's "The Saints Rock 'N' Roll."

He was constantly experimenting with *effect*, the sound that would make a record stand out from its surroundings, to attract the ear before the ear knows. For marching feet in Anne Shelton's "Lay Down Your Arms," he shook a box of gravel. He thrust a semi-honking saxophone solo to the fore in Frankie Vaughn's "Green Door," jump-started Lonnie Donegan's "Cumberland Gap," and had to wait three years before Chris Barber's Jazz Band had a hit with the sonorous clarinet of "Petite Fleur." He pinpointed instruments within an orchestra to exaggerate, adding and blending different microphones, shaving off frequencies so that others could come to the fore, echoing and manipulating and sure that he could do a lot more if he was given his due. Increasingly obstreperous and demanding, he soon left to become a personal engineer for jazz producer Denis Preston, designing the first stereo studio in England near the Holland Park tube station in Lansdowne Road in 1958.

There was, and always will be, ongoing controversy about the science of technology versus the art of performance, especially for jazz purists who preferred a more natural reproduction. "Electronic product" was how Meek artist John Leyton was denounced, his voice sounding "like it was recorded at the bottom of a well." The inevitable clashes with Preston, and an insistence on his own compositions after the surprise success of "Put a Ring on His Finger" by Les Paul and Mary Ford, led to a hasty exit in November 1959 when he stormed out of a session at Lansdowne. He then partnered with Saga Records, founding the Triumph label in February 1960 and constructing the first of his home-built and jerry-rigged studios where he allowed his audio imagination free range, whether orbiting the moon with the Blue Men in *I Hear a New World* or finding the perfect romantic song in Michael Cox's version of John Loudermilk's "Angela Jones" (*I'll meet you at your locker / When school is dismissed*). He was not unaware of the commercial concerns of his adolescent audience ("Records with Teenage Appeal" was one of the company's slogans), as well as the problems he faced as a label entrepreneur. When Triumph's biggest hit proved their ruin, unable to press enough copies of Cox's single to meet demand in the tail-chasing outflow and inflow that was the lot of the struggling independent, he decided that only he could be the one making creative decisions, that he would lease his productions directly to established record companies; that he would find artists and give them songs and record them in his own New World.

He moved into three floors atop a leather bag shop at 304 Holloway Road, converting it into a studio where he might sleep and scheme and record anywhere in the house, at any time he liked, positioning singers in the bathroom, string players up the stairs, drums hidden behind a screen with a dampening woolen blanket, delighting in a chaotic working environment of dangling wires and amplifiers and strewn boxes of tape with markings only he could interpret. Only he knew how to produce his record under such haphazard conditions, on his own customized equipment, experimenting at will. More than anyone, he dragged British recording techniques into a new decade.

Meek's renegade streak didn't extend to the artists he worked with, or the material they warbled. Mostly they were pretty boys, with passable voices and bland personalities; Joe liked that they were malleable. He'd already engineered a hit with Marty Wilde's cover of "Sea of Love," and admired Larry Parnes's stable of stars. When aspiring manager Robert Stigwood asked Joe to supply a song for his client, the actor John Leyton playing a singer on a television series, Meek and songwriter Geoff Goddard came up with "Johnny Remember Me," an entreaty from a dead lover to the boy she's left behind, its macabre appeal heightened by Joe's interest in séances in which he invariably tried to contact the spirit of Buddy Holly. The only tangible result would be Mike Berry's "Tribute to Buddy Holly," which added credibility to Joe's RGM productions when it was a mild hit in 1961.

To say that Meek was prolific is an understatement. In the time it took Phil Spector to release 24 records on Philles, Joe produced 141 sides, according to John Repsch's comprehensive and detailed biography, *The Legendary Joe Meek*, which might account for why Joe slammed down the phone when Phil called Holloway Road to arrange a meeting. Often compared to each other in ambitious vision and temperament, both believed artists were subservient to soundscape. Unfortunately for Joe, most of his productions did not have the epic scale of Spector's, and he very seldom worked with singers or musicians who could match his audio breakthroughs. The songs were generally trifles, and it didn't help that many of his demos consisted of him humming a snatch of out-of-pitch melody and expecting his musicians to make sense of it.

On one occasion, it worked far beyond anything even Joe might have dreamed possible. "Telstar," its airborne uplift of melody expressed on one of Meek's favorite keyboard instruments, the Clavioline, given the pulsating rhythmic undercurrent of Leyton's "Johnny Remember Me," and sounding as in-orbit as its producer, caught the imagination of a world mesmerized by the space age, becoming a worldwide smash in the fall of 1962, even topping the charts in America. Any gains he might have made were stymied by ultimately frivolous copyright suits, and Larry Parnes contracting the Tornados as Billy Fury's backing band even as "Telstar" became a hit, the band relegated to a minor spot on Parnes's package shows. Perhaps Larry was aware of Joe's infatuation with the Tornados' bass player, Heinz Burt. Meek had high hopes for Heinz, whom he convinced to dye his hair bright blond, go solo, and share his apartment; but the last thing Parnes needed, in these waning days of the stand-alone teen idol, was competition. Heinz's only hit was "Just Like Eddie," and in comparison to Cochran, he was found wanting.

Like most of the British record industry, Joe was unaware of the coming boom in beat groups. He was visited by the manager of one of these bands in January 1962, making the rounds of record companies to little encouragement. He turned Brian Epstein down, and except for the Honeycombs' "Have I the Right," with its backward sweep of shimmering guitar and pound-for-pound beat delivered Dave Clark Five–style by femme drummer Honey Lantree, Meek would not have an entrant in the upcoming Invasion. Even as future stars like Steve Howe, Ritchie Blackmore, Tom Jones, Rod Stewart, and Mitch Mitchell cycled through his bunker on Holloway Road, he seemed unable to make peace with the coming of psychedelia, where his audio imagination might have proved useful. Fueled by stimulants and his own increasing delusional paranoias, he withdrew into his hideaway. Finally, in a scandal that would overshadow his work and reputation, he called his landlady upstairs in February 1967, on the eve of the eighth anniversary of the plane crash that killed Buddy Holly, and shot her. Then himself.

In the early 1990s I visited the site of the Holloway Road studio to pay my respects, standing in the doorway of 304, stepping in his vanished footprint. Behind me, in a red London call box, the phone began to ring. I picked it up. There was no dial tone, only a silence that seemed enclosed, like a reverb chamber waiting for its sound to enter.

|||||

IT'S NOT LONDON.

Liverpool is far enough north that the nearest city seems to be, if not Blackpool, then Hamburg, where the beat groups go to apprentice their trade. The city has ample time to nurture its local heroes, to have a gathering place called the Cavern, underground as befits a cellar, to develop at its own remote pace.

Alan Sytner's prototype for establishing the Cavern was a smoky jazz club in the Latin Quarter of Paris called Le Caveau de la Huchette, itself modeled on one of the original existential *boites* of St.-Germain-des Prés to spring up in the wake of World War II, Le Tabou. Its bohemian atmosphere, where Juliette Gréco was courted by Miles Davis, where Jean-Paul Sartre and Simone de Beauvoir came to carry on first and second sex dialogue after Café Flor and Les Deux Magots shut for the night, where Boris Vian and Albert Camus exchanged metaphors, dazzled the teenage Sytner, and he determined to open a jazz club in his hometown of Liverpool. Looking for a suitable location after he'd turned twenty-one, he found an abandoned and vaulted cellar at 10 Mathew Street underneath a warehouse in Liverpool's center, across from the Grapes, one of the city's venerated pubs. On January 16, 1957, the Cavern opened featuring the Merseysippi Jazz Band and other local attractions. It was a success from the start. A key decision was made not to serve liquor, so as to attract a younger audience, and the club's capacity of six hundred seemed a perfect size, intimate yet expansive, despite the lack of ventilation and the oozing dampness coming off the walls. Underneath the Cavern, undiscovered until its excavation in 1982, a large man-made lake exuded humidity. It was a club made for sweating, loosening inhibitions, releasing the proprieties of its patrons and performers. The atmosphere came first; the bands would follow.

Skiffle began making inroads into the ragtime jazz and less popular "progressive" jazz that Sytner favored as the fifties progressed, even as the characters that would promenade across the Cavern stage slowly gravitated to the fore. In May 1957, Alan Caldwell secured a booking for his Texans Skiffle Group; by August 1959 he had changed their name to Al Storm and the Hurricanes, on the way to the western-themed Rory Storm, with Johnny Guitar (Byrne) and one Ringo Starr (Richard Starkey) on drums. Kingsize Taylor and the Dominoes had begun skiffle-shifting to rock and roll as early as August 1958. Synter had no ear and little patience for the new music. The Quarry Men found this out when they secured a Cavern gig on August 7, 1957, even though only Lennon was able to make it. Drummer Colin Hanton remembered the night for Spencer Leigh's evocatively time-lined re-creation of *The Cavern Club: Rise of the Beatles and Merseybeat*: "We did some skiffle numbers to start with but we also did rock 'n' roll. John Lennon was passed a note and he said to the audience 'We've had a request.' He opened it up and it was Alan Sytner saying 'Cut out the bloody rock 'n roll.'"

Still, there was no stemming the musical tide as it roared up the Mersey estuary. Ray McFall had been watching over the Cavern's finances, and when Sytner went to London to get away from the club's mounting debts, McFall bought the underground warren for 2,750 pounds, reopening in October 1959. He first attempted to maintain the club's jazz character, as well as provide a stopover for folk-ish American acts like Josh White, Cisco Houston, Jesse Fuller, Sonny Terry, and Brownie McGee, but by

May 25 of the following year, when he held his first Rock Night with Rory Storm and the Hurricanes and Cass and the Cassanovas (who would become the Big Three when Cass left), he saw where his future lay. So did the Blue Genes jazz group, who maintained a regular Tuesday night residency. They added Swingin' to their name, taking on a more frontal approach, sharing the bill with "clean beat groups." As for Ken Baldwin of the Merseysippis, "We were so anti-beat music that we never stopped to speak to them." Or hear what they might be singing, in the sectarian wars of musical style.

Rock and roll demarked Liverpool's class wars as well. Filmed in stark black and white on the streets of a city still bearing scars from Europe's last eruption, the 1958 *Violent Playground* gathers a teen gang in the courtyard of Gerard Gardens, a poverty-ridden postwar housing project whose resident youth menace is Johnny, played by pre-Ilya David McCallum. He's brooding, chiseled, with a murderous streak that makes me wish he would have cut a record for Joe Meek. Johnny leads his budding rabble in a spasmodic dance to Johnny Luck's "Play Rough," threatening the "blue bottle" policeman trying to reform them; but it's Freddie Starr as the pint-size hooligan Tommy, with his band the Midniters, that leads to Joe's foray into Merseyside. "It surprised me that the Beatles and Gerry and the Pacemakers did not approach me for a record contract," Meek sulks to Bill Harry in *Mersey Beat* on May 23, 1963, disregarding Epstein's visit more than a year earlier. During the session for "Who Told You" at Holloway Road, "Freddie was one big bundle of energy, impersonating a host of artists, cracking witty jokes and performing funny gestures all around the studio." Starr knows his talent lies in doing anything for a laugh, culminating in the 1986 tabloid *Sun* headline: *Freddie Starr Ate My Hamster.*

||||||

THE QUARRY MEN WEREN'T HAVING much luck. They trian-
gulated in February 1958 when Paul's friend George, a Liverpool
Institute schoolmate with whom he traded guitar chordings, rode
with them on a bus home after one of the group's infrequent gigs
and showed off his grasp of Link Wray's "Raunchy." Harrison,
though a year younger, seemed able to stand up to Lennon's acerbic wit, had honed his guitar solos in a band called the Rebels,
and by mid-year joined the Quarry Men for their first attempt at
recording. For the seventeen shillings and sixpence they scraped
together to visit Percy Phillips and his "Professional Tape & Disc
Recording Service," John sang an agreeable version of Buddy
Holly's "That'll Be the Day." Paul and George wrote a countryish
"Trying to Get to You" for the b-side of the edition-of-one shellac demo. Their attuned harmonies and entwined backing vocals
were promising, though the rest of the year was darkened by the
tragic death of John's mother, Julia, on July 15, killed by a speeding policeman on his way to work. Foundering, the best gig they
could get in 1959 in Liverpool was a short residency at the Casbah
Coffee Club in West Derby, run by Mona Best, whose son, Pete,
was an aspiring drummer.

Strangely, it was the least musical of their fluctuating person-
nel who would have a lasting impact on the nascent group. Stuart
Sutcliffe was a visual artist whom John knew from art school.
Lennon persuaded him to use his earnings from selling an abstract painting to buy a Hofner President bass; though Sutcliffe
never progressed from the rudimentary, his sense of look and
stylish imagination permeated the band. It was he, when they
were searching for yet another new name, who came up with the
Beetles, supposedly after the motorcycle gang that Lee Marvin
rode into town to challenge Marlon Brando in *The Wild Ones*
(though the apocryphal tale doesn't bear carbon-dating since the
movie was banned in England until 1968), saluting Buddy Holly's
Crickets. Holly, even a year after his death, was riding high on

the British charts, and still formed a large part of the Quarry Men's repertoire. Lennon punned *a*, and after a brief flirtation with the modifier Silver, thus they became.

They acquired a manager, Allan Williams, who ran the Jacaranda Coffee Bar and knew Sutcliffe from having him paint murals on the walls. The group had begun hanging around his basement club, and when Larry Parnes came to town looking for a backing band for Billy Fury to tour northern England and Scotland, they auditioned for him. They weren't good enough for Fury—Parnes wanted them to replace Sutcliffe and Lennon refused—but the ever-thrifty Parnes thought they might do well with a lesser Liverpool singer he was managing, Johnny Gentle. The tour proved a disaster, beginning with a car accident that put their temporary drummer, Tommy Moore, in the hospital (the promoter forced him out to do the show), and deteriorated from there. By July the Silver Beatles were backing a stripper at an illegal club in Upper Parliament Street, run by Williams, with Paul on drums. It proved a taste for what was waiting for them in the St. Pauli district, in Hamburg, on August 17, an immersive toss-in-the-deep-end that would last until December. Before they left Liverpool, they asked Pete Best to join them, and set off for the red lights of Germany.

Seven days a week; four, five, six, more sets each night; DM30 to be split when the evening wound down. They didn't like to repeat songs, playing until exhausted, a quick benzedrine pick-me-up, and then on into the dawn. Hamburg was a wide-open vice center, and free from the constraints of being home, the Beatles took advice. They moved along the Grosse Freiheit from the Indra to the Kaiserkeller, both owned by Bruno Koschmider, sharing a bill with fellow Liverpudlians Rory Storm and the Hurricanes, becoming friendly with their be-ringed drummer. But when they wanted to climb the ladder to the rival Top Ten Club, Koschmider reported George, who was underage, to the authorities, and he and then the rest of the band was deported. The setback turned fortuitous when they arrived home in Liverpool, "Direct from Hamburg" at the Litherland Town Hall, and realized the skills they'd acquired in Germany served them well. They'd turned professional. As John would later say, "70 percent of the audience thought we were German," but it was an audience they had learned to cajole over the long Hamburg nights, beckoning sailors off the street, enticing university students to lose their inhibitions, winking at the *frauleins* and free to be as outrageous as their tawdry surroundings. Whenever they lagged, Koschmider goaded them on with a shouted *Mach Schau!* Make a show!

||||||

THEY RETURNED TO A LIVERPOOL fully in thrall with post-skiffle rock and roll. The Cavern was subterfuged by bands taking advantage of a willing venue, especially with jazz waning, and the audience growing more youthful. The Remo Four were an instrumental group in the mode of the Shadows, sporting a full lineup of Fender guitars. Gerry and the Pacemakers were led by the affable Gerry Marsden, making their Cavern debut in October, and had their own PA system and a Watkins Copicat to bounce their vocals around. The Big Three made the loudest noise of all, powered by coffin-sized amplifiers built by guitarist Adrian Barber. The bricked cellar walls of the Cavern had little natural reverb, giving the bottom end room to expand; along with drummer Johnny Hutch, and bassist Johnny Gustafson, the Big Three were regarded as Liverpool's most hard-driving combination, a power trio before the notion existed.

They were second in showmanship to Rory Storm. Known as the Golden Boy, crowned by a sheen of piled hair that he coiffed onstage with a giant comb, he was an indefatigable performer, leaping into the audience, turning the microphone stand upside down, and in one memorable show in New Brighton, high-diving into a swimming pool to climax a song. The Hurricanes spent their summers at a variety of Butlin's holiday camps, impeccably suited in fire engine red and electric blue (Rory would go on to favor gold lamé), choreographing synchronized routines, and allowing their drummer a solo spot—"Ringo Starrtime"—to make up for the fact that he'd given up an apprenticeship with a secure future job offer to take a chance playing music full-time.

"Ritchie" first appeared with the band on March 25, 1959, at the Mardi Gras. In the pocket diaries kept by Johnny Guitar from 1958 through 1963, mostly a scribbled sentence or two on what he did, which girls he was chasing and where he spent the night, the fact goes unremarked. A week later Johnny goes back to the club. "Not bad," he notes. "Went with cloakroom girl." He's similarly circumspect about January 17, 1960. He sees Cliff Richard at the Palladium with "Eileen," then "played good" at the Cavern. What he doesn't mention is that this is the night Rory drops the pretense of skiffle and launches into "Whole Lotta Shakin' Goin' On," earning the ire of the trad jazz audience. Ray McFall fines them ten shillings, adding "We are not going to tolerate that music down here," even as Wednesdays become Rock Night that summer, and bands like Dale Roberts and the Jaywalkers, Wump and His Werbles, Ian and the Zodiacs, and the Delacardoes come out to play.

By October, lunchtime featuring "beat" music is on offer. On February 9, 1961, the Beatles make their first Cavern appearance after returning from Germany at one of these afternoon sessions. They've been playing around town frequently during January, their black leather jackets and newfound cockiness conjuring girlish screams that are beginning to follow them from Aintree Institute in Liverpool to Lathom Hall in Seaforth. They're booked by Bob Wooler, resident master of ceremonies at the Cavern ("the best of cellars" is his signature line). On March 21, McFall adds them to a Blue Genes' guest night, much to the surprise of the resident group, who disapprove of the Beatles' scruffy manner. At this point, the band are already looking beyond Liverpool. Williams has signed them to Peter Eckhorn's Top Ten Club on the Reeperbahn for a thirteen-week booking. They play for Pete's mum at the Casbah on March 26, and leave the next day by train for Hamburg. Neither Sutcliffe nor Williams will be with them when they return. They unceremoniously fire Allan in a contract dispute; perhaps they too are suspicious of the blaze that destroys a Top Ten in Liverpool only six days after Williams opens what is supposed to be the city's first all-beat club. Stuart leaves the band to concentrate on his art and live with his German girlfriend, Astrid Kirchherr. It is she who will convince the Beatles to dress like "what a boy should look like when he plays this kind of music," and takes their before-and-after photographs. Fashion forward.

They leave behind a coming-out party for Liverpool's new breed of bands. On March 11, at the misnamed Liverpool Jazz Society located in the Iron Door Club, promoter Sam Leach puts on an "All Night Rock Ball," a *Rock Around the Clock* featuring twelve bands in twelve hours, from 7:30 p.m. to 7:30 a.m. It is nominally headlined by Gerry and the Pacemakers, abetted by the Beatles, Rory Storm and the Hurricanes, the Big Three, the Remo Four, Kingsize Taylor and the Dominoes, Dale Roberts and the Jaywalkers, Derry and the Seniors, Johnny Rocco and the Jets, Faron and the Tempest Tornadoes (later to become Faron's Flamingoes), Ray and the Del Renas, and the Pressmen. Beat boom.

||||||

BILL HARRY IS MORE FAN than musician, prone to tootle a kazoo with an impromptu skiffle congregation, editing a jazz magazine at the Liverpool College of Art College, and friendly enough with both Sutcliffe and Lennon to introduce them to each other at the dawn of 1960. He becomes acquainted with the byways of the local music venues, starting at the Jacaranda, moving sideways through the Jive Hive to the Casbah, and with Bob Wooler begins to compile a list of homegrown groups that, to their surprise, soon tops three hundred. He sees a fan base eager to be informed of what's happening around town and on July 6, 1961, publishes the first issue of *Mersey Beat*, a fortnightly that chronicles the rise of Liverpool's musician community, providing promotion, encouragement, and the gossip of local stardom. In the first issue, Lennon appears on the front page with a "Short Diversion on the Dubious Origins of the Beatles," alongside a photo of Gene Vincent smoking a cigarette and signing autographs at the Rialto Ballroom between "two young Liverpool beauties, Mary Larkin and Terry Shorrock," and a feature spotlighting Cilla Black "on her road to fame." The print run of five thousand sells out quickly, with the manager of the record department at the North End Music Store on Great Charlotte Street, Brian Epstein, quickly ordering more copies when his first dozen vanish within minutes of putting them on the counter.

The Beatles have just returned from Hamburg and their first proper recording session. *Beatles Sign Recording Contract!* is the headline for issue 2, along with the now iconic Astrid portrait of them moodily sitting on a railway car dressed in black. Stuart wears sunglasses, but by the time the group goes into the studio to provide backing for Tony Sheridan, produced by orchestra leader Bert "Wonderland by Night" Kaempfert, he's relegated himself to the sidelines. The released single, "My Bonnie" b/w "When the Saints Go Marching In," with the group credited as the Beat Brothers, will come out in the fall, prompting "Raymond Jones" (a mythical made-up name put in the order books to justify ordering the import single) to enter NEMS on October 28 and request the record, supposedly alerting Epstein of potential sales and the Beatles' commercial possibilities. Perhaps so, but this was hardly the first time Brian was made aware of the group. He had been writing a column highlighting and reviewing NEMS's new stock of releases since issue 3, the same weekend the Beatles appeared on August 5 at the Cavern with Kenny Ball's Jazzmen and the Remo Four. He reviews show albums, upcoming jazz releases—"Trickling in now are albums from Prestige ('Bluesville,' 'Swingsville,' and 'Moodsville')"—and "pops" from Elvis, Bobby Rydell, and Chubby Checker ("Let's Twist Again"). He can hardly be oblivious to the parade of good-looking young men with guitars that decorate the pages of *Mersey Beat*, or "the scruffy lads in leather and jeans" (as he puts it in his autobiography, *A Cellar Full of Noise*), who frequent his store during the afternoon, spilling out from the music club a hundred paces away, catching up on the latest records, though he has to keep his attraction compartmentalized in an England that criminalizes homosexuality.

The Beatles are spinning their wheels, going nowhere, even though they play almost constantly at the Cavern to excitable crowds. "The Beatles are No. 1 because they resurrected original style rock 'n' roll," enthuses Wooler in issue 4 of *Mersey Beat*, singling out the "mean, moody magnificence of drummer Pete Best," as well as their "remarkable variety of talented voices."

For John's twenty-first birthday on October 9, John and Paul go to Paris to celebrate. There, Jurgen Vollmer, who was part of their artful coterie in Hamburg, cuts their hair in the inverted-bowl forward-brush style favored by the aspiring artist crowd. Astrid had already given Stu a similar makeover, and after initial reticence, Lennon and McCartney take the fateful step. They are still performing in head-to-toe leather outfits, which must have made playing in the steamy Cavern nearly unbearable, and it is this mixture of rough trade and cutting-edge that Brian Epstein sees when he slips in a side door to the lunchtime session at the

Cavern on November 9 to witness the Beatles for the first time. He is wearing a pinstriped suit, feeling decidedly out of place, yet intrigued. "There was clearly an excitement in the otherwise unpleasing dungeon," he remembered, an allure of forbidden desire heightening his business acumen.

The group's casual stage demeanor, eating sandwiches (well, it was lunchtime) and smoking between songs, in-joking and jostling one another, belied the strength and expanse of their repertoire, which would eventually set them apart from other Liverpool groups. Aside from the rock and roll standards all the bands were covering, Holly and Vincent and Presley, the Beatles added Ray Charles ("Hallellujah I Just Love Her So") and the Shirelles ("Boys"), Hank Williams, and Bill Monroe, and could let down their guard with romantic ballads. McCartney took a turn on "Over the Rainbow," and swooned "Til There Was You" from Peggy Lee's version. All the top Liverpool groups had their soft spot: Gerry with "You'll Never Walk Alone," Rory with "Beautiful Dreamer." Then it was back to the rockers, hot off the American charts. There was little original material being tried out; even the Beatles kept their constant songwriting to themselves, uncertain how the audience would receive their own compositions.

Brian offered management in December. The Beatles were ready for his guidance, even if he didn't quite know how he would proceed, having never done it before. They didn't complain when he smartened them up, suit and tie and on-time, knowing there was a world outside Liverpool that needed to be convinced. He wisely stayed out of their musical way. He tightened their presentation, keeping them to a set list, and began making inquiries around the London-based labels for an audition. More because of his managerial position at a record store than the band he represented, he persuaded Decca A&R man Mike Smith to make the trek north to see the Beatles at the Cavern in mid-December. Smith thought them worthy of an audition.

On New Year's Eve, the band got in a van with roadie Neil Aspinall and traveled ten hours through a wintry mix to London, getting lost along the way. At 11 a.m. on the first day of 1962, they played a selection of their stage presentation for a hungover Smith, using unfamiliar studio equipment (they were told their own amps were too shoddy), packing up after little more than an hour. Smith couldn't give them an immediate answer, and besides, he was off to see Brian Poole and the Tremeloes, another of those new beat groups, only this one located closer to London. The latter got the nod (Smith's superior, Dick Rowe, infamously told Epstein that his future was in selling records rather than in management, and that "Groups of guitars are on the way out"). By January 3, the Beatles are back at the Cavern for lunchtime.

They're not their best at Decca's West Hampstead studio, nervous (former Shadows drummer Tony Meehan is present) and bleary from the long drive, without the benefit of a live audience, but their strengths are on display. In the Teddybears' "To Know Him Is to Love Him," their harmonies coo; in Buddy Holly's "Crying Waiting Hoping" George takes a well-nurtured solo, though you can tell he wishes his amplifier would keep the note chiming a bit longer. There's the Coasters' "Besame Mucho" with a cha-cha *boom!* beat, country honk in "Sure to Fall," a bouncy "September in the Rain," John's hollered "Money," and the exotica of "The Sheik of Araby." Fifteen songs in all display versatility. Tellingly, Rowe is drawn to their self-compositions: "Hello Little Girl," "Like Dreamers Do," "Love of the Loved." But no.

Epstein doesn't let that deter him. They're the most popular group in Liverpool when *Mersey Beat* appears on January 4 ("a foregone conclusion" editorializes Harry), beating Gerry and the Pacemakers, the Remo Four, Rory Storm and the Hurricanes, Johnny Sadon and the Searchers. Throughout the winter they are playing somewhere almost every night. As the group readies to return to Hamburg in April, marked by a farewell show at the

Cavern for their fan club—"An evening with John, Paul, George and Pete," a first set where they play in their leathers and a second decked out in suit and tie—and the customary send off from the Casbah, Brian continues working his way through the lower echelon management of London record labels. The group arrives in Hamburg the day after Stuart Sutcliffe shockingly dies of a brain aneurysm; while they're at the Star-Club on Grosse-Freiheit they share a bill with Gene Vincent. They're overtaking their past.

By May 9, the future is made manifest when Epstein meets with Phonogram head of A&R George Martin. Though Phonogram plays second fiddle in the EMI hierarchy, Martin is able to range widely. He is a schooled musician with a leaning toward Rachmaninoff, in possession of a good sense of humor, having worked with the *Beyond the Fringe* comedy troupe and the Peters Sellers and Ustinov. He had tested the waters of the youth market with the Vipers Skiffle Group, though he took on a pseudonym, Ray Cathode, so as to not besmirch his reputation. He sees possibilities in the Decca audition tape, hearing the band through Paul and John's vocals, and agrees to give them a further tryout on June 6. The collaboration would last the life of the Beatles.

The immediate problem was Pete Best, and it fed into frustrations the group—especially George and Paul—had been wrestling with over the year. Pete was known for his "Atom Beat," a four-to-the-bar undercarriage of bass drum that was made for noisy clubs, but as Lennon and McCartney's songwriting grew more sophisticated, his playing felt more and more out of depth, estranged from the group mind-set. They'd felt Ringo Starr behind them when he sat in on February 5 when Best took sick, and in August traveled to Butlin's in Skegness, where he was seasoning with Rory Storm and formally invited him to join the band. Even if he'd suspected it was a possibility—Martin had already asked session drummer Andy White to play on the Beatles' first recordings—it shocked both Best and his fans, who took unkindly to his departure. When the Beatles showed up at Abbey Road for their first proper recording session on September 6, George was still sporting the black eye he'd gotten from an angry Best admirer at the Cavern when Ringo debuted as a Beatle some three weeks earlier.

But they came bearing "Love Me Do," which Martin picked out of the four songs they'd played for him in June. Shortly after they initially recorded it, the Beatles opened Bruce Channel at the Tower Ballroom in New Brighton. Lennon was impressed with the harmonica playing of Delbert McClinton, which helped "Hey Baby" achieve the coveted number one slot in America (Frank Ifield's "I Remember You," with its own harmonica solo, returned the favor in a rare appearance of an English artist on the US pop charts that summer), and he used it to full effect, balancing the elementary nursery rhyme scheme: *Do/You/True/Do.*

"We copied records we liked," said Johnny Guitar of the Hurricanes, and like most Liverpool groups, he left it at that. For the Beatles, their developing songcraft was their passage out of Liverpool and into the world.

IIIIII

BEING A BAND.

What is it about the Fabulist Four, the perfect quartet, that sets them apart, beyond their peers, their generation, even the idea of pop music itself? They sound more randomly weird as we get equidistant from their time frame, untethered from the progression of genres that mark their contemporaries. They lead by example, and yet the results hew to no predictable landscape, blending instruments and style and overreach. That still, after these many years and maddening familiarity with each of their songs, they are capable of surprise; the revealing scope and sophistication of their musical imagination; the way each personality jigsaws together for an all-too-brief decade, and then the inevitable solo albums, individual brilliance showing how much they relied on each other to make a four-ever magic.

Ringo's addition is more than skill on the toms, an intuition of drum fill, though it's said he has trouble with a snare roll. By the time they record their second single, "Please Please Me," his personality has synchronized the band, which is a drummer's job. He's personable, able to be the butt of the joke and yet wiggle his ass leaving the others to preen. As they take on the roles we'll come to know them by—the cute one, the quiet one, the moody one, the one that needs nurturing—they also combine them, four corners squared. Martin had asked them to speed up their first crack at "Please Please Me," to apply tension until release. McCartney pedals his bass as the verse harmony begins in unison and then splits apart like a crack in the earth; there are rousing *c'mon*s, and the double me-aning of *please* when it repeats, entreaty and command.

Their rise is rapid to the point of vertigo. In December, "Love Me Do" hangs on for dear life in the *Pop Weekly* chart, just breaking into the Top Thirty, as the group grumpily goes to Hamburg to finish contractual obligations with the Star Club, ushering in a new year in which "Please Please Me" will be officially released on January 11, heading toward number one the next month. Even as late as the week ending July 20, 1963, with Cliff on the cover, they are underbilled after Wee Willie Harris ("Beatles etc.") beneath a headlined "Giant Double-Page pic of Billy Fury." They are not as novel as hindsight roseates, clambering up the British charts—"From Me to You," "She Loves You," "I Want to Hold Your Hand"—on their way to a benefit command performance for the queen in November. They bow theatrically as one after each song, uniform collarless jackets and matching mop tops and cheeky smiles. Their shrill audience allows them to test out stage moves: the shake of the head, the sudden leap to falsetto, the simplicity of the idea that she loves you, that he wants to hold your hand, that we're in this together. The rise and rush of Beatlemania.

|||||

IN AMERICA THEY'RE RUMORS AT FIRST, despite three singles that have come out to little impression. Epstein has tried to sell them to the major labels, beginning with EMI's US partner, Capitol, who pass. He's forced to license his band through the independents. Vee-Jay, the Chicago r&b independent, has been cash-infused (some might say confused, as the company is ill-equipped to deal with their newfound largesse) by the success of the Four Seasons, and must hear something similar in the Beatles' keening harmonies. They gamble on "Please Please Me," following it with "From Me to You" in the first half of 1963. There is an album should they choose to release it, but it's bumped behind Jimmy Reed, Jerry Butler, and Frank Ifield. Swan, not unfamiliar with the temporality of teen idols, takes their shot with "She Loves You." There is no follow-through.

But by December 1963, the stir they are creating in Britain can't be ignored. Epstein had flown to New York in November to talk with Ed Sullivan, who had witnessed Beatlemania first-hand when he came upon airport chaos at Heathrow on a trip to England, and Brian skillfully negotiated a trio of headline appearances. Capitol, suddenly aware that they have a hot property in their overseas operation, institutes a suit against Vee-Jay, who can ill afford any more legal troubles. A disc jockey named Carroll James breaks their first hit on WDCD in the nation's capital, spurred by a teenage girl, Marsha Albert, calling up to request "I Want to Hold Your Hand" after seeing a CBS evening news brief on December 10. Jack Paar shows blurry film clips of Beatle hysteria. In the final 1963 issue of *Billboard*, there is a full-page ad promising *The Beatles Are Coming!* The official release date is December 26, 1963: "Surf on the Thames sound," is how the trade magazine describes it. By the time they arrive at the Sullivan Theater on Broadway and West Fifty-Second Street, after having gotten off a plane to the kind of command reception reserved for royalty, "I Want to Hold Your Hand" is at number one. As they look out their Plaza hotel windows at a frenzy not seen since Elvis, the hit parade primes for their assault. The Top 40 has been in shock since John F. Kennedy's assassination; the sixties are about to start over. On April 4 they have the top five singles in America, with another seven scattered throughout the Hot 100, along with the number one and two albums, Capitol's *Meet the Beatles* and better-late-than-never *Introducing the Beatles* on Vee-Jay. Fifth Beatles abound. One is savvy promoter Sid Bernstein, who has gotten them a showcase at Carnegie Hall. My favorite is Murray the K, a disc jockey on New York's WINS, who insinuates himself into their coterie with his combination of glad-hand and jive talk (he has his own inclusive lingo, *meusurray*, me-and-us inserted into the interstices of each word). He runs shows at the Brooklyn Fox, uses Olatunji's "Drums of Passion" as his theme, and has broken the news of their Pan Am flight arrival at the newly christened JFK Airport. He shows how easy it is to join their band, or start one in emulation.

I'm watching that storied night of February 9, along with 73.7 million other curiosity-seekers. I'm in the sweet spot of adolescence, just seventeen *you know what I mean*. Old enough, still too young. I've been practicing guitar chords from a *Sing Out!* folk song collection, singing "That's My Desire" and "Blanche" out my bedroom window, a long way from being the Dual-Sonics or the Driftwoods, local instrumental bands plying the basements of Hungarian social clubs or the Linwood Ballroom around New Brunswick, New Jersey, where I'm growing up.

What I see, more than anything, is the concept of a band.

Not a backing group with a singer out front, or the ethnic hierarchy of doo-wop (Italian lead singer, Jewish harmonizers, Afro-American bass, like the Emanons, whom I witness singing "Stormy Weather" on the beach near Coney Island). Each Beatle takes his turn in the limelight, and you are overtaken by their combined synergy. Especially since they're now used to the adulation, playing it like another instrument. The screams may be predominantly female, but the guys look under the hood, at the way the engine is sparking. At least that's how it was for me, and I'm a guy who collects vintage spark plugs.

It's ironic that by the time they get to America, they've left Liverpool far behind, except as place marker. Their ascent is so precipitous that it would be easy to forsake where they come from, except they use it as calling card, playing up their provincial roots. They have their own descriptives—*gear*, *grotty*—and their accent, far removed from the posh inflections of London, filters through a sinus clog, as if they have a nose cold. America hears their snappy comeback first, at a press conference when they've stepped off a plane into the new world, Scouse-ish humor deflecting and winning over doubters. Not that there are many, given the heroic welcome they're afforded, a chorale of "We Love You Beatles" to the sing-song of "We Love You Conrad" from the *Bye Bye Birdie* soundtrack, granted the scepter of idolatry. For a band whose roots fêted rock and roll as it crossed an ocean, this must have been a moment to bewilder and treasure.

Their creation encapsulates the cultural transformations of the 1960s. The voyage between "She Loves You" to the endgame of "I Am the Walrus," with all the magnificent shards of creativity in between, spreads across the take-anything spectrum of popular music, the heart on the sleeve and the bite in the tongue, sound collage and lyrics a-twist with layers of meaning and mnemonic, instruments chosen without regard to what has come before, each phrase and hook and texture of arrangement existing as if it always meant to be there. Decades later we arrive at bio-discography through outtake, remix, remaster. Every anniversary commemorated; the emphasis on process rather than the songs themselves. Snippets of studio conversation, live performances, works in progress, false starts, all show our desire to know *how it was done*, how four musicians could make such incessantly interesting music, and have it change the course of popular music.

It made me want to find out, or at least feel what it felt like. In the summer of 1964, after patiently absorbing barre chords from a friend who could play some of the diminished progressions that Paul brought to "Till There Was You," I bought a cherry red Gibson Les Paul Special and a Magnatone 280 amp (true vibrato, the same kind Buddy Holly played) from a kid down the street who had given up the calling. On November 7 the Vandals (*Bringing Down the House With Your Kind of Music!*) debuted at Chi Psi fraternity on the Rutgers University campus.

The somewhere of start. The start of somewhere.

||||||

THEY'RE EASY TO MERCHANDISE: boots (Cuban heel, elastic side gussets), trinkets, lunchboxes and wall hangings, dolls of all description. Their toylike matched set translates readily to caricature, an emoji before any exist. Beatle wigs appear on the most unlikely of heads, and a movie that both exalts and humanizes them, Richard Lester's *A Hard Day's Night*, documentary as flight of fancy, sets their myth in celluloid.

Epstein moves quickly to consolidate his holdings within Liverpool. Gerry and the Pacemakers had been on the Mersey scene, as well as Hamburg's Top Ten club, almost as long as the Beatles, first playing the Cavern in 1960. In 1962 the *Liverpool Echo* popularity poll placed them in the number two slot, and the Pacemakers could hardly mind runner-up status in Brian's management roster when sloppy seconds included "How Do You Do It?" The Beatles had turned down the potential hit since it was written by professional songsmith Mitch Murray; produced by George Martin, it followed "Please Please Me" into the top slot of the British charts. Gerry wore his guitar high under his chin, in the Liverpudlian manner, and "Don't Let the Sun Catch You Crying," a showcase for the major seventh chord, is for this hopeless romantic the most poignant dawn-breaking song since "When the Blue of the Night Meets the Gold of the Day." Gerry's version of "You'll Never Walk Alone" would be adopted as the sing-along of the Liverpool football club, and his wistful "Ferry Across the Mersey," written for the 1965 film of the same name, captured an enduring *land-I-love* for his hometown.

Billy J. Kramer also profited from Epstein's alliance with the Beatles. Produced by Martin, he started with "Do You Want to Know a Secret" and was given songs from the overflow of the prolific one-upmanship of Lennon-McCartney, "Bad to Me," and "From a Window." With the Dakotas, a backing band he found in Manchester when his former group, the Coasters, refused to leave their day jobs (Kramer himself gave up a position at British Rail), he achieved success on both sides of the Atlantic, and finally broke free from his Beatle associations when he insisted on recording "Little Children," a non-Beatle composition by Mort Shuman and J. Leslie McFarland, which became his biggest hit.

On the femme side, Epstein signed longtime Liverpool song-stress Cilla Black. He had been introduced to her through Bill Harry at the Blue Angel Club after she sang "Boys," reclaiming it for the girls' prerogative of the Shirelles. She dueted the song with Ringo when he was with the Hurricanes, and made a practice of sitting in with the Big Three and Kingsize Taylor and the Dominoes, though she was too young to follow them to Hamburg.

There were few other female singers in the boys' club that was Liverpool. Beryl Marsden gave Barbara George's "I Know" a run for its currency, an Amy Winehouse prototype. In the Beatles' wake the Ladybirds—fresh from Hamburg—delighted the Cavern. Cilla's girlfriend was Pauline Behan, George Harrison's "bird" when the newbie Beatles played the Iron Door, later to marry Gerry Marsden (no relation to Beryl). Black had made the front page of *Mersey Beat*'s first issue in an article opening with a lengthy "the price you pay" preamble ("The sweet smell of success turns bittersweet," fledgling editor Harry wrote, "for a star can rocket overnight into oblivion again," citing Jerry Lee Lewis, Terry Dene, and Marty Wilde). But Cilla "is building up her confidence," and Harry, typing the article moments before deadline, has forgotten the last name of his fashion columnist, Priscilla White. He changes her to Black, allowing Cilla's image to step within a shadowed darkness, wrapping it around her like Peggy Lee, her inspiration, would a sable. Her early publicity emphasized "bright red hair and jet black voice." She had reserves of voice, and a worldwide hit with "You're My World" took her a long way from the Iron Door, though she never lost the bouffant.

The Searchers had momentum when Epstein came calling and didn't need his help. They too began as a skiffle group, their evolution to a rock band compelling lead singer Tony Jackson to concentrate on learning the electric bass. Johnny Sandon, who bore a striking resemblance to the early bespectacled Buddy Holly, took his vocal place when they made their Cavern debut in April 1961, and when Jackson felt comfortable enough to sing and play at the same time, Sandon moved over to the once-instrumental Remo Four. All the Liverpool bands were adjusting to the demands of the new sound. The Searchers did their time at the Star Club in Germany in 1962, and followed the Beatles into the charts with remakes of the confectionary American hits "Sweets for My Sweet" and "Sweet Nuthins," but it was the more jingle-than-jangle folkish rock of "Needles and Pins" (written by those west coast scousers Jack Nietzsche and Sonny Bono), and later "When

You Walk in the Room" and Malvina Reynolds's "What Have You Done to the Rain," which gave them a chiming ring that would preflyte the Byrds.

"Needles and Pins" is atop *Pop Weekly*'s chart on the week ending February 8, 1964, at the moment the Beatles land in America. The Swinging Blue Jeans notch under them at number two with "Hippy Hippy Shake." There's Gerry at four (and between, at number three, an exponent of the "Tottenham Sound," the Dave Clark Five with "Glad All Over," its cataclysm drums having much to do with Joe Meek's sonic breakthroughs) and even a group called the Merseybeats at number 19. All eyes are on Liverpool. Decca, not about to miss another opportunity, sets up a mobile recording unit outside the Cavern to capture the city's second string: the Marauders, the Dennisons, Bern Elliot and the Fenmen, Beryl Marsden, Dave Berry and the Cruisers, the Fortunes. Heinz, Joe Meek's guilt-by-association, gets top billing, though his career is receding in the rearview mirror. Like another snapshot of the sound reverberating from Liverpool at its moment of discovery, *This Is Mersey Beat* (documented in the Rialto Ballroom over two days in May 1963) with Faron's Flamingos, Earl Preston and the TT's, Ian and the Zodiacs, and other combinations that could be found any Saturday night on Mathew Street, *Recorded Live at the Cavern* is full of frantic energy, each hopeful playing a little faster than usual as if to make up for lost time. Liverpool groups were crisp, cracking snare to the forefront, clean and precise in the guitars, and if anything, carried too much respect for the songs they were covering, impersonating, or sound-aliking when they tried to alter chord changes and riffs to write an original.

Then there was the inevitable dilution of live sound when approaching the studio. Brian Epstein had signed the Big Three but they never accommodated his penchant for grooming. Their first single, "Some Other Guy," originally sung by New Yorker Richie

Barrett and done by nearly every band in Liverpool (the Beatles had played it for a visiting television crew in August 1962 when Ringo debuted as their drummer), was taken from a demo tape and scorned by the group. According to those who were there, the Big Three were the most powerful sound-mass to ricochet off the Cavern walls, and their live *At the Cavern* EP, with Brian Griffiths on lead guitar (replacing Adrian Barber, who left to stage-manage the Star Club in Hamburg, and will journey to America, where he will eventually produce the Velvet Underground), captures a raw dynamic lost on their chirpy second single, "By the Way." They sound confined in their new "shiny mohair suits," as noted by an astute Bill Harry. The flip is "Cavern Stomp," a flapping-arms dance step constrained by the club's tight quarters. By then it's almost over, been here and gone.

||||||

RORY STORM IS LOST in the flocking to Liverpool. He couldn't blame Ringo, though he felt a letdown in the rhythm section, and the fact that it put a curse, as would *Spinal Tap* in another era, on the drum stool and those who would inhabit it, marking time on their way to the next band. It was obvious the Beatles were ascendant. They were paying Ringo twenty-five pounds a week, and in return Epstein had suggested Pete Best switch to the Hurricanes, which seemed an accident waiting to happen. Besides, Rory really didn't want to leave Liverpool. His family lived here, and he would, too, because he was the Golden Boy. He liked the locals, and they loved him down at the local.

He had a stutter that didn't impede him when he sang, but would prove unhelpful in his public persona. His athleticism—he was a swimmer, footballer, steeplechase standout—gave his stage presence a physicality that overwhelmed his voice. Oriole gave him a trial run when they used two live tracks from *This Is Mersey*

Beat for a single, but "I Can Tell"/"Dr. Feelgood" (the latter a harbinger of the throwback virtues of seventies pub rock) didn't have much to set them apart from what other Liverpool bands had on offer. You couldn't see the glory of Rory on a record.

The Hurricanes would never get a chance in America, and so his second (and final) single "America," the derisive show tune from *West Side Story*, produced by Epstein (Brian's only foray to the other side of the glass), has Rory looking longingly at the land of opportunity, an outsider twice removed, filtering a faux-Puerto Rican inflection through his westernized drawl and the unfulfilled promise of *I like to be in America*. There are *la-las* galore, and Ringo stops by to lend support to the man who helped him become the drummer he was destined to be. But like Tony in *West Side Story*, Starr has outgrown the old gang. Rory is content to stay a Shark, a Jet, a Hurricane. "Just tell them that the Golden Boy is here," Storm whispers to saxophonist Mike Evans of the Clayton Squares before guesting onstage after the Hurricanes are no more.

When his father dies, Rory moves home to console his mum. He develops a chest infection, takes a couple of drinks as well as sleeping pills, and—it is declared accidental—never wakes on the morning of September 28, 1972. His mother is found lying near him, an apparent suicide. In a final twist of fate's knife, bringing together the two foreshadowed stars of Liverpool, Billy Fury plays "Stormy Tempest" in the 1973 rock and roll aspirational film *That'll Be the Day*, set in a 1950s holiday camp much like Butlin's. Billy sings "A Thousand Stars," he and Rory taking their place within the firmament.

||||||

LONDON IMMEDIATELY EXERTS its gravitational pull on Liverpool's major players. Within a month of the Beatles conquering

America, Brian relocates NEMS Enterprises Ltd. to Argyll Street in Mayfair, next door to the Palladium, and the group members move en masse to the seat of monarchy and the Isle's beating heart. They'll only return to whence they came through the nostalgic retrospectives of "In My Life," "Penny Lane," and "Strawberry Fields Forever."

A darker wellspring of influence is emerging, a result of the capital's sophistication and specialist record stores. The Liverpool groups hearkened to an American rock and roll that may have begun with Chuck Berry and Little Richard but emulated a more tuneful pop strata, incorporating the fringes of Tamla-Motown and country music—unlike the emerging Rolling Stones or Yardbirds, who delve deeper in their quest for source. Mick Jagger and Keith Richards bond over a Muddy Waters record, and though happy to take a Lennon-McCartney song as calling card—"I Wanna Be Your Man" puts them on the British chart map at the end of 1963—while they figure out how to write their own, their slapdash sound is at once murkier and tougher, threatening, and they contrive a demeanor to match. For some of their listeners, including myself, nurtured in a Northeast surrounded by doo-wop groups, there is the dizzying response of looking in a mirror as the blues reflects back to its homeland; there was little exposure to blues masters on the WMCA pop charts, though Wilbert Harrison's "Kansas City" is about an easy-rolling a number one as can be imagined in 1959, using those selfsame dozen bars. The Animals love their Bo Diddley. A band like the Kinks, whose "You Really Got Me" hammers a riff that links a chain with Muddy Waters's "Hoochie Koochie Man," mates Edwardian foppery to an overdriven Vox amp. And then there was the Who. . . . My generation.

By 1965, the Invasion is at its most invasive. It's often overlooked that the advance guard of the Brits-are-coming are more the plays-on-Anglicisms of Freddie and the Dreamers, Herman's

Hermits, "A Groovy Kind of Love," and anything by the Hollies. They're joined on the pop charts by "Louie Louie" and "Surfer Bird," the ur-texts of garage rock. Temptation took control of me and I fell.

On November 9 of that year I'm at the first all-acappella doo-wop show in Hackensack, New Jersey, bringing together esoteric singing groups like the Savoys, the Five Sharks, and the Zircons, each of whom have garnered a neighborhood following by the defenders of the doo-wop faith. "You might not believe this but many of your well-known recording groups of today are not capable of singing without instruments and 93% of these groups come from Great Britain," say the liner notes of *Acappella All the Way*. As the groups harmonize under a full moon, the Great Blackout descends upon the Northeast, overloading the electric grid and plunging the theater into darkness. When the lights go back on the following morning, the doo-wop era is over.

The Cavern doesn't last much longer. By Sunday, February 27, 1966, Ray McFall can't hold his creditors at bay. An all-night session with Rory, the Big Three, and ending with the Hideaways onstage as police arrive with dogs to confront protesters singing "We Shall Not Be Moved," closes a curtain on one of the hallowed halls of rock and roll. The club would reopen, only to be demolished in May 1973 for a railway ventilation shaft that was never built, then re-created on the other side of Mathew Street, to pay respect to when it was more than just a memory.

SAN FRANCISCO
1967

WE'RE DRIVING ACROSS NEBRASKA WHEN WE RUN OUT of gas. Arguing nonstop in a '56 Ford. Discussing states of being in this year of the Be-In. Heading to San Francisco in the Summer of Love.

The Beatles' creed of "All You Need Is Love" slogans the are-you-going solstice of Scott McKenzie's "San Francisco (Be Sure to Wear Flowers in Your Hair)." But what is Love? It's agreed that it's exhilarating and intoxicating; almost, in fact, as involving as drugs.

Which Larry and I have and then some. The age of psychedelia is upon us. There's been a change in our altered state-to-state, drifting across country, smoking pot to the Byrds' "Eight Miles High" and moving through a gateway song, Bob Dylan's "Sad Eyed Lady of the Lowlands," into speed. We're reliving Kerouac's *On the Road*, that classic beat generation do-it-yourself paint-by-numbers for a next generation cresting out of adolescence. The allure of wander and present tense of highway. We left New Jersey a couple of days ago, knowing we were heading west but little else, just a destination, staying close to the newly sprung hippie enclaves in each city, with their head shops and record stores and

bell-bottom pants and underground press, nodding conspiratori-
ally to fellow long-hairs in the streets, finding a crash pad for the
night, back behind the wheel the next day. On the roam. Next
stop: Denver.

The amphetamine crystal—*almost like a ball*, I free-
associate—is fueling mine and Larry's oft-heated discussion.
We're wondering where to draw the double line in these anything-
goes times, and if you need to. When does your Love cross the
boundaries of another's sense of attraction, or at least manner of
courtship? We pass a swimming pool back near Lincoln, and wonder whether it's okay to jump in. Knock and ask permission from
the owner? Keep driving? Larry feels he has the right to swan
dive without asking; he means no harm to the water or the property; it's all ours. That's the prerogative of Love. I'm less likely to
judge guilt or innocence. I'm for the twilight zone of Being, to
accept all contraries of the human spirit, the cognizance of one's
place in the universe, upholding my share of human consciousness. Zen Len. I wouldn't like anyone to come in and rummage
through my record collection; my Self has its own way of sorting,
how to handle discs or emotions, filed according to a system of
disbelief I've been nurturing over the years. Subculture to sub-
counterculture. *Freak Freely*, says the button I pin to my jacket
on St. Mark's Place in New York's East Village before I hop in the
transcontinental car.

So involved are we in making our metaphysical points that we
hardly notice when the Ford begins to slow, downshift, roll to the
side of the highway. We get out, surrounded by a flat, sunbaked
midwestern landscape, squinting, not sure where we are. Going,
but how do we get there?

Free Love; is such a thing possible?

We're on our way to find out, like too many others.

||||||

SAN FRANCISCO LIES WAITING. The city had long been a destination for the disaffected, well sited culturally, perched peril-
ously on a bay prone to earthquake. Geology and geography come
together on October 7, 1955, when Allen Ginsberg reads his epic
poem *Howl* for the first time at the Six Gallery on Fillmore Street,
a few minutes' walk from where the Fillmore ballroom will host
dance-concerts a decade later. The poem's obscenity trial and consequent publication by Lawrence Ferlinghetti's City Lights book-
shop will solidify the city's reputation as an avant-magnet and
beat capital, as will Lenore Kandel's poetic manifesto for explicit
sexual illumination, *The Love Book*. The University of California,
Berkeley becomes a leading center of the Free Speech Movement
and antiwar dissent; KMPX is the first free-form FM radio station, liberated from Top 40 programming; there is a thriving experimental music community; and LSD has only recently been
criminalized, which makes it more attractive. Eden's forbidden
fruit.

It all points west. Los Angeles has its own siren song—the
"California Dreaming" of The Mamas and The Papas, the "get
here and we'll do the rest" of the Doors, even those all-American
Beach Boys psychedelicized. But it's hardly confined to the west
coast. Sometimes it seems as if the Western world is in kaleidoscopic spin.

In the span of just a couple of mid-sixties years, rock and roll
and its associated musics have grown to represent the arrowhead
of a metamorphosing youth upheaval. Rock (shunning the *roll*,
like a youngster lopping the "y" of a first name in a bid to be
taken seriously) has taken on the conceits of art, no longer teenage, with all loss of innocence and subsequent opening of creative
wellsprings that implies. It has split the radio dial into two opposing frequencies, overground AM and underground FM, though
except for such matters as song length, lyric permissibility, and acceptable amounts of dissonance, the airwaves still rely on a good

hook and catchphrase to encourage a chosen Arbitron to sing along. Sometimes they chorus together. The Beatles release *Sgt. Pepper's Lonely Hearts Club Band* on June 1 to a worldwide phenomenon, regarded as a breakthrough in album conception with hallucinogenic overtones. "Lucy in the Sky with Diamonds"—really, John, inspired by your son Julian?—leads to the sustained chordal mash that closes "A Day in the Life," an on and on and on fading into inaudibility until you, gentle listener, return to this earthly dimension, back where you began, ineffably altered.

A sense of *trip* impels the counterculture, sets it in motion. Art forms meld together, multiplying mediums. The resultant *happening* spills out of bounds—visual, audio, and sensory—and takes pride in violating convention. In the theater, in the movies, in the bedroom, clothes are removed, body parts paraded, barriers between audience and performer erased. The moon is within grasp, and will be strolled upon in a mere two years, a perspective of earth from outer space that affirms we are riding a planet through endless nothingness, all vertigo intact. Generational battle lines fortify; the codex of subculture. Hair length becomes a confrontational political statement, peaceful protest escalating into violence and an increasingly hostile response. Us versus Them; even if Them are Us in a mirror.

|||||

A LONE TROMBONE PLAYS WITHIN the Broadway Tunnel. Cars begin to ballet in North Beach. Books are returned to City Lights. A woman sings Debussy in a storefront window accompanied by a tuxedoed pianist. As light projections are screened on the façade of a Wells Fargo building, a couple in a convertible argue over learning to drive.

For six hours, taking place on the cusp of the full moon, the night of March 9, 1963, it's hard to tell where art leaves off and life begins. The performance piece *City Scale* uses San Francisco as a stage setting, a newly stretched canvas, a spool of magnetic tape incorporating the random and the unforeseen. When the participants arrive in a park overlooking the Mission District, their balloon fest breaks up a brewing street fight between teenage gangs.

City Scale is scored, more map than annotation, by composer Ramon Sender, playwright Ken Dewey, and visual artist Anthony Martin, part of an arts collective called the San Francisco Tape Music Center headquartered in a soon-to-be-demolished Victorian house at 1537 Jones near Russian Hill. On the eve of the Center's relocation to 321 Divisadero east of Haight Street, Sender replaces a fuse to bring electricity to an upper floor, inadvertently resulting in a fire, which might be taken as an art piece all its own. He has been utilizing found sound in his compositions, scraping scissors over a sheet of metal, swirling a washing machine filled with rocks, slowing a recording of a Tibetan gong so that it becomes more *ohm* than *om*. In *Tropical Fish Opera*, from 1962, Sender sets up a ten-gallon fish tank, draws the five lines of a musical staff upon each of its four sides, and with himself on piano, Pauline Oliveros on French horn, Loren Rush on double bass, and Morton Subotnick on clarinet, allows the swimming fish to represent musical notation, to compose melody and dynamics. "We were playing with that sort of chaotic edge, that is between order and chaos," Ramon told David Bernstein. "Isn't that where all the good stuff happens?"

The San Francisco Tape Music Center gathered its component visionaries in 1961, drawn from the world of misfit academia. Sender was studying at the San Francisco Conservatory of Music under Robert Erickson, an encouraging mentor to many within this burgeoning avant-garde. On June 13, 1961, Erickson curated a workshop to provide a showcase for his students and to connect their dots with the ongoing tradition of the farthest reaches of "classical" music. Alongside works by John Cage, Karlheinz Stock-hausen, Harry Partch, and Luciano Berio, aspiring musicians like Subotnick—playing his prophetic *Composition for Synthesizer*—and Terry Riley (bouncing marbles off the strings of a piano) performed. Sender, intrigued by the possibilities of the two-track Ampex tape recorder he had found at the Conservatory, tried his hand at making "sound on sound," overdubbing and transform-ing *Four Sanskrit Hymns* into a jumble of magnetic particles.

The insular world of scholarly composition suddenly seemed too confining for a music newly burst from the classroom. In December, Sender, along with Riley, Philip Wisor, and Pauline Oliveros, organized the *Sonics* Concerts. Terry had worked with drone-ist LaMonte Young when both were at the University of California, Berkeley; Riley's *M . . . Mix* is an early precursor of the looping Mobius strip that would underlay his landmark *In C* in 1964. Oliveros as well was experimenting with sound manipula-tion, debuting her first piece for tape, *Time Perspectives*, filtering vocals with cardboard tubes and frequency modulations. Sender's *Traversals* featured the gurgle of his baby son in his crib. Anything seemed ripe for artistic inclusion, enhanced by a sense of free im-provisation that was hardly confined to the ivory tower. Jazz had long liberated itself from traditional harmony and rhythmic time-keeping, as had painting from the pictorial image. In fact, Riley claimed his music was more aligned with abstract expressionism than the *new thing* of John Coltrane and Ornette Coleman.

Not that categories made much of a difference anymore. The Tape Center—founded by Sender and Subotnick—purposefully encouraged disciplines to conjugally visit. An upstairs space was given over to the Bay Area listener-supported radio station KPFA to broadcast works in progression. The Canyon Cinema, started by Bruce Baillie, screened innovative works by Stan Brakhage, Kenneth Anger, and other uncompromising filmmakers. The Dancer's Workshop, led by Ann Halprin, provided physical interpolation; Anthony Martin referred to himself as a "visual composer," using snatches of film and liquid projections, a technique he learned from the work of Seymour Locks, a professor at San Francisco State who overhead-projected swirling translucent paint and liquid-filled slides in the 1950s to create hypnotic patterns and an immersive environment that verged on hallucination.

The aim was to create a "theater of totality," in the words of László Moholy-Nagy, an early-twentieth-century theorist who sought to bring static painting into a multisensory experience. His treatise on *Vision in Motion* (1946) theorized an idea that had entranced artists for centuries, such as the mathematician Louis Bertrand Castel, who in 1734 built "a harpsichord for the eyes" called the *clavecin oculaire* with the aim of intertwining light with music. Moholy-Nagy imagined a Light Space Modulator, refracting and reflecting beams through Plexiglas, with a desire to create a "kinetic, time-spatial existence." Alexander Scriabin, in 1911, had debuted a "color symphony" called *Prometheus: The Poem of Fire*; Thomas Wilfred wrote his *Lumia* (1922) for a Clavilux, a pipe organ that also contained a keyboard that could trigger prismatic light beams.

New musics require new methods of fabricating sound; or is it the other way around? On a small budget, the Tape Center salvaged electronic equipment wherever it could, from military surplus to the telephone company, chaining tape machines together, dovetailing Hewlett-Packard oscillators and line amplifiers and ring modulators and a contraption called the Chamberlin that had a tape head under every key, a filial ancestor to the Mellotron. Among the most important advances to come from the creative ferment of the Tape Center was Don Buchla's "electronic easel," an idea suggested by Sender and Subotnick in 1963, which, along with the work of Robert Moog, would evolve into one of the first modular synthesizers. The Buchla Box, as it was called, used voltage-controlled oscillators and envelope filters and analog sequencers to shape all manner of timbre and amplitude. The implications for A Flock of Seagulls would be enormous.

During a three-year span lasting until 1966, when the Tape Center moved its centrifuge to Mills College in Oakland, the collective at 321 Divisadero provided a remarkable clearinghouse for ideas and provocative milieu. Breaking down distinctions between popular and high art, blending performance with radical wild-card conception, admiring the random within purposeful and cogent manipulation, they are the framing device as San Francisco begins to ingest the consciousness-altering properties of the chemical compound known as lysergic acid diethylamide-25.

Set and setting.

||||||

THE ACID TESTS TAKE amoebic shape in San Francisco in 1965, orchestrated by Ken Kesey, a bestselling author turned madcap ringmaster. He's gone beyond words, given up trying to paraphrase the inexplicable, preferring instead to put his metaphors and characters into improvised pinball action. "I'd rather be a lightning rod than a seismograph," Kesey tells Tom Wolfe, who goes along for the ride in *The Electric Kool-Aid Acid Test*, which travelogues the too-old-to-be-beatnik / too-young-to-be-hippy Bay-bridging that Kesey's band of cavorting Merry Pranksters bequeaths to San Francisco's emerging psychomimesis.

As a youth, he is by turns wrestler and actor, ventriloquist and magician, roles that serve him well when he assumes captaincy of a bus full of zonked fellow travelers and sets out to circumnavigate the America of 1964. Kesey had entered Stanford's creative writing program six years earlier on a fellowship, but learns more about the byways of creation when he volunteers to take part in psychological experiments held at the Veterans Hospital in Menlo Park. For seventy-five dollars a day he is given a variety of drugs

designed to influence synapses and reroute brain waves, an out-
growth of the pioneering work of Albert Hofmann, who beginning in 1938 attempted to find pharmaceutical uses for a fungus
found in rye kernels. Five years later, on April 19, 1943, Hofmann
accidently ingested some of his LSD-25 and took a now-famous
bicycle ride into the future: "I perceived an uninterrupted stream
of fantastic pictures, extraordinary shapes with intense, kaleidoscopic play of colors." He would later refer to the drug as his
"problem child," feeling that its value as a psychological and spiritual tool was compromised by sensationalism and casual escapist
use; but by then it had entered the bloodstream and was well on
its way to society's medulla oblongata.

Tripping and trancing; a pathway through reality into ur-
reality. Kesey researches his 1962 novel, *One Flew Over the Cuckoo's
Nest*, by working the night shift in a psychiatric ward, conjuring
the persona not only of his main character, Randle McMurphy,
who fakes mental illness, sowing discord among the patients, valiantly resisting control until he is subjected to a lobotomy; but
of his narrator, Chief Broom, an Indian inmate who lives on the
other side of madness, and, at the novel's conclusion, makes his
dramatic escape into freedom. So too Kesey, who writes the first
three pages of the book on peyote to get inside the Broom closet,
moves to Oregon, and later La Honda, south of San Francisco,
and similarly transforms his environment—speakers in the trees
blaring free jazz, recording gear capturing echoing reverberant
sound, an expanding coterie of psychic vagabonds—to scribe *Sometimes a Great Notion*, a mega-novel that provides an excuse to
head to New York for its publication party. For the journey he
buys a 1939 International Harvester D-50 school bus for $1,250,
outfitted with bunks and refrigerator, stocks it with LSD and
Dexedrine and a supporting cast of miscreants, like the Vietnam
vet Ken Babbs, Mike Hagen (known as the Hassler), Gretchen
Fetchin the Slime Queen; and to serve as driver and generational

link, the actual hero of *On the Road*, Neal Cassady. Intrepid Travelers all. On the front of the paint-splashed bus is lettered *FURTHUR*: two U's. You and You. Rhymes with *Cuckoo*, that nest where left and right sides of the brain U-nite, and off the Merry (Band of) Pranksters go . . .

They're on their way to the World's Fair in New York, a vision of the future already out of date, much like meeting with Jack Kerouac at a party on the Upper East Side as he regards them with suspicion and disdain. There is a similar misconstrue when the Pranksters visit Timothy Leary and Richard Alpert in Millbrook, where the League of Spiritual Discovery is centered, hoping to convene with those they believe are allied forces in the psychedelic reinvention. Despite Leary's proselytizing, early mushrooming in 1961, and the Harvard Psychedelic Project he hosts at Marsh Chapel on Good Friday 1962, and Alpert's *Be Here Now* philosophy and subsequent reincarnation as the guru Baba Ram Dass, there is a marked difference in approach. The pages of Leary and Alpert's academic house organ, *Psychedelic Review*, are more clinical than exalted, more research than searching, analytical and distancing, experience once removed. "Expectation, Mood & Psilocybin" is the cover story for the fifth issue, published in 1965, with an emphasis on methodology: "The expectation of 'love' is most strongly related to aggressiveness, insight, and déjà vu experiences," writes a laboratory team headed by Ralph Metzner, ". . . negatively related to various somatic symptoms, such as nausea, throat-chest constriction, and body-melting." Though various issues examine Zen Buddhism and Gurdjieff, "Peyote and Cannabis" ("Of particular interest is what proportion of the population would be attracted to their use and for what purpose"), "Ayahuasca Drinkers Among the Chama Indians," and the interaction of "Bhang and Alcohol: Cultural Factors in the Choice of Intoxicant," there is little element of fun.

The Pranksters are hardly meditative. They want to confront, disrupt, put on, and piss off, anything to upset the stasis they see in normative society. They're unpredictable, which is a self-fulfilling prophecy all its own. On their journey eastward (following in the footsteps of another pilgrimagic text, Hermann Hesse's *A Journey to the East*), they drive into Arizona, where the Republican convention is in the process of nominating Barry Goldwater: *A Vote for Barry is a Vote for Fun* they banner on the side of the bus, flying American flags and driving backward through the Phoenix streets. Cassady careens down the Blue Ridge Mountains in Virginia, not using brakes, talking a mile a minute, matching his internal speedometer with the swerves in the road. They ride through Times Square playing flutes, waving Day-Glo hands, touring the tourists. Back in California, when it comes time for an anti–Vietnam War rally in Berkeley, Kesey and his disciples dress up in quasi-military outfits, place a gun turret atop the bus, fashion machine guns out of wood, and caravan to the demonstration. Kesey tells the crowd "There's only one thing to do . . . And that's everybody just look at it, look at the war, and turn your backs and say . . . *Fuck it!*" as the Pranksters serenade the crowd with "Home on the Range." Ranging back home in La Honda they attempt to edit the hundred hours of film they've shot on their summer vacation, using it as a pretext for screening parties laced with psychedelics.

These become the seedlings of the Acid Tests, as if the Tape Center's multimedias had taken over Kesey's compound and tossed away the illusion that it was a performance. The Pranksters—by now grown to include Hell's Angels and runaways and thrill-seekers in search of a rollicking free-for-all—want to shorten the sensory lag of reaction time, so they are not forever destined to live historically, a microsecond behind behind the unfolding present. The movie resists coherent assemblage, unsynched and out of focus (though Kesey's acid-drenched cinematographers on the bus have their own focal lengths in mind); but it paves a way for an environ in which receptors are bombarded, stimulated, and spun in quark-like overload. Get on board; flip the human light switch of *On* the Bus, or *Off* the Bus, new routes added as ridership skyrockets.

Can You Pass the Acid Test? Locations shift to accommodate the tribal increase of nonstop bacchanal. In November 1965 they haul the projectors over to Ken Babbs's house and begin to unreel; by December 4 they're in San Jose, with music provided by a former jug band who have changed their name for the occasion to an identifier found in a Funk & Wagnalls dictionary: the Grateful Dead. Two weeks later the whole shebang sets up shop at the Big Beat nightclub on San Antonio Road in Palo Alto. In January 1966 the revelry takes over the Fillmore Auditorium, paving the way for a gala Trips Festival by the waterfront at Longshoreman's Hall, a three-day exposition (January 21–23) more convocation than convention. The old Tape Center gang is there, with Ramon Sender and Ann Halprin and Tony Martin given free rein to deconstruct their environments, aided and abetted by anthropologist Stewart Brand, whose polymorphic slide show, "America Needs Indians," as filtered through the peyote rituals he had researched in the Southwest, sets the tone for the festival's opening night. Kesey's Merry Pranksters are on hand to provide creative mayhem. Throngs, tripping on laced ice cream and the realization that they aren't alone in their eccentricities, number in the thousands. Audience participation is not only encouraged, but de rigueur.

Providing soundtrack, mixing in with the pandemonium and the confusion—the "ecstatic dress" of the attendees, the echo-upon-echo looped microphonics and speakers picking up random conversations and ricocheting them around the hall, the nude antics of the Open Theatre, the Chinese Lion Dancers celebrating the Year of the Horse, the blinking traffic lights and strobe lights and liquefied projectiles—are guitar-centric rock bands.

The din, the visual clamor, the psychoactive drugs, all are conducive to exploration, improvising, to see what music might sound like as telepathy. At least for now, the bands here this weekend—the Grateful Dead, Big Brother and the Holding Company, the Loading Zone—are just one component of a spectacle, a funhouse mirror in this carnival of dizzying rides, freak show oddities, burlesque dancers and hustlers and barkers and rubes, the newborn hippies as they are about to be christened, or buddahed, or I Ching'd, out for a night of phantasmagoria. Cotton candy, corn dogs, LSD.

The torch is passing, culmination to beginning. Sender has seen the psychedelic light, and heads for the Mojave Desert with fifty tabs of lysergics and the realization that he could never live in a city again, ultimately joining a commune in Sonoma called the Morning Star Ranch; Brand is on his way toward formulating *The Whole Earth Catalogue*. With Kesey increasingly unwilling to play any part more serious than class clown—he shows up at the Trips Festival in a silver space suit, complete with helmet, flipping the visor down when he doesn't want to answer any questions—and dealing with legal problems of his own (a pair of marijuana busts that will send him on the lam to Mexico), still uncertain whether he'll avoid prison, it's time to move on to yet another astral plane. By Halloween 1966 and the Acid Test Graduation, twenty-five days after LSD becomes illegal, Kesey and the Pranksters will host a commencement ceremony for the Class of '66, San Francisco High. Cassady hands out diplomas. "Beyond LSD" will be "the next step in the psychedelic revolution," Ken tells a skeptical television reporter, though he adds, ever elusive, "Never trust a Prankster."

Meanwhile, Wolodia Grajonca, a refugee from Hitler's Germany now calling himself Bill Graham, has taken over the logistics of running the Trips Festival, though its illogistics disturb him, the drugs and the chaos. There's only so much he can do when the entire audience, as well as performers, are dosed and stoned and getting in for free. He has been organizing benefits for the San Francisco Mime Troupe over the past couple of months, featuring these same bands and others like the Jefferson Airplane, the Great Society, the Charlatans; he sees the income and attendance escalating, and has just signed a lease to hold regular shows at the Fillmore Auditorium for forty-five dollars a night.

All he's got to do is put up a poster.

||||||

IT'S ON MY WALL, twenty-four by fourteen inches, all purples and reds and oranges with bold silver lettering that folds each word within itself like a tri-dimensional jigsaw puzzle. A *New Year Bash*, spanning 1966 into 1967, featuring Jefferson Airplane, Grateful Dead, Quicksilver Messenger Service. A dream bill, and I'm dreaming. I've been trying to write my name in this sinuous Wes Wilson script all semester, my last before college graduation, decorating the margins of textbooks and term papers with whorls and mandalas. My band—the Zoo, dressed in animal-skin shirts and barefoot—has gone from playing Motown covers and extended fraternity favorites like "Shout" and "What'd I Say" while the dance floor is awash in beer, to sitting in lotus position spinning raga-rock through the final throes of the Who's "My Generation," using the guitar's D string as modal drone and piling amplification atop it.

These past couple of years have proved an adolescent growth spurt for rock and roll, genus Garage. The Gar Age may begin with the English Invasion, American bands forming in the role model of the BeatlesRollingStonesPrettyThingsKinksYardbirds; but the transplanting has lately taken on a nativist cast, fuzz atonal and full of yowl, underlaid by reedy electric organs and lyrics that promise angst and anger and repressed frustration in equal measure. All over America, groups—encouraged by the mass production of cheap electric guitars and emulative television shows like *Shindig* and *Hullabaloo*, pharmacological indulgence, a willing audience of their peers, and a yearning self-bravado—are springing up like invasive species. They draw equal influence from guitar instrumentalists like the Ventures or surf riders Dick Dale, the Surfaris, and the Chantays, as they do the Brits, a transatlantic Ping-Pong that pushes the Anglo influence further afield. For a "My" generation, the garage band—a term applied retroactively, when it's recognized as the spark in the combustion-chamber for rock and roll's V-8—is like a fine-tuned engine. Here's the key. Start the motor. Play a song.

San Francisco is bookended by Seattle on the western coast, whence comes the entry-level anthem of the new teen bands— "Louie Louie," a 1956 Richard Berry original covered nigh-simultaneously by the Kingsmen and Paul Revere and the Raiders in 1963; and Los Angeles, where the music business-as-usual is centered, the Seeds meet the Standells meet Love (the group, not the pheromone) as the Sunset Strip riots. San Francisco's growing band community is just far enough away along California's spine to allow it freedom of movement, though there is an element of sibling rivalry, of not wanting to be part of the "commercial" aspects of Los Angeles. It's a tradition derived from folkies, who like to think of themselves as committed idealists, politically aware, their roots deep in the common, above the commercial fray, looking down the necks of their acoustic guitars and banjos at the flighty carryings-on of rock and roll. But let's face it, by 1964 there was only the merest shading of difference between popular and populist. Bob Dylan and Peter, Paul and Mary have only a sliver of Top 40 between them, and Dylan was about to go electric.

Before the two could hyphenate, there had to be a marriage made in heaven. The Byrds aren't often thought of as a garage band, but their emulation, both fore and aft, was central casting to the onrushing band explosion. Jim (later Roger) McGuinn had seen the success of the Beatles and Dylan, apprenticing as a sideman with the Chad Mitchell Trio and the Limelighters, and as an aspiring folkie in Troubadour-laden Los Angeles began singing "I Want to Hold Your Hand" on an acoustic twelve-string guitar. By summer 1964—with the screaming girls of *A Hard Day's Night* as inducement—he joined with David Crosby, Gene Clark, Michael Clarke, and Chris Hillman, and began reinterpreting the folk songbook through electricity. A single under the name of the Beefeaters released by Elektra in that same year shows the group attempting to ride the redcoat-tails of the British beat boom, but they had yet to develop their signature accessory, the jingle-jangle chimes-of-freedom that is the Rickenbacker twelve-string as it heralds "Mr. Tambourine Man."

The Byrds would advance-scout many incarnations to come—psychedelia and space rock in "Eight Miles High" and *Fifth Dimension*, country rock with *Sweetheart of the Rodeo*—but the idea that folk and rock could be joined at the hip gave legitimacy to both. It would reach an apotheosis in Barry McGuire's "Eve of Destruction," written by P. F. Sloan, a bizarre chart-topper in September 1965, with lyrics that reach for the apocalyptic and offer not much in the way of hope or redemption: *Even the Jordan River has bodies a-floating.* . . . Sloan would also pen Johnny Rivers's "Secret Agent Man," the Grass Roots' "Where Were You When I Needed You," and the Turtles' "You Baby," as well as riposting the opening guitar cadenza of "California Dreaming."

||||||

WHILE "EVE OF DESTRUCTION" IS still riding high on the airwaves, I get a telephone call from my uncle, Larry Kusik, a lyricist who writes with title and genre in mind. He will later specialize in cinematic love themes—"A Time for Us" from *Romeo and Juliet*, "Speak Softly Love" from *The Godfather*—but now he's a journeyman, on staff at publishing companies, a rhyme for hire. I find his name on 45s from the Crystals, Rick Nelson (no *y*), Ruby and the Romantics; as well as might-have-beens like Judee Persia, the Kittens, the Lollipops, the Charmers. And soon, Link Cromwell.

He knows I've been in a band, playing college mixers and VFW halls, venturing as far west as the fraternities of Lehigh and Lafayette, and then back to Rutgers in central New Jersey, where we provide chorus for the Greeks on the weekend. He asks me to sing "Eve of Destruction" over the phone. Two weeks later I'm in Associated Studios in New York City, on the east flank of Times Square, making a record.

It is—naturally enough—a folk-protest tune. Uncle "Q" has written it with Ritchie Adams, the voice of the Fireflies' "You Are Mine," a hit in 1959, a songwriter who has his first success with Bobby Lewis's "Tossin' and Turnin'" in 1962. By the seventies he will be a lead singer of the Archies and write Engelbert Humperdinck's "After the Lovin'," a man of many guises.

As am I. We've crafted the persona of Link Cromwell, with an extra touch of subliminal Brit. I'll be "Crazy Like a Fox." *They call me neurotic / they say I'm psychotic / because I let my hair grow long*. Ritchie plays most of the instruments, a twelve-string guitar, sings background harmonies, even honks a couple of saxes buried in a mix he hopes will stir the consistency of Phil Spector's Wall of Sound. *While they're working on the inside / I'm having fun on the outside* . . . Unwitting, I tell my own fortune, the anticipation of finding myself a decade later *outside of society*, strumming another folk-protest anthem. *Is where I want to be*. I play bass on the flip side, "Shock Me" (*You tell me that you know what love is all about / Well c'mon baby show me what you're putting out*), with my uncle on harmonica and Alan Gordon of the Magicians drumming. I have crossed the line between hope and becoming. Anything can happen after this.

"Crazy Like a Fox" winds up on Hollywood Records (1107), sandwiched between the Chargers' "Saxafire" (1106) and the Pac-Keys "Dig In" (1108) with "Stone Fox" as its b-side. Foxy! Hollywood is a division of Nashville's Starday, who have revived a venerable r&b label dormant since 1957, and are looking for a way into the teen market. Link Cromwell is revealed to the world on March 9, 1966, confronting a pop chart dominated by "The Ballad of the Green Berets," Staff Sergeant Barry Sadler's Vietnam hero-worship retort to the peaceniks. The anticipated showdown between the forces of war and make-love-not-war stalemates. Despite a Newcomer Pick of the Week from *Cash Box*—"a bluesy rocker with a real slick repeating riff"—I only hear the record on the radio once, spinning the dial toward WAEB in Allentown, Pennsylvania. But it's enough to make me think that I can be a part of this. As I am, as I will be.

||||||

DOWN IN LOS ANGELES, Brian Wilson works on the only-knowing-God of *Pet Sounds* on his way to the infinitude of *Smile*. Groups like Love and the Leaves tangle over "Hey Joe." The Mothers (of Invention) orchestrate shock value; Frank Zappa knows how to read music. The Doors reach and then moonlight-drive past "The End." As Buffalo Springfield witness the curfew upheavals on Sunset Strip in November 1966 and newsreel it in "For What It's Worth," it's left to Ed Cobb and the film *Riot on Sunset Strip* to screen it at the drive-in.

Once a member of the Four Preps, writer of soul standards "Tainted Love" for Gloria Jones and "Every Little Bit Hurts" for Brenda Holloway, Cobb produces the Standells' most-garagic

"Dirty Water," and then takes his tune-up skills north, to San Jose, fifty miles south of San Francisco, where there is a flourishing teen-rendezvous band circuit. The Chocolate Watch Band, led by Dave Aguilar shaking a mean pair of maracas, are firmly in the Rolling Stones wing of English emulation; as opposed to Count Five's ornithology ("Psychotic Reaction," complete with Yardbirds' "I'm a Man" rave-up); and Syndicate of Sound's "Hey Little Girl," a synthesis of sound that will encapsulate all the tropes of what will be called garage rock, now broken free from Britain's colonies. Ed Cobb will manipulate the Watch Band, bringing in studio musicians, eviscerating the group by their third album, *One Step Beyond*, but not before the original band can be Scopitoned in *Riot on Sunset Strip*, wailing "Don't Need Your Lovin'" as Mimsy Farmer writhes about the room in psych-splendor, hair like Medusa, the Cramps waiting in the wings.

San Francisco's nascent bands pay scant heed to the adolescent shenanigans in the South Bay, an exception being made for Joan Baez, who has come out of Palo Alto to grace the cover of *Time* magazine. The music of choice in the Franciscan city is more likely to be folk-based, geared around North Beach coffeehouses and nightspots such as the hungry i and the Purple Onion, from which the Kingston Trio and the Smothers Brothers have launched careers. But Jerry Garcia—a fleet-fingered bluegrass banjo picker also from Palo Alto whose spiky clarity of tone amplifies as he goes ever more electric—begins to be attracted to the clamor of the local bands. He has drawn from the well of the Harry Smith *Anthology of American Folk Music*, lending his plaintive voice to murder ballads and Appalachian porch melodies, and has even made a pilgrimage to Indiana in hopes of meeting Bill Monroe. By January 1964 he is part of Mother McCree's Uptown Jug Champions, threading Gus Cannon through Jim Kweskin, along with Ron "Pigpen" McKernan, a gruff blues enthusiast who plays harmonica and keyboards, and Bob Weir on washtub bass, a local high school student who has sat at the feet of Jorma Kaukonen, another local coffeehouse regular wondering whether to go electric, unraveling his secrets of how to play guitar. In mid-1965, at the instigation of Pigpen, they trade in their Jug for amps, deciding to become the Warlocks, an electric blues band. Bill Kreutzmann, also from Palo Alto, is recruited as drummer, and in an auspicious and crucial move, Jerry invites an old acquaintance who stops by their regular Wednesday night gig at Magoo's Pizza Parlor in Menlo Park to play bass guitar. They're not much more than a cover band—Chuck Berry, Sam the Sham, Bob Dylan's "Subterranean Homesick Blues"—but Phil Lesh's sinuous bass, comping and restless, insinuating melodies and loosening rhythm, will give the Warlocks an improvisatory nudge and room to move.

Garcia and Lesh had befriended each other as far back as 1959, bonding in 1962 when Phil brought him onto KPFA's folk music show, *The Midnight Special*, to sing "Long Black Veil," but had followed separate musical paths since. While Jerry immersed himself in folkways, Lesh—a jazz trumpeter with a classical bent—was attracted to composition courses at Mills College in Oakland, where he audited the seminar of artist-in-residence Luciano Berio. An exponent of postwar *avanti*, the Italian brought with him a Dantesque theory of "labyrinths of listening," deconstructing interpretation, collaging musical quotations from all eras and styles, finding tonal in the atonal: beyondo Berio. His exemplar puts Lesh on the periphery of the San Francisco Tape Center; in 1964 he collaborates with Steve Reich in the "Music Now Koncerts" at the San Francisco Mime Troupe's theater, the cross-referencing begun.

There's little snarl in the Warlocks' music. Except for Pigpen's blues exhortations, which are encouraged by the Rolling Stones, Weir would allow that "[t]he Beatles were why we turned from a jug band into a rock-and-roll band," he and Garcia leaving their folk purism behind. Despite his mop-top bangs, Lesh feels the Beatles are not "serious enough." But then the Beatles don't think they're serious enough. After the overtly zany *Help!* they've gone into Abbey Road and are recording *Rubber Soul* for Christmas 1965 release, the first album where they make the studio their own.

The Warlocks climb north along the peninsula as Thanksgiving approaches, through the Sans of Mateo and Carlos to Francisco, where they have a live-in-the-studio demo session set for Autumn Records on November 3, only hinting at how they'll transform. "Caution, Do Not Stop on Tracks" fades just as Jerry is warming his solo, Pigpen's harmonica in the spotlight. "Don't Come Down" is "Subterranean Homesick Blues" gone overground. Most tuneful is an early version of the traditional "I Know You Rider" that will stay with the group throughout their lifeline, along with an unexpected emphasis on harmony, Gordon Lightfoot's "Early Morning Rain" filtered through Ian and Sylvia, lead vocals sung in tandem, even if pitch is a bit suspect. "The Only Time Is Now" mingles the Byrds with the Beau Brummels, Autumn's 1965 claim to fame, whose early adoption of British tunefulness—they have the same wistful yearning as Gerry and the Pacemakers, the triumphal choruses of the Searchers—has given them two transcendent hits, "Just a Little" and "Laugh Laugh," and a brief for them to be considered the first of San Francisco's new breed. Produced by Sly Stewart, soon to be (Family) Stone, what the Brummels don't have is LSD, which, as the year progresses, becomes the Warlocks' (and most of San Francisco's musicians-in-the-making) mind-bending ("Mindbender" another song from the Warlocks' session) drug of choice.

They need a new name; there's a lot of Warlocks out there, including a group from New York contemplating a change of identity (the similarly psychosomatic Velvet Underground). There's those go-anywhere late sets at the clubs they've been playing under the influence of psychedelics, the visits to Kesey's freewheeling campgrounds and subsequent Acid Tests, the way their music seems to have a will of its own, to stretch and become elastic, to float and meld, its own segue. They will forever be the Grateful Dead, life as perceived from afterlife, a just reward.

"Our best expectations are now the problem," someone mutters into an open microphone at the Acid Test held inside the Fillmore on January 8, 1966, precursor to the upcoming gala event at Longshoreman's Hall. "Confusion, dread confusion," says another disembodied voice amid calls to *turn on the power!*, optimistically adding "Seems as though it may work yet." The band goes into Slim Harpo's "King Bee" and then meanders into a long version of "Caution, Do Not Stop on Tracks," clattering along, focused on the effect the music is having on the shimmying dancers, shimmering lights, cameras, action. The Dead's arc disembodies the unstable mass of traditional and free thinking that will be the hallmark of San Francisco's music. At the Trips Festival, it all comes together. Or apart.

||||||

A FAMILY PORTRAIT. The bands gather in Golden Gate Park in the fall of 1966. The trees are still in full bloom. Photographer Jim Marshall, like Mathew Brady before him, snaps the shutter. From left to right: Quicksilver Messenger Service, the Grateful Dead, Big Brother and the Holding Company, Jefferson Airplane, the Charlatans. Maybe it should be read right to left, since the Charlatans were first.

Long after the silver lodes had run out in the mining town of Virginia City, Nevada, the Charlatans were the house band in a faux-frontier revival at the Red Dog Saloon in the summer of 1965. More style than musical substance, the group dressed as if the Old West had never left the turn of the twentieth century.

Though they'd formed in San Francisco, the ghostville ambience of Virginia City and loose thematic revelry of the Red Dog seemed to suit their Victoriana haberdashery and penchant for LSD ingestion. Singer and autoharpist George Hunter, who had conceived of the Charlatans before learning a note of music, chose his members on feel, sartorial look, and happenstance: he met bassist Richard Olson at a bus stop, and amateur pianist Mike Ferguson in the antique mart (with a sideline in marijuana) that Ferguson ran called Magic Theater for Madmen Only. The actual musicians were guitarist Mike Wilhelm and drummer Dan Hicks, their old-timey sound—"Codine Blues," "Alabama Bound," "Wabash Cannonball"—enhanced by regular Tuesday excursions with the Red Dog crew to the local hot springs, drugs a-bubbling and a-boiling. By the time the Charlatans returned to San Francisco in the fall, they discovered a cauldron of like-minded musical oddballs sorting into band alliances, inventing places to play.

Everyone knew or had heard of each other, planetary masses solidifying from the space dust permeating San Francisco and its emergent solar system, centered in the convergence of Haight and Ashbury Streets. They met at coffeehouses like the Drinking Gourd on Union, where Paul Kantner ran into Marty Balin and heard singer Signe Tole to start the seedlings of Jefferson Airplane. Sam Andrew walked past a rooming house at 1090 Page and was drawn inside by a guitar played by Peter Albin as Big Brother and the Holding Company coalesce; John Cipollina similarly wandered by to encounter Gary Duncan and Greg Elmore, who will join him in Quicksilver. There are basement jam sessions at Page, encouraged by Chet Helms, soon to take more formal shape as the Family Dog, event planners who throw a dance at Longshoreman's Hall on October 16 that brings some of these newly hatched combinations—such as the Great Society, with a vocalist named Grace Slick—out of the pizza parlor at 3138 Fillmore Street that Balin has converted into the Matrix. The Family

Dog debuts with "A Tribute to Dr. Strange," named after a comic book character low on the totemic pole of the alternative (to DC's more overground superheros) Marvel Comics (Superman's more-than-human against Spiderman's all-too-human). And when over a thousand freshly enfranchised freaks show up, showing out and off, a community reveals itself, much to its own delight.

The Jefferson Airplane are the first to mark their territory. Like most of San Francisco's clans, their contradictions work in their favor. Balin is a balladeer, a romantic who channels his inner Gene Pitney on his 1964 debut for Challenge Records, "Nobody but You," and the Kingston Trio–esque Town Criers before becoming attracted to folk rock. Or fo-jazz, as the Airplane's new manager, Matthew Katz, calls it, presenting them to RCA Records. Jorma Kaukonen brings a harder finger-picked edge, and when he imports r&b bassist Jack Casady from Washington, D.C., the Jefferson Airplane (condensed from Jorma's secret identity, Blind Lemon Jefferson Airplane) find their flight path, eventually coming to land in the studio with engineer Dave Hassinger (who is recording the Rolling Stones' *Aftermath* at about the same time) in early 1966. They make a first album hardly representative of the maelstrom that is San Francisco, not surprising since at this point the Lovin' Spoonful is the model Airplane. Balin's co-vocalist, Signe, blends too easily with Balin's crooning style. What the Airplane need is abrasive tension, an attractive opposite.

They find that in Grace Slick, whose Great Society shares bills with the Airplane at the Matrix and then Longshoreman's Hall, and whose brother-in-law, Darby, is letting his fascination with Indian music overshadow her keening, shattering glass of a voice. In 1966, she shifts her allegiance to the Airplane, taking with her two of the Great Society's signature songs, "White Rabbit" and "Somebody to Love." Written by Darby Slick, the Society's version of "Somebody" is melancholic, inner-directed, imbued with a sense of loss. The Airplane's invocation becomes a call to arms, a rallying cry increasingly anthemic as the media begin to discover San Francisco, while the "Ask Alice" of "White Rabbit" is answered by Grace's imperious commandment of "Feed Your Head," prying open psychedelia's Pandora's box. Wonderland, as Alice learns, is as much nightmare as otherworldly dream sequence.

Big Brother and the Holding Company are made of harsher stuff. Their sound is galvanized by James Gurley, who fixates on John Coltrane, spending hours in a closet with a stethoscope attached to his unplugged electric guitar, trying to find his own heartbeat. His father was a stunt car driver who used his son as a battering ram through a wall of flame; Gurley plays the guitar much the same, a voltage barely contained even when he finally plugs into an amp. It's left to Andrew, bassist Albin, and drummer Dave Getz to keep up with his roar, and they're doing just fine on the local circuit under Helms's encouragement when they decide to take on a co-female singer, much like the Airplane and the Society. The only problem is finding someone to match their aggressive and roughhewn blast of sonics.

Helms originally hailed from Texas, and was aware of the psychotropic Austin scene where the 13th Floor Elevators held court. He remembered a girl he had hitchhiked with to San Francisco in early 1963, who had made the round of coffeehouses singing blues that harked back to Bessie Smith and had developed a pronounced addiction to methedrine, so much so that she had prodigal-returned to her hometown of Port Arthur to try to once more fit in. She couldn't. She made it as far back to bohemia as Austin, where she watched Roky Erickson of the Elevators scream at the top of his lungs, and found her ideas of folksinging suddenly transformed. When Chet contacted Janis Joplin in June 1966 and convinced her to return to San Francisco, she was ready for a band.

It took a while to integrate her into Big Brother's roar. As

Janis learned to ride swells of volume and "Light Is Faster Than Sound" rhythms, the group crafted songs that showcased her. By the time they traveled to Chicago in August for an ill-advised week at Mother Blues on Wells Street, losing money, getting stranded, and signing with Bob Shad's lower-echelon Mainstream Records to generate money for gas home (a move they would come to regret), they were beginning—in the words of a later Big Brother song—to sound like "A Combination of the Two." It spilled over to their choice of intoxicants—alcohol and speed as opposed to LSD. "Alkydelic," Janis characterized it. The Mainstream album has its problems, not the least of which was the perennial bedevilment of San Francisco's bands to translate their live energy into the static enshrinement of a record—but Joplin's voice even then cut through like a banshee, the band's fury barely self-contained. By the time of its release, not until after Big Brother's groundbreaking appearance at the Monterey Pop Festival the following June, they had already grown immeasurably. Until then they were only rumors wafting from the Bay Area, another name on a poster from the dueling ballrooms that were the Fillmore and the Avalon.

The posters awarded status as well as spreading word beyond Northern California, a visual iconography that put hallucinatory ambience over legibility. The main artists—Rick Griffin, Victor Moscoso, Stanley Mouse, Wes Wilson, Alton Kelly—were art nouveau-rich, their illustrations blindingly Day-Glo and particularly appealing under black light. They beckoned even as they advertised, a far cry from the generic boxing posters once used to billboard rock appearances.

Like the wall hangings they commissioned, concert promoters Bill Graham and Chet Helms provided a steady stream of showcase opportunities for the local bands, as well as a light-show environment and eclectic booking (the Fillmore in 1966 not only headlined Otis Redding and the Four Tops, but brought in poets

Allen Ginsberg and Andrei Voznesensky, put on plays by Michael McClure and LeRoi Jones, even hosted Lenny Bruce on June 24, 1966, along with visiting progressive rock bands like the Paul Butterfield Blues Band and the Blues Project) that not only uplifted a ready-and-willing audience but also enhanced the profile of the local acts. The concept of the "dance concert" was as much a part of the ballroom experience as the bands themselves. Ironically, this began to change as the groups became more of a main attraction, the encompassing environments of the Trips Festival giving way to a hierarchy of star that shifted the relationship between audience and band. Even the characteristic liquid light shows, exemplified by Bill Ham's residency at the Fillmore, seemed to fade into the background as bands became more of a known entity and consequent draw.

Despite partnering together in the early days of the ballrooms, Graham and Helms found themselves at opposing ends of the booking spectrum. After a particularly financially successful Paul Butterfield Blues Band show at the Fillmore in March 1966 which Bill and Chet co-promoted, Graham was on the phone the next morning to secure their next appearance for himself. "You want to stay in this business, get up early," Graham told an affronted Helms, who in turn realized what he wanted to do was stay up late. Chet found an old swing ballroom with a sprung dance floor on the corner of Sutter and Van Ness and opened the Avalon, creating a yin-yang of venues that broadened San Francisco's attitudes toward the encroaching music business. Where Bill reveled in his cutthroat competitiveness, perhaps necessary in the acid haze of San Francisco, Helms was more casual, looking on his presentations as chances for the community—including the bands—to interact.

And by now, there were more than enough bands to go around. Despite their array of differences, the groupings within Marshall's Civil War daguerreotype share a curious mixture of old-trad (blues formalisms, three or four chords per verse and chorus when not droning modally) and a penchant for spatial odyssey. They're learning to write songs that encompass their disparate elements, but until then they fall back on covers and old familiars. Some, like Quicksilver Messenger Service, named for the mercurial planet that represents their collective Virgo constellation (and in these astrological times, when "what's your sign?" reveals as much identity as one's hometown, this seems prescient), preferred to turn Bo Diddley inside out rather than compose their own fields of exploration.

Drums skitter on the snare more than they whack, an offshoot of the jazz training that most of the band percussionists—Kreutzmann, the Airplane's Spencer Dryden, Big Brother's Getz—have absorbed. Guitar tones, with the exception of James Gurley's squall, are clean, precise, and pointed, a firm twist of the volume knob up from their folk origins. By and large the groups are wary of the recording process—"plastic" is the sneering adjective applied to the studio Babylon that is Los Angeles—preferring the spontaneity of live experience, even though this reveals an innate and hidebound conservatism in a time when technological breakthroughs in recording promise expansive possibilities. The Dead try to have it both ways, collaging hundreds of edits of live performances for their second album, *Anthem of the Sun*, in reaction to the amphetamine rush of their debut, recorded in three days and composed of a majority of covers. The Airplane keep trying to subvert the concept of an album after the Top Ten success of *Surrealistic Pillow*, and their follow-up, the overtly contrary *After Bathing at Baxter's*, seems determined to upend any expectations of commercialism, Balin's heart-on-sleeve receding as Grace's acerbic mischief-making, abetted by Paul Kantner's scientifictional bent, is on the ascendant. Much of Big Brother's long-awaited major label debut is recorded live, even to re-creating their stage setup in the studio, with Bill Graham acting as master of ceremonies: ". . . *four gentlemen and one great-great broad.*" The bands all profess to be anti-showbiz, but their casual approach to performance has its own theatrics. There are tuning problems—in this epoch before strobe tuners were invented—that are sometimes as maddening and mesmerizing as the songs that follow. It doesn't help that the guitar is an instrument impossible to perfectly temper. *In tune, man . . . that's what we all strive for . . .* Or, as Darby Slick notes, "the string sounds too sharp, or maybe way too flat, all at the same time." And then there were five other strings. Life in a band.

A Fillmore soundboard tape from February 1967, given John Cipollina's way with a sway bar (also known as a vibrato bar; a whammy bar; and a guaranteed-to-throw-your guitar-out-of-tune bar), allows Quicksilver several *plink-plank* minutes to avoid dissonance before counting off. Not a chance. Cipollina's guitar, erasing pitch with anguished cries and bends, trebled by six Wurlitzer horns atop his amp, instills in their gunmetal version of Buffy Sainte-Marie's "Codeine" an overtone of fist-clenched need, adrenal rush held off to the bursting point, teetering on the edge. They perform it for the quasi-hippy documentary *Revolution*, released in 1968, in a murky ballroom that captures on grainy millimetered film the blurred lights and deepening shadows in which the bands grow, like nightshades, no spotlights, only pinwheels and random dancers caught between flashes, mid-swoop. You could get lost in this spinning universe, especially if you're a runaway from somewhere you never wanted to be, getting up the nerve to put it all behind, meeting a friend who got here before you, or maybe just a meeting. You don't know where you're going to sleep tonight. But Quicksilver is keeping the last song going, "Babe I'm Gonna Leave You," one chord on overdrive, building to the climax. You don't want them to leave. You don't want it to end.

||||||

IF THERE'S A BEGINNING TO the endgame, it is the Human Be-In in Golden Gate Park on January 14, 1967. "A gathering of the Tribes," proclaims the lavishly illuminated *San Francisco Oracle* in four-color newsprint, its cover *sadhu* opening his third eye, "a union of love and activism," bringing together "Berkeley political activists and hip community and San Francisco's spiritual generation . . . ," "Heroes" like Timothy Leary and Dick Gregory; poets like Allen Ginsberg, Michael McClure, Gary Snyder. "All the Bay Area rock bands." "Costumes, blankets, bells, flags, symbols, cymbals, drums, beads, feathers, flowers." One-stop shopping. It's a "pow-wow," and we all know what happened to the last indigenous people in America gathering tribes against an implacable adversary.

Seen from a golden anniversary, it's easy to cartoon the oft-naive and post-innocent presumptions of counterculture, its beads and bring-downs, the revolution that seemed so close and yet only got further, like Kesey's bus. If it was a privilege to *turnontunein-dropout*, it was privileged young adults who were able to take advantage of the dash for freedom, as ghettos began to combust, as protests against the Vietnam War and the draft grew more vehement, as an upsurge of violence and the harshness of living on the streets turned into desperation. But at this moment, held in suspension, twenty thousand bedecked souls frolic on the Polo Field on a sunlit Saturday, beginning a long-promised Age of Aquarius, the Water Bearer pausing and considering the follies of mankind before dousing the flames of youthful indulgence, hubris, and a beyond-how belief that love could change the world.

It was a message too good for its own good. Instantly the concept of Love as universal solution was easily wrapped, packaged, and proselytized. Held aloft by both mainstream and underground outlets, Haight-Ashbury was suddenly the At of Where, the gold of pot at the end of the rainbow, unprepared for the open invitation. But you didn't have to go to San Francisco to feel an alternative culture making its mark in the popular arts. New Journalism emphasized the subjective amid imagistic wordplay, and a flourishing underground press—from the *East Village Other* to London's *International Times*—presented an alternative spin on counterculture concerns. In particular, comics, still bound and gagged by a censorship code instigated by the infamous psychologist Frederick Wertham with his *Seduction of the Innocent* in the early 1950s, dived underground: artisans like Robert Crumb, Vaughn Bode, S. Clay Wilson, Trina Robbins, Spain Rodriguez, and Gilbert Shelton did much to unlock the collective id of the funny papers, the ink blots of subconscious urge.

The hope for karmic resolution, the quest for spiritual enlightenment that underlay hedonism, the communal yearning for a "Get Together"—the words of Dino Valenti made sing-a-long by the Youngbloods—that could heal a schismatic world, all attempted to find common ground in a world increasingly at odds. By 1968, with political assassinations rife in America, with student riots in Paris and police brutality in Chicago's Grant Park during the Democratic convention, perhaps the vulnerability of Love—that sense of opening heart and letting down defenses—becomes a fatal liability.

Over in Berkeley, a bay away from San Francisco, Country Joe McDonald mused over this conflict of interest. His band—the Fish, named after Mao Zedong's "swim among the people as a fish"—had started as jug band protesters, politicos by birth and affiliation, both Joe and guitarist Barry Melton progeny of communist workers. Their first release, *Songs of Opposition*, with an early version of the LBJ-skewering "Superbird," was a self-funded four-song EP that was antiwar; their second, with a prototype of "Bass Strings," was pro-LSD. Both strains would show up in altered state on the group's debut Vanguard album, *Electric Music for the Mind and Body*, with its eerie organ beds played by David Cohen, and Melton's guitar excursions, a voyage into the real as it infiltrates surreal. "Section 43," based on a theme of Grieg, contrasts pacifist arpeggios against militaristic chopped chords, trying to find coexistence between the political and the personal.

It is Janis Joplin who draws out Joe's tender side, the one that allows him to write a love letter to Grace Slick in "Grace," to pen an ode to "Janis" that balances the F-U-C-K cheer prefacing "I-Feel-Like-I'm-Fixin'-To-Die Rag," a sloganeering *what's-that-spell* that will rouse the Woodstock festival in 1969, a brief lifetime away. Joe and Janis have a romantic encounter in the spring of 1967, when Country Joe opens for Big Brother at the Fillmore. It starts to fall apart almost immediately, but McDonald sees her vulnerability beneath the bravado, puts it in waltz time, and loves her for it. As will the world.

|||||

SHE IS THE STAR OF the Monterey Pop Festival, inhabiting lyrics so filled with newfound sensual power, her ability to channel all her many conflictions into one howl of release, that they ask her to repeat her incandescent performance from Saturday afternoon on Sunday night, so the movie cameras can catch it. It is her coming out; a debutante at last.

The San Francisco bands are almost an afterthought at the Monterey Pop Festival in June 1967, put on more from proximity than having earned their gold records in the marketplace, like headliners the Mamas and the Papas, Otis Redding, the Who, the Association, or the Animals, whose Eric Burdon appears to have ingested San Francisco's communion wafer whole: *To the city and people of San Francisco / Who may not know it but they are beautiful* . . . Big Brother and the Holding Company steal the show, or at least as much of it that remains for the taking after Jimi Hendrix pyrotechnics his guitar. The Summer of Love is about to solstice.

Even as the bands venture out into the world at large, signing lucrative record deals and embarking on national tours, they also flee Haight-Ashbury, escaping an avalanche of sightseers and curiosity-seekers. The Dead's rooming house at 710 Ashbury is busted for marijuana; Big Brother relocate to Marin County and take on Albert Grossman as manager, who views the Holding Company through the prism of Janis, and encourages accordingly; Jefferson Airplane, riding the platinum success of *Surrealistic Pillow*, move into a mansion at 2400 Fulton Street. The neighborhood is overrun with the summer's first onslaught of psychedelic tourists, clutching cover stories in hand, wannabes wanting to be in the place to be. Be-in.

It's not just runaways that are drawn to San Francisco. It's bands of all perspective, flourishing like so many variations on a theme, lured by the action and the talent scouts. Where to start? My Top Seven includes Moby Grape, Sons of Champlin, Serpent Power, Steve Miller Band, Santana, United States of America, Flamin' Groovies. The Grape for being a three-guitar powerhouse whose "Omaha" is a headlong rush of foot-on-the-accelerator; Sons of Champlin harnessing horns and a decorous sense of arrangement ("Why Do People Run from the Rain?"); Serpent Power, headed by poet David Meltzer, "just following tracks" in "Endless Tunnel," accompanied by the ominous click-clack of railway banjo; Santana bringing Latin arithmetic into Carlos's blues guitar, Gregg Rolie trading Leslie'd organ solos with a rhythm section driven by timbales and tireless drummer Michael Shrieve, versioning Olatunji's "Jingo" and Willie Bobo's "Evil Ways"; Steve Miller, Chicago blues-based, fashioning a song cycle of rare delicacy with "Children of the Future," on his way to having the last laugh as the Joker, rhymes with *toker*; United States of America with their ring-modulator and hint of approaching electronica; Flamin' Groovies resurrecting rock *and roll*'s golden-age virtues, the tributary of echoplex and past perfect, stroking against the current. All deserve further elucidation, past semicolons. But time is counting down in the Haight, and for many of the most popular groups, San Francisco is a stopover on their way to grander things.

The two biggest successes of the San Francisco renaissance take an end run around the ballrooms, going straight to radio. The Golliwogs are a struggling garage band when John Fogerty heeds the dominant performance style in San Francisco. He's a staunch traditionalist, but bold and savvy enough to stretch Dale Hawkins's "Suzie Q" over ten minutes of solo, a safe haven of horizontal exploration that quickly makes the aptly-renamed Creedence Clearwater Revival an FM favorite. They will become America's premier rock band throughout the late 1960s and early 1970s.

Sly and the Family Stone are also made for the airwaves, steeped in r&b showmanship and a relentless downbeat, each band member a character in their own right, though Sly is the puppet master. Psychedelia has infiltrated soul, funk, and jazz, with the Temptations ("Psychedelic Shack") and the Chambers Brothers ("Time Has Come Today") turning up the sound effects, George Clinton looking past the Parliaments to Funkadelic, and even Miles Davis modernizing his cool to attract the tripped-out, enhancing his 1969 *Bitches Brew* with tape loops and intensive editing, heralding a fusion of jazz and rock, emphasis on the latter. The message of Sly's Family Stone is multiracial, multi-gender, inclusive, at least until it turns into the bleak narcotic tableaux of 1971's *There's a Riot Goin' On*, opening with the down-and-downward slope of "Love 'n Haight." But before Sly gets tangled up in his own strings, sometime around his public wedding in Madison Square Garden on June 5, 1974, he unifies the body-mind duality in his exhortation to *c'mon* in "Dance to the Music." All you need is a drummer, time keeping more reliable than love.

Call the roll. The Mystery Trend. Ace of Cups. Mother Earth.

It's A Beautiful Day. Mad River. Frumious Bandersnatch. Each band its own world, a tale that begs reissue, preferably with liner notes. Alternate takes. Like the one in which they become the next San Francisco sensation, to play the Fillmore on both coasts, West and East, and everything in between.

||||||

I'VE GOT MY OWN ROLE-PLAY. Audience member. I'm watching James Gurley of Big Brother stagger around the Avalon stage with his amplifier hugged to his guitar, cradled to his chest, shrieks emitting, releasing unearthly bellows and billows of crushing feedback. He opens his arms and the Fender Twin topples to the floor, reverb tank crashing, immolating. The instrumental is "Roadblock." Janis is offstage. I have a crush on the band before I have a chance to be transfigured by her moan in "Love Is Like a Ball and Chain," to dream about ways I could be there for her, to ease her pain, to comfort her if only to buy her records and witness her shows and remember her for always.

I'll stay up all night. The next day is a wake for Chocolate George in Golden Gate Park, a Hell's Angel killed after his motorcycle is hit by a car on Haight Street (he's buried with a carton of his beverage of choice, chocolate milk), an early inkling of the collision course in an unholy alliance of outlaw bikers and in-law hippies that will culminate at Altamont Speedway. Big Brother is scheduled to appear. So's the Grateful Dead. I'm here. As the acid of the night before slowly dissipates in the afternoon afterglow, I sway dizzily as the Dead spin "Viola Lee Blues" into a vertigo of dervish whirl, as Big Brother wail to their hometown and what it's become. And where they're taking me. These are the bands that I want to be like.

Larry and I had pulled into Oak Street on the Panhandle a couple of mornings before, stopping along the way to swim in the Great Salt Lake. I felt encrusted with saline. There was an undetermined amount of people living in the four-story house; I bedded down in a windowless room on the third floor, mattress on the floor, though I could sit at the kitchen table and watch the morning approach, trying to write an appropriate song that always seemed just out of grasp. We were two blocks down from Haight, four blocks from Ashbury. Though I had pictured the getting-here for so long, as I turned left on the corner of Shrader for the first time I was stunned, overwhelmed by the burst of color and costumery, the rampant thronging crowds of a New Jerusalem; the bubbling hubbub, so like a bong. The upcoming equinox might yet portend an end of days, but here in late August, me wide-eyed with the conviction that I have come to the promised land, it was still summer. Not yet bummer.

|||||

MORE IN SELF-DEFENSE THAN RENUNCIATION of principle, a mock-funeral processions down Haight Street from the All-Saints Episcopal Church on October 6, 1967 proclaiming *Death of the Hippie / Birth of a Free Man*, filling a coffin with beads, long hair, and flowers before it is ritually conflagrated on a pyre. A fortnight later the Pentagon fails to levitate even under the combined mind-and-media power of Yippies Abbie Hoffman and Jerry Rubin, the Fugs and Allen Ginsberg. The pre-industrial Arcadia of communal coexistence, the promise of world peace through psychedelics, the hope that history recognizes the error of its ways, the planetary conjunctions. Over before it's begun.

The filigree guitars of San Francisco are traded for heavier, more primordial firepower emanating out of England, the Marshall and Hi-Wattage amplitude arms race of British rock, Cream and Jimi Hendrix in particular. By 1968, Blue Cheer (named for a street version of LSD) would spit forth a meaner rendering of

"Summertime Blues" that ricocheted the implosion of the previous summer, when 100,000 bedraggled supplicants came to San Francisco needing to be fed, housed, entertained, drugged, and saved from overdosing. Pharmaceuticals of choice pivot toward harder pleasures, as heroin begins its beckon. The casualty rate is bound to increase.

Out in the world, the bands seem unmoored, attempting to find ways to stay true to themselves on a larger, less forgiving stage. The Charlatans, who barely made it out of the Red Dog Saloon, immediately begin shedding members. By the time of their debut single in 1966, "The Shadow Knows," they're a shadow of themselves, and when a long-awaited debut album trickles out in 1969, with Michael Ferguson gone, Dan Hicks off with his Hot Licks, and George Hunter only contributing cover art, they have long since ceased to matter, even to themselves, though history will treat them kindly.

Jefferson Airplane have the opposing problem. They've been in the crosshairs of a hit record, and feel the weight of infamy. They appear on the cover of the June 28, 1968, issue of *Life* magazine as representatives of "Music That's Hooked the Whole Vibrating World," along with peers the Doors, the Mothers of Invention, Cream, and other now-enshrined names. The band may want to uphold San Francisco's way of doing things—the shambling informal stage presence, the avoidance of commercialism, the belief that they're not in "show business," that they're first and foremost family—but component parts are beginning to shear away. Jack and Jorma increasingly gravitate toward the bro-jam they call Hot Tuna, especially after watching Eric Clapton and Jack Bruce up each other's ante in Cream. Grace and Paul push shock value and a caustic sense of humor. Marty is shunted aside, laughed at for his sentimental streak by the band he founded (he will have his revenge when "Miracles," the 1975 ballad from a reconstituted Jefferson Starship, surmounts even "Somebody to Love" as the group's top hit single). *Surrealistic Pillow* was made in two weeks; *After Bathing at Baxter's* takes six months and eight times the budget, and sells a quarter less. There's no business without show business. The Airplane will continue to rabble-rouse— "Volunteers of America" is a call-to-arms for the estranged and alienated, and *Crown of Creation* restores their emphasis on song, especially their take on David Crosby's sweetly realized ode to ménage-à-trois, "Trinity." But their parting is commemorated by *Bless Your Pointy Little Head*, recorded live in October and November 1968 at the Fillmores on each coast, their divisive directions held in abeyance in the exult that the Wright Brothers must have felt as they achieved liftoff and altitude.

Perhaps the split is foretold when Grace becomes the face and de facto spokesmodel of Jefferson Airplane. The inevitable focus on a charismatic lead singer will write Big Brother's epitaph as well, just when they seem to have it all. Janis, alternately dismayed and empowered by her overnight fame and its attendant flamboyance, her insecurities hiding behind Southern Comfort swilling and her feather-boa'd good-time cackle, is elevated on an unattainable pedestal, while the band struggles to keep up with her runaway overnight stardom. *Cheap Thrills*, the group's Columbia debut, is recorded under considerable internal and external pressure, not to mention a ravenous release date, the band's ramshackle attitude undermined by producer John Simon's fastidious approach. It's not all his fault, though he declines to take credit for the released version, deeming unusable two hundred tape reels of concert performance and studio frustration. Heroin use and the downtown Manhattan party scene around the Chelsea Hotel hardly help matters, nor does an attempt to replicate the rowdy atmosphere of Big Brother live, complete with dubbed audience applause (only one of the tracks, "Ball and Chain," is recorded on location). Nonetheless the album forcefully conveys Big Brother's elemental power, the gutsy dueling of Andrew and Gurley throughout, their foreplay in "Summertime" (derived from a Bach prelude) as much evocation of Haight-Ashbury's solar moment before night descended as the album's definitive "(Love Is Like a) Ball and Chain," Janis at her most vulnerable. For all their imperfections, perhaps because of them, the Holding Company are Joplin's perfect foil and complement, their recklessness matching her own.

Cheap Thrills went gold within the first month of release, in August 1968, but Janis didn't last the year. She longed for the precision of a lockstep soul revue that Big Brother's shambolic hurly-burly hardly promised. She ventured to be an Otis Redding, the Franklins Aretha and Erma; and hastily assembled a horns-and-soul Kozmic Blues Band ready to showcase to the Memphis Stax-Volt community at their annual hometown Yuletide celebration. But the Soulsville audience had seen it all before, and a raggedy performance skewed her new direction. Though the band did get tighter, she seemed uneasy at the helm, and was gathering about her a more compatible Full Tilt Boogie Band—seen to advantage on the televised *Dick Cavett Show* on June 25, 1970, with an astonishing "Get It While You Can"—when she closed herself off in her room at the Landmark Motel in Los Angeles in October 1971 while recording *Pearl*, under the guiding and empathic hand of Paul Rothchild. She never finished it.

Posthumous. Always a hard word to write when talking about an artist who's beginning to understand who she needs to be and you're just getting to know. *Freedom's just another word for nothin' left to lose*, Janis sings in Kris Kristofferson's roadworthy "Me and Bobby McGee," but freedom also means everything to gain, and sometimes that's too much freedom for the choosing. I think of my friend Larry, and how he never wanted to commit to one path in life, preferring to have all options open to him at any one time, and only has his beatific smile to show for it. Choice, or are you chosen?

It's the same with a band. Who do you choose? After Quicksilver runs the gamut of Bo Diddley—*Happy Trails*, their second album, features an extensive workout on "Who Do You Love," adding "Mona" for good measure—Gary Duncan's epic "Cavalry" maps a possible future, twin guitars that spiral and entwine, allowing open improvisation rife with interpretive possibilities, especially with Cipollina's soaring lyricism. Instead, Duncan leaves the band, by his own admission burnt-out, only to return with a new singer in tow who happens to be their old singer. Dino Valenti had discussed forming a band with Cipollina when Quicksilver was in its formative stages, before being jailed for selling marijuana, before his "Get Together" became the Summer of Love's come-hither. Invited back into the fold after 1969's unadventurous *Shady Grove*, centered on British session pianist Nicky Hopkins, Valenti treats Quicksilver as his backing band. At first he seems to revitalize their torpor, especially when "Fresh Air" from *Just for Love* becomes an unlikely hit single in 1970. It only postpones and disguises the decline. Recording sessions in Hawaii dilute Quicksilver's essence and motivation, and Cipollina begins to seem a distraction rather than a linchpin of their sound. He leaves the band in October 1970, on the same night at Winterland that Marty Balin departs the Airplane, and news of Janis Joplin's death reaches the stunned audience, an epitaph for the San Francisco Sound in the making. John's renown is such that the Welsh group Man flies him to the London Roadhouse in May 1975 to replicate his bar shivers for a live album. True to form, he is out of tune, as if tuning matters in his moving target of temperament. He is my favorite guitarist. What more can I say?

The Grateful Dead carry on, amassing a definitive live recording in *Live Dead* (the reviewer from *Rolling Stone*, daring to seer, notes that this is "where music will be in five years," when he will appear at the Whisky a Go Go with an improvisatory trio headed by a rock poet, and then travel to San Francisco, where he will have his picture taken with said poet and John Cipollina); then simplifying with the return-to-folkever of *Workingman's Dead* and *American Beauty*. Adding the spectral lyrics of Robert Hunter and the clattering polyrhythms of drummer Mickey Hart joining Bill Kreutzmann, a succession of keyboard players and female vocalists, a songbook that encompasses classic rock and roll and country and western and rhythm and blues and their own vehicular meanderings like the canonical "St. Stephen" and "Dark Star," to the gypsy encampment that follows in the wake of their concerts, they manage to keep alive the idealism and continuance of psychedelic community that the Haight once promised in its purest form; or formlessness, those languid unfolding hours of performance, intermission, and sense of mission—until Jerry Garcia's passing on August 9, 1995.

Two months before, on June 2, at the Shoreline Amphitheater in Mountain View, California, he's singing "Standing on the Moon," *be with you be with you be with you* trailing into the distance until he is no longer there. His eyes are closed, imagining life on earth from a distant crater, as the Grateful Dead live out their legacy, each member his own configuration, playing the songs and filling stadiums and keeping alive a shared Eden perched precariously between Woodstock and Altamont, when I, like too many others, hung my life in the balance.

||||||

IT'S NEW YEAR'S EVE. Going on half a century. I have become the poster on my teenage wall.

To play the Fillmore, for me, is always a homecoming. We're the band opening ourselves up on this countdown to 2016 as it passes into 1967, conjuring the phantasm of the night which began the Year of Love, when Jim Haynie took LSD and was carried into the Fillmore on a litter clad only in a diaper as the Dead played "In the Midnight Hour." I'm dressed in the duds of that summer: headband, paisley shirt, leather vest. My hair is as long as it's been, *getting good in the back*. We're doing "San Franciscan Nights," a Monkees tune, even "Crazy Like a Fox," where I imagine an alternate universe in which Link Cromwell brought his folk-protest hit to San Francisco and wigged out. I stand where John Cipollina worked his magic, where I sent out a salute to Sam Andrew in the last moments of his life, where we played a Love two-fer for rock visionary Sandy Pearlman ("Little Red Book" into "Seven and Seven Is"), and where in a few minutes we'll embark on a medley of "Somebody to Love" into "White Rabbit." Patti saunters out from the wings to join us in resurrecting the spirit of a time that, if the cosmos didn't wobble on its axis, at least showed us how to spin the galactic wheel of fortune.

You can dwell on what didn't happen. Half-empty. Or you can drink the love potion that remains.

DETROIT

1969

IT WAS THE TALLEST STRUCTURE OF THE 1964–65 WORLD'S
Fair in Queens, New York City, looming over the avowed future
of better living through international imperialism and corporate
technology. "Man's achievement on a Shrinking Globe in an Expanding Universe" is the fair's motto. The New York State pavilion,
designed by Phillip Johnson in the style of "Googie" architecture,
mingles space age imagery befitting an episode of *The Jetsons* with
its Tent of Tomorrow, multicolored Plexiglas roof, speedy "Sky-
streak" capsule elevators promising an "Astro-View" of the surrounding exposition, and a 360-degree cylindrical Theaterama
decorated with pop-art images: a Roy Lichtenstein cartoon *Girl
At Window*, Robert Rauschenberg's *Skyway* with a prominently
collaged JFK, James Rosenquist's all-American *World's Fair Mural*, Robert Indiana's electric signage *Eat*, an *Unnamed* explosion
of metal parts by John Chamberlain. Andy Warhol's contribution
is a silk-screen titled *Thirteen Most Wanted Men*, a collection of
criminal mug shots deemed so offensive that Robert Moses has it
painted over silver (with Warhol's approval) before the fair's opening, a collaboration as unlikely and too-perfect as the homoerotic
dual meaning of *Most Wanted*.

With the future's abandoned promise now lying in ruins around the pavilion, the open-air rotunda begins hosting rock concerts in 1969. Chuck Berry, the Grateful Dead, Led Zeppelin, and Three Dog Night ("One" *is the loneliest number that you'll ever do*) have all headlined this summer. On September 3, the night after Ho Chi Minh's passing a world and a war away, it's a Detroit visitation with the MC5 and the much-anticipated New York debut of the Stooges.

Iggy draws first blood, poking at his bare chest with a broken drumstick while the band stolidly hammers around him. The morning-afterglow of the Woodstock festival is wearing off, a mood ring darkening on its way to Altamont. The Stooges weren't invited anyway. Not anywhere.

Oh last year I was twenty one
Didn't have a lot of fun
And now I'm gonna be twenty two
Another year with nothin' to do . . .
1969, baaybee. . . .

The Five give no quarter. They have always had a spaceways bent, free jazz melded to precision rock and roll. Tonight, away from the politics and rhetoric that has both elevated and undercut them, the MC5 are the show band they were always meant to be: Fred "Sonic" Smith and Wayne Kramer bending backward like a strung bow, Rob Tyner with his cloud of hair exhorting, the auto-plant rhythm section of Dennis Thompson and Michael Davis pistoning louder and louder until liftoff loosens their force of gravity.

They are proud, the High Energy they espouse, the Trans-Love message they propaganda. But it's only going to get meaner from here, if it's not mean enough already.

||||||

COMIN' DOWN. INNER CITIES SCORCH, colleges strike, streets fill with riot and tear gas. Police are "pigs," the government an *Animal Farm* tribunal, as the underclass wallows in the muck. Any chance of union seems distant naiveté, giving way to the rhetoric of armed insurrection, the default solution. *Are you part of the problem or part of the solution?* goes the trick question. The either/or of rebellion.

Vietnam never ends, a half million US troops committed and climbing, the ruling order tightening a stranglehold around its own neck. Lives are lost, sacrificed. Sometimes music seems beside the point. On April 5, 1968, the Jimi Hendrix Experience is scheduled to appear at Newark's Symphony Hall. Martin Luther King Jr. has been murdered the day before. Hendrix has always bridged the worlds of black and white, hoping to make a rainbow-hued music, but tonight he feels his race, in a city that answered the Summer of Love the year before with a four-day funeral pyre of resentment and seething frustration. The late show is canceled due to a wary curfew. I'm at the early performance, wearing my Nehru shirt and plenty of *looove* beads, still wanting to believe in the power of enlightenment through guitar feedback. Jimi doesn't want to be there. He looks at his watch, regards the too-white audience with a resignation bordering on weariness, trapped by the trappings, and contemptuously shatters his guitar, as if it's expected of him; as it is. As he will recast "The Star-Spangled Banner" in his own image at Woodstock, reclaiming the tattered flag of disillusion. The Days of Rage approach, when self-appointed Weathermen rampage through the streets to revenge, wreak havoc, and provoke retaliation.

Detroit erupts the week after Newark in July 1967. The city has become ever more racially split since the Chrysler Freeway first condemned then paved over the Paradise Valley stroll that was Hastings Street in the urban renewal 1950s. Along with the surrounding and thriving black neighborhood, this entertainment hub, the Black Bottom, where John Lee Hooker single-chorded in bars like the Palms, Sportee's Lounge, the Horseshoe Bar, and most famously, the Flame; where Duke Ellington, Cab Calloway, and Billie Holiday routed to and from Chicago; where Berry Gordy ran numbers and watched how Joe Von Battle ran his record store and JVB label—all is now as lost as Joe's charred stock and tape library strewn across the ruins of his burnt-out building. There is nothing left to rebuild.

In *The Algiers Motel Incident*, John Hersey recounts the heightened night of July 25 when Detroit cracked apart, when three black youth were slain in the heat of atrocity by white police officers. The scenes from the uprising, as survivors prefer to call it, are eerily reminiscent of the nightly television newsreels from Vietnam: tanks in the street, helicopters hovering in the air, napalm blazes, snipers positioning for the kill. After this conflagration Detroit will choose sides, the suburbs beckoning white flight, a schism reenacted in later years each eve before Halloween, Devil's Night, when arson becomes Detroit's trick-or-treat.

The tragedy is that it doesn't have to be. Ethnic groups of all stars and stripes flowed to Detroit when it became the assembly line of the automotive industry. They came from the Deep South of Georgia and Mississippi, the mid-south of Kentucky and Tennessee, bringing their polkas and their reels and their blues and hollers. Beyond the titans of industry castled in Grosse Pointe, the Diego Rivera frescos that surround the inner courtyard of the Detroit Institute of Art bear witness to the collective melding. Set in the Dearborn Ford plant, the mural shows the working class at work, from birth to Last Judgment, raw material to finished juggernaut, each racial color a necessary ingredient in the making of steel: red iron ore; black carbon coal; white limestone; the yellow silica of sand. His is a multiracial workforce, a conveyer belt twisting through Detroit's neighborhoods, its salt-box houses and "sprawl," as Hersey describes it, "the resident nations of black

and white [who] had for years been encroaching and elbowing
and giving way to each other . . . pockets of prosperity, of ethnic
identity, of miserable poverty, of labor, of seedy entertainment and
sometime joy," and the music they make.

There is no better record label to hear this pot a-melting than
Fortune Records, run by a Jewish couple, Jack and Devora Brown,
who opened their studio in the late 1940s to anyone who might
walk into their storefront: r&b vocal quar-and-quintets, blues
hustlers, hillbilly ramblers, white and black gospel evangelists,
gypsy violins. They had a microphone in the back room and sold
records behind the counter. A mom-and-pop operation.

Mom had met Pop on a blind date. She told him she was an
aspiring songwriter, and he courted her by hiring Artie Fields's
sixteen-piece orchestra to duet with a singer named Russ Titus on
her compositions "Jane (Sweet as Summer Rain)" and "Texas Tess
Down Texas Way" at the studios of Vogue Records, then known
for their colorful picture discs. There was little interest from the
major labels, and so in 1947 the Browns began releasing 78s under their own imprimatur, "for TRULY GREAT MUSIC," keeping things as in-house as possible, in fact from their own home at
11839 Twelfth Street (later Rosa Parks Boulevard). When pop records became too expensive to record, they turned their attention
to the blues and country music that seemed in abundance around
them. The nearby neighborhood of Hazel Park was nicknamed
Hazeltucky, and one of the Browns' first hits couldn't have been
more local, the neighborhood shout-out of the York Brothers'
1949 "Hamtramck Mama" and "Highland Park Girl." Blues was
even closer, and when Jack brought a few records into Elmer Bar-
bee's record store at 3530 Hastings, he saw a small backroom
studio where John Lee Hooker was trying his luck. Hooker had
come to Detroit, working the day shift at Comco Steel and the
night shift at the Apex Bar on Monroe when, in 1948, he recorded solo for a small label owned by record distributor Bernie

Besman. Leased to the Bihari brothers, "Boogie Chillen" went to number one in 1949, with references to *walking down Hastings Street / I heard everybody talking about the Henry Swing Club*, an off-the-cufflink narrative suiting the relentless drone and pulsate of Hooker's amplified guitar and an improvised echo chamber using a speaker placed inside a toilet bowl. It's almost too rudimentary, and yet forms the foundation on which Bo Diddley and Chuck Berry and all of rock and roll will build. Original sin.

The Browns open their own outlet at 11629 Linwood, across from Central High School, and work both sides of de facto segregation. There is white country-bop and black blues and vocal groups. Skeets McDonald has Fortune's first jukebox favorite, a burlesque "The Tattooed Lady" ("Upon her butt was West Virginny"), and Roy Hall follows the same stream of consciousness with "Dirty Boogie." Both are on their way to grander things, cresting slightly ahead of rockabilly. By the time McDonald gets to Capitol Records in 1951 he's tamed considerably, and Hall will write "A Whole Lotta Shakin' Goin' On" and let Jerry Lee have the spotlight. But the bars are full of bands waiting to display a steel guitar break and a mournful harmony: for the former see Chuck Hatfield's "Steel Wool"; for the latter the Davis Sisters' "Jealous Love," of which Skeeter will go on to Nashville and "The End of the World." Or any record by the Cherokee Chief and his Oklahoma Buddies.

It was a complementary relationship, Jack at the controls and the accounting books and Devora out in the rudimentary cinderblock studio, no headphones, voices and instruments clustered around an Electrovoice 666R microphone, one of the first female record producers, guiding harmonies and lyrics, especially when Detroit's vocal groups show up unannounced. High tenor Nolan Strong, tenor Juan Gutierrez, baritone Willie Hunter, bassist Quentin Eubanks, and guitarist Bob "Chico" Edwards walked across from Central High in late 1953, and Devora gave them

"Adios My Desert Love," three *cha*'s with Nolan's voice sliding between the maracas' shakey and Edwards's snaky guitar solo, along with a basso profundo from Eubanks. The dying notes of Strong's trailing falsetto segue into the Diablos' 1954 master-piece, "The Wind," the group strolling around Belle Isle in the mist of the Detroit River, harmonizing with the breeze. A spooky tremoloed guitar introduces the Bflatmaj7 chord that allows No-lan his tale of lost love while the Diablos lament in back of him. When Strong begins the somber recitation of his woeful tale, it's as if he's reading from a Ouija board predicting his fate. His gen-der blurs, and you can hear Michael Jackson in his inflection: *Darling, when a star falls . . . when I see lovers making love. . . .* The Diablos were reliable mainstays of Fortune, both up and down-tempo, with songs like "Daddy Rocking Strong," "The Way You Dog Me Around," and "Route 16," though when Nolan had to go into the army in 1956, the traumatic experience scarred a voice that everyone from Lou Reed to Smokey Robinson regarded as the finest of his era. "They caged a canary," Fortune collector Tone "the Bone" Fusco once told me, settling the needle on a 78 of the Whirlwind Evangelists' "Climbin' Higher." We sit back to savor another slice of Fortune.

They moved their headquarters to 3942 Third Avenue, along the Cass Corridor, and there was a house band, pianist Joe Weaver and the Blue Notes, to back up the Earthquakes, the Swans, and the Royal Jokers, who, as Weaver remembered, "did a whole show" when they recorded. "That's a gasser," Devora would say when she heard what she liked, and the Browns would press up five hundred copies at a time and sell them, servicing a regional belt increasingly rusting. Their only hope of crossover came when the lead singer of the Five Dollars, Andre Williams, delivered a tongue-waggling sermon on underage sex in 1957, "Jail Bait," that was picked up by Epic, until they realized his tongue wasn't in his cheek.

There is rockabilly galore when Elvis opens up the independent market to country boppers. Fortune meets Sun halfway with Pete De Bree's "Hey Mr. Presley" and Dell Vaughn's "Rock the Universe," and sets up a subsidiary, Hi-Q, devoted to rebel-rousers like Loyd Howells's "Don't Make Me Stop Drinking" and Don Rader's "Rock and Roll Grandpa." Johnny Powers looks like he's on the verge of breaking out with "Honey Let's Go to a Rock and Roll Show" but he's snatched up by Sun. The Browns get Dr. Ross from Sam Phillips on the rebound, and his "Cat Squirrel," from 1960, will prove one of Fortune's most enduring releases, rediscovered and standardized in the British blues boom, especially in the hands of Eric Clapton and Cream.

Salvation was awaiting at Fortune, a penitential path trodden by Johnny Buckett, whose "Griddle Greasin' Daddy" and "Let Me Play with Your Poodle" lead him to the dashboard see-the-light of "I'm Using My Bible for a Road Map." Fortune's gospel series is especially faith-healing, local choirs and congregations and preachers stopping by to hallelujah a chorus. Black worship with the Gospel Believers of Detroit ("Bless This House") and the Silver Harps ("I Found the Lord") joins palmed hands with the white Tennessee Harmony Boys' "Don't Forget to Kneel" and Frankie and Nancy Webb's "You'll Regret You Didn't Pray." Mary Frazier soars on "I Believe," her faith a testament. Jack and Devora were believers.

But belief goes unrewarded. The closest Fortune comes to a real hit is Nathaniel Mayer's 1962 "Village of Love," leased to United Artists and on the national charts for twelve weeks, scraping its way to number 22. The Browns are not properly paid, Mayer disappears into a hardscrabble life on the streets of East Detroit, pop music is changing (despite their attempt to keep up with the times through Dave Hamilton and His Peppers' "Beatle Walk"), and Fortune will never outgrow Third Avenue. The decayed shell will still be standing in 2001 when a Detroit raunch 'n' blues band, the Demolition Doll Rods, goes down to the ruins to reprise Fortune's hardly heard classics—the Creators' "Booga Bear," Roy Hall's "She Sure Can Rock Me"—before the building becomes a vacant lot.

Wind, blow. . . .

||||||

BERRY GORDY JR. WAS SURELY aware of Fortune's long presence in the city, and took care not to make the same mistakes as the Browns when he laid the groundwork for his Tamla-Motown empire. Unlike Jack and Devora's resolutely local preoccupation, he sets his sights outside Detroit's city limitations—*The Sound of Young America*—and runs his Hitsville U.S.A. with an ear and a business model primed for maximum efficiency. If you don't want to go back to the factory, you'd better start one.

Gordy, an aspiring featherweight before answering the bell of the music business, has the instincts of a pugilist. His first coulda-been-a-contender is Jackie Wilson, a Golden Glove teen newly out of reform school on his way to three years with Billy Ward and the Dominoes, where Wilson replaces and absorbs much of Clyde McPhatter's lilting delivery. Berry writes, along with Roquel Davis and Gordy's sister Gwendolyn, "Reet Petite (The Finest Girl You Ever Want to Meet)," Jackie's first solo hit in 1957, and goes on to songcraft the career of Mr. Excitement through the epiglottal "Lonely Teardrops" in 1959. Wilson had a four-octave range and didn't hesitate to use it.

But Berry felt he wasn't reaping the greater rewards of songwriting. He wanted to oversee his own hits, emphasis on *own*. In 1959, he headquartered in a wood-frame house at 2648 West Grand Boulevard. Gordy lived on the second floor, recorded in the basement, and eventually controlled all his means of mass production, much like the Ford assembly line on which he once time-clocked, from songwriting to publishing to session to finished recording to booking to grooming to stage presentation.

This might have resulted in the *same old song* but for the *different meaning* artists Berry discovered in and around Detroit. The Motor Town Revue would come to include Smokey Robinson and the Miracles, the Four Tops, the Temptations, the Supremes, (Little) Stevie Wonder, the marvelocity of Marvin Gaye, Martha and the Vandellas, the Marvelettes, all and so many more contained within the edifice Gordy built with single-minded deliberation, one hit at a time. There were shadings of delivery in each artist, underscored by the writing of the brothers Brian and Eddie Holland with Lamont Dozier, and the behind-the-scenes musicians in the engine room of Motown. Hosannas can be written about James Jamerson's thumb on the bass. The in-house Funk Brothers' ensemble playing, uncredited at the time, contributed to the sense of Motown as monolith, its mono aimed straight at the radial speaker of the car radio. Even within the confines of formula, there could be incisive and telling differences, like an auto manufacturer unveiling different models each new year, altering a signature accessory of detail, adding chrome trim, more horsepower.

"Motown was essentially a bridge between gospel and popular music which virtually by-passed traditional rhythm and blues," David Morse astutely notes, citing a reliance on percussive handclaps, tambourines, responsive calling, and the example of Ray Charles, but even such a reductive point of departure underestimates the conceptual unity of the Motown sound, its encapsulation of the hit parade in the early 1960s. By the time the Supremes' "Where Did Our Love Go" conquered the summer of 1964, only Motown offered a viable alternative to the Beatles' chart dominance, and that group more than acknowledged its debt to Gordy's urbane determination: on their *Second Album*, there are three from Hitsville: "Money," the Contours' "Twist and Shout," and the Marvelettes' "Please Mr. Postman."

Though Berry would eventually oversee the enterprises of Motown from eight buildings along West Grand before moving to Los Angeles in 1972, any hometown pride he generated would prove elusive to those following his lead. A Motown hit was meant for the wider world, to leap over barriers of race, class, dance floor. To randomly draw from the hat of Motown classics, songs like Martha and the Vandellas' "Dancing in the Street," Smokey's "Tears of a Clown," the Four Tops' "Bernadette" are much like the Temptations' "Papa Was a Rolling Stone" with Gordy as father figure. Wherever he laid his hat was his home.

||||||

MEANWHILE, BACK IN THE GARAGE. . . .

Mid-America was swarming with bands getting their driver's licenses. Faced with choosing between the factory or the upward mobility of college (with its own intimations of factory), many white would-be rock musicians opted for the self-gratifying pleasures promised by the English beat groups. There were plenty of opportunities for bands unsteadily learning how to play in VFW halls and backyard parties, as well as franchised clubs aimed at teenagers like the *Hullabaloo* circuit. Sometimes a one-off single for a local label would break nationally—Minneapolis and the Castaways ("Liar Liar"), Chicago and the Shadows of Knight ("Gloria"), Cleveland and the Outsiders ("Time Won't Let Me"). Michigan seemed especially fertile territory when Tommy James and the Shondells' "Hanky Panky" (from Niles) and ? and the Mysterians' "96 Tears" (from Saginaw) both topped the charts in 1966.

The Rationals, from Ann Arbor, bottomed those charts (number 97) for a week in November 1966 with their version of Otis Redding's "Respect," soon to be erased from remembrance by fellow Detroiter Aretha Franklin's 1967 cover of a cover of a cover (the Vagrants from Long Island); but their blend of r&b sieved through British sources, much as England filtered American r&b, was emblematic of Detroit's approach. The first song Scott Morgan of the Rationals had sung in public was Barrett Strong's "Money," and he'd learned it from the Beatles.

There was an aggressive inbred streak to the Midwest, the souped-up rev of a muscle car wrenched down the street. Mitch Ryder was the first to break out. As Billy Lee he had been working in a black soul club called the Village—ostensibly the setting for Nathaniel Mayer's "Village of Love"—with his band, the Rivieras (including drummer Johnny Badanjek and guitarist Jim McCarty). Disc jockey Bob Prince introduced them to Four Seasons producer Bob Crewe, who changed their name to the Detroit Wheels with "Mitch Ryder" picked from a phone book, and souped up their live intensity with well-chosen covers. They first hit in 1965 with "Latin Lupe Lu," and then followed with clever medleys: "Devil with the Blue Dress" paired with Little Richard's "Good Golly Miss Molly," "Jenny Jenny" with "C.C. Rider," a sommelier's delight.

Bob Seger and the Last Heard; Ted Nugent and the Amboy Dukes; Terry Knight and the Pack; the all-femme Pleasure Seekers with the Quatro sisters, Suzi, Patti, Arlene, and the Ball sisters, Nancy and Mary Lou. Their coming-of-age could be tracked at the Elks Club, the Hideout, the Crow's Nest, a high school dance or battle of the bands. The Palace in Grand Rapids. Tanzhouse in Traverse City. Sometimes the groups would travel west to the university town of Ann Arbor, to play the Fifth Dimension and stop into Discount Records on State Street, where Hugh "Jeep" Holland kept track of the new releases.

Holland was a record collector who expanded his passion into promoting and publicizing live appearances. He managed the Rationals when they were still high school students, releasing their singles on his A-Square label, along with another homegrown

Ann Arbor band, SRC. (A case can be made for Ann Arbor as more fertile soil than Detroit for burgeoning combos.) Both had promising lead singers named Scott (Morgan, and Richard Case), always on the verge of breaking out of regional airplay. Despite nudging the national charts and garnering Best Local Band honors on WKNR, Detroit's Top 40 outlet, the Rationals took until 1970 to release a proper album, and then under the watchful eye of Bob Crewe; by then their café au lait r&b had been outgunned. The Rationals can't capitalize on their early prominence, left behind as bands grow more combative, though Morgan's voice will ring true in Detroit's genealogy.

SRC bequeaths Holland a cover of Skip James's "I'm So Glad" through the lens of Cream, and the Pretty Things' "Get the Picture," which Jeep petulantly credits to the Old Exciting Scot Richard Case. SRC feel cramped in Holland's garage, and their debut album for Capitol in 1968 is expansive in the manner of British psychedelia, songs more train of thought than verse and chorus, whimsy and exaltation and ribbons of overtoned guitar (Glenn) and embedded organ (Gary) woven by the Quackenbush brothers. Their lack of recognition at the time, a lysergic adventurism only heard late at night over CKLW across the Detroit River, or WABX, the progressive rock voice, is to wonder at the peculiarities of fate, which chooses one band over another.

But it's an A-Square 45 I receive in the mail in September 1968 that allows me to hear firsthand the tremors from Michigan, radio signals only bouncing so far. Bob Rudnick and Dennis Frawley shorten the antenna when they sign on as disc jockeys at the tiny Upsala College radio station in South Orange, New Jersey, which over the summer vacation has been overtaken by a free-form collective. (Astonishingly, WFMU still broadcasts at 91.1 on the dial, outliving its college, still resolutely free of format, still one of the most inventive call letters in the world. Still listener-supported.) This is not the newly stratifying alternative of Top 40 progressive FM, substituting album cuts for singles. Anything goes at 91.1 on the dial, 1500 watts, nineteen hours a day, from the Velvet Underground to John Coltrane. Rudnick and Frawley share a kolumn, "Kokaine Karma," in my hometown newspaper, the *East Village Other*, who's playing where and why attention must be paid, with news notes and rumors, along with doses of agit-propaganda: "Music is the revolution," they write in the August 23, 1968, issue, as Chicago readies for warfare. "The Yippies are destroying the doddering Democratic convention with a Festival of Life," to be held in Lincoln Park, with the Fugs, Allen Ginsberg, Country Joe and the Fish, Phil Ochs. It devolves into acute confrontation, even as they report a week later that "the MC5, a veteran band of many love-ins and free outdoor concerts, displayed a primitive, exciting, ballsy R & R and makes one wonder if Detroit is not being ignored as a major rock band city by the music industry."

In the September 13 issue, with Pharoah Sanders at Slug's, the Nazz (featuring Todd Rundgren) and Wind in the Willows (led by a willowy Deborah Harry) at the Cafe Au-Go-Go, and the Children of God at the Electric Circus, they shout the praises of this band of "musical guerrillas, a fusion of avant-garde jazz and primitive rock," which is all the in-between I need to send the requested dollar to Trans-Love Energies, 1510 Hill Street, Ann Arbor, Michigan. "The MC5 from Detroit create an absolute spiritual energy force literally smashing the listener against the wall."

"Looking at You" / "Borderline" arrives a few days later, part of an edition of five hundred. It's barely contained by needle and groove, a blurred chaos of overload and distortion. Ignore no more.

||||||

THE ROOF OPENS TO THE SKY, allowing the elements to wreak vengeance on the wooden dance floor, built on springs to add bounce to ballroom stepping, debris covering the stage in lost hopes. The Grande Ballroom, on Grand Rapid near the corner of Joy, may today lie in ruins, but its storied history on the west side of Detroit, built in 1928, a Moorish deco façade in a once-predominantly Jewish neighborhood attracting the underworld of the Purple Gang and the more sedate pleasures of foxtrot and waltz, has yet another incarnation in store when it becomes psychedelicized in 1966.

Russ Gibb was a part-time disc jockey who taught social studies at Maples Junior High School in Dearborn. He had been trying his promoter's hand at record hops, and witnessed sociology in action when he visited San Francisco earlier in the year, seeing the Byrds at the Fillmore. There was a growth opportunity for a hallucinogenic venue in Detroit. Gibb opened the Grande on the weekend of October 6; ten weeks later "Uncle Russ" was in the black, having acquired a poster artist, Gary Grimshaw, a liquefied light show projected by Robin Sommers, and a house band aligned with a hippie-politico commune, Trans-Love Energies, whose leader, John Sinclair, not only had a media outlet in the local underground newspaper, the Fifth Estate, but seemed to have a charismatic knack for proselytizing and rabble-rousing.

The MC5 kick-started like any other disaffected teen combo in the Midwest, with Fred Smith and Wayne Kramer, from blue-collar Lincoln Park, channeling their penchant for troublemaking (and in Fred's case, baseball) into learning the guitar. They were equals in challenge and daring, spiraling leads and chopped chords, like street rods revving at a light. Gonna race. They were trio'd by vocalist Rob Tyner, who chose his stage surname in tribute to McCoy Tyner, and a frenetic rhythm section of drummer Dennis Thompson and bassist Michael Davis, which pushed and pulsed them. "It's a being," Davis remembered of their togetherness years later, five fingers curling to make a fist, the strange alchemical of a band come to life.

The MC5—for motor city, or motorcycle, or motochronic—had begun playing in 1964, mixing James Brown's "I Don't Mind" and "It's a Man's World" with accelerated takes on the English Invasion. The influences were less Beatlesque than rave-up and auto-destruct, leaning toward Van Morrison, the Who, and the Yardbirds. The group's first single, on the small-town AMG label in 1965, covered Them's "I Can Only Give You Everything"; they had originally wanted to record "Gloria," but Chicago's Shadows of Knight beat them to it (another Detroit area standard was Muddy Waters's "Baby Please Don't Go," by way of Them, later a showpiece for the Amboy Dukes). On a rehearsal recording in Wayne's mother's house, from 1965, the frantic interlock between Fred and Wayne bursts in horn-section precision, spurred by their love of jazz, each flurry of phrase reaching for the astral. "We could solo simultaneously," said Kramer.

It was unearthly explorations like "Black to Comm" that separated the Five from their peers. A two-bar riff, one note on the pickup, another seven up an interval and out. Ascend into bedlam. One day in Wayne's basement Fred twisted the volume knob on his Vox Super Beatle amp until it became "unbearable, right," as Rob recalled, "and started playing the chords to 'Comm' spontaneously and smashed a jar across the room." It enhanced Fred's nickname, "Sonic," his penchant for finding new harmonics in the simplest of chords. The MC5 were used to the outer limits of noise, the freedom of a jazz that seemed to have no limits at all, every sound and squeal and rhythmic space in commotion at any given present. They aspired to Coltrane's spiritual purity, Sun Ra's interplanetary cosmos, Albert Ayler's *skronk*, and the group unity and dedication to craft of the Art Ensemble of Chicago. It heightened the concentration of their arrangements, the excitement as they would approach the precipice of "Black to Comm." Tyner would take his microphone and point it at the speaker column, riding the shrieks; the guitars would cannibalize the sound, as

Thompson and Davis locked the chant of "Love Is Real." It could go anywhere.

They drove around in Tyner's 1960 blue Chevy and schemed, even coming to blows once in the parking lot of the Ball & Cue, Fred and Rob rolling around on the ground, arguing about their artistic responsibilities. As Wayne tells it, in the cinematic MC5 documentary, *A True Testimonial*, Fred deliberately smashed a glass, saying he wanted a band that was "strong, and arrogant. We just knock shit over." "That ain't cool," Rob answered, "you're not proving anything by that." As they fought they realized violence was antithetical to what they could achieve as a band of brothers.

John Sinclair saw in the Five the revolutionary music he had been awaiting and predicting; musically, politically, culturally. There was no difference in his mind. Born in 1941, growing up in Davison, Michigan, where his father worked in the nearby Buick factory, he felt that "rock and roll destroyed history," as he wrote in *Guitar Army*, an anthology of manifestos that underpinned the revolutionary philosophy of the commune he led. Trans-Love Energies grew out of his involvement with the Detroit Artists Workshop at Wayne State University in 1964, a collective that encompassed poetry, visual arts, jazz, and an underground newspaper called *Guerrilla*. Jailed for marijuana possession in 1965, he resisted the countercultural call to the west coast, and with his wife, Leni, headquartered in a building at the corner of John Lodge and Warren. He watched and cheered on the Detroit riots with a sense that the time had come for "revolution, rock and roll, dope and fucking in the streets," and hung a banner encouraging "Burn Baby Burn" (echoing the Mighty Montague's mantra from the Los Angeles Watts riots).

"We were on the side of the black people," he told Steve Miller in the eyewitness accountings that make up *Detroit Rock City*. "The only white people we had any use for were hippies." A police rampage at a Belle Isle Love-In on April 30, 1967, showed that authoritarian crackdown was equally opportunistic. Outlawry—or any perception of it—became a shared risk, with police harassment and repression a given, as Trans-Love's presence became an increasingly disruptive and eruptive force in the community.

The Five needed a manager, and more, a philosophy that could encompass their disregard of boundary. Sinclair enlisted them in the cultural revolution their music prefigured and in so doing gave them a mission beyond entertainment. It would be a hard burden for any band to live up to, much less in the dog-eat-god world of the music business. The MC5 took up the challenge, fought their good fight, and paid the price.

The group moved into the Trans-Love commune in time to suffer the backlash of the riots. Their equipment van was fire-bombed; they were subjected to random police provocation and accused of disturbing the peace, which was the stated intent. There was no distance between being a target and their no-quarter-notes-given stage show. They were used to Battles of the Bands, and they challenged touring superstars who made Detroit a stop-over at the Grande, daring anyone—Cream, Blue Cheer, the Yardbirds in the months before they became Led Zeppelin—to top their raw volatility. Trans-Love preacher "Brother" J. C. Crawford worked the body heat of the hometown crowd, urging *to see a sea of hands, rise up, take control, a true testimonial* as he emcee'd the MC5. They launched from the stage like a landing party hitting a beach, a rush of battle joined. Kramer falsetto'd Ted Taylor's "Rambling Rose," Tyner shouted the call to arms of *Kick out the jams, motherfucker!*, and then they pressurized John Lee Hooker's "Motor City Is Burning," Sun Ra's "Starship #9," and their own "Rocket Reducer No. 62," putting the *Rama Lama* in the *Fa Fa Fa*. Spangled, strobed, stun-gunned.

It was getting too dangerous in Detroit, even as the MC5's residency at the Grande created a homing signal for the estranged.

In the spring of 1968 Sinclair moved Trans-Love to 1510 Hill Street in Ann Arbor. The university town had a reputation for political resistance—as did most colleges then, especially with the military draft only a letter grade away—and over the course of the summer, like the contrarian culture surrounding them, Trans-Love turned militant, armed and combat ready, at least in photographs where the MC5 brandish guns for guitars, one weapon and the same.

If it was a pose, stationed at the barricades of Sinclair's "total assault on the culture," it was reactive to a world where student demonstrations fought Paris to a standstill, assassinations—from King to Robert Kennedy and even an attempt on Andy Warhol—split the screen, and "police versus young people" waged their courtroom drama outside the legal system. Suffering an all-too-real body count, the Black Panthers were willfully dismissive of the White Panthers, as the political arm of Trans-Love called itself in solidarity, dismissing them as "psychedelic clowns." There was some truth to this, Trans-Love playing court jester in the face of oppression. "We were the furthest thing from a political organization that you could possibly imagine," Sinclair admits today, but he doesn't recant his belief in the White Panthers' ten-point program: freedom the power of all people to determine their own destinies free planet free food free media freedom of all political prisoners free world economy free access to all information free educational system free free free.

The MC5 took this free-for-all to Chicago's Lincoln Park on August 25, 1968, for a "Festival of Love," entertaining Yippee troops journeying from across the nation to protest the Democratic caucuses for president in a country perennially bisected down the middle. The Five, along with Phil Ochs, and the Fugs, were one of the few promised bands to show up, managing to play an incendiary set (captured on film by the FBI) before tear gas and flailing police brutality took "Black to Comm" to a more ominous mayhem. Among those swept up in the melee is Fred. On his twentieth birthday, he is in a downtown Detroit jail cell, charged with assaulting a police officer. When he's released, there are crowds awaiting outside, cheering him, or so he thinks until he realizes pitcher Denny McLain has just sealed his thirtieth win of the season for the Tigers. An ex-shortstop, Fred can appreciate one for the home team.

It was a fantasy insurrection enhanced by hallucinogenic drugs and an overload of underestimation. "LSD was the catalyst that transformed rock & roll from a music of simple rebellion to a revolutionary music," Sinclair apotheosized, as the MC5's notoriety began to generate national publicity. Increasingly the Five were promoted as a mouthpiece of the propaganda wing of the White Panther party rather than a cataclysmic rock and roll band; turvy topsy. It's hard to fault their enthusiasm and idealism, barely out of their teens, swept up in the trench warfare of clashing ideologies. Was it music or message, jacked up or hijacked?

"MUSIC IS REVOLUTION," Sinclair capitalized in December 1968. For the MC5, whose quest for purity of sound had begun nondenominational, they were about to discover that the overthrow of a system was going to take more than a major label record contract.

||||||

DANNY FIELDS WAS a company freak. His job description was "a kept hippie, mediating between the turtle-necked titans of the record industry and the unpunctual, crazy monsters called musicians." He was translator and advance scout, goad and go-between, straddling the chasm between creation and distribution, or, as the cage match is usually carded, art versus business. In 1968, with counterculture-oriented rock music a significant shareholder of marketing strategy, a credible liaison to the underground press, FM rock stations, and word-on-the-street was not only needed but given its own wing in the building. "The record industry is establishment in form, but anti-establishment in content," Danny believed, and he had the antidisestablishmentarianism to prove it.

A habitué of the Warhol circle centered in Max's Kansas City's back room, Fields had written the headline for John Lennon's "We're more popular than Jesus" brouhaha when he was an editor at *Datebook*. He watched as the Velvet Underground plied their demimonde, introduced Jim Morrison to Nico, and from his loft on West Twentieth Street in Manhattan, just a few blocks from Max's, gathered strands of intersecting outsiders to see how their DNA spliced. Danny was a sometimes press agent and confidant-to-the-stars at Elektra Records, founded by Jac Holzman in 1950 as an outlet for traditional folk ("it was inexpensive to record," Jac would say as he shuttled his Vespa around Manhattan delivering Elektra's catalog in the early years), growing into a major player in the folklore revival around Bleecker and Mac-Dougal, now making a successful transition to highbrow rock in the 1960s with Love, the Doors, Tim Buckley, and *The Zodiac: Cosmic Sounds*.

Rudnick and Frawley alerted Fields to the MC5 when he guest-programmed their radio show. After the Five's trial-by-fire in Chicago, Danny traveled to the Grande to see the group on Friday, September 22. "I was incredibly impressed by the energy and power and love and adoration that the audience was directing at them." He took their urban guerrilla infatuation with a grain of schtick, seeing it through the lens of style. Coming from "the most effete crowd, from the most effete city," Fields was "poised for being slammed by something that was full of blood, and lust, and sweat and cum and smell and vigor . . . they were like Vikings," and he was further impressed by the Trans-Love organization, Sinclair barking orders, a willing cadre fanning out to poster and promote, a grasp of show business all the way down to the basement of the Trans-Love building where a multicolor printing press was spreading the word, a media network in readiness.

"If you like us, you'll love our little brother band," Wayne Kramer told Danny. The Psychedelic Stooges were at the University of Michigan Student Union in Ann Arbor that Sunday. He climbed the same stairs he'd ascended two years earlier to see the Velvet Underground for the first time (and was then asked by Andy Warhol to impersonate him to a reporter). Called Jac on Monday morning. Told him what he found. "Offer the big band $20,000 as a signing bonus, and the little band $5,000," Holzman responded. By ten o'clock, says Danny today with the same bemused palms-up sense of wonder that allows him to perceive arcane greatness, he had gotten "two of the greatest bands in history with a phone call."

In early October, at the Trans-Love commune, flanked by Holzman and yet-to-be-convinced Elektra vice president Bill Harvey, the MC5 and the Stooges officially enlist in the armed forces of the music biz. "Our idea was to take over the world," John Sinclair said. The MC5 was set to be the vanguard of cultural overthrow, a live album arranged at the Grande over Halloween, a promotional tour set up to introduce the band to the rest of the country late in the year.

And then: *motherfucker*. The ultimate transgressive, an all-too-common epithet ranging from casual to causal, applicable in any number of descriptive situations, to shock or defame or merely marvel. A word with its own barbed hook.

||||||

IT'S THE ZENTA NEW YEAR, to celebrate a mid-week All Hallows Eve and evening of October 30 and 31, 1968. Trans-Love Energies is concocting its own trick-or-treat religion. Elektra has decided to capture the immaculate conception. It is not only the MC5 we will be hearing, but the walled enclosure of the Grande, the community the MC5 spearheads, the future as awaiting listener. They're not making a record; they're making a moment. Free admission.

It's felt the only way to harness the Five's battering ram is in performance, spotlit. No studio can contain their fierce uproar, their extreme volume. Engineer Bruce Botnick flies in a pair of eight-track machines from California, and Holzman oversees the audio, much as he did when he set up one of the first binaural Magnecord tape recorders in the living rooms of folk singers when he was starting out. He is still very much an audiophile and anthropologist. Sinclair thinks Holzman is part of the revolution, but Jac is more "interested in documenting what you do with music in the context of that."

Kick Out the Jams has it both ways. Not only does it snapshoot the MC5 at the height of their rising, a force-field of incineration, but the album's overkill cauterizes a country tearing apart. "There is no separation," Sinclair insists again and again in the liner notes, all evidence to the contrary. The MC5's "Come Together" predates the Beatles' variation on a theme. Despite the crossed cartridge belts and White Panther pins affixed to bare chests, they're vaulting over politics. *Let us dance the dance from which all dances come / Let me give tongue to it yes*, Rob sings. Fucking in the streets: the MC5 have one-upped Martha and the Vandellas.

The galactic expanse of "Starship" closes the album. On November 1 the group is brought down to earth by the formal inauguration of the White Panther Party, "an arm of the Youth International Party." Sinclair is minister of information. There is a minister of defense, Pun Plamondon, along with his wife, Genie, as minister of foreign affairs, and a unity platform that allies with the Black Panthers, calling for, among other inflammables, the *end of money*, which is a strange way to start a career in the music business.

The scheduled promotional foray in advance of the album's release in January 1969 only reveals how exposed and vulnerable the MC5 are as standard-bearers of upheaval outside their home ballroom. Now it's they who are the visiting upstarts, and when they open for the Velvet Underground at the Boston Tea Party for a three-night stand starting December 12, their showboating and professed anarchism—one follower gets onstage urging the audience to "burn the place down"—draws Lou Reed's acerbic disdain. "We had nothing to do with what went on earlier and in fact we consider it very stupid." Promoter Don Law promptly bans them in Boston.

Things fall further apart in New York on December 26 when a militant East Village coalition called the Motherfuckers, perhaps in homage to the Five, has demanded that Bill Graham create a Free Night at the Fillmore East for the "community," though whether that includes the resident Ukrainian population or those left over from the heyday of Yiddish theater is unclear. Organized by Danny, Elektra has rented the theater as both media event and curtain-parting, though the Fillmore, fearful of disruption, withholds free tickets meant for the Motherfuckers. In a miscalculation, the MC5 don't help matters by arriving at the Fillmore in a pair of limousines hired by the record company. There is immediate chaos, the crowd using the incitement of "Kick Out the Jams" to clamber onto the stage, howling and threatening and waiting for a signal from the band to self-destruct. Equipment is trashed, stolen, the backdrop screen knifed and shredded. Bill Graham, trying to calm the situation, is punched in the face. The MC5 retreat, leaving behind a wreckage that will prove toxic to future bookings.

I'm watching from somewhere in mid-orchestra. It's the first time I've seen them, the "revolutionary theater" promised by Rudnick and Frawley, awed by the Five's ferocity and showmanship and volumetric assault. But by the third song, when the group is overrun by mobocracy, it's clear that music is taking second place to mindless destruction. My memory is still seared by the sight of a chain wielded over the drum set, coming down to whiplash the cymbals, a tolling bell of impending apocalypse.

It's not over yet. The MC5 make the cover of *Rolling Stone* in January through the intercession of editor/aspiring record producer Jon Landau, though the release of the album in February is marred by a dispute with Hudson's department store in Detroit, which refuses to stock the album because of the word *motherfucker* and the inflammatory liner notes by Sinclair spread across the inner gatefold. When Trans-Love responds by taking out an ad proclaiming "Fuck Hudson's," affixing Elektra's logo on it, the store returns all Elektra product, a chill that translates to retailers across America. The company had released a single version of "Kick Out the Jams," substituting *brothers and sisters*—recorded at an afternoon run-through at the Grande—for the perceived obscenity, and by March has decided to cut its losses by placing the expurgated cut on the album, removing Sinclair's notes. This is unacceptable to John and the band. Though the group had begun sessions with Bruce Botnick in Los Angeles for a proper studio album, the relationship with Holzman is frayed beyond repair, and in April their Elektra contract is mutually rendered null and void.

It will prove a turning point for the MC5, one that will alter not only their working relationship with Sinclair but their musical direction. They quickly sign with Atlantic Records and begin to distance themselves from Sinclair's control, moving out of the Trans-Love house and eventually John's management (he has his own problems, notably a pending trial in July for possession of two marijuana joints that will send him to the penitentiary with a sentence of nine and a half years until a rally two years later featuring John Lennon and Stevie Wonder generates enough outrage to have him released on bond; eventually the charges are dismissed).

The band had been less than happy with their performance on their debut, and though Elektra had told them they could re-record the shows, the album was rush-released to take advantage of the publicity. "The night we recorded *Kick Out the Jams* was actually the end of the band for me," Michael Davis professed nearly forty years later. "Before that night, the MC5 was totally experimental. Every time we went up onstage, it was like we were making the sound up . . ." And then: "Although we never got any more experimental, we got better musically. We were better musicians, better writers, we were able to make recordings that sound more professional. . . . It's kind of a bittersweet victory."

The agent of change was Jon Landau. He had been observing the Five since just before they made their debut album. In a memo to Fields on October 21, he outlined his enthusiasms ("The MC5 are the most historically perfect group in history, right?") and his reservations about their presentation. ("It is my belief that the ability of the 5 is dependent largely on whether or not they have mastered their craft.") He identified Thompson as a "weak link," and when he began working with the band as producer, focused on tightening the rhythm section, carving out space for guitar parts, taming their unruly elements into a streamlined version of the Five. He wants to teach them "self-control" and discipline, qualities their debut album steamrollered. "The group has got to be an either/or thing," Jon believes, and so their follow-up will overcompensate in a whipsaw that puts the band's skill set on the spot. If *Kick Out the Jams* was obliterating in its aural attack, Landau hopes *Back in the USA* will restore a faith in rock and roll's traditional values, in his view represented by Chuck Berry and Little Richard, the Nazz and the Remains. The album opens with "Tutti Frutti" and closes with "Back in the USA," looking over its shoulder when it should point forward; wasn't it the Remains who sang "Don't Look Back"?

The sessions are fraught, divisive, as the group confronts the inner scope of the studio. For those who revel in the MC5's unruly dynamism, the loss of fury is a principle betrayed. Comparing the re-recorded version of "Looking at You" on *Back in the USA* with it's A-Square predecessor barters precision for passion, cleanliness for godliness. Yet the album's relative orthodoxy at the time overlooks strengths the band needed to encourage if they were to grow beyond the Grande, the doctrinaire revolutionary corner in which they had been painted, the effort it would take to hone musicianship into practicing what they preached. The clarity helps focus Tyner as a singer ("Let Me Try"), the dynamics of "The American Ruse" and "Human Being Lawnmower" favorably impact their cultural critique, and "Shakin' Street" allows Fred an opening thoroughfare into the epic riff-on-a-grid that will be "City Slang" when he fronts Sonic's Rendezvous Band in the later seventies.

Back in the USA proves a misnomer when the band departs for England and then the rest of Europe in the summer of 1970, a half year after the album's release. They'll spend a good portion of their next two years overseas, stopping home to finish an album, *High Time* (1971), which finally understands who they are, could be, and will be as their influence seeps through rock and roll's onrushing strata. Their reputation—as touchstone and sacrifice—serves notice that the path they've taken to the dissonances of "Skunk (Sonically Speaking)" and the flat-out pound of "Baby Won't Ya" and Wayne's moody "Miss X" and Tyner's "Future/Now" are the Five as they should be remembered, and venerated.

But like the shattered alarm clock on the cover of *High Time*, it's too late. Injurious drugs subvert the band, and they shed members, first Davis, then Tyner (who doesn't approve), then Dennis, until it's finally just Wayne and Fred, like they once began. In the fall of 1972 they're somewhere in Denmark with a ringer rhythm section, the crowd waiting for the riot they have come to expect as part of the show. They've never sung the songs before, or played them without Dennis's thrash, Michael's bedrock. The ignoble finale comes on New Year's Eve, no Zenta now, at the Grande, a fifth of the crowd and a quarter of the money, getting the band back together in a caricature of what they once were. Halfway through the set Wayne leaves the stage, heading to the "dope house," a spiral that will soon lead him and later Davis to prison. "I just can't play anymore," he tells Fred.

"Sonic" nods that he understands. This is not why they became the MC5.

||||||

WHAT TO DO WITH THE STOOGES?

They don't have many songs, just bludgeoning riffs and ascetic rhythms and Jim Osterberg in the alter ego he was born to play, writhing and contorting and hanging from the microphone stand, finding ever-new ways to attract and repel and antagonize. He hardly sings, the band grinding out rudiments behind him, a sound that lowers rock and roll's common denominator until it's skeletal, bared to the bone.

They are insular, in-jokes and *o-mind*, a descriptive they apply to the groupthink that has made them an unlikely band. Compared with the MC5's effusive invitation, the Stooges are party crashers, getting by on sheer nerve, the *what-will-he-do-next* of Jim-as-Iggy, surrounded by a ruthless monochrome noise approaching hypnosis. This mesmerizing spectacle and soundtrack would appear to be even more difficult to replicate on record than the MC5.

Osterberg craved attention; that much was assured when, as a drummer in his first band, the Iguanas, he perched atop a seven-foot scaffold at the 1965 Senior Talent Show at Pioneer High in Ypsilanti, towering over his bandmates. The Iguanas self-released a tribal rendition of Bo Diddley's "Mona," a prophetic template for the underpinnings of the Stooges, and then Jim moved over to the Prime Movers, an Ann Arbor band that also contained Scot Richard Case, and for a brief moment, future Stooge Ron Asheton on bass. He followed the blues to Chicago, where he soaked up lyrical plain-speak and the cumulative impact of repetition. He was far more well informed than he liked to appear, about serial music and Artaud and art happenings at the University of Michigan, where he also witnessed the antics of a drunken Jim Morrison when the Doors came through Ann Arbor in October 1967, cross-stitching it with the frontal leer of a Mick Jagger. Best of all, Iggy knew how to entice a fair damsel of either gender. Pan-sexy. The pharaohs never wear a shirt on their hieroglyphs; why should he?

He pranced, menaced, outraged; for the band's early appearances at the Grande in 1968 he would emerge in whiteface makeup, dolled up in a Victorian nightdress and a sparkly silver wig, dragging a vacuum cleaner in his wake. The Stooges gave him the ruckus he needed to make it believable. As a guitar player, Ron Asheton leaned heavily on the drone, the sympathetic string inside a vibrating chord, rhythm matching sustain. His doggedly simple riffs—who hasn't barked along to "I Wanna Be Your Dog"?—are skewered by a wha-wha pedal inducing vertigo, one sweep of frequency removed from "Papa Was a Rolling Stone." It is the first sound you hear on *The Stooges*, which begins recording on April Fool's Day, 1969, in New York's Hit Factory with John Cale as producer. Brokered by Danny, he's too perfect a choice, a disciple of LaMonte Young's *Dream Music*, an omniscient viola in the Velvet Underground, the mad scientist who has brought Nico's femme fatale to the wayward dissonances of *The Marble Index*. Cale is not afraid to let the Stooges be themselves, and will seek to enhance their monotone, their deadpan, their simplistic aphorisms with sanitarium touches: the jingle bells and one-note piano that madden "I Wanna Be Your Dog," the veiled threat of "Real Cool Time," the downer chant-a-long of "We Will Fall."

Ennui pervades the album. "1969" sublimates a two-note chord sequence Ron has lifted from the Byrds' "Tribal Gathering," and its recorded release on the eve of the Woodstock festival seems like a slap in the face to the counterculture. Three days of peace and love? Who's kidding who? I go to Woodstock and my camera is stolen while I sleep. I hitchhike home and the Stooges' album is awaiting. Inspired by *Crawdaddy* magazine, with its coterie of rock writers inventing a new journalism beyond fan fare—Paul Williams, Sandy Pearlman, Richard Meltzer, Jon Landau—I've become a record reviewer for *Jazz and Pop*, which seems to encompass the adventurism of rock and free jazz. The editor, Patricia Kennealy, is the girlfriend of a college classmate, David Walley, though this affair comes to an abrupt halt when she weds Jim Morrison in a Celtic hand-fasting ceremony. I write about Nico and the Velvets, Pearls Before Swine and Tyrannosaurus Rex, the Small Faces and the Dillards, learning my trade. I'm primed for the Stooges.

Initial critical response is favorable. "You may not like it, but you can't escape it." I seal my approval that August in Boston's rock newspaper, *Fusion*, noting "a total negation of anything," "Unpretty, unhopeful," the "lethargic limbo" of "Ann," the "sinking gratefully into the mud surrounding them, embracing the inevitable decadence to follow." My prescience is luck of the draw. A few days later my phone rings. It's Danny Fields, thanking me for my support. "Who *are* you?" he queries (a question I've been asking myself), inviting me to a press party that will pave my entry into a select New York coterie of "rock writers," pointing me toward an opening for a music columnist in *Cavalier*, a monthly men's magazine with intellectual pretensions where early Stephen

King tries out plot lines, cartoonist Vaughn Bode displays his erotic reptilian fantasies, and I can write about anything I please. "Sound Scene" will pay my rent for the next six years. Now he's discovering me.

For all its appealing dumbness (the Ashetons and Alexander even call themselves the Dum Dum Boys), a half century of listening to *The Stooges* only makes their thuggish debut the more remarkable in its confidence and cohesion. Scott's drumming sidesteps bash in favor of surprisingly crisp and disciplined rhythmic patterns, Iggy fitting yowls of exquisite boredom over the precision hammering. Ron leans on the wha-wha and Dave dumdums to connect the dots.

It is the birth contraction of what will be known as punk rock, reductive insolence and purposeful antagonism that threads the Stooges' deconstruction through the approaching decade as surely as Jim crisscrosses the dividing line between Osterberg and Iggy and opts to stay with his Frankenstein's bride. He changes his last moniker, Stooge to Pop, for *Fun House*, the group's second album, recorded in Los Angeles over the spring of "1970," an auld lang syne—*Till I blow away / I feel alright, I feel alright*—exposing Iggy's reckless willingness to put himself in the path of annihilation.

They come to Ungano's in February 1970, a small club in the limbo of Manhattan's Upper West Side, on the same West Seventieth Street block where Bill Haley recorded "Rock Around The Clock" at the Pythian Temple, an even shorter stroll to the Continental Baths, where ambisexual immersion is on offer. "Needle Park" is at the crossroads of Broadway and Amsterdam, two streets away. The Stooges couldn't help but feel at home. The club is small, dark, with a stage more raised dance floor than proscenium. Arnie and Nicky Ungano have strategically installed mirrors on the wall so the joint looks larger, but it's enough hole-in-the-wall to host Junior Wells, the Vagrants, Captain Beefheart, the Amboy Dukes, the MC5, and for six weeks the previous summer, an opening act folk singer named John Braden plugging his debut album for A&M. I'm his bass player, a Fender VI.

Iggy roams the crowd a-taunting, grabbing fishnet candle lamps from tables and pouring hot wax over his bare chest, time allotted for the Stooges to improvise and unravel at will. They're working on the songs that will comprise *Fun House*, learning what they want from a record. What they don't want is to get less loud. If they need to take a break from the action, Mr. Pop lies on the stage, jeans ripped at the knees and silver opera gloves over his elbows, crooning "The Shadow of Your Smile." Then it's time for the unholy bleat of slaughter.

Don Gallucci, a record producer flown in from Los Angeles at Holzman's request, watches with growing interest. Once a keyboardist in the Kingsmen, he can relate to the simpleton appeal of austerity. "Louie Louie" is redux-a-go-go. But Jac also knows Gallucci has produced a craftsman's hit for Elektra with an unlikely group called Crabby Appleton, whose "Go Back" is a model of tight hook and exactitude, as pop as Iggy's newly adopted last name and the direction the Stooges are moving toward; or rather, pop moves toward them.

Gallucci sees the songcraft behind the Stooges' performance art. When he takes them into Elektra's Los Angeles studio on La Cienega, he goes right to the gristle of the matter, setting the band up as if they were onstage, getting rid of headphones, baffles, bringing in PA speakers, and giving Iggy a handheld microphone. Engineer Brian Ross-Myring has just come from a Barbra Streisand session. If there's bleed between the instruments and distortion on the vocals, so much the better. The Stooges like their type O.

The studio had been built and proofed for solid-state sound, "clean, crisp recordings" as Gallucci describes on the fortieth anniversary of *Fun House*, the antithesis commemorated by a connoisseur's edition that documents all fourteen hours of the session, the entire twelve reels of eight-track tape, take after take after take, minor adjustments and false starts, and most telling, concentration. The difference between each run-through is minimal, like the Stooges' subtractive. Rock at the turn of the seventies is full of *grand mal* ambition, exclusionary, complacent, virtuosity for its own forsake. Time to start over from scratch.

Iggy sharpens his claws, yips, and caterwauls. The Stooges live together in a farmhouse on the outskirts of Ann Arbor called the Fun House, twelve rooms devoted to bacchanal, Iggy in the attic. Like a television reality show, they move the revelry into the boob tube hall of mirrors that is "T.V. Eye." "Down on the Street," "Loose," "Dirt," "Fun House" into the cataclysm (rhymes with orgasm) of "L.A. Blues," where Steve McKay inducts his shrieking saxophone into the band. You don't need more than a jump-start title to know what each song is about. The Stooges' extreme deliberation fills in the blanks. No waste, nothing wasted. That comes later.

Jim calls Danny after it's done. "Nobody will ever say again that we can't play." A couple of weeks later, in the middle of a field in Vermont, where an alternative-media conference is wandering the woods taking acid between gung-hos of solidarity, Fields holds up a pay phone and I hear the first notes of *Fun House*. Over the wire it is like a dial tone to the future. Two months later Iggy, at the Cincinnati Pop Festival, smears peanut butter on his pectorals and like a Mayan prince walks upon the outstretched hands of the crowd, ritual sacrifice about to begin.

||||||

"THE ALTERNATIVE CULTURE IN THE Detroit/Ann Arbor community is first and foremost a rock 'n roll culture," writes Dave Marsh in *Creem* magazine in 1970. "It is around the music that the community has grown and it is the music which holds the community together." And it's *Creem* that mirrors Detroit's blowback with a literary provocateur's slant. They are not *Rolling Stone*, which is the accepted arbiter of taste, perhaps rightly so given the in-depth reportage and access editor Jann Wenner encourages, savvy enough to have the MC5 on-the-cover-of in January 1969, along with fear-and-loathing journalese by Hunter Thompson and by the end of the year, detailed coverage of the tragedy at Altamont. Their outreach to a rock-adjacent audience comes at a price, making *Rolling Stone* more aware of its coveted placement on the newsstand, unwilling to jeopardize a broader readership or advertisers. They're not underground anymore.

Creem wants to bait and switch. The staff lives together in a communal loft at 3729 Cass Avenue, a run-down three-story warehouse just a few blocks from where Fortune Records has its storefront. It's a seedy part of town, even then, and attracts the new subgenre of rock critics who use album releases like musicians use instruments, occasions for raving or ranting, the gone-to-gonzo circumlocution of a Lester Bangs, Nick Tosches, Richard Meltzer. Their critical analysis is anything but the inverted pyramid of proper journalism; *Creem*'s irreverence invents a magazine that revels in juvenilia as well as expertise, an immersion into music where it's not merely soundtrack but a reason for living. Lest it become too full of its own pretensions, *Creem* revels in self-deprecating humor, poking fun at itself and the absurdities of the artists they cover. It is the first place where the phrase "punk rock" comes into print, when Marsh, writing in May 1971, applies it to ? and the Mysterians.

The first issue is published in March 1969 out of a head shop prophetically named Mixed Media, owned by Barry Kramer and staffed by Tony Reay, an employee who thinks up the *Creem* name and concept, encouraged by Jeep Holland and Russ Gibb, who are looking for a local promotional outlet. Kramer was a businessman—he also owned Full Circle Records on Cass—but had a passion for music, and he soon takes charge of publishing *Creem*. With all the sudden spotlight on Detroit, it seems propitious to give the bands a voice, and there are surely enough bands to go around. Mitch Ryder's newest combination, the foreshortened Detroit, even rehearses upstairs at the *Creem* building. Early on Barry decides that the magazine deserves a national audience, competing with *Rolling Stone* for the hard-core rock fans it is leaving behind. With editor Marsh, and a mascot drawn by Robert Crumb called *Boy Howdy!*, *Creem* is as pugnacious as the volatized brand of rock it evangelizes.

The bands come out to play on April 7, 1969. As David A. Carson locates in *Grit, Noise, and Revolution*, the Detroit Pop Festival at Olympia Stadium is a watershed of the city's claimants to fame. The MC5 headline, the Stooges have pride of place, and over ten hours, on two stages, the overdriven and misbegotten parade.

The Amboy Dukes have last summer's hit single in hand with "Journey to the Center of the Mind," feedback like a laser scope tracking prey, though their guitarist abjures psychedelic drugs; Ted Nugent will go full-on native a year later, draped in loincloth and faux fur. Bob Seger doesn't care for such trappings. He has come tantalizingly close to the big time since his debut record in 1966, "East Side Story," recorded with his first group, the Last Heard, sold fifty thousand copies around Detroit. A year later they have a near-national hit with "Heavy Music," though his record company, Cameo-Parkway, folds too soon to take advantage of it. His dogged determination and work ethic, continuing to tour the blue-collar heartland until his journeyman Silver Bullet Band builds an arena following in the mid-seventies, makes believable the here-nor-there road weariness of "Turn the Page," *the sound of the amplifiers ringing in your ears*, the well-worn path to that ol' time religion, "Old Time Rock and Roll." Glenn Frey, one of his best friends and another Detroiter, decides not to form a group with him and takes his diaspora to the Sunset Strip, where he lost-and-founds the Eagles.

All the bands, stripped down as they are, showcase outstanding guitarists who are versatile skilled craftsmen and inspired soloists. Despite Detroit's powerhouse reputation, their albums alternate flat-out roar and dappled romanticism, often in the same song. Ron Koos knows his way around a guitar, having backed Wilson Pickett, and co-leads Savage Grace with classically trained keyboardist John Seanor, resulting in a whiplash between chomping clusters of hammer-ons amid florid harpsichord arpeggios. Their only album—highlighted by the dystopian "1984"—before moving to Southern California is a portrait of a band not feeling at home, that wants to do more in a city that would prefer them to do less.

The Frost share a record label with the Third Power. Compared with the majors, Vanguard's scale of promotion and thin studio production works against them. The company has rock-oriented success with Country Joe and the Fish, but they're still tied to the folk era. Lead guitarist Dick Wagner possesses a fine-tuned sense of composition and production, though the finessed arrangements of the group's debut, *Frost Music*, feels like the band wants to let loose. Most of the follow-up, *Rock and Roll Music* and its title track affirmation, is recorded live at the Grande, Wagner's slipstream fingering distilled in a pyrotechnic burst at 3:05 of "Help Me Baby," followed by a blood-curdling scream. There's eleven minutes of the Animals' "We Gotta Get Out of This Place," though they won't be getting out of Detroit. By the Frost's third album, the Beatlesque *Through the Eyes of Love*, the group is disheartened by the lack of records in stores and respect outside their home territory. Both Dick and guitarist Steve Hunter from Mitch Ryder's band will twin their guitars to Lou Reed's manifestation of *Rock n Roll Animal* at New York's Academy of Music, appropriately an old vaudeville theater, where on December 21, 1973, they breathe new majesty into Velvet Underground hymns like "Sweet Jane" and "Rock and Roll." When Lou plays Detroit, it's Wagner and Hunter who get the biggest cheers.

The Third Power are guitarist Drew Abbot, Jem Targal on bass and lead vocal, and drummer Jim Craig; that's all you need to nip at the heels of Hendrix and Cream. They manage one album, 1970's *Believe*, promising in its stylistic dexterity, especially the divergence between the heavier-than-thou "Gettin' Together" and the falsetto-on-helium "Passed By," before dividing by three. Abbot will become Bob Seger's long-standing guitarist, local boys made good.

There are retro rockers Früt with an umlaut, the Rationals on their last grab at the brass ring, and SRC, whose 1969 album, *Milestones*, recorded in their home studio, moves further toward the ambitious overreach of prog-rock. The Pleasure Seekers are still femme outliers in a male-dominated landscape, donning see-through for the occasion; Suzi Quatro will soon be making her way to London to find fame and fortune, eventually to return to America as Leather Tuscadero on *Happy Days*, a role she was, sisterly speaking, born to play. Each band is on the roller coaster of their rising fall, and most won't survive the onset of the seventies.

It's the unanticipated success of Frijid Pink in the spring of 1970 with a rendition of "House of the Rising Sun" that sets the bar for Michigan's homecoming. It's got the Stooges' wha-wha, the crunch solo that fuzz-faces the melody, and a folk ballad reinventing itself every time it's brought out of retirement. Like the many versions of "Train Kept A Rollin'," its lineage only reflects back one generation: the Pink are more Animals than Bob Dylan and Dave Van Ronk, who nod to Texas Alexander, Josh White, and Nina Simone. In April 1970, "House of the Rising Sun" is the biggest hit out of Detroit. Until Grand Funk Railroad.

They're from Flint, sixty miles northwest, a "Vehicle City"

where General Motors builds Chevrolets and Buicks and where a half century later the waters will turn poisonous. They started as Terry Knight and the Pack, which included Mark Farner on guitar and drummer Don Brewer, working up and down the peninsula until Sir Terry realized he didn't have to play in the band, that he could do a lot more as manager because that's where the money lay in wait. He found Mel Schacher subbing on bass in ? and the Mysterians, and svengali'd Grand Funk's image, requiring constant stage motion. No time to breathe; *On Time*, as their debut album proclaims in October 1969. They sneak up on the cognoscenti, as I'm thinking of myself far too seriously, seeing them open for Canned Heat somewhere in New Jersey shortly after their first album comes out. I don't get it, but I live in Manhattan, hang out in Max's Kansas City. Terry Knight doesn't care about me. He knows that when Grand Funk played the Atlanta Pop Festival for free on July Fourth weekend in 1969 as an undiscovered band, the audience—estimated at well over a hundred thousand screaming fans—didn't want them to leave. That he has what they want.

The first album doesn't stray too far from source material, plundering the Yardbirds' "Happenings Ten Years Time Ago" for "Into the Sun," Vanilla Fudge for "Heartbreaker," the mirror image of "T.N.U.C" along with well-worn blues familiars. They have the ability to switch gears, to season the overwrought with the earnest, bending notes downward, dragging songs into the national mood deflation. Their "Paranoid" comes out a year before Black Sabbath, on a follow-up album released in December 1969, introduced by the ominous static of a radio broadcast, an air raid siren, fuzz bass, and a butcher's block of doomed chords. Farner's solo within Grand Funk's deconstruction of the Animals' "Inside Looking Out" is compression looking for an escape.

Knight rents a billboard for $100,000 stretching the entire length of Forty-Fifth to Forty-Sixth Street in Times Square to announce the June 15, 1970, release of the group's third album in six months, *Closer to Home*. It's top ten by August, three gold rewards in a row, and its FM-friendly title track, "I'm Your Captain," fully orchestrated with sound effects of lapping waves, follows as an AM hit single soon after. Michigan gone mega.

||||||

"GRAND FUNK TOOK OUR SPOT." Dennis Thompson ruefully shakes his head in *Detroit Rock City*. "That's cruel." He's too right. At their core the MC5 were about showmanship and commitment, projecting solidarity to their mainstay audience, peers in the workers' class. They may have overreached, gone beyond immediate gratification, caught up in hope and the intoxicating rush of revolutionary change. Things are blunter now.

The style that results has been given hindsight definition: proto-metal, or as the subtitle of the *Brown Acid* compilation series of seventies obscurities has it, the "American Comedown." It's the harsher sound of the new English heavy bands, Black Sabbath and Budgie with Deep Purple thrown in, meeting American forebears like Sir Lord Baltimore and Dust; volume-quaking amplifiers, tubes glowing and blowing. Grand Funk replace their matched pairs after each show, sometimes during the show, as roadies stand behind amps in readiness wearing asbestos gloves, reaching into the flames. On July 9, 1971, I'm up in the press box at Shea Stadium in Queens, across from the remains of the World's Fair. The last show I saw here was the Beatles in 1965. A *memento mori* to Jim Morrison's passing flashes on the scoreboard. Turn out the lights. Grand Funk sprints to second base, hands aloft flashing peace signs. A sold-out audience bays allegiance, a din to equal the roar of 8,000 watts of hulking amps. The last time the group were in town, I went to Madison Square Garden to review their *Live Album*, collecting quotes from fans waiting outside, a tailgate party for the end of the sixties. They've sold out Shea in seventy-two hours; it took the Beatles six weeks. Mark Farner sheds his shirt, steps atop the organ, spreads his arms wide, and declares "You're the Best Fuckin' Audience in the World!" The stadium arc-lights blaze on. I'm convinced. They are living proof that seals the promise, the rock and roll dream a gift for the taking.

Or the taken. Terry Knight is president, director, and general manager of GFR Enterprises Ltd., with "an undisclosed percentage of the group's earnings believed to be on a par with Col. Tom Parker's deal with Elvis and the late Brian Epstein's contract with the Beatles," this from a press release he oversees on April 17, 1972, after the group sues for divorce in March, asking for accounting and independence. "I knew there was going to be trouble when Mark came to me and said he didn't want to fall down on his knees during the show anymore." Knight gets the private jet, the oil field investments. The group keeps the road, immortalized in their 1973 tour diary, "We're an American Band," playing poker with Freddie King and *fine ladies* importuning *c'mon dudes let's get it on*, an invitational lifestyle that has made *rock star* an ideogram for high living and hijinks.

Within Detroit, the Goose Lake Festival is the downer. Held over the weekend of August 7–9, 1970, with international acts like Jethro Tull and Ten Years After abetting Detroit's own, promoter Richard Songer envisions a get-together theme park where brothers-and-sisters mingle as if in Eden. The reality, when an expected crowd of 60,000 swells to over 200,000, the fences topped with barbed wire, is that there is no leaving once you're inside, a helicopter strafing overhead and mounted police protecting the stage and a profusion of drugs that places music secondary to carnival attraction; this is when it begins to decay from within. Speed and heroin have come to town. Detroit ravages. Pretty soon everyone is wheeling and dealing.

Sinclair receives his out-of-jail card three days after John Lennon topical-songs him at a rally in Ann Arbor on December 10, 1971—*it ain't fair, John Sinclair / In the stir for breathing air*. He walks out to greet Leni and the daughter he has never known, into a world post-revolution, pre-tribal; the theme song of "Just Like an Aborigine" that the Up, house band of Trans-Love, banner. The Rainbow People's Party are Somewhere Over. Pun in prison, graduated from the FBI's 10 Most Wanted List; Genie gone to Texas to found a chapter of the Red Star Sisters. The scattering is under way.

Two bands, however, have seen enough to make a spectacle of themselves. Alice Cooper has traveled from Los Angeles, where their surrealist (Alice will someday be photographed with Salvador Dalí) pastiche of glam-on-the-lam proves too strange even for Hollywood. The eponymous lead singer, once Vincent Furnier, was born in Detroit, though the band gathered in Phoenix, Arizona. After two unsuccessful and quirky albums on Frank Zappa's Straight Records, attracted by the city's growing reputation for flamboyant hard rock and their unexpected popularity in the Midwest, they take up residence in an old farmhouse north of the city in Pontiac. Working with aspiring producer Bob Ezrin, they craft the teenage battle cry of "I'm Eighteen," and embellish it with a horror movie stage set and show that includes all manner of execution: guillotines, electric chairs, hanging scaffolds; Alice in Neverland.

George Clinton gets freakier. He's been leading the Parliaments since they started harmonizing in Plainfield, New Jersey, in 1959, had a brief fling with Motown and a break-through when "(I Wanna) Testify" grazes the Top 20 in 1967. Clinton sees a way to funkify in the mode of Sly Stone, space out like Sun Ra. Funkadelic: the psyche of beat, centered on a bass that pops and slides and grunts. *Free Your Mind and Your Ass Will Follow* in 1970 keeps both Parliaments and Funkadelic in concentric orbit. With *Maggot Brain*, released in July 1971, its scorching Eddie Hazel guitar solos and Bernie Worrell's skittering keyboards, George is on his way to ring-mastering the P-Funk pledge of allegiance that is 1978's *One Nation Under a Groove*. All rise.

||||||

IT IS A FAR DIFFERENT Stooges that emerges from the carnage of Detroit. They've effectively disabled themselves, bought and sold into their own myth, temptation's temptation. Alexander forgets the chords to their songs at Goose Lake and is fired by Iggy as they come offstage. Elektra dumps the band, and even a plea from their new talent scout, my impressionable self, that they be kept on for a third album falls on deaf ears (in more ways than one) when Bill Harvey visits the farmhouse and is met by Ron in full Nazi regalia, Iggy and Scott in the throes of addiction.

James Williamson has been a Stooge waiting in the wings since before the band took shape. He has a determined alpha dog sense of riffage that bends the substructure of the Stooges his way. For a time Scott and Ron are out of the band, Jim and James taken under the wing of MainMan Productions, overseer of David Bowie, who sees himself as the *trois* of a *ménage* with Iggy and Lou Reed. They are flown to England, where they write songs and frameworks of ostinato, and finally call the Ashetons to join them; Ron on bass, which he regards as a demotion, though in reality he has always ridden the bottom strings. In 1973, *Raw Power* bridges a Detroit that is now influence, the impending it implies and inspires.

The MC5 find it harder to gather their shattered pieces. After the collapse of his band and his dream, Wayne will serve time in Lexington Narcotics Farm for selling cocaine to an undercover officer, though he uses "inside" to take music lessons from another inmate, bebop trumpeter Red Rodney, an education he will repay when he starts a foundation in later years, Jail Guitar Doors, that supplies free guitars for prisoners who use music as rehabilitation. Rob will write a song, "Grande Days," that déjà-vu's the *I-had-some-wild-nights* ghosts of the Ballroom, when *the music roared and thundered / Like fireworks from hell.*

Fred Smith follows the most mercurial path of all. He remembers a conversation he once had with Jim Morrison in Ungano's, Wild Turkey for Fred, Jim swigging from a bottle of Jim Beam, where they spoke of collaboration. They feel confined in their respective bands, imagining working together with Bruce Botnick, blending poetry and improvisation amid a new beginning for both. Morrison goes off to Paris, Fred back to Detroit. Over before it's begun, and he mourns lost opportunity.

Smith then joins forces with the crème of the many exes now inhabiting Detroit: the Rationals' Scott Morgan, the Stooges' Scott Asheton, the Up's Gary Rasmussen. He is wary of the music business, its promises and betrayals; his Sonic's Rendezvous stays close to home turf. On March 9, 1976, I come to Detroit with the band I am playing in that night at Ford Auditorium. Our record company holds an informal welcome party at Lafayette Coney Island, a local landmark for hot dogs with chili, onions, mustard, for the debut album we have newly released, *Horses*, which merges poetry with improvisation, as well as a shared sense of what music can accomplish to elevate the human spirit.

He stands by a radiator, off to the side. We always invite a local guitarist to play the finale of "My Generation," and knowing how much the MC5 mean to me, I bring our lead singer over to meet him. That night, after the show, they sit together backstage, slightly stunned, deer caught in each other's headlights, enfolded by love.

Patti Smith and Fred Smith will marry. She will move to Detroit and they will raise their family, and sing together as couples will. One day Fred comes into the kitchen, where Patti, so she likes to tell it, is peeling potatoes. "People Have the Power," he says simply. "Write it." She says "Aye, Aye, Captain," and they record it in 1987 on *Dream of Life*, a testament to the commitment they have fused together.

Despite Fred's untimely passing on November 4, 1994, "People Have the Power" has now been sung all over the world, at rallies and festivals and jubilees, with its rousing call to action, the hope and glory it uplifts, the union it offers one voice that is all voices . . .

So MC5.

|||||

IT'S THE NEW MODEL YEAR. Out go the tailfins, the two-tone paint-jobs, the bench seats, the gas guzzling and lack of muffling, the reckoning of unplanned obsolescence. Bands continue to sprout like weeds through the city's bombed-out rubble, abandoned by automakers and a parochial public, mutations asserting their will to survive, thriving in hostile conditions. Frank Gagen's was a gay drag bar on West McNichols in the Highland Park section when Scott Campbell of the Sillies and Vince Bannon took it over, hoping to emulate the punk-rock emanations from New York. By 1978 the revamped Bookie's was home to Destroy All Monsters, who have ensnared Ron Asheton to play guitar alongside the sultry Niagra, the red-leather Romantics, the Mutants and Flirt and the Cubes. Except for Gang War, a tag team between Wayne Kramer, newly sprung, and Johnny Thunders of the New York Dolls and Heartbreakers, the sound veers radio-anticipatory, pending the abrasive corrective of hard-core.

When LA's Black Flag stage-dives at Bookie's in 1981, a freshly nihilistic generation is imminent. Purposefully affronting the skinny-tie and synth-pop crowd, they turn up the violence: bands like L-Seven, the Necros, the Fix, the Meatmen; Cass Corridor dungeons like the Freezer, Cobb's Corner, City Club; a record label called Touch and Go that lets them tape their noise untrammeled. Negative Approach is led by John Bannon, who wants to make "nothing out of nothing." While their only studio album, *Tied Down* (1982), doesn't dare approach their amplitude live, its frantic mosh speed and sheer effrontery give Bannon a sense of destiny, of impending holocaust.

When he sees Nick Cave at the Graystone in 1983, he abruptly tacks leeward, gathering in his girlfriend Larissa Strickland from L-Seven, who is just beginning to play guitar, six strings of strung out. The Laughing Hyenas lead Detroit's rock to the precipice and then—John and Larissa hand in hand—gladly leap off. He shreds his voice, corrosive, she gouges at her guitar, and the baying audiences are a seething mass of flung bodies and sharp elbows, collision as spectator sport. The White Panther T-shirt he dons at the Khyber Pass Pub in Philadelphia on June 20, 1992, is a holy relic, like the preserved wrist bone of a forgotten saint.

The era of the Grande seems ancient history. Dan Kroha of the Demolition Doll Rods thinks of John Sinclair and the MC5 as hippies, which is not untrue. In the 1990s bands strip off anything that gets in their way, even clothes; the Doll Rods wear as little as possible, stark exposure, the adrenaline of nerve and sex, which describes early rock and roll as well as anything. They could've been on Fortune, but they're too late, or too early. The garage-rock renaissance that sweeps Detroit in the 1990s finds its lodestone in geologic compilations (*Nuggets, Boulders, Pebbles*, the mine shaft of *Back to the Grave*). Bands like the Gories, the Dirtbombs, the Von Bondies, the Detroit Cobras want to restore the raucous blur of noise from an amp before it turns into recognizable notes.

The White Stripes gather in the chips. Jack White understands a framing device; he's an upholsterer before taking up guitar, fitting fabric to padding and deck. He thinks in contrasting primary colors, designing a duo with his then-wife Meg, though he calls her his sister, sibling rivalry a good hook, like the pointed phrases to which he attaches songs. He concocts a catechism, she whacks the drums in the solar plexus. They're the ones who get out of Detroit.

Beyond guitars. Detroit's techno innovations also travel well, especially to a Europe where electronic manipulation elevates once-functional disc jockeys to center stage. Taking a sine wave from Kraftwerk and Giorgio Moroder, filtering new wave synth-pop through Parliament-Funkadelic, techno sacrifices verse-chorus to the pulsating control freak of the dance floor. The Belleville Three—Juan Atkins, Derrick May, Kevin Saunderson—meet in high school in the early 1980s, at a moment when synthesizers become handy as well as cheap (Roland's TB-300). Bleeps and whooshes are comfortingly futuristic (the Ran-Dells' 1962 "Martian Hop," Popcorn's 1972 "Hot Butter," Afrika Bambaataa's "Planet Rock" ten years later), and within the warehouse parties that spring up in Detroit's devastated cityscape, the trio are the driving force of an electronica that will spawn its own DM, *party people* heard 'round the world. Tracks are skeletal, loop-de-looping, the Cybotron throb of Atkins and Richard Davis's "Clear," May's "Nude Photo," Saunderson with Inner City's "Good Life." Subwoofers to raves everywhere.

Hip-hop's parallel universe lives only a rhyme scream away. Insane Clown Posse is scary-movies and spectre'd nightmare out of Stephen King, though their Juggalo rhythms crunch hard enough to prove menacing to guardians of morality. Kid Rock is a proud hedonist. In *8-Mile*, Marshall Mathers practices his lingual halo'd by the proscenium of the Michigan Theater, now a parking lot, tying word torrents into *shibari* knots of precise cadence and self-determination, splitting infinitives. M and M, M in M, Eminem.

The music the moment. One shot. Take it.

NEW YORK CITY
1975

THERE'S NOWHERE LEFT TO GO. IT'S NOT MUCH OF A bar, here among the dissolute and the dispossessed. Skid Row. The street that gives it number 315 is wide; an elevated railway once ran overhead. Though the tracks were torn down in the 1950s, exposing the avenue and scurrying the inhabitants to seek refuge, it still feels hidden, a subterranean jungle within the city surrounding, weeds entangling urban undergrowth.

The Bowery (from *bouwerij*, running north up the spine of olde Nieuw Amsterdam) is T-boned by Bleecker Street as it migrates from quaintly named Greenwich Village, where it intersects MacDougal in a crossroads central to folk tradition, much like Robert Johnson's solitaire with the devil. There, radiating outward, could be found the Night Owl Cafe, the Café Wha, the Café Au-Go-Go, the Café Bizarre, the Gaslight Café, the Village Gate, Gerde's Folk City, the Bitter End; Izzy Young's Folklore Center for broadsides and songbooks, the Kettle of Fish for late-night drinkers. The once of was. Those plucked from its midst are gone, moved on to legend or loss.

There are no places to play in New York for a new rock band. None. There are folkish clubs; cabarets where Broadway show tunes are camped and encored; stages where national acts stop over. Madison Square Garden. The Academy of Music. Central Park in the summer. The new breed of disco. New York has outgrown itself, as it always does.

Downtown is left to its own amusements. Raw loft spaces amenable to noise, storefront theaters, street corner pharmacies, the city's *avanti* clustered in apartments with bathtubs in the kitchen and an armada of cockroaches. You can do whatever you want.

||||||

IN JUNE 1970, THE VELVET Underground begin a residency in Max's Kansas City, a watering hole for the arts crowd that orbits Andy Warhol, screen-testing in a tiny back room on Park Avenue South lit by Dan Flavin's red neon light sculpture. Red tablecloths, red lobsters. A suffusion of infra.

It will be the group's last stand, though nobody suspects this when the Velvets begin what is intended as a two-week residency upstairs (where the owner, Mickey Ruskin, usually seats tourists who come for the steak and stay for the chickpeas). Wednesday through Sunday, June 24–28 and July 1–5. This is their first New York appearance in three years, and will be extended through the summer. The group is making an album uptown, their fourth, and the first for Atlantic Records, the one that's supposed to be *Loaded* with hits, their pop album; but then all their albums are pop in retrospect. Lou Reed realizes that you have to sing songs in your head first, and then you're hooked. Addiction, perversion, salvation. It's one and the same to him, each album set apart in tone and texture, a fateful quartet consistent in shapeshifting. The Velvet Underground will mirror Lou as he once mirrored Nico. Be your mirror.

They've been shedding members, only Sterling Morrison on guitar left from the band playing at the Café Bizarre when Andy

Warhol stopped by in the final days of 1965 with his entourage and invited the group to join the frolic. The Velvets' transgressive monotone and effrontery fit immediately into Warhol's theme park; his deca-dance band. Warhol added the gyrations of Gerard Malanga and Edie Sedgwick, his consigliere Paul Morrissey suggested Nico as aluminum foil, and happenings—by then noun'd, much in the manner of the San Francisco ballrooms, though the coasts could not be more psychically opposed—stoked media agitation.

The Velvets are black-on-black, obsidian in a time of spectral hue. They soak up color, opaque and urban. The Summer of Love, with its aspirations of flower-bedecked rural commune, is two summers away when they begin; the Velvet Underground its prequel and sequel. They revel in their sense of city, the nervous amped-up amphetamine gliss of time in a rush, orbiting the ninth circle of lower Manhattan, though in fact they don't perform within New York for two or more years at the height of their infamy. This is where they start and finish, their hometown.

Fifty-Six Ludlow Street is two blocks south of Delancey, on a Lower East Side once crowded with immigrant pushcarts and tenement dwellings. In the fall of 1964, John Cale, a Welsh classical music scholar operating on the fringes of postmodern music (he sits next to John Cage at a piano playing Satie) lives there in a coldwater flat—"a marginal existence," he remembers—with Tony Conrad, a fellow member of downtown microtonist LaMonte Young's Dream Syndicate. With his Theater of Eternal Music, Young is obsessed with slowing the passage of a perambulating drone much as Warhol stations a movie camera "to see time go by" in the eight hours of *Empire*, his silent interdimensional observation of the Empire State Building.

John and Tony live on the top floor, electricity supplied by an extension cord run from a next-door apartment occupied by Angus MacLise, a drummer with an interest in Far Eastern polyrhythms.

On more than one occasion society heiress Isabelle Eberstadt pulls up in her white Rolls-Royce Shadow and climbs the five flights of stairs to hear Conrad's work-in-progress soundscape for a Jack Smith avant-film. Jack himself might be there, stopping at Warhol superstar Mario Montez's apartment just below. Smith's *Flaming Creatures*, and Mario's (not Maria's) cross-gendered acting ability, is an underground cinema forefronting the mediums in New York. Art has come off the walls and onto the screen, visual and kinetic motion, no longer painting, pop art come to life. It is the central focus of site-specific art phenomena taking place in low-end lofts and makeshift performance spaces like the Film-Makers Cinematheque run by Jonas Mekas, then located at 434 Lafayette Street, abetted by Barbara Rubin, who will bring Warhol down to meet the Velvets as the band begins to gather momentum.

Lou Reed visits John and Tony on leave from Long Island and his parents' supervision, emotionally fragile after a stay at Syracuse University, where he has been mentored by the tragic poet Delmore Schwartz. He's allowed out on weekends, a "trial period" enhanced by his current job as songwriter-on-demand for Pickwick Records, a budget label operating out of Long Island City. When he two-steps a humorous dance craze for them called "Do the Ostrich"—*you put your head on the floor and have somebody step on it!*—the company puts it out under the band *de plume* of the Primitives. To promote it Lou recruits John and Tony, who are amazed when the song calls for them to tune all their strings to the same note; it's what they've been doing with LaMonte. The company wants to sign them to a seven-year contract; Pickwick as locust. They leave, taking their idea of a band with them.

Conrad moves out as Lou moves in, but right before Tony departs for a career wanderlust that will take him as far afield as the German progressivism of Faust, he brings home a tattered paperback book he's found on the Bowery, a risqué exposé of outsider sexual subculture by Michael Leigh that gives the newly formed group a name that is perversely subliminal. Guitarist Sterling Morrison had known Lou from Syracuse three years before, and when he re-meets Reed on the D train, he gains entry into a soupçon of outré music, theater, film, dance, poetry, and hedonism, centered at Piero Heliczer's loft at 450 Grand Street, where the group are the behind-the-screen musicians providing ambient soundtrack, much like the pianists who accompanied silent films. Morrison is the most traditional musician of the Velvets' instrumentalists; he links Cale's academia and Reed's transistor-under-the-pillow classicism.

Maureen Tucker gives them a beat. They're not sure if she's a boy or a girl when she comes around, but she has practiced along to Bo Diddley records and they need a drummer for the next night, a gig arranged by journalist Al Aronowitz at Summit High School in New Jersey opening for a local folk-rock band called the Myddle Class. It's the first night they bill themselves as the Velvet Underground. The teenage audience is not impressed by nascent versions of "Heroin" and "Venus in Furs," and even the owner of the Bizarre threatens to fire them if they play "The Black Angel's Death Song" one more time. They do, he does, and as the new year of 1966 begins, the Velvets sound-effect Andy Warhol's vision of the Exploding Plastic Inevitable. Mixed Me-dia.

It won't be easy being the Velvet Underground, despite a legacy they will into being by the sheer effrontery of their commitment to intemperance, the penance they pay in pursuit of ultimate truth. Their stay with Warhol gives them second billing when their concerns are more than voyeuristic manipulation. They aren't willing to perform with quotes around their music, the Factory's ironic detachment. The sybaritic indulgence of their first album, Andy's banana cover peeling erectile fruit, gives way to the death's head that graces their second, *White Light White Heat*. They go beyond satyriasis in "Sister Ray," poking at their mainline like a junkie who can't find a free vein among the track marks, turning their instruments up until noise turns catatonic. Cale leaves; Lou renews his vows with the transfiguration of "Pale Blue Eyes" and "I'm Beginning to See the Light" in a third album that just bears their name as title, as if they're a new band. Born again. "Help me find my proper place," Reed asks in "Jesus," his confessional begun.

Now they have come for closure, a floor above Max's back room, once removed. Lou looks out at the crowd and realizes he's seen this movie before, plying his songs in a hideaway to those who know him all too well. As for me, I'm just getting to have a know, a Velvets-friendly rock writer invited upstairs by Danny Fields, given the secret handshake. Lou and I talk about doo-wop records and pre-Code EC comics like *Crypt of Terror* and *Haunt of Fear*. Harmony and horror.

There's two sets a night. The second one for shing-a-linging. Sometimes it's the new songs, "Sweet Jane" or "Rock and Roll," and sometimes one of their canon will keep unwinding, the nodding trance of "Heroin" or "Some Kinda Love" as bodies flail in time.

I find myself dancing to the Velvet Underground. As I always will.

||||||

I CAN'T HELP BUT NOTICE her on the inbred New York circuit, sometimes stepping into Max's late at night, or with her boyfriend Robert Mapplethorpe near the Chelsea Hotel. She's friendly with Steve Paul, impresario of the Scene up on West Forty-Sixth Street, though he's shuttered it—the mob wants him to pay protection—by the time I'm ready to enter its after-hours dominion. I've gone to witness Pink Floyd there, or Jerry Lee Lewis, but only the early show, before they clear the house for late night hijinks.

I've seen Patti Smith in a play at the off-off-Broadway La Mama Theater in May 1970, Jackie Curtis's *Femme Fatale*, where she plays a tough-talking speed freak, all bones and slashed black hair and unfettered attitude, no distance between her role and self. I have an instant crush, and when I watch her and Robert across the room later in Ratner's, next door to the Fillmore East, a Jewish dairy restaurant that still gives the East Village a shtetel flavor, he in fur vest, skull necklace, rockabilly curls, she with the same thin cotton blouse knotted at the midriff she wore in the play, I can only look on in admiration.

I'm between apartments, living with the writers Richard and Lisa Robinson on the Upper West Side, having given up my downtown lease in the fall of 1969 with grandiose ideas of heading to Europe, leading a footloose life and open to come what may. But right before I embark Danny Fields finds me a monthly gig at *Cavalier*, a skin magazine with literary pretensions. I'm asked to associate edit a countercultural journal called *Changes*. Grande dame Lillian Roxon of the *Sydney Herald* champions me and writes an article about how rock writers are the new rock stars, turning heads as they walk through the lobby of the Fillmore East. Well, surely a stretch, but here I am trading repartee with *littérateurs* I'd only read in New York underground magazines or *Crawdaddy*, all elevating the discourse of rock and roll to a heightened level, writing about music as if it were the music itself. Sandy Pearlman, Richard Meltzer, Jim Fouratt, Vince Aletti, Robert Christgau, Richard Goldstein; these are the ones I single out for inspiration.

Richard Robinson is for emulation. He's editing six magazines at a time, including *Hit Parader*, has just been fired by progressive rock flagship WNEW-FM for adding "and roll" to his on-air persona, and is working as a tastemaker for Neil Bogart at Kama Sutra Records, where he will produce the Flamin' Groovies. He teaches me to write fast and humoresque, tabloid journalism as a higher calling, and if you make up quotes, well, just be sure the artist would've said them. We're all fans, that's why we're here. It was good to think of myself as a beat reporter, especially when hitmakers moved so fast up and down the charts, and you had to get the story in before the next one came along, all tied to the release schedules of record companies and the vagaries of fashion.

The phone rings at the Robinsons one day. "Hi," says a small, almost shy voice, introducing herself. She's gotten the number from Steve Paul, to tell me she's read an article I've written for *Jazz and Pop* and how it touched her. Patti is from South Jersey, pretty close to my central Jersey, and she knows the music I celebrated, the heartbeat behind it. We both lived close enough to Philadelphia to hear Jerry Blavat over the radio late at night, the Blue Notes' "My Hero" or Maureen Gray's "Today's The Day." We knew how to do the Strand.

I've been working behind the counter at a record store called Village Oldies for Bleecker Bob and Broadway Al for about a year now, ten dollars a shift and all the records I can filch, rummaging through the stacks to cull cuts that might fit on a compilation called *Nuggets* that Jac Holzman of Elektra has asked me to assemble, from albums that have that one special track. He hasn't given me much direction, which is his genius as a record company president, allowing things to happen and then framing them for the world. He has a title, and I invent a sub- , *Original Artyfacts from the First Psychedelic Era*, that defines my own coming of age as a musician and writer, though I don't realize this at the time. I'm still becoming, the history so recent I've only begun to grasp that there's an era ended and another on the way.

I feel it my duty to write "The Best of Acappella," published in the December 1969 issue of *Jazz and Pop*, because only I seem to be aware of the perfection of its niche existence, a clustering of street-corner groups in a doo-wop afterthought in which instruments were dispensed with, the human voice unadorned, in the moments before and after the British Invasion when it effectively disappears except for revival shows. Originated and promoted by record stores—"oldie" emporiums implying past—the groups stayed resolutely within the bounds of the New Jersey Turnpike. The Zircons from the Bronx with "Lonely Way"; the Velvet Angels—the Diablos without Nolan Strong—visiting from Detroit and "recorded in a Jersey City Hotel room"; the Young Ones' "Marie" and the Vi-Tones' "The Storm." Treasures of beauty, and it was my responsibility to preserve their names for the ages. Which, in a way, was my brief for *Nuggets*. To make sure my favorite records kept on living.

Patti started stopping into the store after that, sometimes with her sister Linda. I'd put on our shared discography and we'd do the Bristol Stomp when things got quiet. One night she came in with a strange request. She'd heard I played a little guitar, and might I back her in a poetry reading at St. Marks Church she wanted to shake up. Could I do a car crash? Free jazz had taught me that. She was hanging out with playwright and Holy Modal Rounder drummer Sam Shepard at the Village Gate, who suggested she might recruit the guy at the record store across the street. I went over to her loft on the second floor over the Oasis Bar, overlooking West Twenty-Third Street, bringing my Fender Champ amp and a Gibson Melody Maker, the last equipment I had left after a particularly larcenous summer (o where is my Fender VI now?). She chanted poems and I followed along, watching how she breathed. Simple chords, all I knew.

On February 10, 1971, Patti opened for Gerard Malanga at the weekly Wednesday reading sponsored by the Poetry Project at St. Mark's Church. The house of worship, there since before Manhattan mapped its grids, catty-corner to Second Avenue on Tenth Street, was a haven for the arts, open-minded and bohemian. It being Bertolt Brecht's birthday, after Anne Waldman's introduction we began with "Mack the Knife": Lotte Lenya and Lenny.

Patti dedicates the night to *all that is criminal, the great pit of babel . . . the petty thief, the whores of mexico . . . the rhythms of prison, the pirate saint, the masters of russian roulette . . .* and reads poems typed out feverishly on her red Remington, finding swagger in words and imagery that don't have time for capitals, that proclaim arrival and a mutinous seize of the helm. It won't be the last time I will hear "Oath's" opening line of *christ died for somebody's sins but not mine.* There is a tender "Cry Me a River" for Robert and her sister Linda that catches at the throat, and then the music. We offer a quasi-pop song that almost has a chorus—"Picture Hanging Blues," about Jesse James and Billy the Kid and the woman who goads them into a duel over her; a languorous minor-key blues called "Fire of Unknown Origin"; and the immolation of "Ballad of a Bad Boy," *wrecking cars is my art . . . fenders hot as angels they blazed inside me . . . that boy is evil he's too bad for parole . . . his mama killed him, his papa grieved for him, his little sister annalea wept under the almond tree. . . .*

It was only supposed to happen once.

||||||

THERE'S A HOT NEW BAND in town. The first poster appears out of nowhere on the wall of Village Oldies in the spring of 1972. They're playing at the Mercer Street Arts Center, two minutes walk away, a nightclub with a couple of different-sized showrooms built onto the back of the decrepit Broadway Central Hotel, where there seems to be an encouraging interaction between avant-theater and rock harnessed to machines. I've been to the Oscar Wilde Room to see Bob Mason's Stardrive, heirs to the duo of Silver Apples who synthesized when it was still called *electronic* music; and Suicide, the coupling of Alan Vega and Marty Rev, who enact that tensile moment when the countdown runs out and you have to pull the trigger.

They have a great name, New York Dolls, and I'm immediately in their fan club. The one thing that's been missing amid all the creative synergy in downtown Manhattan is musical accompaniment. Despite the fact that Max's has become a hangout for touring rockers and their attached-at-the-hip coterie, including journalists and publicists, its Warholian roots are now more reverential than omnipresent, except when Andrea "Whipps" Feldman—who sometimes calls herself Andrea Warhol—announces *showtime!* and climbs up on a table to lift her dress. The upstairs performance space features national attractions making their New York *this-is-a-nice-town-wasn't-it?* stopover. It could be anywhere; even Kansas City.

The Dolls could only be birthed from Manhattan. Comprised of refugees from the outer boroughs, they gathered in Rusty's Bicycle Shop in the West Eighties after closing time during the summer of 1971, locked in until morning with a couple of amps, a drum set, a bottle of vodka, trying their hand at r&b covers by Archie Bell and the Drells and Sonny Boy Williamson, writing songs about how it felt to be a new mutation in the making: "Personality Crisis," "Trash," "Frankenstein," and "Looking for a Kiss." Carting their equipment and worldview across Columbus Avenue to the welfare recipients of the Hotel Endicott on Christmas Day, 1971, their first gig, they borrowed haphazardly from rock's messier side, joyously chaotic, reveling in affront and belief in their own reinvention. Six months later, they were to be seen each Tuesday night at the Mercer. Right on time.

Blurred gender and costumery, posing and put-on and courting outrage, gay culture infiltrated theatrical trope and prop. Charles Ludlam's Ridiculous Theatrical Company and its sibling rivalry with John Vaccaro's Play-House of the Ridiculous echoed across the country in San Francisco with the Cockettes, spangling stages, leaving glitter in its wake. In England, the emergence of Marc Bolan, with David Bowie close behind in an androgynous arms race, pop-starred a new look, dandyish, gold lamé and artifice taking over from downmarket denim and fringe, makeup de rigueur. This was Hollywood Boulevard reclaimed, glamour spelled with a "you," image first, music to follow, like a film script in development. As Ray Davies of the Kinks noted in "Celluloid Heroes," released in the summer of 1972, *Everybody's in movies, it doesn't matter who you are.* "Lola" two years earlier had made porous the dividing line between sexes, the arched eyebrow of camp plucked and penciled, persona meeting personification.

Malleable gender had been part of New York rock since Eric Emerson's Magic Tramps and Wayne County's sassy southern belle, both Warhol habitués. Bowie met Iggy in the back room of Max's, put his arms around Lou, and "Walk on the Wild Side" was a hit single. Alice Cooper set an arena standard for shock-rock theatricality, along with an early penchant for drag—it wasn't by accident that Frank Zappa's motherly love gave them first encouragement—even if the band's pronounced maleness read more unisex gimmick than cross-dressage. Bowie had worn a full-on gown on the cover of his album *The Man Who Sold the World* in 1970, though his impressionistic Bacall didn't attract too many Bogies in the heartland of America. A dalliance with homosexuality, especially after the Stonewall riots in 1969 resulted in a resurgent gay pride, was viewed as a curious flirting with the many forms sexuality could perceive itself. If you wanted to go to a party, you could do worse than attend the polysexual fest at Z-Man's (the x and y chromosome transexualized in a new letter) in Russ Meyer's 1970 *Beyond the Valley of the Dolls*, scripted by film critic Roger Ebert, where the innocent singer in an all-girl band called the Carrie Nations looks wide-eyed at the group onstage: "I've been to parties where they've played Strawberry Alarm Clock records, but I've never been to a party where the Strawberry Alarm Clock played!"

The Dolls' pastiche took what they needed from flamboyance,

yet their pop leanings were reactionary. They respected the Velvet Underground (though city-bred, they didn't aspire to wilful dissonance), appreciated the Stooges (though weren't about to put themselves in harm's way, at least for now), they liked old blues and Brill Building three-minute anthems. "The bands that were big then," said David Johansen, lead singer, ". . . to go see them was too laborious. The songs would drag on for twenty minutes, hours of nothing happening." He recalled the package shows put on by Murray the K at the Brooklyn Fox. The acts "would come on for six minutes, do three songs, and destroy the place. Scorched. To me, that was what rock and roll was about."

That they were visual was no surprise, since guitarist Sylvain Sylvain and original drummer Billy Murcia had been in the *shmatte* trade, running a hand-knit sweater company called Truth and Soul. Cairo-born Syl and Bogotá-bred Billy met third-generation Italian Johnny Genzale at their high school in Bayside, Queens, a couple of neighborhoods over from Forest Hills, where a band who hoped to be like the New York Dolls, the Ramones, would coalesce a few years later. They gravitated to Manhattan, cutting classes from Quintano's School for Young Professionals off Times Square, a holding pen for public school outcasts, and hung out on the fringes of Nobody's, a bar on Bleecker Street that catered to bridge-and-tunnel kids hoping to pass as English rock stars. Arthur Kane drifted down from the Bronx to join them in a band called Actress. David Johansen took the ferry from Staten Island to live on East Sixth Street in the East Village with his girlfriend Diane Podlewski, a Warhol supporting actress in *Trash*, and played harmonica in Village clubs with the Vagabond Missionaries. The magnetic poles of the Dolls—uniting the world of Max's with Nobody's—were match-made. Syl walked past the New York Doll Hospital on East Sixtieth Street and saw their future.

They were more ambient than trained. Sylvain remembered the ambient oud of his childhood, and his chopping plectrum on the strings did much to keep Arthur and Johnny from flying off-kilter. Kane, and the newly monikered Thunders, flurrying and clustering notes between breaths, gave the songs a hill-and-dale singsong that David could *shpiel* over, vaudevillian in the best of senses, comic timing and sly asides and winks at the audience and himself even as the frontal thrust of the music showed they weren't fooling around. The mirrored walls of the Oscar Wilde Room as they built a following over the summer of 1972 were perfect for showing off and showing out a couture whose *eleganza*—Lisa Robinson's well-chosen descriptive—seemed another way of finding like-minded outlanders in a year when *fabulous* became the compliment *du jour*.

Their rise was precipitous, steep in a way both vertiginous and ultimately harrowing. It is to their askew credit that they kept a sense of humor about them even in the darkest of times. The Dolls' tale is fraught with fuckup. And it doesn't matter. It wasn't an act for them, no artifice in their flair for the dramatic, and if they were irresponsible and self-destructive and hardly punctual, they stayed in character. I like to think of them answering the casting call of *West Side Story*: Tony (David), Riff (first Billy Murcia, then Jerry Nolan), Bernardo (Johnny), Anybody's (Arthur), Syl as Maria; the Shakespearean aria of juvenile delinquency. *We like to be in America*. But Manhattan as an island can seem as remote as Bali Hai when it crosses the Hudson to northern America. As I saw the band, week after week, legging and wiggling to "Bad Girl" with Miss Elvis and Miss Ohio, scribing appreciative paeans in the rock press, feeling like something new was cresting, it seemed only a matter of time before the Dolls would achieve national recognition.

They acquired a manager, Marty Thau, whose background was hit-driven and quirky, first as a promotion man for Cameo-Parkway in its ? and the Mysterians days, and then Neil Bogart's Buddah label in the bubble-gum era; and signed with a management company run by Steve Leber and David Krebs, who had also corraled Boston's Aerosmith in their quest for the most-likely-to-succeed east coast band. Rolling Stones comparisons were impossible to ignore, both lead singers resembling and even aping Mick Jagger, moody saturnine guitarists to stage left with edgy Keith Richards vibes. Same rock-as-credo. When record companies in America proved reticent, not helped by the Dolls' chaotic presentation, easy prey to drugs and alcohol, the band took to England, where peacockery was in fashion and the Dolls were already fan magazine favorites, heralded and eagerly awaited by *Melody Maker* and *New Musical Express*. They landed in England in late October, played a handful of shows to acclaim and bewilderment, and were on the verge of a contract offer by Kit Lambert at Track Records. But two weeks into the tour, Murcia's death by misadventure, claimed by a lethal mixture of Mandrax and alcohol, made them aware of the loaded dice they were playing with. Not that it changed their mission.

Back in New York, they found a new drummer. Jerry Nolan had been mentored by Gene Krupa and added crisp precision to the Dolls' driveshaft. They also discovered a champion at Mercury Records in writer Paul Nelson, originally from Minneapolis, where he'd edited the folk music magazine *Little Sandy Review* and known Bob Dylan in his formative years. He applauded Dylan's conversion at Newport, and understood the charm of the Dolls, that they had shrugged off the frippery of rock—that they were not one of those *horn bands*—and the world deserved to hear them. Despite misgivings, Mercury found it hard to resist the waves of press coverage or Nelson's entreaties. After a triumphant show at the Mercer celebrating Valentine's Day, gathering the local ragtags in one beating heart—along with the Dolls, there was Wayne County's Queen Elizabeth, Suicide, and Eric Emerson's Magic Tramps—Mercury signed the band in March; by April they had taken over Studio B at the Record Plant on West

Forty-Fourth Street, with producer Todd Rundgren in tow. His philosophy as a recording overseer was "If you know what you want I'll get it for you. If you don't know what you want, I'll do it for you." The Dolls did know what they wanted, which was a nonstop eight-day party with full entourage, stimulants a-flowing, and the ribald atmosphere of the Mercer. *New York Dolls*, released at the end of July, contained all their nascent hits—with David's barking vocals, Johnny and Syl's guitars colliding with each other like atoms in a centrifuge, the rhythm section thrashing, with the occasional addition of keyboards and stacked backing vocals. At the time it was regarded as roughshod, without quite the impact of the group live, usually the case when it's not live, not pumped out at 120 decibels to a frothing crowd, but performed under the watchful ears of magnetic tape. A record is the illusion of a perfect performance, or can be, at least in these days of endless overdub and edit. Yet I must say that once past the halfway notch on my Marantz, needle in the groove, the Dolls' long player is a fitting representation of the band in all its strut and glorious miasma of exulting in the transformative, the changeling that is rock and roll; and the songs were catchy.

The front cover, by fashion photographer Toshi, emphasized the feminine, full makeup and accessorizing, perhaps more than necessary when their rough trade might have proved less controversial outside Manhattan, wading into the midstream of the country at large. The album was shadowed by portents; a week after it came out, the Broadway Central Hotel collapsed, taking with it four lives and the Mercer Street Arts Center. Aside from heartening and rabid followers in Detroit, Los Angeles—where they were guests of honor at Rodney Bingenheimer's English Disco and its nubile delights—and San Francisco, their impact was less than headlines promised. The Dolls found it slower going than they'd hoped, and so went faster, sex and drugs overtaking rock and roll. A second album, *Too Much Too Soon*, produced by Shadow Morton of Shangri-Las and Vanilla Fudge fame, attempted to streamline them for the radio, but the Dolls were already having trouble coming up with material, hierarchical cracks in the group beginning to surface, not helped by the realization that they'd been bridesmaids too long, awaiting the *I Do* of mass acclaim or at least a steady paycheck.

The "Trash" *go-pick-it-up* of low-rent pleasure might have one-upped them from the grindhouse, but the accompanying avoidance of emotional commitment and subsequent devaluation of any deeper meanings in a fan favorite (at least *this* fan) like "Puss 'n Boots" or "Vietnamese Baby" left them little room to grow. Johansen was too knowing, Johnny and Jerry were beyond knowing, and Syl tried valiantly to carry on while Arthur was among the walking wounded. Regarded as a reincarnation of the garage ethic of the 1960s, rock journalists on both sides of the Atlantic had put their faith in the Dolls as a renaissance of the music's eternal verities. *Real* musicians predictably dismissed them, some from jealousy, some from snobbery. "Mock rock," tut-tutted compère Bob Harris when the group was on the *Old Grey Whistle Test*, all too right and for the wrong reasons; it was reminiscent of the jazz wars of the 1940s that pitted "moldy fig" traditionalists against the manic flat fifths of bebop. The critical wave that buoyed them stayed impounded in the pages of *Creem* and *Rock Scene*, the *NME* or *Melody Maker*, preachers to the converted.

Malcolm McLaren, a haberdasher from London with a taste for the lurid—his King's Road shop Let It Rock had begun its metamorphosis from Teddy Boy rock revival to SEX, an emporium specializing in fetish gear—was fascinated by the group, and when the Dolls' management set them adrift, he offered his stylistic and paternal advice. Among the few songs the group had written for a proposed third album was "Red Patent Leather," and in February 1975 they brought a communistic dressage concept to the Little Hippodrome on East Fifty-Fifth Street. In the year the Vietnam War shuddered to a close, nobody in America got the joke, even the band. Two months later, on tour in Florida in various stages of withdrawal—Johnny and Jerry junk-sick, David laying the groundwork for a solo career—the Dolls gave up the ghost.

Their spirit would haunt the future, offering inspiration and emulation, though they would have to wait for absolution. There were more offspring out there listening and watching than they knew. In the meanwhile, the coterie of bands that had gathered around the Dolls seemed lost without their example to follow: the Harlots of Forty-Second Street, the Brats, the Fast, Teenage Lust, Streetpunk (a phrase already in the air); fun while it lasted, dropping in on their oh-so-local shows after midnight, especially when they played Club 82, the butch bar on East Fourth Street whose low rectangle of burlesque stage jutting onto the dance floor made everything just tawdry enough to pretend that starshine was still a-glimmer. Only KISS, who painted themselves as monsters and determined to learn from the Dolls' miscues, were able to escape New York, relying on rabble-rousing spectacle and one-dimensional sloganeering to make their impact, anti-art and proud of it.

Which wasn't the case at CBGB, a few blocks and another world away.

|||||

ON EASTER SUNDAY, 1974, Patti and I leave a preview screening of *Ladies and Gentlemen, The Rolling Stones*, at the Ziegfeld Theater on West Fifty-Fourth Street, get in a cab, and travel to a newish hole-in-the-wall on the Bowery where a group called Television is playing.

I've met Richard Lloyd in Max's. He's told me he's a guitarist in a group called Crossfire, and so that's how I nickname him, even though he's now joined Television. Richard Hell, once Meyers, has invited Patti to see his band, also Television. They're playing Sunday nights on the Bowery. I've never been to CBGB— initialed for Country, Bluegrass, and Blues—but they've convinced the owner, Hilly Krystal, to let them have a stage once a week, like a television show, on Sunday nights right after Ed Sullivan. Come on down.

We're a band as well. Sort of. Actually we're more suited to the folk circuit and cabaret, now a trio with Richard Sohl on piano, the first keyboard player who looks as if he might last more than one gig. It's starting to be a thing, much to my surprise, though I can't imagine what kind of a thing it could be given that it's not like anything else. The previous November Patti asked me to reprise our greatest hits for her *Rock 'N Rimbaud* celebration at Le Jardin, atop the Hotel Diplomat off Times Square. In place of "Mack the Knife" would be "Annie Had a Baby." It's been over two and a half years since St. Marks, and I can't say I'd never picked out the chords of "Picture Hanging Blues" sitting on the couch, guitar in hand, imagining doing it again.

I come on at the end of her performance, after poems interspersed with standards played by pianist Bill Elliott. I am unaccountably wearing a sequined Gene Vincent and the Blue Caps T-shirt that I've bought over in England from Let It Rock. She doesn't hold it against me. A month later Patti has a reading at the West End Café near Columbia University, a fabled stop on my beat generation itinerary where Jack Kerouac and Allen Ginsberg and Lucien Carr interacted, and asks me to bring my guitar along. Same greatest hits. Twice in a row.

I've known Patti's new manager, Jane Friedman, from her days as a publicist, most notably for the Woodstock festival. Among other events she's invited me to is the farewell performance of Vanilla Fudge at the Action House on Long Island, for which I am forever grateful, and a circuitous traverse around Times Square blindfolded to arrive at a recording studio for a preview of Stevie Wonder's new album. Jane has arranged an opening slot with Phil Ochs at Max's over the holiday week ending 1973, in the span of both Patti's and my birthdays, separated by three days. We will each be 27, my lucky number. As 1974 dawns, we are onstage together; allowing it to happen.

It takes a while to find the right isosceles to our triangle. Patti's savant friend Matthew Reich sits in on keyboard for a weekend where we open folkies Happy and Artie Traum at the Metro on West Fourth Street, but his rudiments and my rudiments are too simplistic a backing. We've been offered a slot with Holly Woodlawn at Reno Sweeney's on West Thirteenth Street at the beginning of March, a prestigious cabaret-centric venue that *de rigueurs* the feather boa. Patti wants to include standards like "I Get a Kick Out of You" and "I Ain't Got Nobody" along with our doo-wop take on the Blenders' "Don't Fuck Around with Love." We need the just-a-gigolo. Danny Fields suggests Richard to us, and he shows up at our rehearsal room dressed in a sailor suit, blond curls, an off-hand flaunt of his own beauty reminding us of Tadzio in *Death in Venice*. He is DNV even before he shows off his skills, flourishing show tunes, a touch of Rachmaninoff, or hypnotically pounding three chords underneath Patti's chanting. Andy Warhol is in the audience that Sunday night of March 3, our screen test in reverse.

We are trio: piano, guitar, voice.

|||||

"**EACH BAND WAS LIKE AN IDEA,**" Tom Verlaine of Television said of that time when the low-rise stage of CBGB was on the left as you walked into the long narrow room, backdropped by photos of turn-of-the-century bathing belles. Past the stage was the pool table, the bathrooms, even a kitchen where the owner's wife made hamburgers, the grease hood still in what passes for a dressing room thirty-three years later when the end was nigh. The owner slept in the back with his dog, a Saluki named Jonathan. At the start there was no consensus of style, only less accoutrement. Ripped jeans, T-shirts worn through with holes, sneakers. The motorcycle jackets came later. The bands played for each other, on stage and off. The Stilettos emulated the classic Brill Building girl groups, Elda Gentile coquettish, Debbie Harry on her way to being the platinum face of Blondie. The Miamis, diminutive brothers with wide smiles who also backed W(J)ayne County, had the catchiest song, "We Deliver (Twenty Fours a Day)." Soon there would be the Ramones, emulsifying rock and roll down to its primate, all downstrokes and lyrics one step removed from the asylum; the Shirts commuting from Brooklyn, led by the elfin Annie Golden, whose powerful voice and aw-shucks cuteness would take her to film (*Hair*) and Broadway; the art-savvy and paranormal Talking Heads; the Heartbreakers featuring ex-Dolls and ex-Television members; and hundreds more, migrating from across the country to act out fantasies on the scarred wood of the stage, reaching a high/low point with the sonic reduction of the Dead Boys, transplants from Cleveland, whose lead singer, Stiv Bators, wrapped the microphone cord so tightly around his neck that he passed out mid-song. By then Punk, capital *P*, was the ruling party. In 1974, it was still sensibility, not yet formalized.

Of them all, we were closest with Television. They were as literary-minded as musical, drawn to the St. Mark's Poetry Project, and both Tom Miller and Richard Meyers had worked alongside each other at the Strand Bookstore on lower Broadway. They shared upbringings in Wilmington, Delaware, escaping from the same private prep school to arrive separately in New York in the later sixties, gravitating to the Lower East Side's renegade artisan community. In the late sixties, this meant encampment on the literary edges, with poets like Ted Berrigan, Ed Sanders (who had already sutured poetry and rock with the Fugs and his publication *Fuck You: A Magazine of the Arts*), and Anne Waldman keeping poesy aflame with the oral traditions of beatnik lineage. From a small apartment on Elizabeth Street, Richard cranked out an offset poetry magazine called *Genesis: Grasp*, and Miller joined in the wordplay. "Of course there is no art, only life," Meyers proclaimed in the first issue, which is the way artists usually validate their distance from life. By the final issue, in 1971, with three head shots on the cover—Arthur Rimbaud, Antonin Artaud, and a composite of Richard's and Tom's faces in makeup and wig assuming the switched-gender pseudonym of Theresa Stern, they had fabricated a collaborative persona whose poems would be gathered in the 1973 *Wanna Go Out?*, credited to Stern, now biographed as an ex-prostitute living in Hoboken.

Rock and roll gave them a vehicle to live art viscerally. With the poetry cabal increasingly insular, that they were still unwilling to let go their poetic sensibilities would be revelated in an upcoming switch of identities: Miller became Verlaine, Meyers took on a Rimbaudian Hell. All that remained was to play out the future history of the band they would become, friendship and collaboration split asunder much like their namesakes on the Rue des Brasseurs in Brussels, Verlaine shooting Rimbaud in the wrist and both living to tell the tale.

Tom was the musician, free-forming John Coltrane and Albert Ayler as a teenager, taking up saxophone—"I liked to make noise"—before embracing the guitar. In Delaware he met Billy Ficca, a jazz drummer, though there was no audience for what Billy called their "crazy music." When Tom invited him to New York to join a band, he was only too willing to see what Miller had in mind. Richard viewed the music as a vehicle for self-reinvention, an image starting with his scalloped hair, modeled on Rimbaud's, though it would mean he would have to learn an instrument from the fundamentals up. Their expected influences were the Velvet

Underground and the New York Dolls, as much attitude as ante-
cedent; Verlaine was attracted to English Invasion groups—"the
first rock song that really knocked me out was '19th Nervous
Breakdown' by the Stones"—and the American garage bands that
took notice and upped the frenzy. Early Television would feature
covers of Count Five's "Psychotic Reaction" and 13th Floor Elevators' "Fire Engine."

The three-piece Neon Boys never made it out of the rehearsal
room. From fall of 1972 until April 1973 they aligned Tom's guitar with Richard's bass even though they had at first envisioned a
twin-guitar band. The only record of their Siamese togetherness
as Neon Boys is a six-song studio preservation as adieu, divvying
up the songs. Richard's share admits his learning curve: "That's
All I Know (Right Now)" sneeringly adds "I don't care," spit-
tling the microphone. He'll take "Love Comes in Spurts" into
his solo career, and in the held tensile chord over which Verlaine
(call him that) reels out his guitar line is a precursor to the cre-
scendo of "Marquee Moon." Tom gets romping room in "High
Heel Wheels," though his three compositions—"Tramp," "Hot
Dog," and "Poor Circulation"—remain unheard. I assume that's
the way he wants it, and I respect his wishes.

In a bizarre turnabout worthy of vaudeville, Richard becomes
Tom's manager, setting up a brief fifteen-minute showcase at
Reno Sweeney's. The cabaret was known for high-toned preten-
sion, a civilized re-creation of a nightclub type that existed when
floor shows were in fashion, ripe for the *is-the-camera-ready-Mr.
DeMille* divas of the Warhol set. On March 10, 1973, Verlaine
ambles onstage, takes his time adjusting his amplifier, tuning,
getting comfortable in his seat—he hasn't really changed in all
these years—and plays three songs. Hell rips Tom's shirt for effect
before he goes on. There is a song about falling into the arms of
"Venus De Milo," one that becomes "Double Exposure." Richard Lloyd, an obsessive guitarist who sits in his room practicing

all day before staying out all night taking drugs and pleasurings where he may, is in the sparse audience. He is looking for someone he could "embellish or augment," a fellow misfit also obsessed with guitar, approaching it from afar.

The meeting is not happenstance. Lloyd has been staying at the loft of Terry Ork, a west coast transplant who trails the Warhol constellation back to New York after sidling up to them in January 1968 while they're shooting *San Diego Surf*, the follow-up to *Lonesome Cowboys*, shelved after Andy's own shooting. He understands the one thing you need to keep up with the Warhol crew is "wit, whether it be savage or brilliant." He becomes Gerard Malanga's assistant, hothousing in the homoerotic air of tricks and tots around Max's, turning the closet inside out. He lasts as long as Malanga at the Factory, until a shadowy dispute over silk-screen forgeries leads to his firing; but he knew movies, writing about them in the first issues of *Inter/View*, and manages Cinemabilia, a bookstore where posters and esoteric film ephemera attract a knowing clientele. Richard Hell works there, envisioning the cinematography of a movie yet to be storyboarded.

Terry has a loft on East Broadway where the assembling band can practice. Unlike Hell, Lloyd is versed in his instrument, and when he plays with Tom he has the ability to entwine and ground and carve his own space, a hallmark of future Television. By default Meyers returns on bass, his bursts of bottom goading Billy Ficca's skittering on the drums. On March 2, 1974, Television debuts at the Townhouse Theater on West Forty-Fourth Street. "Four cats with a passion," blurbs director Nicholas Ray on the poster; he likes rebellion without a cause. Their name is chosen because "it's something that's in every home in America. It's so obtrusive," says Hell, "it's unobtrusive." Change the channel.

||||||

ACCORDING TO POST-APOCALYPSE TALES told through the ages, it was Verlaine and Lloyd who wandered past the run-down nineteenth-century saloon once known as Hilly's On The Bowery and suggested to the owner, standing on a ladder adjusting the soon-iconic canopy, that the venue might consider hiring rock bands, especially theirs. Even though the music Hilly Krystal had named his club for—Country, BlueGrass, and Blues—showed his musical leanings, he was more interested in originality, and cared little for technique. He was no stranger to the neighborhood locals, and with the collapse of the Mercer Arts Center only four blocks away, was starting to get spillover interest. He'd changed the name to CBGB, underlining it with OMFUG (Other Music For Uplifting Gourmandizers, which shows his askew humor), in December 1973 (the official date given is the eleventh, but like most attempts to pin down acts of fate, the crossover is elusive), as stray combinations led by Eric Emerson and Wayne County commingle among the countryesque acts and poetry readings Hilly favored. Who is Band Zero? All of us.

Born in 1931, Hillel Krystal had been a chorus singer at Radio City Music Hall, knew a bit of violin (he liked a good fiddlers' convention), but had maneuvered behind the scenes in the West Village, managing the Village Vanguard in 1959 before opening his own club, Hilly's, at 104 West Thirteenth Street. Noise complaints forced him east and south into the "drab and ugly and unsavory" Bowery, and in 1969 he took over a run-down bum's bar on the first floor of a flophouse, the Palace Hotel, where he opened the door to the Hell's Angels, headquartered nearby on East Third Street, which helped keep some semblance of order. "Mostly, knives were the weapon of choice," he recalled, streets strewn with those "just lost in life or down on their luck." He was not unaware of the artists colonizing the area—William Burroughs had a bunker at 222 Bowery, between Spring and Prince, the same former YMCA in which the painter Mark Rothko had his studio. The rent was low, and the empty lots and industrial buildings around him meant he could make as much racket as he liked after the restaurant equipment stores closed and the street left to desolation. Yet it did have a sense of beacon, a lone light amid darkness, a row of neon beer signs along the bar beckoning you inward; and noise.

Patti and I walk down the aisle, toward the stage. There is Television, herky-jerky shifts of mood and mannerism, each member protonic. The one we haven't met is Verlaine. He looks rural, a hayseed cupping his slyness behind a cigarette, squinting out through the smoke, slightly bemused. He wrenches at his guitar, pulling it out of tune and keeping it there, possessed, battering chords and bending strings past the point of breakage, though he appears stock still next to Hell, who is leaping about, spasming, not so much note-ing his bass as slapping and flapping at it, as if he'd put his finger in an electric socket.

Along with Tom and Richard, there is the other Richard, Lloyd, who seems proficient, even confident on his instrument, if somewhat spacy; not so Tom and Richard reaching for something yet to be configured in their playing. Lloyd stands in the middle, bookended by the opposing poles of Hell and Verlaine. Ficca impels and diffuses them, catching off-beats the front line favor, each twitch and involuntary shudder. Hell sings, Verlaine sings, voices that yelp cut-up lyrics, followed by long open-ended guitar solos. Alien beings. Our kind of band.

Our band—might we call it that?—is beginning to figure itself out. Over the spring, as we merry-go-round the Metro and back again to Reno Sweeney's, our set takes on contour. Patti declaims her poetry, we segue into song, and then she sings her poetry, making it up as she goes along. Richard and I follow her persona-shifting, up volume, down volume, slowing, speeding, dark, light, dual equilaterals. She is learning to be a singer. Sandy

Pearlman had asked her after the St. Mark's reading if she wanted to sing with Blue Öyster Cult. Steve Paul similarly offered his Blue Sky record imprint and possible collaborators. But Patti is just beginning to see how to make it her own.

We are aware of the effect we're having on an audience, not just localized friends and hangers-on, but curiosity seekers won over and mesmerized though they—like us—aren't quite sure why. Writing and performance, Patti understands both; her poems are clear, accessible, funny, sexy, shocking, redemptive, and then she inhabits them. It is uncanny to watch the audience fall under her spell, hypnotically following a trail of thought as she spirals outward, and then reels the tangent back to earth to reprise a final chorus.

We're practicing almost every day, up four flights of stairs behind a movie billboard on the west side of Times Square at Forty-Sixth Street, in an empty office down the hall from Jane's Wartoke PR firm. There is a piano there, and we spend afternoons trying out songs we like: Smokey Robinson's "Hunter Gets Captured by the Game," Bessie Smith's "I'm Wild About That Thing," the Velvet Underground's "We're Gonna Have a Real Good Time Together," and those we're beginning to write. Richard has a moody keyboard piece we call the "Harbor Song" (*I went down to the harbor / The ships were comin'* . . .), "Picture Hanging Blues" has taken on formal structure, and "Ballad of a Bad Boy" closes our set with enough noise to declare our intentions. Sometimes we just rotate chords underneath Patti's storytelling, Richard comping changes, me fingering lead lines that originate from the Fender VI, as much bass as guitar. We set to music "Piss Factory," which Patti has been proclaiming since St. Mark's the previous New Year's Day, her escape from south Jersey as metaphor and mission: *james brown singing I lost someone / georgie woods the guy with the goods and guided missiles* our shared discography, given a rolling underlay by Richard, and I jazz along.

What's most intriguing as a direction is the way we're starting to link poem with song, or introduce a song with a long preamble that might well be a poem. Such synthesis begins to emerge from the second stanza of "Witt," the title piece of Patti's second collection—*look at this land where we am. Lost souls. Failed moon over the carnival*—and off we au-go-go to the "Land of a Thousand Dances." She knows Chris Kenner's original, I remember East LA versions by Thee Midniters and Cannibal and the Headhunters, and "DNV" loves to dance. William Burroughs had given Patti a copy of *The Wild Boys*, and from it has grown the feral character of Johnny, his Homeric wanderings, each dance never the same. She always liked telling stories to her siblings, to Robert, to the gang at the Chelsea. Now she's story-timing a growing downtown audience.

Like most of America and its nascent revolutionary cells, we are captivated in early 1974 by the plight of Patty Hearst, granddaughter to William Randolph of the newspaper dynasty and the roman à clef *Citizen Kane*. She was eighteen years old, a sophomore at UC Berkeley, when on February 4 she was kidnapped at machine gun–point by the paramilitary Symbionese Liberation Army. When she surfaces two months later, she has assumed the name of Tania, declared allegiance to the SLA, and is seen in a black wig, toting an M1 carbine as honor guard while the Hibernia Bank in San Francisco is robbed. When a photo is released to the press of her in full battle dress, jaunty beret, pointed rifle, the SLA flag unfurling hydra-headed behind, its guerrilla pinup ensures prominent cover placement on newsstands and tabloid hand-wringing.

Patti focuses not on the sensational but an intuition of Patty as a young girl swirled into the unimaginable. She understands surrender, placing it in musical context—*honey the way you play guitar makes me feel so masochistic*—and the allure of giving oneself over to a noble crusade. In our case it's rock and roll's transformative power, traditional abandon, exaltation, reinvention, now in danger of losing its way. Like the critics of the French *nouvelle vague* in *Cahiers du Cinéma*, there comes a time when we realize we have to take matters into our own hands. I'm increasingly unable as a writer to pretend objectivity, championing to the point of proselytizing not only favored artists but the virtues that need a constancy of reminder; the why of why we do it, to express hidden longings, aberrations, paths to glory. The guitar for us is emblematic of a band lineup honed for frontal motion, rhythm ascendant, and the need for drummers to take notice. We don't have a drummer as yet.

For Patti, it's more concentric. She has seen herself as art's comprehension, its mistress, the elevated muse, providing motivation. With Robert she abetted his vision, and yet in the disarray of her room in their shared loft on Twenty-Third Street is her own altar to self-preservation, walls filled with pinned photos of hero worship—Dylan, Mayakovsky, Edie Sedgwick—and artistic aspiration. She sees it in others before herself. Bobby Neuwirth, Dylan's alter-ego in *Don't Look Back*, emboldens her strut and writing. Sam Shepard tells her you can't make a mistake improvising: "If you miss a beat, create another." When she first encounters Sam drumming with the Holy Modal Rounders at the Village Gate, hollering a song called "Blind Rage," she has no idea who he is. Despite his theatrical Obie bonafides, he introduces himself as Slim Shadow, and as Patti relates in *Just Kids*, "This guy truly embodies the heart and soul of rock and roll." The music has already shown her holy awakening: "It's the only religion I got," she rejoinders with Sam in their coauthored play *Cowboy Mouth* in 1971. "Any great motherfucker rock 'n' roll song can raise me higher than all of *Revelations*."

She perceives this halo in Television, and hails them in the October 1974 *Rock Scene* (full disclosure: the Robinsons edit, I'm on the masthead): *Someday somewhere must stand naked. . . . A*

*group called TELEVISION who refuse to be a latent image but the
image itself! The picture they transmit is shockingly honest. . . . Dive
clubs anywhere at all. They play undulating rhythm like ocean. They
play pissed off psychotic reaction. They play like they got knife fight
in the alley after the set. They play like they make it with chicks. They
play like they're in space but still can dig the immediate charge and
contact of lighting a match.*

Patti and Tom spark, the undeniable of attraction. They share
a belief in flying saucers and spherical music, their dance beguiling
to watch as it unfolds, incrementally slow, over the spring of 1974.
It is circumspect, as each is, as much as you can be in a small club
where there is no back room, all shifting downward glances and
secret lingo, encouragements, mutual respect. *Every night I would
go down to the bar / Where he played guitar,* Patti would preface
"We Three" over the next decades, reminiscing the moment and
bringing it back to stage left front where Tom stood, just within
reach. The third party is enigmatic: Is it Allen Lanier of the Blue
Öyster Cult whom she lives with, or Richard Hell who wishes he
could live with her? Or her own commitment to art, which must
be delicately held in balance in any relationship?

On June 5 we book a session at Electric Lady Studios to see
what we sound like on a record, with its own imbalanced relationship, where you sing to yourself and hope it's heard beyond the
microphone. I've been dabbling in record production, tried my
hand with a Boston band called the Sidewinders, signed to RCA,
that has the same virtues as my *Nuggets* curations, hook choruses,
punchy guitars, short songs, acceleration and youthful fervor; and
I'm familiar with homegrown 45s from seeing oldie record stores
press their own singles. Robert stakes us to the tune of a thousand
dollars and we're ready to press play.

It's 9 p.m. in Studio B of Electric Lady, in the back, eight-
track, and we won't use all of them. Five years before, Patti was

sitting on the stairs of the newly opened West Eighth Street recording studio designed by Jimi Hendrix, in the space where a hoedown club called the Village Barn sub-basemented since 1930, too shy to go into the party, when Jimi walked up the stairs, on his way out the door, off to the Isle of Wight, not much more lifeline left. He told her of his dream of an abstract universal musical language, beyond key and tempo. Now we're attempting to crack its code. Because Richard and I are key and tempo, we bring Tom Verlaine with us to provide abstraction. "Hi Jimi," Patti whispers into the microphone before we begin his slowed version of "Hey Joe" (through Tim Rose) that we are attaching to Patti's poem, now called "60 Days": *Sixty days ago she was just a little girl / And now here she is with a gun her hand*. When it's Tom's turn, we encourage him to spiral as far outré as he can go, mixing his two takes together for a maelstrom of double helix. With fifteen minutes left in the three-hour session, Patti recites "Piss Factory," me and DNV tap-dancing beneath her, emphasizing the *never return* and *I will travel light* and the *be somebody*, which, at least in recorded form, we are now. At midnight, Tom and Patti take a ride on the Staten Island Ferry, marrying our bands.

At the end of July I drive to Philadelphia to pick up 1,500 seven-inch copies of Mer 601, black label with silver print, a small swan as logo. The disc is slightly pie-plated, and I can tell by looking sideways at its rim that the pressing plant has used recycled vinyl, its grayish tinge a clue to tell the original from future bootlegs. By August it resides on Max's upstairs jukebox, where "Piss Factory" seems to be a hit, where we will begin on the twenty-eighth a one-week extended-to-two stand with Television as co-headliners. It speaks to our—and their—escalating audience, many well-meaning friends but also those drawn by word-of-mouth, or the not-so-underground press (the *Soho Weekly News* and the *Village Voice*, and national publications like *Creem*), or the records we've dropped off at bookstores and record stores, never getting around to pick up the proceeds, or Patti's ability to hypnotize both herself and the audience.

Photographer Bob Gruen points his Sony Portapack half-inch reel-to-reel video recorder at us on a random Sunday night, September 8, late show, second set in the second week, when we've settled into the ritual of alternating with Television. I remember us as a work in progress, but the ten-song set list is focused, tightly segued, not far from where we would arrive a year later when we again walked down the stairs of Electric Lady to make our first album.

We open with the Velvets' "Real Good Time Together," Patti in a shiny silken dress shirt and tie spinning off to take an excursion to Harlem *where the blackest thing . . . is white*, shooting up Lou as I scrub at my Melody Maker. There's a change of pace: *This is from our first album, Mink in Hi-Fi.* She lowers her voice into Chris Connor range, torches "I'm Wild About That Thing," and turns on the sultry as DNV takes the verse about *jelly roll.* She undoes her windsor knot, tells a story of Jeanne Moreau in a black slip wandering down to the harbor, as Richard guides her along the water, the waves and crescendos of *everyone-got-someone-but-not-me* that is the "Harbor Song." There's the Marvelettes' "Hunter Gets Captured by the Game," and a "Piss Factory" that hews to the recorded poem, Patti swiping her right hand downward for emphasis, pace, the underlined resolve of *I will / get out / of here . . .* until she's on the outside where she belongs. There's a poem about Marianne Faithfull *sweetness in your little girl mouth . . . sacred heart bleeds . . .* that leads into "Paint It Black." The triplets of "We Three," Patti's bony shoulder twitching in time. "Picture Hanging Blues," and then "Land," which has yet to mount its saddle but has learned how to pony, lyrics already settling in place, *the place called space* and how *it's across the tracks* and *I like it like that* and *penknives and jackknives and switchblades preferred* and *twistalet* and *got to lose control and then you take control* knees open *come on in johnny.* . . .

We climax with our a-side. The poem that led to "Hey Joe" is yesterday's newsprint, Patty Hearst now replaced by a processional in the crosshairs of a pistol. Patti points Joe's gun: Charlie Baudelaire *gets it in the spleen goes down on one knee*; Arthur Rimbaud *bang in the groin, down on one knee*; the *T.A.M.I. Show* on the silver screen as Jan and Dean slide in on their surfboards *come down on one knee*; Lesley Gore in her pink Easter suit and corsage *going down on one knee*; the silver lamé Supremes *down on one knee*; Chuck Jackson, Marvin Gaye, James Brown, those boys who sing "Time Is on My Side" waiting in the wings, Arthur Lee, all *bow down on one knee*, Huey Newton shot falling *to one knee*, Lee Harvey Oswald running into the Texas movie theater *T.A.M.I. Show* on-screen, our generation *come down on one knee*. Like an angel Jimi Hendrix *he falls down on both knees*: kerosene, a match, his guitar *in flames kisses the sky*, annunciating the prophecy of desperate children awaiting *a new language, a new rhythm, a new tongue.*

Go down on one knee. Our genuflect to the lineage of which we are becoming a part.

||||||

TO WATCH THE BANDS GROW. That is CBGB's charm. It's enough off the beaten path to be its own path, the groups congregating there shot through with spyrogyric genes past and future. For a while it's only the various ideas playing for each other, the club as much practice space as performance outlet, in fact better for rehearsal because it allows response, how each band's music looks from the outside. It's assumed you like classic pop but skew into the *twinkie zone*, that mind-meld named by event promoter Mike Quashie, who hosts late night Manhattan after-hour parties in the realm between real and surreal. Anything goes, nothing to lose.

One of the first to show up is the Ramones. It's hard to imagine three more ill-fits: gawky Jeff Hyman, blitzed Douglas Colvin, militant John Cummings. It's Tommy Erdélyi who sees their potential as a grouping, though he'd known them all for years as Forest Hills High classmates who moved on to the peripheries of rock, looking for an entry point. Johnny and Tommy have played together in high school, something called the Tangerine Puppets; then Johnny and Dee Dee alliance; Joey drums in a Queens glam-rock outfit called Sniper, walks around in towering platform heels and a satin jumpsuit. Tommy, impressed with the hook-driven British glitter scene, takes heart from the redux of the New York Dolls. He is more interested in being a recording engineer, and after apprenticing at the Record Plant, partners in Performance rehearsal studio on East Twentieth Street. Future Ramones gather there, including their to-be road manager, Monte Melnick. After debuting as a trio on March 30, 1974, it's deemed Joey is more suited to front the band, the skeletal already in place. They've written seven songs, most of which have *don't* in the title: "I Don't Want to Go Down to The Basement," "I Don't Wanna Walk Around with You," "I Don't Wanna Be Learned / I Don't Wanna Be Tamed," "I Don't Want to Get Involved with You," "I Don't Like Nobody That Don't Like Me." What do they wanna do? *Now I wanna sniff some glue.* Got it. Tommy takes up managerial guidance and drums. They play what they know, which is hardly anything at all, each downstroke counting-off *1–2–3–faw.* Their careening accelerant and gift for chant makes them emblematic of what CBGB will become to the world, songs distilled to fundamentals and then subtracted. What keeps their songs from negative energy, from what Joey calls their cores of "alienation and isolation," is the joy of playing them.

Don't underestimate their savvy. Beyond the need for breakneck stamina, Ramones' songs twist and skid, sudden shifts in rhythm cued by crash cymbal, no solos, blunt force lyrics, constant chords, no chance to breathe, next one under way. "Eliminate the unnecessary and focus on the substance" is the band's credo. Johnny and Dee Dee's relentless amp overload toughens Joey's romantic nihilism, Tommy eschews frills and fills, and their brotherhood extends to the choosing of a collective name and uniform: sneakers, tattered jeans, Brando motorcycle jackets, sullen concentration. The Ramones' cretin hop, so easily demarcated, will resound through punk rock as it will come to be characterized, and caricatured, and karaoke'd.

Half-hour sets stay the same length but more songs are crammed in. Their arrival at CB's over the weekend of August 16–17 prompts Hilly to say "nobody's [ever] going to like you guys," but he likes them well enough. Danny Fields is the first to take notice, asking to be formal manager, buying the group a set of drums as a token of good faith. Their frontal minimalism and moronic sloganeering fit well with the more artsy elements of the club's b-movie casting, *Beat on the Brat with a baseball bat* to "Blitzkrieg Bop." The latter's *hey-ho* chant, now a staple at sporting events, will become a distant reverb harking back to the Ramones as they pass the New York Mets' stadium on the 7 subway line from Forest Hills into Manhattan, carrying their guitars in paper bags.

A lifetime later, backstage on a Massachusetts rock festival summer afternoon, me and Johnny jaw about the Boston Red Sox. Me and Joey watch ? and the Mysterians at Coney Island High, him shouting *yeah baybee*, head bobbing on his giraffe-like frame. I meet Dee Dee on Second Avenue with my eight-year-old daughter, he in his blond rapper (Dee Dee King) phase, her look of bewildered fascination. Hearing Tommy play bluegrass with Uncle Monk, his last band, in his mandolin picking the Ramones' early percussive. All no longer, and yet ever.

On the same night the Ramones debut at CBGB, they share the bill with Angel and the Snake. Debbie Harry has come out of the Stilettos with boyfriend Chris Stein in tow, and together they will build Blondie into a world pop phenomenon. Right now, it's more character building. The Stilettos had been engendered by Elda Gentile, who visited Warhol's factory on an art school class trip and fell for Chelsea boy Eric Emerson, later having his child, Branch. She appeared in underground plays and bonded with cross-dressing Holly Woodlawn, joining Holly's pastiche of a band, Pure Garbage, before putting her idea of a classic girl group in motion. Along with Harry, who had been the chanteuse in Wind in the Willows, a hippy folk aggregation with an inoffensive 1968 album on Capitol before working briefly as a Playboy bunny and fringing on the Warhol scene as a Max's waitress, and another vocalist, Rosie Perez, they are a girl group in quotes, with a theatricality that borders on camp and vestiges of glitter. Their first appearances are in a bar-and-grill called Bobern on West Twenty-Eighth Street, between Broadway and Sixth Avenue, the same block that sported New York's first Tin Pan Alley. By May 5, 1974, they move up to supporting Television at CBGB, but Debbie and Chris are becoming dissatisfied with Elda's stage direction. They break off from the Stilettos, taking bassist Fred Smith and drummer Billy O'Connor with them, assuming the name of Angel and the Snake for a couple of shows before officially becoming Blondie. Though Debbie has the deadpan charm of a Keely Smith, the spotlight heightens her good-humored kitten-with-claws, and the songs have a knowing awareness of their *good-bad-but-not-evil* beguile, more Shangri-Las than Ronettes. The songs she writes with Chris are traditional in a way that makes them seem retro, even though all the bands are looking backward for inspiration, a reevaluation of pop's original enticements. Undervalued in the CBGB hierarchy, at least at the start, Blondie will ultimately prove the most amenable to mass adulation, amassing records as platinum as Debbie Harry's hair.

The word spreads. A place to play.

What was it like? What it was really like, there at three in the morning when the last band is done and you're thinking after-hours. Hindsight is knowing how it's going to turn out. It's the out of finding that keeps the night young.

Have another beer, Rolling Rock the verdigris bottle of choice at the bar, and see who picks up who, whose turn onstage. Once inside, hand-stamped, you enter and leave at will, shoot the breeze on the sidewalk, dodge the occasional tossed bottle from the upstairs flophouse, look in on a few songs, wait for the band to blow up onstage, storm off and back, start the song again. It's a way of testing inclination, measuring the night's temper, competence enhanced as mistakes are made, learned from, as bands swap members, as everyone gets better over 1974.

IIIIII

IT'S OUR TURN TO PLAY CBGB. On February 13, 1975, we initiate a Thursday-through-Sunday stint with Television, a Valentine's weekend that reprises on the first day of spring, when we continue for another five weeks, allowing room to explore improvisations, expand our sound, and integrate our newest member, the guitarist and bassist Ivan Kral.

Our Manhattan-centric reputation has grown to the point where our *Rock and Rimbaud III*, held in the incongruous tiki-bar setting of the Hotel Roosevelt's Blue Hawaii Room up by Grand Central Terminal, has a line wrapped around the block in early November 1974, the first anniversary of our performance art. The virtuoso guitarist Sandy Bull opens for us, accompanying Patti on the oud for "All the Hipsters Go to the Movies." We kick off with another Hank Ballard song, "Let's Go Let's Go," and have added new craftings still figuring out destinations: "Free Money," beamed to her, as Patti says, when she looked into the ice-blue eyes of a husky dog; "Birdland," a poem derived from the Peter Reich memoir of his orgone-proselytizing father, Wilhelm, being taken from him by extraterrestrial visitation; and a version of the archetypal "Gloria" that began when Richard Hell sold us his Danelectro bass for forty dollars. Patti strapped it on, hit a low E note and as it vibrated, intoned the opening lines of "Oath": *Christ died for somebody's sins but not mine.* There is only one song that can be communioned with, and I'd been playing it since 1966: "Gloria," *in excelsis deo.*

We leave for our first official road trip the next morning, on our way to California. Jane has booked us a week at the Whisky a Go Go, opening for a band called Fancy from England that has a one-hit wonder with a remake of "Wild Thing," and then a trip up to San Francisco. While the dressing room overlooking Sunset is filled with various well-wishing Stooges and garage-rock aficionados who scrawl *Standells* on the wall, and the shows go over well, Richard and I are straining to keep up with the way the songs are developing; to pace Patti's sense of headlong discovery of who she can be. She's singing more, enjoying the room she has to move onstage, and we're hearing the need for another musician, overtone and scaffold. When we land in the Bay Area, we debut in a record store—Rather Ripped—in Berkeley, play a club called the Longbranch with Eddie Money, and finish our run on a Tuesday audition night at Winterland. Jonathan Richman of the Modern Lovers sits in on drums during our set (I'm exasperatingly out of tune throughout, in these last moments before guitar tuners are invented): "Gloria," "Piss Factory," and "Land." He's our first percussion, though we're not ready for that yet. We're looking for a bridge.

Back in the practice room in mid-December, we sift through the guitarists who have come to audition from our classified casting call in the *Village Voice*. I'm not sure what the unhopefuls make of us, telling them we want them to get *out there* and *assassinatin' rhythm* and they're usually packing up before we ask them to leave. On the third day, when we're despairing of finding someone suitable, Ivan Kral comes by. Though he's been playing in bands downtown, including the rock-basic Luger and a stint with Debbie Harry's new offshoot of the Stilettos, I've never met him. A Czech refugee with a Kafkaesque moodiness and a love of the Beatles and Rolling Stones, he has an appealing accent, good bone structure and haircut, and plays both bass and guitar. When we embark on "Gloria" he resolutely follows along, unflinching, steadfast, and we realize how other guitarists altered our approach. Ivan enlarges it, so we still sound like ourselves.

Jane books us a gig at the Main Point outside Philadelphia, opening for Eric Burdon, our first as a quartet, and then we move into CBGB, two sets a night, swapping turns onstage with Television. We bring our art crowd to CBGB, and the club starts to fill, gathering momentum beyond the bands and their followings. The night-after-night allows us freedom to explore, to embark on patient journeys within the songs—especially those with a story to tell. "Gloria" climbs out of *her blue t-bird, knock-knock-knocks* on the club's front door where *anything's allowed*; Johnny follows Hilly's Saluki, Jonathan, out that front door, where he's hit by a car and resurrected time and again in "Land." Each night takes on individual sheen, to see what Patti can draw from the shimmering air and the silence that comes over the room when she begins to dreamscape. William Burroughs or Lou Reed witness rite's passage. Sometimes I open my eyes in the middle of one of our voyages and wonder where I've been transported, emerging as if from a faint, the stage set reappearing in shards around me.

We have new songs, and with the expanded lineup we can enhance them. "Redondo Beach" is a poem from Patti's small-press book *Kodak* (an edition of 100), set to a reggae beat. "Distant

Fingers" is an imagined song title from Nick Tosches who writes a semi-fictional profile of Patti for *Penthouse* and cites that as one of her hits. "Break It Up," from a dream Patti has of Jim Morrison rising from his grave, is enhanced by Tom Verlaine's guitar aviary. "Kimberly" grows from a Booker T. and the MGs riff into a backdrop for the cataclysmic birth of Patti's youngest sister.

Television is also transforming. Over the fall of 1974, the schism between Tom's and Richard's idea of the band's directive has grown into trench warfare. Tom wants to stand center-stage, to put only his songs on the demo that Richard Williams of Island Records UK has offered them, with a precondition that Brian Eno, once of Roxy Music, produce. It's all Tom compositions on the demo—five in all, "Venus De Milo," "Prove It," "Double Exposure," "Friction," and an in-process stage epic, "Marquee Moon"—though Verlaine is displeased with the results, the guitars hard and dry where they should be warm, wet. It's the same onstage with Hell; as Tom moves deeper into the well of his songs, finding new parts and subtleties, Richard outthrusts his emotions, relying on sheer audacity. There is no common ground, a wire connective to prevent reversed polarity. Richard foresees the *leave it in time* of "Blank Generation," and is about to fill in another band name. For Verlaine, it's too soon. Television isn't ready to make a record yet, at least how he perceives it should be, as each song breeds elaboration.

Two weeks into our residency, at the beginning of April, they part ways and means. Fred Smith, taking leave of Blondie, moves over to bass and fits into resolute place. His alert reflexive allows Verlaine and Lloyd to ripple guitar lines, chop chords, warble. The songs lengthen, intricate and extricate, tie themselves in knots; Tom's character one part conjuror, one part voyeur. It is the waxing "Marquee Moon" that I remember most from that spring, hearing its strains, each movement unfolding successively as I walk along the bar back past the pool table, knowing it's going to be their last song, maybe the last song of the night, or we'll go on next to see what awaits.

Offstage is a record contract, and there is interest. ESP-Disk offers its universal language (it was begun as an Esperanto label), and though it's tempting to be on the same roster as Albert Ayler, the Fugs, Pearls Before Swine, Patty Waters, and Sun Ra, we do have a mainstream streak. RCA Victor gives us an in-house audition, but before they have a chance to make up their querulous minds, Clive Davis of newly founded Arista Records comes to CBGB. He knows of Patti, has just begun a label that needs a maverick presence; he also respects performance, and believes an artist must give all and more onstage, regardless of where they slot on the pop spectrum. All we ask is creative freedom. Signed. By the end of our April stay at CBGB, they're turning people away over weekends.

Saigon falls on April 30 and the Vietnam War convulses to a close. Eleven days later, in Central Park's Sheep Meadow, Phil Ochs delivers a victory speech, we play "Land," and Johnny comes marchin' home. It's time for a parade in his honor; we need the cadence of a drum major. Jay Dee Daugherty has been running the sound system at CBGB with components scrounged from his home stereo, and is also the drummer in the Mumps, led by Lance Loud, both California transplants. Sometimes during "Land" Jay Dee gets behind Billy Ficca's kit and keeps timing. On May 28 we play a concert over the airwaves of WBAI-FM, the free-form Pacifica radio station, in a church on the Upper East Side. During "Gloria," Patti relives the history of the band, each jigsaw interlock. When she gets to the where of the drummer *we know you're out there*, he's already there. In June, Jay Dee joins us in the practice room, and is made official when we play the Other End on June 26, the Bleecker Street folk mecca, once the Bitter End. In the audience is the prime number of the Village folk scene, the infidel Bob Dylan. He comes backstage, is photographed joking with Patti, an acknowledgment that we are going electric at last, a rock and roll band, as we always desired, on our own terms.

We spend that summer inducting Jay Dee into our midst, though the adjustment goes both ways. We are used to blurring the beat, slowing and accelerating and staggering. He is the beat. It's not all we'll have to get used to. Keeping tempo in the up-coming recording sessions will be our choice of producer, John Cale, picked for artistic sensibility, radical edge, confrontation, and urban chaos. He will forcefully be all that, though we have our own agenda, which is to stay true to ourselves.

He's never heard our music, and so we take him to the Joyous Lake in Woodstock to show what we can do. On the way up, in my red '64 Chevy Impala, we listen to reggae, a constantly ac-companying soundtrack. "That sounds like Radio Ethiopia," says John, fulfilling a producer's job of paving a path ahead even while the present is yet to be accomplished.

On September 2, we move our equipment into Electric Lady's Studio A. Interstellar space murals surround us, the recording chamber lit by the glowing dials of the control room with its navi-gational mixing board, like the prow of a solar ship. We're on the night shift, arriving after dark and staying till the sky lightens. As the clock tolls twelve, we press play on "Gloria," try our hand at "Redondo Beach." Begun.

Every record, but especially the first, is a psycho-drama, look-ing in the mirror of your music and hearing it as if for the first time. The songs are still new to us, the addition of drums and the self-conscious awareness of making a record, that day, that take, that version that doesn't vanish into the air when you've hit the last chord. It's not enough to just play. You listen to yourself play, a peculiar split personality, and sometimes your voice, your in-strument, your *feel* isn't what you think it sounds like, as you hear it inside your head. There's matters of tone, frequency response, building blocks of overdub and seeing how onboard enhancement, echoes and reverbs and a multiplicity of tracks might create something unheard before.

Early on, we had to decide how much of a record to make: that is, to layer and edit and cross-fade in the quest to represent a perfect illusion of a live performance, or try to catch the incandescence in a bottle that is live performance on the fly, a document as it happens in the moment, as if you are there. "As if" is the tricky part.

The best records can be both. We were determined to keep freestyle improvisation at the forefront for songs that called for it. Our more structured material, like "Redondo Beach," "Free Money," "Break It Up" with its spiraling Tom Verlaine lead lines, even "Gloria" itself, which had evolved into a sculpted arrangement, could be tracked and overdubbed. Others in our repertoire had little but a starting point. We wanted to see where the adrenal energy of songs like "Land" and "Birdland" might voyage as they took flight in a room with science fictional murals of space travel on the walls. *There's a little place / A place called space*, sang Patti, as we made ready to explore the cosmos.

A producer, more than anything, is a standard by which an artist measures who they want to be, as well as how close they are to achieving that wanting. It's a mirror-mirror reflection of a trusted advisor, sometimes a naysayer needing to be convinced. I believe John had in mind a more arranged record, one fleshed out with intriguing sound palettes and melodic lines, as well as making sure our rickety instruments stayed in tune; and we defending our turf, wanting things looser, less premeditated. In the end, especially within the improvisations, he challenged us to not settle for anything less than as far as we could go.

"Birdland" had begun as a short poem. As we explored it over and again, proving to John that it only needed our collective will to take flight, the song expanded past the six-minute mark, gathering whirlwind imageries in its stormy wake; finally cross-ing the nine-minute meridian, attaining the length and breathless breakthrough it achieves on *Horses*. For "Land," Patti provided the propulsion of a three-stage rocket to the basic track. When her initial rush of wordplay tailed off, she urged the band on—*Build it! Build it!*—later weaving strands of poetry-in-motion through-out, as Johnny's consciousness pinwheeled through the thousand dances on offer.

There is a narrative arc to *Horses*, a vision called forth in the album's making, enhanced by the presence of Jimi's ghost in Elec-tric Lady, its spectral appearance at the end of "Land," lying *be-tween the sheets* following *a long Fender whine* to *a sweet young thing humping on the parking meter leaning on the parking meter*, returning to the beginning of the record as if asking to be played again. "Elegie," a memorial tribute to Hendrix, with music writ-ten by Allen Lanier, closes the album, the departed remembered and honored, and an acknowledgment of the long line of rock and roll chronology within which we had just somewhat presump-tuously placed ourselves. We had wanted Chet Baker to play a trumpet solo over its coda, but were unable to afford the fee his manager asked from our small budget. Some things are best left to the imagination.

As mixing and final touches to *Horses* spilled over into Octo-ber, we ran out of studio time. The record was due to be released in America on November 10, the passing day of Arthur Rimbaud. I remember waking at two in the morning to head to Electric Lady, working until the next session was due to come in and then trying to catch a few hours' sleep.

On the morning of October 11, we mixed a final version of "Redondo Beach." As dawn broke over lower Manhattan, we walked up the stairs, out of the studio, into the future.

||||||

CBGB HAS BUILT A NEW STAGE, seventeen by seventeen, moved the proscenium to the right side of the room, raised to heart level if you stand in the cleared space before it, equipped with a barrel-chested sound system befitting the club's newfound prominence as a showcase.

The bands rise to the occasion. Hilly decides to take advantage of the sudden swarming around CBGB and stages an Unsigned Band Festival that begins on July 16 and stretches until the first of August, two weeks and three weekends, accompanied by press coverage that is more than willing to be convinced. During the past months journalists have been drawn to the club like fish to a shiny lure, not only local papers like the *Soho Weekly News*, where Danny Fields not-so-coincidentally writes a column extolling the implosion of native fauna, but as far as England, *New Musical Express* and *Melody Maker* sensing some new sustenance for pop's insatiable appetite.

Inevitably a hierarchy develops. The Ramones have been attracting the most attention, as much for their one-dimensional image as their dumbed-down songs, though Television is tipped as the band to watch. Blondie has been energized by the addition of drummer Clem Burke, a crisp and enthusiastic hard-hitter, and the group has been doing demos with Alan Betrock, one of the first journalists to understand the pop implications, as opposed to the high-minded and literary aspirations of CBGB's art wing, of what this assemblage could be, and soon propagandize it in his *New York Rocker* monthly. Blondie is also prescient. One of the songs they test out is "The Disco Song," which, reconfigured as "Heart of Glass" three years later, will symbolize the rapprochment of these two diametrically opposed genres with more in common than they think.

The club is not only attracting outliers, but those who place themselves within venerated tradition. Willy Deville is an old-school sharp dresser, sharkskin suit, slicked-back hair, pencil mustache, and his band Mink Deville hearkens to soul and blues more than anything resembling punk. He is in San Francisco when he hears about the commotion at CBGB and decides to relocate to the Lower East Side, immortalizing it in his songs "Venus of Avenue D" and "Spanish Stroll," produced by Jack Nietzsche in time-honored castanet tradition. Tuff Darts, led by Robert Gordon, are even more of a flashback, parameters ordained by the anthemic "All for the Love of Rock and Roll" and Gordon's impending spearhead of the 1980s rockabilly revival.

This "Conservative Impulse of the New Rock Underground," as James Wolcott captions it in the *Village Voice* reviewing the CBGB festival, seems to find illustration in the accompanying photograph of the Talking Heads on the cover; but aside from their preppy look and Rhode Island School of Design self-awareness, theirs will be a radical maturation. The initial focus might be on "Psycho Killer," David Byrne's jittery impression of agitated mania, but the rhythm section—Chris Frantz on drums and Tina Weymouth on bass—is made of sterner stuff. They listen to Hamilton Bohannon, underpinning the Heads' songs with a solidity that will allow them endless experimentation, as Byrne explores world musics and incorporates them into his increasingly theatrical presentations.

I'm standing outside CBGB with Sire Records president Seymour Stein singing doo-wop classics when he hears the first pealing notes of the Talking Heads' "Love → Building on Fire"—*when my love stands next to your love*—and rushes inside. Stein is the first record company honcho to take note of the CBGB bands, in the mold of his mentor, Syd Nathan, of scrappy independent King Records in Cincinnati, home of artists from Cowboy Copas to James Brown, where Seymour apprenticed when he was eighteen. Nathan had an ear for the bottom-up, and worked distributors like musicians play instruments. Seymour learns from him that he has "shellac in his veins," and that he "belonged in the music business." Stein begins Sire by licensing hits from abroad—their first success is the Dutch import "Hocus Pocus" by Focus—and the label's importance to the scene will be such that his patronage will allow bands to flourish, his interest sparking other labels to take note, offering credibility if not immediate sales. It is Seymour, under the urging of junior producer and talent scout Craig Leon, who signs the Ramones, puts them in Plaza Studio deep in the recesses of Radio City Music Hall for seventeen days in January 1976 with a budget of sixty-four hundred dollars, and thus releases the first album that can be officially subheaded punk.

The festival is also a coming out party for Richard Hell and his new alliance with Johnny Thunders and Jerry Nolan. Television had opened for the Dolls at the Hippodrome Theater in the beginning of March and Hell traded complaints with Thunders and Nolan backstage. They departed their bands at the same time; Johnny saw in Richard a foil and songwriter, someone with a shared interest in hard drugs and dissolute living. Hell's thumping bass braced Thunder's string-swipes, and adding guitarist Walter Lure from the Demons provided necessary collagen. The Heartbreakers would embody the dissipated lifestyle they hailed in song—from "Chinese Rocks," written with Dee Dee Ramone about ditch-digging in one's veins and *shoulda-been-rich* to the joyful nihilistic embrace of "Born to Lose," their career-careen a paean to self-destruction and its fountain-of-youth appeal in rock and roll. This will become evident when they travel to England in 1976 to join the Anarchy Tour with the Sex Pistols, the Clash, and the Damned.

But for Richard it's too much in the opposing direction; he's still a symbolist poet at heart. Television's cerebral leanings have been swapped for the "too brutish" Heartbreakers and a year after leaving Television, he's on his own again. This time he's ready to have it all his way, sealing leadership by using his name frontally, forming the rawboned and spiky Voidoids: Bob Quine stabbing Micky Baker guitar lines in dissonance, Ivan Julian a resilient rhythm guitarist, Marc Bell importing his drumming from Brooklyn heavy-rockers Dust (Bell will continue streamlining his style as he moves into the role of Marky Ramone). They make their album for Sire in 1977, and then Hell tires of being Hell. He wants to return to Richard Meyers, a writer, perhaps a screen actor, who doesn't go on the road, who recognizes its temptations and distractions.

Television bides its time, seasoning their new lineup live and experimenting with how they sound recorded. A few weeks before the festival they come by our practice space and Jay Dee tapes them with his TEAC four-track. Though Lloyd threatens to quit the band when Tom chooses the seven minute "Little Johnny Jewel" to release as a two-part 45 single on Terry Ork's label, it sets them apart from the catechism of faster-louder that is the burgeoning CBGB style. It's almost contemplative. Tom blips his guitar, the band clatters haphazardly, then defiantly as the song emerges into the light. Another Johnny, *just trying to tell a vision*.

Released in August, the eddying guitar solos, crescendos, sly wordplay, and crafty arrangement augurs well for their upcoming album. Verlaine holds out until Elektra agrees to let him produce. Working with engineer Andy Johns, *Marquee Moon*, released in February 1977, is the product of two simmering years, the title track recorded in one live take so long that it fades out on the album because of vinyl's spatial limitation, a climax restored in later editions, of which there would be many. There is no lack of songs to choose from, "See No Evil" and "Friction" (*How does a snake crawl out of its skin*) and the phantom limbs of "Venus De Milo" delivered *jus' the facts ma'am* in the deadpan of a private eye, Verlaine wringing his guitar neck until it releases into the starburst of "Marquee Moon"'s final arpeggiations.

But its very prowess signals the coming of age for a CBGB

generation, as well as Television itself. Lloyd wants to write songs, and Verlaine is ever more intrigued with the filament tubes of the studio. If their first album was a live set on a magical night, the follow-up *Adventure* would prove more aurally expansive, Tom in the forefront, Richard sidelined. They are verging on separation even as they peak in concert—for me, a night at My Father's Place in Roslyn, Long Island, on March 20, 1978, Tom's shivering guitar a needle and thread from the full moon over CBGB, April 25, 1975, when the marquee sheds its light on those forthcoming.

In 1976 Hilly records his summer festival for a double LP that features the upwardly mobile and the also-rans: the Shirts, Mink DeVille, and Tuff Darts among the former, the Laughing Dogs, Manster, and, unfortunately, the Miamis among the latter. If it seems a patchy affair, especially since by now the leading lights of the Bowery have been culled and gifted major label recording contracts, it is a fair representation of what CBGB will offer over the next three decades on any given night, the parade of wannabes, could-bes, the inspired and conspired, a band gathering for one show before breaking up, those embarking on a lifelong allegiance to music, never less than four wild-card attractions a night, sometimes more, whether the room is full or a dozen friends of the band come to urge them on, if nothing else creating a memory when a sacred stage is trod. The acoustic overflow is given performance space next door in CBGB Gallery, and for a few years on the other side of the entrance is a pizza and record emporium. It's quite an empire, the most open-minded rock club in the world for a third of a century, its paw print worn proudly on an allegiant T-shirt, now a theme restaurant in Newark International Airport, where I have a shot and a beer on my way somewhere, listening to the soundtrack of my friends, as bemused as Hilly might be.

Max's Kansas City yins CBGB's yang, or vice versa. Original owner Mickey Ruskin opened a restaurant on nondescript Park Avenue South just north of Union Square in December 1965, and was forced to close his not-in-Kansas-anymore nine years later when the electricity was turned off for nonpayment. Ruskin had an interest in visual artists who in turn liked the fact that they could charge meals and run up a bar tab for work in progress. When Warhol's Factory moved across the Square, Mickey became de facto maître d'. This let-it-happen in the face of chaos is a mark of a great club impresario, something he would share with Krystal, and later, Steve Maas of the Mudd Club. Ruskin was unaware of musicians and watched from afar as the upstairs music venue hosted memorable performances by Alice Cooper, Bruce Springsteen (opened by Bob Marley and the Wailers), the Stooges' infamous "Open Up and Bleed" theater of cruelty where Iggy slashes at his chest with a broken bottle, Waylon Jennings; he even dipped a toe into the New York talent pool with the Dolls. But an ill-timed attempt to expand uptown with Max's Terra Haute, linking the two by shuttle bus, left him stranded somewhere near Des Moines.

Tommy Dean Mills, an inveterate gambler known in every casino from Las Vegas to Cannes, who had previously run a Queens restaurant out near JFK Airport, took over the location and attempted to remake Max's as a Long Island–styled disco the following summer. This was disastrous, and so he brought in booker Peter Crowley from Mother's, a hard rock bar on Route 23 in Wayne, New Jersey, to bookend CBGB. "The first thing I tried to do was steal Hilly's acts," Crowley remembers. By Easter 1976, Max's felt confident enough to go head-to-head with CBGB with their own festival. Wayne County, in "Down at Max's," checks off the many bands, more than enough to go around, and around, and around, like the studio compilation album from 1976 that bears Max's logo, highlighting the Fast, Pere Ubu from Cleveland, the Senders, the Stilettos, Suicide. CBGB has its own theme song, Startoon's "Rockin' on the Bowery," and though the clubs maintain wary codependence, bands easily migrate between the two, as they will for the next five years until Max's once again shutters. It will host its share of Heartbreakers' monthly rent parties, allow the Brats to fantasize about being the "First Rock Star on the Moon," and be a homing beacon for visiting punk role models (Sid Vicious). Even stranger creatures of the night flourish there (Von LMO, Kongress), along with rockabilly savants (Buzz and the Flyers, Levi and the Rockats, the Bloodless Pharoahs with Brian Setzer), legends (Bo Diddley, Link Wray), marriage vows (Sirius Trixon of the Motor City Bad Boys saying "I Do" in 1977), soon-to-be's (B-52s, Devo), and could they ever-be's (Superdude Party and "Gorilla Rock").

The atmosphere of each club is slightly different—Max's with a bridge-and-tunnel vibe, CBGB's *la bohème* scruff—but in reality each needs the other's magnetic pole, regardless of where the bands place themselves conceptually. Representing the "fuck art let's rock" wing are the Dictators, led by the wrestlemania of Handsome Dick Manitoba, their 1975 debut album *Go Girl Crazy* a humoresque template for the lowbrow ethos that will hallmark John Holmstrom's *Punk* magazine, ribald cartoon satire that—like all good caricature—helps adjective and delineate as punk's hegemony becomes law.

The band Suicide will prove the biggest surprise with the partisans. Alan Vega thrives on the dare of confrontation as much as Marty Rev's synthesized keyboards provoke discordance, and the fall of the Mercer forces them to reevaluate how to present their music, notwithstanding the fact that Hilly can't stand them. Marty Thau, who had moved on from the Dolls to attempting to sign Richard Hell to forming his own record label, Red Star, heard the oscilloscope thrumming that underlay Vega's narration of con men, ghosts, miscreants, romantic losers, and the disturbing, strangely soothing industrial hypnosis it could be. Craig Leon took them to a small studio fittingly called Ultimate Sound over a weekend and hard-stereo-ed the pair, leaning on overmodulation and rebounding echo to enhance the trance. Suicide's first album, released in December 1977, not only presages all of synth-pop, demoting the guitar to nonexistence, but their racket predicts No Wave. Theirs is the ultimate question, to be or not to be, and what will be.

Every night is New Year's Eve. As 1976 turns the celestial speedometer, Ivan Kral takes his movie camera into CBGB and points it along the bar. There we all are, me and Jay Dee whooping it up, honking noisemakers like saxophones, a glimpse of Patti, John Cale, Terry Ork, Verlaine and Hell and Blondies and Talking Heads and Ramones, Hilly chatting with Richard Robinson, and those on the edge of memory, the girl with the high cheekbones lighting a cigarette, the dark-haired bartendress, the whole gang and shebang, regardless of where we go from here in this new annum. The togetherness will replicate across the country, dens of iniquity forming a circuit—the Rat in Boston, Madame Wong's and the Masque in Los Angeles, Mabuhay Gardens in San Francisco, Bookie's in Detroit—each neural pathway connective. The bands trade amp settings and dress codes, put their regional spin on the din, and take heart from increasing numbers, the combined strength of a moving part.

||||||

IT'S A RANDOM NIGHT OUT, always will be. Flick a pinball, start somewhere, end up who knows where. Let's say summer of '78, August, no particular date, when New York empties because of the heat, only animals left to roam the Manhattan streets. I'm wandering along Fourth Avenue, stopping at one hangout after another, seventeen blocks to Max's from CBGBs, back again, the trad-rock Gildersleeves at East Fourth along the way to scope groups from the boroughs, see who's playing where, who you know or will know, in the band or not. I have a hit record in hand with Patti, crisscrossed the nation and Europe, and yet I feel I haven't left where I started, the rest of it happening somewhere out there, across the Hudson or the Atlantic. Tonight I'm back where I belong.

The last years have been a wild ride, when we left New York for the world. We took *Horses* on the road and are met in each stopover with an underclass forming bands, awaiting the crack of the starter pistol that will spring them into action. The crowds look around the room at themselves as much as they do us, the *sea of possibility* we espouse, that we've taken up as missionary duty, because it's been gifted to us as well, this flip of the changeling switch.

We always invite local guitarists to join our encore to reclaim the Who's "My Generation." When we play Detroit on March 9, 1976, Arista throws a welcome bash for us at Lafayette Coney Island, renowned for its chili hot dogs and down-market ambience. There I introduce Patti to Fred "Sonic" Smith, once of the MC5. After the show they sit together backstage, dazzled, taken with each other, embarking upon their family-to-be.

In May we head to Europe. Our first touchdown is Copenhagen, Daddy's Dance Hall, where I look out the dressing room window at train tracks from every foreign film I've ever seen, in wonderment at where music appreciation has taken me. At the press conference they ask when the next *Nuggets* is coming out. I'm surprised, not only that *Nuggets* has transited the world, but that we represent the next incarnation of *Nuggets*, whoever and whatever that might be. We play seven shows in seven days. By the time we get to London for a pair of appearances at the Roundhouse, our batteries are running low. No matter. We sing to who will be the Clash, the Sex Pistols, the Slits, Generation X, the Pretenders; the imminence of new.

Where do you go from there? *Radio Ethiopia*, our black sheep second album, is where we fully embrace rock and roll's imperious calling, Jack Douglas as producer urging us to a trio of key changes in "Ask the Angels," building unbearable tension in "Pissin' in a River," shaking sugar packets to simulate alien landing in "Distant Fingers," as we negotiate the live-in-studio *kingdom of zion-lion-ion* that is "Ain't It Strange." Patti wants to venture beyond comprehensibility, pre-Babel. In the title track she slurs her words beyond recognition, action-painting her guitar as language reaches limitation. We record "Radio Ethiopia" in a hurricane at the Record Plant, the eye of which is its coda, "Abyssinia." When the album is released, to much consternation and backlash from those who previously championed us, we react as always, upping the ante. The tours get more feverish, Patti racing across tables in the Bottom Line, glasses shattering in her wake, banned from radio for profanity, monitors shoved offstage as we get more disruptive, testing the limits of control. When Patti falls from a high stage in Tampa in January 1977 during "Ain't It Strange," fracturing her neck, at the moment in the song in which she challenges God to make a move, our forward motion stops long enough to consider consequences.

We are thus disabled when the music we helped seed begins to take over airwaves and underground outcroppings. If the opening of *Horses* asserts personal responsibility, *Easter* renews our vows beyond confrontation. Working with Jimmy Iovine in his first solo flight as producer, we trade obfuscation for clarity. There can be no mistaking our message this time, from the opening "Till Victory" through to "Rock and Roll Nigger," where we reclaim the pejorative and stance it outside society, *nigger no color it is made for the plague,* to the final walk to Easter Sunday church with Arthur Rimbaud and his sister Vitalie, iron bells tolling, *the scarred transfigured child of Cain.*

Iovine is looking for a hit single; of that he makes no apologies, nor do we. I'll be out playing guitar in the recording room, half-consciously cycling a set of chords, when he'll rush out and say keep going, hoping for the grand chorus. But our tastes run more esoteric, as the chords I'm playing turn into the acoustic tribal afterlife of "Ghost Dance," not likely to be played on Top 40, which is still the arbiter of numeric achievement, whether we like it or not (we do). While in the Record Plant we're visited by Bruce Springsteen, working on what will be *Darkness at the Edge of Town* down the hall. Jimmy has engineered for him, and Iovine puts his fast-talking persuasives to good use by asking for a track that seems left by the wayside as Bruce piles up song ideas. Springsteen has already written us a couple of shots in the dark, but they sound like him trying to be us, which is not the point. Jimmy gets Patti a cassette of "Because the Night"; one night she plays it over the phone to me, waiting for Fred to call from Detroit, its chorus undeniable. She writes at the verses until his voice comes over the wire, and by then the song of this night, this love, this eternity, has been aria'd. Bruce's demo had more Latin in the rhythm, a sway to the hips. The Patti Smith Group arrows it forward, Cupid's bow, and it does what is intended, which is to be the song that soundtracks your life.

But we never stray too far from CBGB and its environs. In 1977 when Patti first returns to performance after her fall from grace, neck still immobile and moving gingerly, it is where we begin our physical therapy: *out of traction back in action.* When Hilly takes over the old Anderson Theater as 1977 winds to a close, a remnant of Second Avenue's Yiddish Rialto, he stocks it with the top shelf of CBGB's talent: Talking Heads, the Shirts, and Tuff Darts on December 27, the Dictators and the Dead Boys on the second night, and we have three in hand to pop the cork with Richard Hell, the Erasers, Mars. But there's no heat, the electrical system can't handle more than it could when the great *tummeler* Boris Tomashevsky reached the back rows, and even a capacity of 1,500 proves not enough, the crowd overflowing the aisles. On Patti's birthday Bruce comes to help blow out the candles on the first public performance of "Because the Night," just before the fire marshals arrive to extinguish the show.

And CBGB is the site of our last performance as the Patti Smith Group in New York City, in America. On August 11 we play Central Park's Dr Pepper Music Festival, and then, as we used to, haul our equipment downtown. We are tired, spent from the last four years, Patti's voice ragged, and she is distracted, imagining the start of a new life in Detroit with Fred. *Off we go to the land of love* she rhapsodizes in "Frederick," from an album beginning to seem ever more a farewell, *Wave* goodbye. We record at Bearsville in Woodstock, during a remote winter that buries us in snow. Todd Rundgren is producing, his philosophy laissez-faire. When we decide to record "Seven Ways of Going" live and choose the best performance, he leaves us a lump of hash and tells us to have a good time. He deftly stacks Patti's swirl of vocals in "Frederick," plays bass on "Dancing Barefoot," places the martial cymbal crashes within "Broken Flag." But it is Patti's pilgrimage that is the album's thread, the rueful realization of the Byrds' "So You Want to Be a Rock and Roll Star" with the image of her brother Todd bearing the scars of a bottle attack by the Sex Pistols' Sid Vicious. If the opening words of *Horses* bespeak rebellion, the closure of *Wave*, Patti walking along the shore with Pope John Paul I to the accompaniment of DNV's tidal Moog, signifies rapprochement, that in return for her self-determination she is free to start over.

We finish up the seventies in a soccer stadium in Florence, the only band on the bill, walking through lines of armed security to the stage amid the clamor of riot outside. Rock and roll has been banned from Italy for many years, much like Spain, and our arrival fills the stands to overflowing, by far the biggest audience we have ever confronted. We raise the American flag and they jeer; the pope's words over the loudspeaker are drowned out; we have a conflict of symbolism. But symbols, like dogma, obscure truth, and we all look to the celestial when we play "My Genera-tion" to finale the show, the crowd pressing ever closer, climbing onstage. They are not threatening, in fact, surprisingly, I feel their comfort, their enfolding, their respect for the amplifiers and in-struments, sitting and surrounding us, awaiting their turn as we ascend into the purity of noise.

Begun February 1971 in a small church on New York's Lower East Side, perhaps 150 in attendance. Ending here in front of 70,000. Our movie.

IIIIII

THE GROUPS SEEM TO START over from scratch every five years or so, a regeneration long enough to court and discover an audience too young to know Before, that wants to mark their destiny. Perhaps New York moves more quickly than most, but I doubt it. It's just compressed, new wave no wave now wave. In the early eighties, I watch from the fire escape of my fourth-floor apartment across the street a mutant breed of kids line up in the afternoon for Hardcore Sunday at CB's, taking advantage of Hilly's open-door policy. Teenage Jesus and the Jerks, DNA, the Cramps, the Contortions all deconstruct; Sonic Youth comes to town, picking up where *Radio Ethiopia* leaves off; the Bush Tetras complain about "Too Many Creeps," wonder "Who's Gonna Pay My Rent?" Post-punking. On lazy afternoons I'll walk over and play the Gorf video game by Hilly's desk at the entrance, to see who shows up for sound check, because you never know.

This is only my quadrant of the city. In the 1970s each neigh-borhood of New York City claims its own principality. At first there is little cross-breeding. Up in the South Bronx, Jamaican-born disc jockey Kool Herc-ules spins dual turntables and breaks beats, extending percussives in what he calls "The Merry Go Round," beginning with the opening countdown at 2:21 of the

Incredible Bongo Band's "Apache" that bedrocks the uptown variant of Kingston's vocal "toasting." DJ Grand Wizard Theodore invents scratching when his mom yells at him, slicing and sliding the disc back and forth to create a beat beyond the beat. Those who play records assert primacy, add posses: Grandmaster Flash, the Rock Steady Crew, Afrika Bambaataa. In Hollis, Queens, Darryl McDaniels of Run-DMC is reading comic books, feeling like he can tell graphic stories, too. Hip-hop will be a new way of singing; less melody, more rhyme and rhythm and wordplay. Tongue twisting.

In Spanish Harlem, as all the growing Hispanic enclaves of the boroughs, Latin music has traded mambo for karate boogaloo for salsa. Celia Cruz is the queen, Eddie Palmieri king, Larry Harlow the provocateur, Hector Lavoe the doomed lothario, Fania the label to contend with. At Studio Rivbea, just two blocks away from CBGB at 24 Bond Street, Sam Rivers hosts spillover free jazz from the Tin Palace and Slug's in his ground-floor loft, matched on Greene Street by drummer Rashied Ali's Alley. There is a wing of classically trained experimentalists shrinking and expanding duration and volume—Philip Glass, Rhys Chatham, John Zorn, Glen Branca. Disco is all over rampant, from gay clubs in the West Village and Chelsea like David Mancuso's Loft and Nicky Stavros's Gallery, to outer-borough dance halls with refractive mirrored balls far removed from Manhattan, the Bay Ridge captured in *Saturday Night Fever*, Tony Manero as Vinnie Barbarino as John Travolta. Genres stick to their own turf until ready to merge. It's the New York City of *The Warriors*, a 1979 Walter Hill film in which each gang is garbed like a different music, slipping under the ears of the major labels, a turnstile leap into the tunnels of a subway system reclaimed with graffiti's tag-along, through a cityscape bordering on decay. Hybrids adjoin. *Warriors, come out to play-ay-ay* . . .

We weave our now and move on. Presentiment. An aphorism

comes to us somewhere in Europe in 1976. I write it in a notebook: "The guardians of history are soon rewarded with history themselves."

Repeat and ricochet. It's the last night of CBGB all over again. Guitar in hand, I played its final curtain on October 15, 2006, with Patti and the band, she role-calling a litany of shades no longer here to share the occasion, those departed, those still onstage. A recurring dream. Tonight I'll re-create the ghost of CBGB at the Bowery Electric, on the corner of Bowery and Joey Ramone Place, two minutes up from its old location. The annual Johnny Thunders' Birthday Bash. I'm here every year. He was a good friend, a never-say-die-until-you-do rock and roller, and I miss him.

Strike the chord, sing the song, as Gloria walks through the door.

LONDON
1977

EACH TRIBE IN UNIFORM, SERENADING THE APPROACH of battle. Brits in pith helmets and blood-red tunics, affixing bayonet to rifle; Zulus brandishing shields and spears, bone necklaces, bare chests. "They've got a very good bass section, mind, but no top tenors, that's for sure," says one appreciative Anglo as the opposing Africans sing as they advance, the beleaguered regiment hoisting the Welsh parade-ground anthem "Men of Harlech" in reply. For a brief moment the martial airs come together, triumphant choruses in tandem, and then the 1879 Battle of Rorke's Drift is joined, a concert before the carnage much like the riot that follows the September 1956 showing of *Rock Around the Clock* at the Trocadero cinema in London, or the Anarchy Tour's stopover in Manchester two decades later, the stage awash in broken beer bottles and hurled fruit, a hostile crowd waiting outside chanting, "Get the punks. Kill the bastards."

We're watching *Zulu*—the 1964 movie starring Michael Caine—in the flat of Clash guitarist Mick Jones. He's just given me a pair of d-ringed zippered trousers with leather cuffs that suit my skinny. It goes with the Haile Selassie badge and Ethiopian cross I wear, symbol of a colonial war still being fought a century after, though we're on the side of the indigenous, the shared call to arms that is Bob Marley's "Punky Reggae Party." I have yet to chop my hair, though it's considerably shorter than when I began with Patti, befitting the straddle of musical generations we seem to embrace, as much beholden to the sprawling improvisations of the sixties as the current coif of razored cultural overthrow.

These are war games of musical allegiance. Mods and rockers rush toward each other on the slippery stones of Brighton's beach. Skinheads and punks aggro on the streets. In *Subculture: The Meaning of Style*, Dick Hebdige traces conflicting ideologies as they reveal oblique signals of nuanced dress code, setting apart even as they connote belonging: the signifiers of "mundane objects which have a double meaning." The point of a shoe, a collar's angle, modes of transportation and drugs taken, all are "a form of stigmata, tokens of a self-imposed exile." In the last internecine war, Teddy Boys and their echo-plexed rockabilly fantasies of a distant America faced off against jazz Mod-erns gone Jamaican ska and northern soul, both united in opposition to the mainstream pop charts. Now class conflict—more horizontal than vertical since it pits working yobs against each other—is again garbed for confrontation.

IIIIII

IT'S FITTING THAT THE BRITISH response to the nascent underground in America—inflamed by press coverage in weekly music papers eager to stay one step ahead of the next in line—begins in a clothing shop. Across from a pub called the World's End, a sharp left and then right from the main drag of Carnaby Street's successor as a promenade for youthcult finery and foppery, 430 King's Road is a hole in the wall that would be easy to miss except for its window display. In 1971, shortly after it opened, this would feature the latest, or rather retro-est, Teddy Boy clobber modeled on Edwardian style: long draped jackets, ripple-soled brothel creepers, brocade vests, bolo ties and zoot key chains, along with a jukebox stocked with Eddie Cochran and Billy Fury. "Authentic rock and roll culture," in the words of the orange-haired proprietor. Anything but hippy.

Sylvain Sylvain, spending money earned all winter knitting sweaters, stopped by Let It Rock on summer holiday that year before returning to New York to claim his place within the New York Dolls. He made the acquaintance of the owners, the odd couple of Malcolm McLaren and Vivienne Westwood, and when the two traveled to New York City in August 1973, showing their wares at a hotel boutique exhibition in New York, one of the only visitors to appreciate their sense of stylish was Syl and his bandmates. On display were some of Malcolm and Vivienne's newer creations, girl's blouses seared with cigarette burns, T-shirts cut on the angle, illustrated with murderers and Marxists, part of a "destructive" line they were conceiving called *Too Fast to Live Too Young to Die*. The Dolls played them their just-recorded debut album. "It made me laugh so much," Malcolm remembered to Dolls historian Nina Antonia. "I was actually shocked. I suddenly thought that you can be brilliant at being bad and there were people loving them for it." For Malcolm, it was "better than being bad at being bad, or being good at being good."

His contrarian philosophy—echoed by his friend the photographer Ray Stevenson, who told him to "Observe the trend and do the opposite"—was honed by his embrace of Situationism as provocation and guiding manifesto. Guy Debord's *La Société du Spectacle* (1967) had helped provide philosophical rationale for the Paris students riots of 1968, emphasizing the hollow ring of modern society with its emphasis on appearance and not *being*, the false sense of security that is *having*. To confront this was to create a *situation* in which battle lines were drawn and quartered, though Malcolm, running a clothes emporium that thrived on appearance and *having*, intuited both the disruptive and capitalist opportunities within this construct. He could bank it both ways. Soon he would bring to market Vivienne Westwood's most popular garment, the Anarchy shirt, with its straitjacket clasps, metal zipperings, and silk-screened inverted crucifixion and swastika on cheesecloth muslin; the revolution commodified. "I invented the Sex Pistols to sell trousers, man," he tells Tom Hibbert in 1989, when it all seems so foregone. "And I sold a lot of trousers, hahaha."

But right now he didn't know anything about the music business, and his attachment to rock's ability to antagonize was more visceral than he'd like to admit. He knew that it was over for glam; he could see that on King's Road, where the sectarianism of style had accelerated in rapid turnover, the trending lemmings of fashion past tense. He and Vivienne had fallen in infatuation with the Dolls, and when they came to London in the fall of 1973, promoting their album, playing a show in the Rainbow Room of the department store and vogueish arbiter of the moment, Biba, they attached themselves to the group's entourage. The band continued on to Paris, with Malcolm following them like a groupie, going to dinners at La Coupole where the bill was absconded from, taking their drugs and indulging their whims.

In the winter of 1975, Malcolm came to New York to assume the tangled management of the New York Dolls, who had just gone adrift from their record company and previous handlers. They were severely on the downslide. He thought CBGB a bit too tatty, and booked them on the Upper East Side in a club called the Little Hippodrome. During this time I spend a piece of evening with him at a loft party across from Madison Square. He tells me of the car accident that claimed Eddie Cochran, Gene Vincent plying the taxi driver with drink; and it seems like he's foretelling the future, though he's yet to meet John Ritchie, whom John

Lydon will give the moniker of Sid Vicious, in the spirit of the Rotten to come.

He hangs around the fringes of the rapidly evolving lower Manhattan scene, more observer than participant. The Dolls need a makeover, a fresh start. David Johansen knows his moment is receding, Johnny and Jerry have chimpanzees on their back, and Arthur—whom Malcolm always considered the intellectual one—has more problems than all combined. Only Syl seems to muster the will to keep the band moving forward. The Dolls are too established, "too big" to play CBGB, but they need to start from scratch. They've had their chance, and it hasn't happened. That didn't mean it couldn't happen with new songs, a new look, a new sense of togetherness, the last most elusive of all.

Better red than dead. At the end of February, the Dolls premiere their revamped incarnation, the song "Red Patent Leather" inspiring new plumage, the conceit carried even further by the hammer-and-sickle flag that is their backdrop, the open letter that calls their former management "paper tigers," the communist trappings and red-dyed drink menu. Vivienne has designed the costumes, but it's Malcolm who elevates the surfeit of concept to grandiosity, guaranteed to bewilder and even piss off their followers, packaging ascendant. The muted reception—the Dolls play well, but what is this contrived artifice?—causes them to flee outside the city, down to Florida, where Jerry's mother has a trailer they can stay in while they hone their material. But that's where it all falls apart, fault lines exposed, the end only a formality. In despair, Malcolm and Sylvain take off for New Orleans, drowning their sorrows in indulgence. Malcolm gets VD not once, but twice.

But he's understood the next step. He wants Sylvain to come to London, to form a band with these kids hanging around his shop, starting to scheme a way of "presenting the look of the music and the sound of the clothes." While Sylvain mulls this over, undertaking a lucrative New York Dolls tour of Japan and wondering if Malcolm is to be believed, he does entrust him with his white Les Paul to carry to England, to be waiting there for use when he comes over. He never does, and neither can McLaren convince Richard Hell, whom he's seen at the Little Hippodrome with Television, and who has the same kind of ripped and slashed look that Malcolm, in his fashion prescience, envisions as the next step in assertive youth rebellion.

The band is already at hand. When Malcolm arrives at Heathrow, back from his American adventures, aspiring guitarist Steve Jones and drummer Paul Cook are there to meet him. They've been hanging around what has become SEX—Malcolm and Vivienne's newest shop designation, rhymes with assignation, reveling in humankind's latent desire for forbidden fabric seen through the prism of fetish sex shops. On impulse, Malcolm gives Jones Syl's Gibson with the pinup decals and tells him to learn how to use it. There's another kid working Saturdays at the store, Glen Matlock, humming along with the Rock-Ola. The band needs a front human, and Malcolm isn't sure where he will come from. Only that he knows he can do this.

||||||

LET'S GO DOWN THE PUB for a pint. Glam is strutting and fanning feathers, a bowerbird pitching woo by dangling trash and tinsel in the mating nest, aspiration measured by chart performance and *Top of the Pops* mime. Nineteen seventy-three proffers a bouncy succession of impossible-to-resist teen chorales (mostly written by Mike Chapman and Nicky Chinn: see Suzi Quatro, Mud, the Sweet), in the wake of Bolan and Bowie, Slade, Roxy Music, Roy Wood's Wizzard singing "I Wish It Could Be Christmas Everyday"; pop's regifting.

Dr. Feelgood is back-to-basic-black. Led by Wilko Johnson's lurching chop-shop guitar and Lee Brilleaux's nicotine yap, it's old r&b and songs that sound like old r&b, only faster. Down to earth, beyond glitter; even Bowie has brought his "Starman" back from space, retiring the Spiders from Mars. Pub rock is last orders and the rush to the bar, nothing fancy, no poncing about, just lay it down, spit it out.

The Feelgoods are from Canvey Island, sporting the dour appeal of dockworkers in this floodplain estuary southeast of London. They reset the clock, not much different than the Stones or Pretty Things in r&b fundamentals, the lineage of their handle tracked from Tampa Red's 1962 incarnation as Dr. Feelgood and the Interns, further animated by an obscure Johnny Kidd and the Pirates' 1964 b-side. Wilko doesn't use a pick, his fingers raw and bloody by the end of the night, and the band's intensity has a claustrophobia, as if they're trying to break out of formulation. There is a recognition of the need to switch the dial on the time machine from past to future. Or No Future, as the case may be.

Pub rock and the crammed sweat-stained venues it hot-houses turn the hourglass upside down on Olympian superegos best regarded from an arena's distance, preferably with awe. Shorn of trappings, revealed like the Wizard of Oz, the music can make its way back to Kansas, Technicolor to b&w. Andrew Lauder, a talent-spotting exec at United Artists in Britain, understands this restoration, colonizing his Liberty label with heritage-upholding bands like the Flamin' Groovies and Brinsley Schwartz, transplanting former Quicksilver guitarist John Cipollina into the lineup of Welsh classicists Man, allowing Hawkwind their full solar wind, and signing the Feelgoods. His taste is in the right place, though his American West Coast leanings means he can only transition the coming tremors, ceding pride of place to those more invested in severing continuity.

Britain's bleak-house social cleavage is mirrored in J. G. Ballard's inexorable dystopias of drought or drowning, isolating tower blocks and marooning traffic islands and high-gloss automotives. The sixties' buoyancy after wartime privation and the amputations of colonial empire has run out of excuses. It's not going to get better. There is an end-of-days mood, miners constantly on strike, IRA bombings, the workweek hacked in half, the pound devaluing and even a new currency that seems less British. England fails to qualify for the soccer World Cup in 1974, underdog champion only eight years before, and is cheered on by a new breed of football hooligan bent on disruption, not unlike the gathering punks.

The bands that will follow in Doctor Feelgood's wake like the strip-down, but it's too much retrenchment, the done of before. A new tuning waits in the wings.

|||||

IT'S A HEADLESS BODY, this band that Malcolm imagines will overthrow the established hierarchy, and in truth, their revolutionary potential would be hard to discern in the summer of 1975 as they look for someone to be their singer. The repertoire of Jones-Matlock-Cook is grounded in Small Faces and the Who, notable forebears, though in each case the groups emulated have gone on to grander things. Both splinters of the Small Faces— Steve Marriott's Humble Pie and the rest of the band adding Ron Wood and Rod Stewart to become the Faces—are now comfortable arena headliners, while the Who is more concerned with cinematic epics that blend spiritual discovery with socio-peerage, the 1971 *Who's Next* salvaged from the ruins of Pete Townshend's *Lifehouse* opera, or the Mod pilgrim's progress of *Quadrophenia*.

John Lydon, nineteen years old from Finsbury Park in North London, has decided where he stands. He takes a Pink Floyd

T-shirt (a garment so expressive of allegiance within the rock universe that it will over the next decades come to occupy its own honored space within the live show, the merch stand, revenue-streaming a declarative bit of cloth allowing one to become an honorary member—or not—of a band, and one that Malcolm has turned to his own billboard uses in SEX); and scrawls *I hate* over the band's name. Anti. But Lydon is more than spiteful negativity. His barely controlled fury only goads him further to challenge performance limitations within sound and its effect on an audience. His willfulness, his theatrical cleverness, allows the forming group to spearhead upheaval, not only providing a starting point, but predicating the end, the built-in auto-destruct of Situationism as it meets pop music's uxorious spectacle.

He sidles into SEX in August 1975 with two friends named John, each in the process of constructing alternate identities: Jah Wobble (Wardle) and Sid Vicious (Ritchie). A new name for a new game. Lydon is convinced to sing along with the jukebox, Alice Cooper's "I'm 18," its *I don't know what I want* soon filched for the rousing teen anthem "Anarchy in the UK," audition passed and rehearsals begun in a back room on Denmark Street. His green Hell-like spikey hair and mottled teeth are enough intrigue for McLaren, and now Johnny—as Larry Parnes might have waved his wand—needs a pet name, the time-honored pseudonymic of the English music biz: see Fury, Eager, Wilde, Faith. He will be Rotten, its intimation of decay and disability elaborating his confessed character study of Sir Laurence Olivier in *Richard III*, hunchbacked over the microphone, the caustic insult and piss-take, wielding the contempt of those who have lost patience but not their sense of humor.

Paul Cook and Steve Jones had been trying to get a band together since 1973, playing instruments that Jones pickpocketed from local music shops. They frequented McLaren's establishment and fumbled around with a guitarist named Wally Nightingale until Glen Matlock tried his hand at bass. At about the time Malcolm and Vivienne convert their shop to SEX, McLaren has taken an interest in these local strivers. When he returns to England after the Dolls' debacle, and after Jones tries his hand at singing, they decide Wally doesn't look the part, starting their quest for a lead vocalist.

With CBGB's summer festival and its new breed running rampant through the British music press, a London funhouse mirror is inevitable. Luckily for the nascent Sex Pistols, neither Sylvain or Hell takes up Malcolm's offer, so the United Kingdom can have its own homegrown provocateur. By October 1975 the Sex Pistols have a set list in the making, covering the Modern Lovers' "Roadrunner," the Count Five's "Psychotic Reaction," a slew of Small Faces, Who, and the Kinks' "I'm Not Like Everybody Else." To prove the last, they've started writing their own songs: "Younger Generation," "I Did You No Wrong," "Submission," "We're Pretty Vacant." In guitar overload and chord structure there's not a lot of difference between their inspirations and their aspirations. What will set them apart will be Johnny Rotten's (let's call him that) piercing stare-down, mischievous gift for causing trouble, and ability to clotheshorse the part, an English dandy never out of character despite increasingly bizarre adornments.

In November, on the same week that an album called *Horses* is released in America, the newly named Sex Pistols (as if they're the house band at Malcolm's shop) play their first gigs, tellingly at arts colleges (St. Martin's School of Art on Charing Cross Road, Holborn's Central School of Art & Design) where they might be viewed as much installation as entertainment. Pop art: McLaren, like Warhol, now has his Velvet Underground. Through the winter and spring of 1976 he pop-ups the group in unlikely places—the Xmas Ball of Queen Elizabeth College, the Bucks College of Higher Education Valentine's Dance, the El Paradise strip club in

Soho, a "New Band Night" at the vaunted 100 Club in Oxford Street—attracting an entourage of miscreants who will become Siouxsie Sioux, Steve Severin, Adam Ant, Chrissie Hynde, Howard Devoto and Pete Shelley, Tony James, Peter Perrett, Billy Idol, Vic Godard, band names yet to be announced, camp followers soon to decamp into their own personas.

Over the three months that transpire before Neil Spencer in the February 21, 1976, issue of *NME* warns "Don't look over your shoulder, but the Sex Pistols are coming"—the first paragraph about an "orgy on stage," the next with "chairs arcing gracefully through the air," reviewing the group's appearance at the Marquee Club trashing the equipment of the headline band, Eddie and the Hot Rods, while SEX spokesmodel Jordan removes layers of shiny clothing—the Pistols establish a new wing of British pop, claiming the outskirts. The music has to be abrasive yet irresistible, cut to the bone, impossible to ignore, inviting to those looking for reinvention, and if chaotic and ear-splitting, by the time they play the Nashville in West Kensington on April 3 they've found a sound engineer who is able to carve the wayward frequencies coming offstage. Dave Goodman gives them a full-frontal decibel roar that will set a high bar for how they must come off on record.

The headline band at the Nashville, more a billing formality since the 101ers are themselves just starting out, though they've already recorded a first single, are led by Joe Strummer. Born John Mellors in Ankara, Turkey, where his father was stationed with the diplomatic corps, he devises a stage name by calling himself Woody Strummer, a nod to Woody Guthrie and a nascent sense that music could be turned to social protest and political action. The 101ers publican-rock had been noticed by Ted Carroll's Chiswick label, whose Rock On record shop in Camden is a haven for collectors and classicists, but the group wouldn't last long enough to take "Keys to Your Heart" on the road, though you can hear future Strummer in the hoarsely barked mid-song recitative. Standing in the Nashville watching the Pistols onstage, "Five seconds into their first song I knew we were like yesterday's papers . . . that the future was here somehow." Overcome, he kicked in the monitors when it was his turn with the 101ers, much to Goodman's displeasure. "A cog in the universe shifted there." he told Sean Egan, and immediately set out to find his own constellation. In Julien Temple's campfire cinema-biograph, Joe says that he looked around at the casualties of the sixties as if a war zone, viewing the strewn bodies of dead illusions. He'd come to the battle after it was over, but vowed to fight on.

Another band caught up in the vortex of momentum was on the lookout for just such a committed personality. T-shirt designer Bernard Rhodes had traded Situationist tips and tops with Malcolm—one was sloganed *You're Gonna Wake Up One Morning and Know Which Side of the Bed You've Been Lying On*—and was scouting for his own group to manage. He came upon London SS, yet to play a gig but seemingly cut from the same agitating haberdasher's cloth as the Pistols, meeting guitarist Tony James wearing one of his T-shirts at Dingwall's Dancehall, then introduced to guitarist Mick Jones and yet another guitarist Brian James, and secured them rehearsal space in Paddington to start auditioning a rhythm section. Dissatisfied with Mick's "arty ideas . . . He was into concepts and I just like to get up and play," he told early punk journalist supporter Caroline Coon, Brian subsequently went off with one of the would-be drummers, Chris "Rat Scabies" Millar, to form the Damned. The bass slot went to Paul Simonon, who brought a brooding reggae dub sensibility and a visual artist's paintball style to the band, though he had yet to negotiate four strings. He painstakingly writes the notes alongside his fretboard, and in so doing, shows how immediate and yet a lifetime is the learning of an instrument.

Strummer's hot-wired stage presence proves the missing link between Jones and Simonon. James and yet another potential guitarist, Keith Levene, will soon be gone, with Terry Chimes filling in as drummer (though he's resolutely anti-political) as Rhodes provides inflammatory rhetoric to use as ammunition. Paul monikers them the Clash, and Mick provides melodic verse-and-chorus in the same way Glen Matlock brings a tunefulness to the Pistols' repertoire. Where the bands conceptually split apart is their approach to Britain's cultural conflict. Rotten rhymes Antichrist with *anarchiist*, while the Clash hope to effect change unraveling the system from within. One to destroy, the other rebuild. Can you have it both ways?

Despite their flagship song, "Anarchy in the UK," Sex Pistols music hews to familiar tropes, heavy guitar riffs that owe much to Rory Gallagher and Paul Kossoff, minus solos, the bass pushing eighth notes, drums a-bash, crash cymbals underlining clever rhyme-schemed lyrics over guitar hooks as insinuating as, well, ABBA, from which Matlock transcribes the chorus of "SOS" for one of their first originals, "Pretty Vacant." What sets the group apart is their cheek, baring bottoms, daring the audience to kiss their ass. It may be Lydon who's charged with provocation, though the Pistols won't rise to the top of the heap by posturing and insulting. There's no denying they have the musical assault and tight interlock to back up their attitude.

The Clash take it more seriously, no piss-taking, no abrasive name-calling, no fucking around. They're about solidarity with the estranged, rousing through emulation, earnest to the point where they will become the Only Band That Matters in the dawning 1980s. They flaunt their guitars as weaponry, trying to kickstart a Britain that is like a Triumph Bonneville stuck by the side of the A1, let down by its electrics, oil leaking from a faulty gasket, needing a good wrenching.

But first the American Invasion has to come to town.

||||||

WE LAND IN LONDON ON May 16, 1976, on the way back from
Amsterdam. Seven shows have been scheduled for seven nights
in Europe, kind of like the way Buddy Holly once toured for
the Winter Dance Party. But, hey, we've made it overseas, gonna
be on the *Old Grey Whistle Test*, stopover in Copenhagenparis-
brusselsamsterdam and back to London. In Amsterdam we play
the fabled Paradiso, where they sell hashish upstairs. As I limp
through customs in Heathrow, a Moroccan lump in my boot,
both Ivan Kral and Richard Sohl are pulled from the line to be
strip-searched.

Both shows at the Camden Roundhouse are sold out, and
we're due to play the night we arrive. The tour has been eye-
opening, not only for the level of support from the crowds—two
nights at the Elysée Montmartre in Paris, and an unexpected triumph in Brussels, which will prove a stronghold for us over the
next forty years—but the furor of our arrival to the United Kingdom, where they speak our language. Or, as my father used to
say, a "similar" one. Keith Relf of the Yardbirds dies on the night
of our show; "Land" becomes his elegy, and we feel comfortable
within the tradition of the music that has given us courage over
the years, what is known in America as the English Invasion, and
in England as the United Kingdom taking its rightful place on
the world rock and roll stage. Welcome.

My instinctual remembrance is that we weren't at our best at
the Roundhouse, batteries running low after nonstop shows; but
I'm not sure that's the point of who we were deemed to represent
for those attending. A *sea of possibility*, as Patti would pronounce
in "Land," encouraging a next generation—our record label named
Mer—to *dip in*, a chance to step outside the social register of the
pop universe. *Outside of society*. Where we wanna be.

But we're between generations. We've taken to encore with

the Who's "My Generation," claiming it for our own—*we created it / let's take it over* Patti heralds in Cleveland on January 30—and it seems like insurrection is in the air. On the night after our two shows, supported by the up-and-coming Stranglers, I opt to check reggae mystics Ras Michael and the Sons of Negus at Hammersmith Palais with Chrissie Hynde (seeing both of those names in the same sentence fills me with great joy), and after to catch the Sex Pistols at the 100 Club. It's that kind of night. I come in on the last couple of songs, assaulted by a band that is coarse, brusque, overloud, and argumentative, my kind of group; though I miss the part, as our drummer Jay Dee recalls, where the lead singer sneers "did you go down to the Roundhouse to see the hippies? Horses, horses, *horseshit* . . . !" Guilty as charged. I may be a hippy, proudly so, but that doesn't mean I can't be a punk. We're all miscegenated.

And granted, for a band like ours that resists easy definition, which likes sprawling improvisations as well as manic acceleration, we can only offer belief in the future and emotional support. Our message, as Clinton Heylin writes in *Anarchy in the Year Zero*, is "overtly redemptive—the kids taking things over, not kicking things over." The Ramones are more the blunt and bludgeon, a homogeneous look-see easier to mutate rebellion, headlong momentum and cartoon songs with curt lyrics that sloganeer alienation, boredom, whose speed matches the sulfate rush of Britain's eager acolytes. As a band, they're easy to figure out, to decipher chords and insolence, to emulate in the practice room. When the group touches down in London on American Independence Day for their Roundhouse debut, opening for the Flamin' Groovies (then in their Beatlesque incarnation), sporting a battle-hardened professionalism from their first outside-CBGB tours and debut album, they give the foundling English bands something to shoot for. Or shoot at. At Dingwall's the night after the Roundhouse, Glen Matlock is among those who toss plastic beer glasses toward the group as they go onstage. "Let's see how tough you are," he yells, though it only gets the Pistols further banned from London venues.

By summer 1976 English punk is aware of itself as a crusade. The bands are starting to coalesce, the same faces at the same gigs and the same fistfights, the sorting of who-plays-what. Joe Strummer is given an ultimatum by Rhodes—in or out—but he's bought his one-way ticket. The Clash will play their first gig with Strummer on vocals at the Black Swan in Sheffield, opening for the Pistols on the same night the Ramones startle the Roundhouse. Joining a band, which is like a gang, which is like a family.

Though the Ramones' visit seems to battle-cry an emerging punk spirit in Britain—or, to an equal number of commentators, confirm the counterweight of an authentic English punk beyond the imported self-conscious artiness of the CBGB contingent— the group's visitation merely validates what is already under way in the United Kingdom, combusted by the Sex Pistols' sudden notoriety and the us-versus-them band formations they leave in their wake. On June 4, fully a month before the Ramones' appearance, Lesser Free Trade Hall in Manchester is the site of a northern foray for the Pistols booked by two fans who have read about the group in the *NME* and have made the five-hour trek to London on February 20 to see them at the Buckinghamshire College of Higher Education, opening for Screaming Lord Sutch, himself no stranger to controversial stage antics. Howard "Devoto" Trafford and Pete "Shelley" McNeish are attracted by the comparison of the Pistols to the Stooges, and Rotten's quote in the Spencer review: "We're not into music, we're into chaos." Art-conceptual students themselves, they've toyed with the idea of having their own band, and Shelley especially picked up on the humor of what the Pistols were propositioning. "The comedy part of punk always got lost in the translation," he said later. "It was

Theater of the Absurd in some respects, making a Godawful noise to get a reaction."

They rented Lesser Free Trade Hall—McLaren advanced them the 26-pound fee—and depending on who's counting, attracted anywhere from thirty to a hundred futures-in-the-making: the Fall, Joy Division, Steven Morrissey of the Smiths, television presenter Tony Wilson looking for something "absolutely real" for his *So It Goes* program, aspiring writer Paul Morley, filmmaker Julien Temple, and others who would be the advance guard of a growing audience, the theatrical fifth wall. McLaren, outfitted top-to-toe in black leather, sells tickets at the door. The official tally is twenty-eight paid, but when Bernard Dickens, soon to be Sumner, pays his fifty pence, he observes Malcolm cagily putting half in the till and pocketing the rest.

More important for the gestating Buzzcocks, the gig hardens their resolve to be a proper band. They had made a less-than-convincing debut at Devoto and Shelley's art college on April Fool's Day, but it only revealed how far they had to go to take on the Pistols at their own game. There was no way they would be able to open the visiting Londoners in June as they had hoped, though an important cog was added when (bass) guitarist Steve Diggle came to Lesser Free Trade Hall to meet a prospective band member for his own group, was introduced to Shelley by Malcolm, and ended up joining Pete and Howard in their new venture. By the time the Sex Pistols returned to Manchester on July 20, Buzzcocks were ready, with a clutch of original popish songs and an ethos that would allow them to bypass major record companies six months later, pressing up their own *Spiral Scratch* EP and encouraging a do-it-yourself independent streak in what was beginning to seem less a random grouping of bands than a movement with a mission statement.

The Pistols are well timed for unveiling. With more than forty gigs undertaken and endless rehearsals, they have become a disciplined juggernaut that belies the carping *can't play, moronic vocalist, unmusical, nihilistic* backhanded compliments as sides increasingly opposition. Guitarist Chris Spedding ushers the group into a proper studio in mid-May for an afternoon to try their hand at demos, not understanding why the Pistols were getting such a reputation for musical ineptitude; his first-take versions of "Pretty Vacant," "No Feelings," and "Problems" are straightforward, rockist, and no-fooling-around. They then spend a week in the early part of July recording with Dave Goodman at their rehearsal space on Denmark Street, overloading an old Teac four-track, using claustrophobia to their advantage, bouncing to eight-track to overdub and mix in a proper studio. Used to live performance, Goodman tries to reproduce their volumetric power, thickening textures, adding instruments—a T. Rex-ish rhythm guitar in "Just Me" ("I Wanna Be Me"), a steaming teakettle under "Submission" to simulate the *submarine mission* that is Matlock and Rotten's riposte to Malcolm's request for a bondage anthem; but he faces the same problems as the New York Dolls did transferring the mayhem of live performance to magnetism. "(No) Feelings" could be a Dolls outtake, so close does it hew to a Thunders riff, Johansen vocal range and narrative spiel, and the debt the Pistols owe their New York forebears, though in "New York" they deny all: *You poor little faggot . . . A lookin' for a kiss, kiss this . . .*

The barrage of press attracts major labels, and by October, the Pistols are being warily watched by Polydor and EMI. McLaren employs some of his rag trade bargaining skills, and even though Polydor thinks it has a deal, going as far as to book them into a studio, EMI matches McLaren's asking advance of 40,000 pounds at the last minute. This is not just any major label. EMI is the home of Cliff Richard, the Beatles, Queen. And they want to make good on their investment.

"Anarchy" is the obvious front-runner for a single, but EMI, worried that its lyric will create controversy (is that a problem?), hopes for "Pretty Vacant." Goodman is given his shot, as he deserves, but he overthinks it; or at least that's how it seems in retrospect. Malcolm isn't making it any easier, telling him to push "Anarchy" faster, more aggressive, more . . . well, more. The loping groove that the Pistols found back in July is bashed away, and the song bogs down, too angry for its own good. They work for a week, take after trying take, the group losing heart. When the final burst of noise climaxes the version Goodman hands into EMI, it seems more frustration than escalation. A remix by company A&R rep and aspiring producer Mike Thorne, who would go on to oversee Wire and Soft Cell's worldwide hit, "Tainted Love," clears some of the murk, only to reveal that the song has yet to find its balance.

Chris Thomas is brought in by EMI, a known quantity having engineered for the Beatles on the *White Album* (including the raucous "Birthday") and negotiating the mixing poles of Pink Floyd, producing Roxy Music, John Cale, and Badfinger. He has a defter touch, a musician himself, orchestrating Steve Jones's guitar so it layers and underlines, a top-of-the-bar sweep to announce each power chord (no third), whining feedback in the third verse that tensions release, boosting Rotten's voice in the mix so enunciation can play with the lyrics, spittle their sarcasm and shaming, the vitriol and go-for-the-jugular. Thomas makes it a pop record, sleek and streamlined.

This will prove counterintuitive as the group becomes more adept at what they set out to *destroy*, the final commandment of "Anarchy." Sessions starting on October 17 go quicker this time, a basic track stitched from Take 3 to Take 5. Following the trail of versions to the released, "Anarchy" shows a refinement of purpose worthy of EMI's most stellar act, the Beatles. The song's structure is already set in stone from the time of Goodman's Denmark Street demos, even to interjection (Rotten's *no dogsbody*). But

Jones's solos now pull back into the rhythmic thrust, Matlock's melodic bass line revolves the chords, Cookie cymbals the punch line in each lyric and nails the ruckus to the floor. It is a powerful piece of rock and roll.

With a final remix at Wessex Studios on October 17, "Anarchy" is ready to meet its rabble at the end of November. But neither the Pistols nor the Clash will strike Britain's first blow for this newly be-knighted *punk rock*. On October 22, 1976, the Damned release "New Rose." Brian James and Rat Scabies have put their band together from the shards of another of Malcolm's insurrectionary schemes, Masters of the Backside, intended to showcase American expatriate Chrissie Hynde; and attract a madcap bassist in Ray Burns, who will assume the anything-but nickname of Captain Sensible. They spot the ghoulish visage of singer Dave Vanian at the Nashville in April, and by July 6 make their official debut opening for the Pistols at the 100 Club. McLaren realizes that a movement needs more than one band and bandwagon.

The Damned have their own agenda, taking "sackloads of speed" and not above playing the fool. Even at the blur and seeming cacophony in which they're delivered, James's songs stick in the rib cage. When they travel to Mont-de-Marsan for the First European Punk Festival on August 21, they are the lone standard-bearers of *le punk* in a coach filled with pub rockers. The event is promoted by Marc Zermati, an early convert to the Stooges, MC5, Flamin' Groovies, whom he conduits to Europe via his Open Market Skydog headquarters in Paris. When he can't obtain the records he presses them himself, thus spreading the word if not the royalties. He had wanted to headline Richard Hell (whose new band is not ready) and the Clash (ditto). "I refuse the Sex Pistols," he said at the time. "The Damned were the only punk band there."

Mont-de-Marsan segues pub into punk. Nick Lowe, also on the bill, had been the bass player for Brinsley Schwartz, his agreeable *So It Goes* announcing Jake Riviera and Dave Robinson's new label, Stiff Records, that summer, b/w a full-on "Heart of the City," which showed he wouldn't be intimidated by the Damned's velocity. Stiff was independent, provocatively so, and on the ride back across the Channel Riviera approached the band and fledgling manager Andy Czezowski. James's snappy riffage keeps "New Rose" from outrunning itself; Lowe pumps the rpm's when it goes to disc.

Breaking the speed limit. Now it's a race.

||||||

THERE IS A MOMENT WHEN everyone looks around and sees themselves, who they'll be when the lone *I* becomes *we*. On August 29, swiveling the spotlight from Mont-de-Marsan, McLaren books the Screen on the Green in Islington for a midnight performance by three bands. It's a bank holiday, though he's banking on scandal to impress the record companies, compounding interest. Buzzcocks will open, the Clash—in their third ever gig, their first public appearance in London—are supporting; the Sex Pistols headline.

But the audience steals the show. *Is* the show. With the Bromley Contingent, an entourage that has coalesced around Malcolm's shop and a lesbian club called Louise's, now cheerleading the Pistols like a parallel band themselves (clothes as instruments), they fashion-preview the fall 1976 collection. The new black: Siouxsie (still Suzie) bare-chested, swastika armband and *Clockwork Orange* makeup, with her boyfriend Steven Severin (last name chosen from Sacher-Masoch's *Venus in Furs*); Debbie "Juvenile" Wilson (only fifteen at the time); Soo Catwoman, with raven wings sprouting from her ash-blond crop top; dominatrix Linda Ashby; Philip Salon's flamboy, others like Billy Idol, Brian Berlin, herded by formidable den mother Jordan, SEX's first shopgirl.

Garments are slashed, fastened by safety pin, imaging Christopher Isherwood's *Cabaret* or a Warhol silk screen. Kenneth Anger films are shown as the crowd sidles in, *Kustom Kar Kommandos* and *Scorpio Rising*, shimmers of polished bodywork set to rock's demonic soundtrack. There is even a typeface—Jamie Reid cuts and jumbles newspaper letters as if the promotional flyers were ransom notes and invents a logo, villainy matched by font.

The Clash sport their own spattered look-see, doing it on the cheap since they don't have Malcolm's clothing racks to drape them. Rhodes makes the group paint their practice space and they Pollock their look from there, changing in the alley behind the theater before the show after helping to build the stage. They've hardly left the rehearsal room all summer, a three-guitar lineup at this point, though Mick Jones and Keith Levene will soon spar for control, and the latter won't last much past the Screen gig. He and Mick had met toward the end of 1975, their musical influences quick to conflict. Levene doesn't like verse and choruses, or the band's new song, "White Riot," about the Notting Hill run-amok that pits black youth against police violence on that same bank holiday, and three guitars—including Strummer's thrash—prove unwieldy. Rhodes had arranged a successful press preview for the group in mid-August at their practice room ("the first new group to come along who can really scare the Sex Pistols shitless," says *Sound*'s Giovanni Dadamo), but by all accounts their set at the Screen on the Green is undermined by poor equipment, a sound mix that reserves volume and clarity for the main attraction, and their own unreadiness for a battle of the bands.

The Pistols have nothing to fear at this point. Their audience instigation is backed by hard-won confidence, the cresting wave an acknowledgment that it's high time for something *new*, announced by Goodman's smoke bombs and heightened by Rotten breaking a tooth on the microphone. "It fucking hurts," he bemoans, driving the band into overkill. They begin with a blur of noise, then it's "Anarchy" sounding like the sing-a-long it is. Just like the record it will be.

Let's keep moving. On September 1 the Pistols videotape *So It Goes* for Manchester's Granada TV. Compere Tony Wilson's "literate rock show" is not *Top of the Pops* or the staid *Old Grey Whistle Test*, and after Lesser Free Trade Hall Wilson sees a chance to take his chance; but even he doesn't foresee how the Pistols and McLaren will make sure turmoil underscores "Anarchy," a far cry from the staid afternoon run-through for camera angles. They trash feedback over Wilson's introduction, snarl *get up off your ass*, Rotten's tattered pink jacket and ear piercings ogling the camera, Jordan storm-trooping on the side, mike stand (Matlock) and chair (Jones) kicked over, refusing to stop to let credits roll. They head to Paris before it airs, debuting Vivienne and Malcolm's new bondage look for the couture capital (knees and elbows attached by hobble straps, trousers garnished by "bum flap" and zippered crotch seam) at the Club de Chalet du Lac, to a discotheque crowd alternately outraged by the brandished Third Reich imagery in a Paris that still remembers Occupation, and aware of the power of a good runway look. Two weeks later Paul Cook is confident enough of his no-future to quit his day job as an electrician's mate, plugged into electricity's source, no longer needing to rewire.

The press has taken up punk's cause with a fervor unmatched since, well, glam rock. There is the usual in-house jockeying to angle the narrative, for and against, dogma versus heresy, but who's better suited to tabloid headline, to make the paper first grab on the newsstand? Champions include *Melody Maker*'s Caroline Coon, a former social activist who founded Release in the late 1960s to provide legal recourse to youths caught up in drug offenses, writing in the August 7 issue, "The time is right for an aggressive infusion of life blood into rock . . . the gloriously raucous, uninhibited melee of British Punk Rock"; Jonh Ingham of *Sounds*, first out of the gate after seeing the Pistols at the El Paradise in April, applauds their "quantum leap in ability" and his belief in "chopped and channeled teenagers . . . People sick of nostalgia . . . People wanting forward motion." He is the first to interview the group. "I want people to go out and start something," Johnny tells him, "or else I'm just wasting my time." At *NME*, probably the most influential weekly at this point, combining snarky commentary with cogent analysis, star journalist Charles Shaar Murray comes away from the Screen on the Green performance declaring "Any halfway competent rock and roll pulse-fingerer knows this is The Year of the Punk." Fanzines tell the punter's point of view, Mark Perry's *Sniffin' Glue* soon joined by *Ripped and Torn, White Stuff, Up Yours!*

There are finally enough bands to make a "Festival," though Malcolm abjures notions of Woodstock by calling it a "Special." Spread over two nights at the 100 Club, September 20 and 21, the Sex Pistols headline Monday, with the Clash, Stinky Toys from Paris, and "Suzie" and the Banshees, at this point guitarist Marco Pirroni (Billy Idol dropping out before the show on his way to Generation X), Steve Severin on bass, Sid Vicious on drums. The next night the Damned top, with Buzzcocks, Chris Spedding joining the Vibrators, and Vic Goddard's newly turnstyled Subway Sect. The Banshees intend to desecrate "The Lord's Prayer" until pulled offstage, but it's offstage on the second night that Vicious will steal the show, sow the seed of self-destruct. He's already invented a dance called the pogo, leaping up and down in the crowd to get a better view, *boing boing boing*, the jostle and push begetting the mosh pit. On the second night, he lobs a beer glass at the Damned, shattering it on a pillar, blinding a girl in one eye. Police are called, Sid hauled off to jail. I'll be reminded of this two years later when he attacks Patti's brother Todd at Hurrah's with a broken beer bottle, the glassine splinters of death wish.

On the first night the Pistols get three encores, bidding war begun.

|||||||

IT'S AN OLD-FASHIONED PACKAGE TOUR. From the start it lives up to its hit single, "Anarchy in the UK," released on November 26, a Friday, in a plain black sleeve, selling out its initial pressing of five thousand by the end of the weekend. When the Sex Pistols are asked to last-minute substitute for Queen on Bill Grundy's Thames-televised *Today* (live at 6:15 p.m. on December 1), their ascent to the top of the charts is assured. Steve Jones and Siouxsie's good cop–bad cop routine taunts out Grundy's seedier side—"I always wanted to meet you," Sioux teases. "You dirty fucker," Steve rejoinders, Johnny uncharacteristically sheepish as he mutters his "rude word." By the time the group return from the television studio to rehearsals for the opening show two days later in Norwich, nineteen scheduled dates in just over three weeks, climaxing on Boxing Day at London's Roxy theater, they own the front pages of Britain's Fleet Street scandal sheets.

It boils down to the Clash, the Damned, and from America, Johnny Thunders' Heartbreakers bearing the last will and testament of the New York Dolls. With Richard Hell's departure, manager Leee Black Childers hopes that going to London will improve the group's chances of getting a record deal as well as distance them from their drug suppliers ("Chinese Rocks" is not just poetic license). McLaren had originally hoped to partner with Sire Records and combine forces with the Ramones and Talking Heads, but already the CBGB bands were starting to leapfrog over each other in draw and potential appeal. With two leading British punk outfits, and a third helmed by an iconic guitarist ready to receive his overseas due, Malcolm felt the tour could fill medium-size halls and present a united front; and might've, had not sixteen of the dates been cancelled in moral indignation by local councils, the bands outgrowing solidarity even as they cram onto the tour bus together, the harsh glare of spotlight exaggerating and emboldening defiance, leaving nuance behind.

The Clash have toughened since the 100 Club punk-a-thon, a regimen of live shows, constant rehearsing, and frontline chemistry. Levene's exit hardens their political backbone and speed-shifts tempos, though Jones, with his grounding in bluebeat ska and Mott the Hoople, keeps the chords chipper, giving Strummer a speaker's corner dais to preach Rhodes's theory of class mutation. The songs get to the point—*in love with rock and roll* and *No Elvis, Beatles or Rolling Stones in 1977*, communards of *garageland* and *so bored with the USA*, wanting *a riot of our own*.

There is already a schism between the Damned and the Pistols, and McLaren, despite offering his initial invite, is intent on belittling them, pushing them further down the bill, knowing he doesn't need them after the fanfare of the Grundy show. They last only until the first gig the tour is able to play, in Leeds, and their rancorous departure elevates the Clash and adds Buzzcocks when they get to Manchester. By then the tour has become a shambles, the bands confined to their rooms in hotels to avoid threats and violence, spending money they don't have, and McLaren's frantic calls to EMI to pick up the tab is not helping matters at a record company whose parent conglomerate is more concerned with corporate image and ancillary venture capitalism, in particular its developing CAT scan technology, despite the fact that "Anarchy in the UK" is the most talked-about record in England.

The Pistols seem burdened by their disrepute, Rotten's constant audience-jibing distracting from their inherent power as a band, the pressure of being in the crosshairs of infuriation making them less playful, more caustic, self-protective. The Clash use the Anarchy Tour to show they're ready to cross swords with the Pistols, gaining in forceful confidence as the truncated itinerary continues. The Heartbreakers, having arrived unaware on the morning after the Grundy incident to wonder what insanity they've gotten themselves into, that makes their lives in New York seem low-key, are missing their girlfriends and drug connections back home, wondering what they might do next.

As the Advent calendar winds down, the tour falls apart, the Electric Circus in Manchester surrounded by a mob of jeering brick-tossing louts, the groups fleeing (Paul Cook in the trunk of a car), Caerphilly's Castle Cinema picketed by religious groups decrying "Satan's Children" (good name for a band), even the planned triumphant London homecoming show crossed out. For the tour finale, in Plymouth, a second night added because there is nowhere left to go, the Clash and Pistols and Heartbreakers play for each other to an audience of less than twenty attendees. Matlock remembers it as the best gig of the whole tour, as if they're finally free to just be a band, to simply play music. Back at the hotel they bacchanal: water fights and pool frolics and Steve Jones walking naked out of the elevator until police are called. They arrive back in London on Christmas Eve. Everyone is broke. Joe Strummer has no place to live. The Heartbreakers have to score. The Pistols are due in the recording studio in three days to see if their new demos can placate EMI, one of which salutes the upcoming Silver Jubilee of Elizabeth II, "God Save the Queen." *We mean it maaan* . . .

|||||

ON THE FIRST DAY OF January 1977, the Roxy formally opens in Covent Garden. 41–43 Neal Street is in a decaying warehouse district off Seven Dials, with an upstairs bar and a basement where the stage is set amid cauterized crimson lighting and mirrored walls, the better to see who everyone wants to be. Andy Czezowski has given up managing the Damned, assuming stewardship of Billy

Idol and Tony James's new band, and decides to try his luck at being an impresario by taking over a down-market gay club about to lose its license called Chagueramas (aka Shagarama's) to provide punk with its first venue of its own, "White Riot" coming home to roost.

The area has a seedy reputation as a former red-light district, of bawdy music halls abutting the Royal Opera House, Cockney proudly rhymed, home to a once-thriving fruit and vegetable market shuttered in 1974, in the crosshairs of imminent gentrification. Idol and James had been playing with Gene October's newly formed Chelsea, part of the swirling mass of hopefuls coalescing into respective alliances, and the two split off to become Generation X, theme song to follow ("Your Generation"). On December 14, they are the first band to plant punk's flag on the Roxy stage, followed by the Heartbreakers, who have stayed in London to advantage their infamy from the Anarchy Tour, and a week later by Siouxsie and the Banshees, a long way from their chaotic debut at the 100 Club. By New Year's Day, resolution has become the Roxy; its hundred nights to unfold, in the words of Mick Jones, "the lifespan of punk."

The year arrives with portents of numerological conjunction. Revered in Jamaica as a back-to-Africa prophet, Marcus Garvey's prediction that July 7, 1977 would prove apocalyptic has a hit reggae single in Culture's "Two Sevens Clash." Strummer scrawls 1977 on his shirt, and aspiring filmmaker Julien Temple captures the Clash in a blistering affirmation at the Roxy on New Year's night. A student at the National Film School attracted to Jean Vigo's *Zero for Conduct*, Temple aligns its raffish schoolboys declaring war on their teachers to the scabrous visuals of the new bands, documenting early Sex Pistols and taking his half-inch video Portapak to the Clash's Camden rehearsal space for further cinema verité. The triad of Jones, Strummer, and Simonon (currently auditioning drummers) are self-aware of how a band

should properly present itself, visually as well as politically, positioning back to front for a formal photo shoot, mussing their
hair, distressing shirts spray-painted with Situationist buzzwords
and gleefully watching themselves on-screen for the first time. Joe
talks about pent-up rage and no-hope unemployment even as the
band readies to sign with a major label less than a month later for
an advance of 100,000 pounds.

It's better than being on the dole. The soon-to-be's crowd
up front watching the Clash set the bar, opportune their career,
Shane McGowan leaping, Sid Vicious grinning, Chrissie Hynde,
Glen Matlock (at fractured odds with Johnny Rotten), the pun-
kette with bow tie and sunglasses, and those just here for the
night, which may be the night of their lives.

Until April 23, when the former owner of the club wrests
control back from Czezowski and his partner Sue Carrington, the
Roxy gives home field advantage to a newly tabled punk Premier
League. Band profiles have been hoisted by the Anarchy Tour,
and groups formed in the irradiation of the 100 Club the previous
fall are ready to Variac the blueprint like a voltage transformer,
faster better, slower likely to be left behind.

A week after the Clash—the club is still only booking
Saturdays—the Jam and Wire share the bill. What might seem to
an outside ear a monolithic noise begins to differentiate punk's
linkage with its past and future. The three-piece Jam, despite
shorn hair and scythed chords, are a throwback to mod style,
matching black suits and relying on old r&b favorites ("Little
Queenie," "Heatwave," Lee Dorsey's "Ride Your Pony") while
they gather their own material. "It's not nostalgia," leader Paul
Weller defends to Chas de Whalley in *Sounds.* "I'm too young to
remember what it was like then," though he references the Who's
first album and the Lambretta motor scooter he buys soon after hearing it. They've trimmed their lineup since supporting the
Sex Pistols last October in Dunstable, ditching the piano player,

attracting quick interest from record companies for their accessible *look-back-in* anger, and are snapped up by Polydor's Chris Parry, who failed to land the Pistols first time around. The Jam's introductory single, "In the City," will come out the same week the Roxy ends its run.

Wire are moving forward from punk's rapidly hardening artery, songs cut even closer to the bone, that stop abruptly when out of phrase, cold precision set against punk's heated agitation. They are an indication of how punk might have flourished artistically if the Grundy incident and subsequent tour hysteria hadn't stunted it into catchphrase and caricature, if it had time to grow beyond mere shock value. Wire begins to put the *post-* in punk, which may be arriving sooner than anyone believes here at the Roxy. At the moment they're simply ahead of their time.

Over the next three months, contenders fill in the blanks as they take turns on the Roxy proscenium, curating greatest-hits anthologies to come. The Adverts' "One Chord Wonder" sums up aspirational possibilities, "Bored Teenagers" provides rationale, "Gary Gilmore's Eyes" imagines life on the receiving end of a firing squad. Singer T. V. Smith is lyrically adept, looking through bassist Gaye Advert's smoke-ringed corneas, adding sultry to the mix along with the required velocity and effrontery. They arrive from Devon in the nick, playing at the Roxy nine times during its short run; after the third, Stiff's Jake Rivera signs them to a single, released just after the Roxy folds. Eater, managed by Dave Goodman, out-youths the competition, average age sixteen, with a fourteen-year-old drummer, Dee Generate, once Rat Scabies's student. They aren't political—"What's the point of having political beliefs when we can't even vote," shrugs songwriter Andy Blade—and Goodman lets them Pistol-it-up as the first release on his The Label. The bass line of "Outside View" is propellant enough to reward them with midweek top billing at the Roxy, and "Thinking of the USA" is pretty much what all the English bands are hoping, to challenge the Ramones on their turf. Eater have only one gear, but that's enough for now.

Chelsea's "Right to Work" is labor intensive, Gene October cast as a strident union organizer, though in suggesting the Roxy location to Czezowski he helps create its assembly line. Vic Goddard has Subway Sect, managed by Bernie Rhodes; blurred 8mm video shot by Roxy disc jockey Don Letts shows him uneasily wandering the stage during "Why Don't You Shoot Me" as if trying to defuse rock's tendency to self-parody. *Sniffin' Glue*'s Mark Perry, soon to take the leap and form his own band, Alternative TV, is struck by Subway Sect's "anti-rock" stance, but it's hard to see how Godard can keep a distance when so imbedded in the Roxy milieu. Sham 69 and their frontman Jimmy Pursey unvarnish punk, less art school and more chants from the football terraces, skirting the edge of skinhead on their way to suedehead: "We're Gonna Have a Borstal Breakout." The Boys are romantics at heart ("The First Time" is one of me personal faves), pop within punk, soon to be power-pop. And what more pop than straighter-ahead rock and roll, encouraged by the Heartbreakers, cross-overed by Slaughter and the Dogs and the Stranglers, adapting the new veneer to rockist inclinations? Even Shakin' Stevens stops by on March 12.

Then there are the curious, which are many. Visiting peers of rock royalty pay court, nodding approval, upping their street savvy: Robert Plant, Marc Bolan, and a supportive and passionate voice on BBC Radio 1, disc jockey John Peel. There is no underestimating Peel's contributions to punk's credibility. He is the first to play the Ramones on his influential show ("the intensity was frightening!" he remembered in 1990) despite the Beeb's antagonism, in the same way he provided encouragement for all manner of adventurous exploration over nearly four decades, regardless of genre, from psychedelia when he was on pirate station Radio London in 1967, to non-Western musics, poets, unsigned artists, and all manner of eccentrics. His favorite record: "Teenage Kicks" by the Undertones.

Female-led presence, still an anomaly on a frontal rock stage, inhabits the Roxy with groups that prove bolder than their male counterparts, confounding gender. Unlike the bad-seed Runaways from Los Angeles, they're not selling salacious. *Some people think little girls should be seen and not heard,* yowls mixed-race Poly Styrene of X-Ray Spex in "Oh, Bondage Up Yours" after seeing the Sex Pistols the previous summer, flashing braces on her teeth, desexualizing and reconfiguring, taking aim at consumerism and conventional beauty. They debut on the Roxy stage in March, set apart by saxophone and what writer Vivien Goldman calls "sassitude," though after a Day-Glo album in 1978, *Germfree Adolescents,* and watching Bromley Contingent adherent Tracie O'Keefe cut her wrists in the Roxy bathroom ("Identity"), Poly begins to feel she's traded one form of proscribed restriction for another. By 1980 she's dropped out of music to join the Hare Krishnas.

The Slits take spirited freedom further, drawing on what guitarist Viv Albertine calls the "sexual revolution in a record" of *Horses.* Fourteen-year-old Arianne Forster (rechristened Ari Up as singer) and Paloma Romeo (drummer Palmolive) attend the Roundhouse for Patti's British debut. Joined by bassist Tessa Pollitt, the Slits mark their first-ever at the Roxy on March 26 opening for Siouxsie and the Banshees, not wanting to be "Typical Girls"—*don't create, don't rebel*—from an album they wait two years to make, the madcap dub-a-rama of *Cut.* "Together," Viv remembers to Paul Morley, "we gave each other the confidence to behave like nutters without really worrying about being girls." Or being girlish if they so chose. They move to an unmale rhythm, "skippy and light" as they describe, leading to the roams of reggae, which Roxy disc jockey Don Letts mood-rings between sets, two rebel musics interacting. Ari's accent shifts from her native German to Jamaican, levitating the Slits' levity.

Letts is the go-between between reggae's rasta revolutionaries and punk's insurrection, an unapologetic black man surrounded by white noise. There are hardly any punk discs yet to spin, so he goes deep into his record collection, much as he did when he ran a clothing stall in the basement of Acme Attractions on King's Road, heavy on spatial dub and talk-over, toasters and boasters, Babylon's redemption through the sacrament of ganja and a patois that lilts language, makes it liquid. My kind of *Nuggets*, and I've lately been voyaging into the far reaches of Brooklyn to reconnoiter a music that seems a world away from CBGB, at least until Bad Brains show up in the early eighties.

Don and I trade tapes across the Atlantic, spellbinding under-rhythms that insinuate into the Patti Smith Group's repertoire. "Redondo Beach" skews ska, a backward swipe of chord, but "Ain't It Strange" on *Radio Ethiopia* allows for our take on reggae's *another dimension*, each night a different seduction. We cover Lloyd Parks's "Me a Mafia" and Carl Malcolm's "No Jestering." When we come to the Hammersmith Odeon in November 1976, toaster Tapper Zukie joins us onstage. I'd found his *Man Ah Warrior* in a Shepherd's Bush record stall a few years back, and with Letts as matchmaker, "Tappa" and Patti fire verbal bolts of brimstone, sparring partners. After, we go down to the ICA, where the Clash version Junior Murvin's "Police and Thieves." No doubt which side we're on.

Reggae is in as much a state of fluxus as rock. Militant and spiritual Rastafarianism—complete with distinctive dread style and roots revival—has been ascending over the slanting r&b backbeat that radio-waved across the Caribbean from New Orleans. In 1961, Fats Domino visits Kingston; in 1962, Millie Small's homegrown "My Boy Lollipop" breaks worldwide. There is affection for Sam Cooke, outlawry, *pum-pums* and the duel-in-the-sun of spaghetti westerns. Jamaica exports home-brewed records to England, where there is a large émigré population brought over to help reconstruct the country after World War II, bluebeat ska crossing the color line, taken up by skinheads doing the Moon Stomp. Chris Blackwell of Island Records westernizes Bob Marley and the Wailers just enough to make them accessible to pop radio, and the catchiness of the Ethiopians and Jimmy Cliff imbues *The Harder They Come* soundtrack with the irresistible come-on of crossover. There are dj sound systems using instrumental b-sides to pre-rap, anticipating and evolving hip-hop, and Rock Against Racism proves more than an empty slogan, though music's power to effect change is up for grabs. As a "(White Man) In Hammersmith Palais," Joe Strummer is disappointed there's not more *roots rock rebel* on display, only showbiz as usual. *White youth, black youth / Better find another solution*, he surmises as *rebellion turns to money*, a moral dilemma the Clash will confront more than any of their peers.

‖‖‖

SIOUXSIE AND THE BANSHEES PLAY the last official night, April 23. Their stay at the Roxy has served them well, maturing from deliberate offense to cajoling tunefulness. Siouxsie sings as well as she temptresses, accompanied by steadfast Severin and a succession of guitarists on songs that will be "Hong Kong Garden," "Happy House," the wall-tumbling Jericho of "Israel." Theirs will cast the longest shadow, that ghost-inhabits goth couture, escapes punk's conception, and unfailingly chills my spine.

The Roxy wasn't meant to last. It's too heated a crucible. "It felt like us against the world," remembers Tony James, but the world wants in. The Damned pull the ceiling down during their set in January. A week later the club is robbed after a Stranglers' gig, and again in February. Drugs are openly flourished; toilets are open for assignation. Marc Bolan press-launches the new T. Rex album, *Dandy in the World*, on March 9. American bands like

Jayne County's Queen Elizabeth and Cherry Vanilla, encouraged by Heartbreakers manager Leee Black Childers, add a dash of Warholian Max's. By then, everyone is wanting to be in the same band, to badge the accoutrements of belonging: garbage bags as outerwear, dog collars, skinny ties loosened, leather and leatherette, safety pins and pinbacks, black eyeliner, hair attacked with a scalpel, spitting on performers to show solidarity.

The owner of the premises, Rene Albert, watches as the club becomes a sensation. He thinks it's worth more than 600 pounds a month rental and damages incurred after every show. The irony is that Andrew and Susan don't even take home enough profit to pay their phone bill, carrying "on from gig to gig, surviving hand to mouth," saved from going under by the Damned filling the place once a month. All cash left over from the night goes to the bands, the staff, floating the booze at the bar, the cleanup after. As Roxy publicist Alan Edwards notes, "they were the true spirit of punk." Punk seems to be only the starting point when Andrew and Susan sign a new production contract with Rene, who wants to book other types of bands, splitting the Roxy down the middle for six months, allowing him into their dominion. Rot has already set in. In *NME*, Tony Parsons and Julie Burchill, the paper's attack dogs, call the clientele "resident fascists" and dilettantes, in an atmosphere that turns punk's boredom back on itself. Andrew admits the club is "finished . . . Somebody's got to cash in and it might well be us." But he and Susan are banned from the Roxy, threatened over rent arrears by Albert as April showers to a close. Siouxsie says "If Andrew and Susan aren't here, it ain't the Roxy no more." In solidarity the Damned and Buzzcocks cancel end-of-month shows. Over and out.

Live at the Roxy releases the day after the club's allotment of mortal coil. In late March producer Mike Thorne puts microphones in bathrooms, eavesdrops on random crowd murmur, and magnetizes X-Ray Spex, the Adverts, Eater, Wire, Johnny

Moped, Slaughter and the Dogs, the Unwanted, and Buzzcocks. The sound clatters off the Roxy mirrors, self-aware of imminent capture and mortality, trying to keep one step ahead of the tape machine. It reminds me of the clandestine wire recordings Dean Benedetti made of Charlie Parker on the bandstand playing "Ornithology" in the 1940s, when the music becomes soundtrack to social engaging, the clink of glasses and surrounding hubbub, and you find yourself in the audience for one brief moment of time travel.

IIIIII

THE PRODIGAL READIES TO LEAVE HOME. In Manchester, where Buzzcocks have kindled local aspiration, the Electric Circus takes heed after the Anarchy Tour stopovers twice the previous December, a nesting ground to Warsaw (later Joy Division) and the Fall, two indications of the city's irascible bent. Ironically, Devoto and Shelley subdivide even as "Spiral Scratch" debuts on their own label in January, its homeschooled nature and pared-down production—two notes of alarm-bell guitar solo and Howard's diminuendo of "Boredom" (he's already seen punk's dead end, and will reemerge outside the boundaries with Magazine)—encouraging independent distribution and a do-it-thou-self attitude, infusing record shops like Geoff Travis's Rough Trade with a steady supply of outlier art.

Liverpool has Eric's Club, another basement lair across Mathew Street from the Cavern Club, where those who will be Echo and the Bunnymen, the Teardrop Explodes, Frankie Goes to Hollywood gather to see visiting bands. In Newcastle, Penetration with Pauline Murray inroads the northeast, "Don't Dictate" a warning to themselves as well as a challenge to society.

The Sex Pistols are conspicuous by their absence. Malcolm, wanting to maintain exclusivity, refuses to play the Roxy, finding himself mired in tactical maneuvering after EMI drops the band in the New Year, citing in its press release an inability "to promote this group's records internationally in view of the adverse publicity which has been generated over the last two months." No one is surprised, least of all McLaren, who gets severance pay and is now free to bargain with other suitors, a Situationist construct beyond his wildest dreams. Richard Branson of Virgin makes an offer, but Malcolm wants no part of the label's hippy vibe, and readies to move the Pistols over to A&M.

But it's a different band configuration that stumbles out of a limousine at A&M's headquarters on March 10 after a publicity signing outside Buckingham Palace to accentuate their new single, "God Save the Queen," greeted by an onslaught of point-and-shoot photographers determined to goad them into ill repute. The original group has fallen apart, or at least been dismembered. The ongoing conflict between Glen Matlock and Johnny Rotten knifes through their adeptness as a songwriting duo, diametric forces that gift their band songcraft. Matlock hooks and melodizes Rotten's invectives, but Johnny thinks their appeal is too close to the Bay City Rollers, on opposing sides of the pop divide. Not that there is that much of a difference. In the always astute words of David Dalton, "With the infusion of Lydon's petulance and narcissism, the Sex Pistols became what the Bay City Rollers pretended to be: a teenage band. The Bay City Rollers were a record company's idea of a teenage band (bubblegum rock). The Sex Pistols were the real thing, charged with sullen, snarling, angsty confusion."

It's been on the boil for a long time. Matlock and Rotten come to blows at the 100 Club one night. He's a "Mummy's boy," according to John; Lydon is his "mum's golden boy," according to Glen. They're still taunting each other in the schoolyard. John doesn't like Glen rooming with Mick Jones on the Anarchy Tour, hanging out with Buzzcocks, suspicious of muso leanings, and

Matlock does harbor them. He likes the Beatles, thinks about harmony and not only within arrangement. Glen's idea of a group is "four guys working together," but the Sex Pistols are founded on Malcolm's dictum of "Cultivated hatred is your greatest asset." It's only a matter of time before they turn that hostility on themselves.

Matlock picks the short straw when they venture to Amsterdam's Paradiso in early January, the band leave-taking Heathrow with enough "rumpus" to alert the press: *shock revolted vomited spat*, shrieks the *Evening News*. As for Jones and Cook, they keep the motor running, content to stay in the engine room. Glen settles for a secondhand metallic blue Sunbeam Alpine, three thousand pounds, and interest from EMI, who will sign the Rich Kids, his new band.

If Matlock's replacement seems typecast punk, it's unsurprising since he invented the prototype. Sid Vicious starts practicing with the Pistols in early February; three weeks later it's official. He'll be Johnny's mate in the band, offsetting the tag team of Jones and Cook, but he has his own agenda. Being Sid. "From the moment Sid joined the band, nothing was ever normal again," grumbled Steve in his autobiography, *Lonely Boy*, truth-telling by degrees, as if anything was normal in the Pistols. They have to adjust to Sid, not the other way around, his rudimentary bass playing, his affinity for violence, his throwdown of how far you can go. He's the true spawn of the devil-may-care. He doesn't give a shit.

Sid is in the hospital weeks after he joins the Pistols, ill with hepatitis, and on the album Steve Jones plays all his parts. Vicious has schooled himself with Ramones records until the doubled-up thrum is his only rhythm. Jones is the backbone of the Pistols, a textured guitarist only too happy to over-and-overdub, his riffage larger than life, spread across the stereo spectrum. When I see him at the Sex Pistols *Filthy Lucre* reunion in 1996—we're only in it for the money, and why not?—shirtless, his butt hanging out of his pants, unreformed, he seems quite chuffed to be who he is, the guy who underpinned the juggernaut that is the Sex Pistols, thence and future history. Jones's chordings doubled an octave lower on bass are key to the Sex Pistols' propulsion, and Cook cracks the whip of the snare behind him. Their guitar 'n' drum duality presages the minimalism of the White Stripes or the Black Keys.

Sid has been searching for ways to make his grand entrance, what with whom, though he'll take it as far as it goes regardless of the instrument he'll play. He's a drummer for a moment, then part of the Flowers of Romance with Keith Levene and Viv Albertine, then tries his honk as a saxophonist, but he has no attention span. Things are moving too fast. He's got the look, porcupine hair and sneer, chain around his neck, the trigger-finger confrontation looking for a fight or to start one. The past June he had been goaded by Rotten—and attacked—journalist Nick Kent. Right after he joins the Pistols he threatens *Old Grey Whistle Test* compere Bob Harris with a beer glass at the Speakeasy, the same month that New York groupie Nancy Spungen fixes her claws into his motorcycle jacket and introduces him to heroin. The bass is just a pulse to whatever comes next. Ask Dee Dee.

It's every obsessive's dream, to become a cog in the object of idolatry. It helps that he's John's protégé, an *It's alive!* manifestation of Mary Shelley's Modern Prometheus. Jones feels he's been demoted to third fiddle. Given Sid's proclivity for setting the bar, attracting mayhem and distraction, maybe Lydon has been shunted aside as well, the sideshow of the Sid show. "God Save the Queen" is indisputably on its way to being a hit record, even if A&M—after the band has dribbled blood in their offices postsigning ceremony, Vicious shedding his first corpuscles as a Pistol trying to kick in a toilet and injuring his foot—has destroyed its pressed copies, given the group 75,000 go-away pounds. Now Virgin—the signatory of a peace treaty between hippie and punk because Malcolm has no choice if he wants to have a record out for the Jubilee—has become the beneficiary of this commemorative souvenir pluperfect for the queen's salvation. When the Pistols and Malcolm and their inner circle take a promotional cruise on the Thames to serenade Her Majesty that June, the record starting its ascent in the charts, everyone gets what they want. Arrests, agitation, attention. Nobody does hard time; they all know what role they play in the psychic payola of the music business.

The studio album that documents the Pistols, *Never Mind the Bollocks*, released in the autumn, achieves all the group might've hoped and no more. It's on-point execution, rife with cynicism, witty wordplays, and lusty sing-a-longing, is power-tube perfection—compressed by engineer Bill Price—that leaves no room for growth; anything else will be variations. Nothing slows Johnny's spew, and he's beginning to feel the need for some space. He plays dub reggae on radio, namechecks Neil Young and Can's Damo Suzuki. Already eyeing the movies, Malcolm would like nothing better than the group be gone before his chicanery is revealed, that the last thing he wants to manage is a rock band that *needs to get to sound check*, that is already a Greatest Hits.

Sid will fuse the bomb. Time for America.

||||||

WE'RE OFF THE ROAD IN early 1977 while Patti rehabilitates her way back from neck injury, observing from afar how planted seeds grow wild. Los Angeles: Weirdos, Zeros, Germs, Fear, Flesh Eaters, Screamers. Portland: Wipers, Ice-9, Neo Boys. San Francisco: Avengers, Crime, Nuns, Dead Kennedys. Boston: Willie Loco, DMZ, Real Kids. Each with its dungeon. The Rat, Madame Wong's or the Masque, Mabuhay Gardens, Bookie's: match the venue with the town. Minneapolis has the Suicide Commandos; Cleveland the Dead Boys. Punk rock will be a life-or-death affair, as will be gruesomely enacted. Anyone left out, band or fan, is name-checked in the pages of *Rock Scene*, a magazine I help edit eight times a year with Richard and Lisa Robinson, which features—among overtly candid backstage footage and photos ("over 200!") that anticipate the social selfie, a column called More New Bands, of which there are a torrent. The look replicates the jagged sound, which in turn creates an underclass connecting the dots of the disaffected, "the alternative to the alternatives," as Richard describes.

The working-class political affectation of Brit punk translates nihilistically the farther west it travels. In such hot spots as Orange County in Southern California, a club called the Cuckoo's Nest accelerates the relatively harmless pogo into the mosh pit slam-dance, the tribal initiation of hardcore. The veneer of pop is stripped from punk. The bands now formulating, Adolescents and Black Flag and Minutemen and T.S.O.L. (True Sons of Liberty), care more about the cyclotronic uplift of rage and tirade, inciting carnage and stage-diving.

The Sex Pistols will end their upcoming US tour in *California über alles*, in the titular of the Dead Kennedys, but they're already outgunned. They've only played a handful of gigs since the release of *Bollocks*, and McLaren, in a movie I'd love to screen, has been interacting with director Russ Meyers (*Vixen, Beyond the Valley of the Dolls*) on an unrealized biopic of the band (it will eventually pass to Julien Temple to direct *The Great Rock and Roll Swindle*, by then postdated). The Damned have already advanced this particular English Invasion (the Dave Clark Five to the Clash's Rolling Stones), but America awaits the Beatlefication of the Pistols, newly signed to Warner Bros. in the United States, tour to start on January 8, 1978. Malcolm has no intention of a traditional capital city swing, palming the promotion machine. He routes the itinerary through the South, locales where the idea of punk is hearsay and heresy, first stop Atlanta, and then to cowboy country.

The spokesmodel is Sid. He's the one who gets the camera angles, invites the bloody nose, the thrown bottle, the after-show melee. At Randy's Rodeo in San Antonio, he hits a heckler with his bass, which he not so much plays as poses, the running gamut of *attitude*; in Dallas, dope-sick at the Longhorn Ballroom, he chisels "Gimme a fix" on his scrawny chest; at Cain's Ballroom in Tulsa, a western swing station-of-the-cross reliquaried with posters of Bob Wills and Hank Penny, he lurches about the stage, oblivious to the song surrounding him. He thinks he's the only Sex Pistol living up to the founding principle, anarchy unleashed, the ur-zombie. Lydon calls him a "living circus" but he won't be for long.

The finale will transpire at San Francisco's Winterland on January 14, a 5,000-capacity hall run by Bill Graham in the heart of the hippie mecca, the largest audience the Pistols have yet confronted, their face-off with the Summer of Love. Jonesy and Cook are in for the beer and birds, Rotten and McClaren are estranged, staying in separate hotels, and the audience slavers to see what Sid will do next. The show is desultory when it's not vengeful, virtually the same set list that they've been hawking for the past year, beginning with "God Save the Queen," ending with "Anarchy," just like a proper band. They encore with a shambling version of the Stooges' "No Fun," Iggy's prophecy come true without the Stoogeling's ability to have fun no matter what, and still does.

They keep those two chords churning, an endless drone of I to IV, no release, losing heart and steam, falling out of time; knowing it could have been their time. "Oh bollocks, why should I go on?" Johnny says, squatting onstage, breaking character. Even stalwart Jones stops playing mid-song, realizing this has come to a standstill. Negative fun lurches toward anticlimax, Rotten declaiming his famous last words as a Pistol, now epigraphed along with other *one giant leap for mankind* declarations. *Ever get the feeling you've been cheated? Good night!* It's thought he's directing it at the rabid audience, but no, it's him he rues. He looks over at Sid with a mixture of sadness and horror. He's known his old friend since he was John Ritchie, watching painfully as he self-immolates. This was not the way it was supposed to turn out. But Rotten can't be surprised. In Leeds at the start of the Anarchy Tour only a year ago, his black necktie needled with safety pins, Johnny baited the hostile crowd. *Ever felt like you've been conned? I 'ope you 'ate it.* Now the mirror catches his own hunched-over boredom, the ultimate mockery of their promise, "No Fun" the encore then as well.

Did they have a choice? Could this karmanic *rise-and-fall* be given new life? Rotten thinks so, and after the show tries to keep Jonesy and Cook aboard and fire Malcolm. But Steve remembers when McLaren gave him a place to live, practice, become the lo-comotion of the Pistols, and he's taken with the thought of go-ing with Malcolm to Rio de Janeiro to meet train robber Ronnie Biggs and lark about, leaving behind a band that has no business being together except business. He turns Johnny down, some-thing he too will regret. The Sex Pistols R.I.P. Rock in peace.

Across the continent, at the Record Plant off Times Square in New York City, the Patti Smith Group are putting finishing touches on *Easter*, an album that signals a comeback from Patti's injury and enforced absence from the road. It's been good for us as a band to have breathing space to write songs, play our home-town, test Patti's endurance, and gather energies for a declaration of principle, no room for misconstrue. In the few days it takes for news of the Sex Pistols' breakup to make its way east, we mix "I'm Set Free" from the movie *Privilege*, the *we shall live again* tribal afterlife of "Ghost Dance," the waiting-for-Godard "Till Victory," the outsider society of "Rock and Roll Nigger," the hit single of "Because the Night." We believe in rock and roll's re-demptive power, its transformation, not its dead end.

The Pistols cleave like split atoms. John (no *ny*) will be Lydon

again, in Public Image Ltd., with his old pals Jah Wobble and
Keith Levene, chanting *Anger is an energy* like a self-help mantra.
Cooky and Jonesy move to Los Angeles. Sid—well, do we need
to hear the gore of his and Nancy's demise again? Gun in hand,
he swan-songs "My Way" in Malcolm's cinematic *his way* retelling
of the Pistols' mythos, *The Great Rock and Roll Swindle*, mowing
down the audience. Vicious should know, because he's the primal Pistols audience, their greatest fan, their suicide. (The group
is quite well documented: another film, *The Filth and the Fury*
[2000], this one witness for the prosecution, will also be directed
by Temple.) McLaren's zany future projects—Bow Wow Wow's
underageous "C30 C60 C90," his "Buffalo Gals" mash-up of
square dance and break dance, a synthed *Madame Butterfly*—are
realized and undermined by the excellence of their soundtracks.
The Sex Pistols turn out to be too good. Bow Wow Wow's version
of the Strangeloves' "I Want Candy" can fill any dance floor at
3 a.m. And *Buffalo Gals go round the outside, round the outside* . . .

||||||

NOW WE'RE TALKING MUSIC BUSINESS.

Unholy assimilation is not for the faint-hearted. The Clash
believe they can beat America at its own game. Their debut album
is so raw that the US wing of Columbia refuses to release it, but
the band takes on the challenge of the recording studio, to hear
what they sound like getting better, bigger, following inclination. Over the next years, in albums like the double-LP *London
Calling* and the triple *Sandinista!*, they sprawl over styles, vora-
ciously Clash-ifying reggae and rockabilly and garage and beatbox
and their beloved punk. Strummer's lyrical volubility thrives amid
Jones's delves into genre, Simonon's fourth gear, and drummer
Topper Headon's pop-the-clutch, laced wheels skidding around
corners.

The chosen producer for their second album, *Give 'Em Enough Rope*, is Sandy Pearlman, a rock theorist specializing in arcane recording gear. He provides a bridge to Columbia, for whom he has co-directed Blue Öyster Cult over five albums into the thinking-person's metal band of "Don't Fear the Reaper," and understands the Clash's need for authenticity, idealism, to make a breakthrough on American radio. Their manager will not like this direction, but Bernie will be gone within the year, as the Clash constantly reconcile and implant agit-prop within their increasing pop sheen, which gives us "Rock the Casbah," "Should I Stay or Should I Go," the joyous chortle of "London Calling."

Many are listening, taking notes. If punk rock is too monotheistic for mainstream America, it's also too confining for the new wavery under way. Punk's main sound effect is to sharpen rhythm and chordings, Elvis Costello and Talking Heads and Devo, until the Knack's "My Sharona" keynotes an angularity that takes it to number one for six weeks in 1979. Power pop. That's what it's come to, always knew it would, and not un-fun. Ask Greg Shaw. Or New Wave, as Sire Records and the press capitalize the gestating styles, which are distracted and then enchanted by the accessibility of inexpensive synthesizer technology, portability and mimicry and ease of operation.

The Clash will be the last punk band standing, to stay righteous, principled, true to who they've willed themselves to be—"A place where the reality, and the art, and the entertainment can all meet," Mick explains to Paul Rambali—and to their fans. There's so many of them now, shutting down Times Square when the group takes over Bond's International Casino for seventeen shows in 1981, or when they look out at the vista of Shea Stadium in October 1982, opening for the Who, torch tossed and them not sure whether to grasp or knock it away. *You have the right not to be killed*, Joe fingerprints in "Know Your Rights," full throttle, from 1982's *Combat Rock*, though by then they're turning on themselves. When Rhodes returns to reassert the group's punk credentials, they'll be a Clash Mk. 2 without Jones, who takes his cut-ups and samplers and sliced chords to Big Audio Dynamite. He and Joe don't share a stage again until a benefit for striking firemen in London's Acton Hall, November 2002. Old mates still looking for a white riot. A month later, Joe gazes into the white light. No reunion.

I get to see him the spring before, in April, at an old warehouse under the Brooklyn Bridge, *by the river*, with his then-group the Mescalaros. It's a five-night stand, Joe noble throughout, *nouveau* and old standards, pushing his young band to step on it, and keep steppin'. After, I go back to say hello. Still here. A hug and a vet's shared nod. He's been at Glastonbury the past few summers, conducting a primeval campfire, flickers of bottles passed around, tales told, battle scars covered by tattoos, new songs coalescing from the clamor of a surrounding festival, several stages at once, all musics in a blur. Joe leans back, dials in a sound from somewhere in the world.

Radio Clash is on the air.

||||||

IN 1979 ROCK DISCO DEMILITARIZES the zone between two once-antagonistic rivals. Generation X's "Dancing with Myself," featuring Billy Idol (of the Bromley Contingent), links punk that grew out of SEX and the sleek 1980s. MTV, successor to Scopitone, needs stars who look good on a Sony Trinitron. New Romantics like Spandau Ballet and Duran Duran dress up the tatters, contrasting the grit that preceded them. Nobody's a mess. Synthetic instruments make their textures known, elbowing guitars aside, algorithms on the rise.

Punk doesn't go away. Hardcore. Now there's a story for another campfire . . .

LOS ANGELES
1984

NORWAY
1993

AH, METAL. HOW DO I LOVE THEE? LET ME COUNT THE ways, thrash to hyperspeed, symphonic to grindcore, allowed to louder. The ultimate rock.

Don't forget power ballads.

Like punk's metamorphosis, there is a New Wave of British heavy metal (NWOBHM) as the eighties ascend, transfusing molten slag from forebears like Black Sabbath, Budgie, Judas Priest, Motörhead. Iron Maiden's zombified Eddie lurches to life, piling on the horror show of predecessors Alice Cooper and KISS, scaled to the gargantuan.

Heaviosity as a concept begins to be applied musical science as the sixties multiply amplitude and speaker cabinets to match. William Burroughs catches the phrase in his 1962 novel *The Soft Machine*—"Uranium Willy, the Heavy Metal Kid"—and takes it a step further two years later in *Nova Express* when his Insect People of Minraud play "metal music." In 1967, an English psychedelic album by poster artists Hapshash and the Coloured Coat features the "Human Host and the Heavy Metal Kids." Steppenwolf calls forth *heavy metal thunder* in "Born to Be Wild." Sandy Pearlman applies Burroughsian logic to the table of elements when he describes the Byrds' "aluminum style of context and effect" in a 1968 issue of *Crawdaddy,* and puts theory into motion when he steers a light-progressive biker band from Long Island called Stalk-Forrest into the astronomy-of-stars that is Blue Öyster Cult, emphasis on the umlauts. There is irony in the *Saturday Night Live* sketch when Christopher Walken, standing in for Pearlman in the studio, requires ever "more cowbell," its metallic clank underpinning BOC's unlikely 1975 hit single "Don't Fear the Reaper."

Blue Cheer is the first American heavy band, whetting the appetite with their transmutation of Eddie Cochran's "Summertime Blues," disaffection as a creed. By the time Iron Butterfly releases *Heavy* in the first month of 1968, the term has genrefied. Led Zeppelin, Humble Pie, Deep Purple are weighted together, and what they have in common is no-nonsense volume, guitar pyrotechnique, impassioned lead singers, and a general lack of appreciation from the intelligentsia of the rock press, who scathe in condemnation, inversely proportioning a loyal fan base that seems oblivious to being looked down upon. In fact, the fans like alienation, because it mirrors the no-future promised by the Stooges, another forerunner.

I first witness the American response to British proto-metal at a Canned Heat concert in New Jersey in 1971. Opening is Grand Funk Railroad, a brainchild of Terry Knight, ex-leader of the Pack turned manager, who wants his band to arouse the feral in their audience. Like many too-cool-for-school rock writers, I find it histrionic, off-putting, here today and gone tomorrow. I'm so wrong. Two years later I stand outside Madison Square Garden collecting quotes for *Rolling Stone* from the capacity crowd as they enter, like the sound-bite film *Heavy Metal Parking Lot* will a decade and a half later at a Capital Centre Judas Priest concert in Washington, D.C. The answers and allegiance are the same, as always when acolytes gather to rejoice in the metal ethos of obliteration and rebirth.

It is hardly simplistic music, though its force-field would suggest otherwise. Metal bands draw on mythos—whether hard partying, *yeah*, or deities dueling on Olympus—and technical craft. It requires concentrated discipline and physical endurance to play, to achieve levitation in the overtones of distortion, vocal or guitar or drums, and do it with split-screen precision. From a pariah music, gleefully so, it has translated across continents and pop charts, racking up the truest of heavy metals: platinum many times over.

Metal's mass appeal invites academic incision, each power chord scoped for socioeconomic, literary, and folk allusion, a sliding scale of interpretation blown to bits when confronted with the beast itself. Letting the music rattle your bones, guitar solo skydiving, eyes seared by lasers and flaunt, one bows from the neck, back and forth, ever faster until escape velocity is achieved, hair flaying, abandon losing. Alchemical.

||||||

THERE ARE PARALLEL WORLDS IN Southern California as the eighties begin. Los Angeles's punk contingent gets the attention, but a new look is coming to town. Its flamboyant roots are two seventies bands once under the imprint of the same management firm, Leber-Krebs. The New York Dolls have the glam and the cross-dress artifice, but Boston's Aerosmith construct honed songs, isn't afraid of production, and will hold off becoming dissolute until they've made it.

Toys in the Attic is their third album, and for most long-lived bands, it's the make-or-break charm. Ensemble playing has tight-ened with road work, initial creativities and influences explored, the blank slate beckons. There is an understanding of the studio as its own process, and producer Jack Douglas walks-this-way with a confident Aerosmith in early 1975 at New York's Record Plant, sixteen tracks to catch the ear, mix, compress. Guitarist Joe Perry hammers and nails riffs, singer Steven Tyler scarves and screams. Dream on.

Exhibitionist lead singer, stolid rhythm section, virtuoso lead guitarist. Build your own band. Van Halen is two émigré brothers from Holland—Alex on drums and Eddie guitaring—adding a bass player when Michael Anthony loans them his PA. David Lee Roth, whose uncle Manny runs the venerable Café Wha in Greenwich Village, steps out front as ringmaster. Eddie's "Eruption," from Van Halen's debut album in 1978, is magmatic in raising the barre for what is possible to be wrung out of six strings. In one minute and twenty-seven seconds, breaking the sound barrier for most notes per bpm (he frequently dazzles in the mid-200s), throwing in a good-measure quote from Rodolphe Kreutzer's second *Caprice étude* for violin, his two-handed fretboard tapping, wrenching harmonics, and kamikaze-diving *whang bar* transform the electric guitar as other tectonics: Les Paul, Jimi Hendrix, the Casters Tele and Strato of Leo Fender, the holy trinities of Moore-Burlison-Gallup, Clapton-Beck-Page, Ramone-Verlaine-Quine, or yourself the first time you play a chord on the instrument (mine was a G).

They join the hordes of bands, trading members like sports franchises—those who will be Quiet Riot, Dokken, Sister, London, Ratt, Mötley Crüe—circling between the Starwood on Santa Monica to Sunset Strip, where a hundred-yard dash from the Roxy and the Rainbow takes you to Gazzarri's, Van Halen onstage nightly, a glitteratti parade that dresses—or undresses—for rock-and-stroll. By 2 a.m., when the bars close, the Strip resembles an underage red-light district, all sexes on display, drugs and backstage access better barter than cash.

Before its closing in 1975, the hedonistic open-door policy of Rodney Bingenheimer's English Disco at 7561 makes it the watering hole of choice for Brit sybarites on California tour. Rodney, once stunt double to Monkee Davy Jones, is a tireless fan and enabler, under the spell of David Bowie, and the dance floor preens when Sweet or T. Rex or Bowie's "Rebel Rebel" reflects its mirrored walls. Led Zeppelin most famously court-and-spark there, and a teen magazine, *Star*, which lasts for five issues in 1973 before the publisher realizes what is going on, is dedicated to giving "Star Girls" pointers on how to seduce the rock god of their choice. Everything is "Foxy," *o* to *u*. Fashion tips: Queenie arrives with "grey-black fishnet stockings, the real short satin hot pants with the Lurex top, and six-inch silver wedgie platforms." Sable Starr says "you have to be flashy, sometimes even sleazy looking," and if another girl tries to outfox you, throw a gin gimlet in her face. Like fishing lures, the celebutantes of Rodney's hook their prey: Lori Maddox lands Jimmy Page, Sable wins Johnny Thunders; Michael Des Barres, whose Silverhead comes over from England and never leaves, finds himself adrift in a sea of trolling nubiles, most of whom still live with their parents. To be a groupie is considered aspirational, though a page after Sable preens about "my looks and the way I dress . . . that's our power," there is graphic short fiction titled "Chain Gang High School," a cautionary script awaiting development.

A *Rolling Stone* feature story in 1969 romanticizes and whambams the phenomenon, interviewing those Michelangelos of late sixties rock members, the Plaster Casters, and the GTOs (Girls Together Outrageously), a band Frank Zappa has assembled from the local groupie population, much as the Spice Girls will be constructed from type a quarter century later. Miss Christine is the waifish Victorian, Miss Sandra the pregnant earth mother, Miss

Cinderella awaits the glass slipper from John Cale, and Miss Pamela will marry Michael and become Des Barres, engagement announced over the loudspeaker at Rodney's, penning *I'm with the Band*, a memoir whose title reveals the ultimate goal of celebrity proximity. Their presence and erotic promise are a powerful fringe benefit and inducement to the job description of Rock Star, today generic for a high-living intemperate lifestyle beyond any strain of music, excess as success. *Party like a Rockstar* toast the hip-hop Shop Boys in 2007, waving bottles of Jack and miming air guitar, sampling two riffs from Ozzy Osbourne's "Crazy Train." *All aboard!*

|||||

POP GOES THE METAL. Not unexpected, given the galore of anthemic choruses and crunchy riffing. When Def Leppard, over-and-over-dubbed by producer Robert "Mutt" Lange, catch newly on-air MTV's eye with "Bringing On the Heartache" in 1981, followed by the Scorpions and Twisted Sister, A&R departments at record companies reconsider pretenders to a throne that Led Zep and Queen have too-long occupied. Van Halen are "Led Zeppelin imitators with a lead singer trying to be Jim Dandy from Black Oak Arkansas" as one A&R thumbs and dumbs them down when the group is starting out, before their World Invasion tour in 1980 rakes in the big bucks. They break pop in 1983 with the salivation of "Hot for Teacher" and "Jump," Eddie on synthesizer, Dave midair, trousers about to split, as Roth will after this album to pursue a vaudeville career.

Mötley Crüe, in an early portent of overindulgence, take two umlauts for their name. Soon it'll be the whole bottle. In 1981 they live in a trashed apartment up the street from the Whisky, where the Strip heads to saturnalia after the clubs shutter. They initially want to call the band Christmas, decorating their family tree with tinsel and spangle in the manner of Sweet and the New York Dolls. Glitter rock has never released its hold on LA. Kevin Dubrow of Quiet Riot has a voice like Slade's Noddy Holder and their most-requested song at the Starwood is "Cum On Feel the Noize." Then there's the Runaways, arch manipulator Kim Fowley's idea of a come-hither girl band who will rock rougher than he's bargained for, overwhelming his notions of schoolgirl pandering. Joan Jett takes tough love from her idol, the glam star Suzi Quatro, Lita Ford is on her way to being an eighties *guitarista*, and Cherie Currie will enact the doomed spandex princess with an abusive policeman father in *Foxes*, a hit 1980 film set among LA hair metal's target demographic, disaffected teens in the San Fernando Valley, before taking up chain saw sculpture.

Guys and Dolls. There's increasingly little visual difference. Hair—that shaggy signifier—begins to tease, perm, primp, visit the beauty parlor and nail salon. It is the west coast version of Britannia's New Romantics, dress-up following the dress-down of punk; Adam Ant walks the pirate plank, Duran Duran yachts in exotic locales. Mötley's full-makeup, *Mad Max* circus costumes and war paint, pole-dances gender, high gloss for a metal that too often resists female inclusion, though sexual willingness is a given. Glam metal will embrace stripper culture, the wriggle until dollar bills are tucked into a g-string, third in open tuning. No wonder glambangers hang out at topless bars on their upwardly mobile climb to the Playboy Mansion. More often than not, it's a dancer girlfriend putting food on the table while her musician boyfriend hopes to snag an opening slot at the Roxy. Role reversal, scored to a libido let loose. The feminized look only heightens performance machismo, the inviting after-party orgy. It's the bait-and-switch of rock and roll, sex and drugs as means to an end. But as Iggy famously cautioned, "Is the fucking you get worth the fucking you take?"

Mötley Crüe are about to find out. Their glory years begin in

1983 when *Shout at the Devil*, their second album, is released after putting-his-job-on-the-line by twenty-year-old Elektra junior A&R rep Tom Zutaut, who drives past the Whisky a Go Go, sees a packed and steaming house besotted with Crüe, and realizes the band's volatile stage presence and self-produced debut on their own Leathur Records has risen them from the pack of other Sunset Strip purveyors. Singer Vince Neil will repay Zutaut's lobbying by having sex with Tom's girlfriend in the band's trailer after their breakthrough appearance at the US Festival in San Bernardino on May 29, 1983, Heavy Metal Day with Van Halen headlining (for a reported $1.5 million), Ozzy, Judas Priest, and Quiet Riot. By then Crüe are on their debauched way. No stopping. They will leave a trail of blackouts and addiction, fatal auto accidents, careening through all the clichés of live-fast-die-young, only Mötley is intent on faster, younger. It makes me wonder how they will muster enough work ethic to sell 100 million records, and still be together after nearly forty years, all members still alive (at this writing).

The band's motivational despot is also their most dissolute cog, declared dead twice from overdoses before he doubles his A's, who impels Mötley Crüe into existence in 1981. Bassist Nikki Sixx has left London, the band he shares with Blackie Lawless (soon to lead W.A.S.P.), psychically shifting geography, and by April, gathers blonde-on-blonde Vince, whose former band has gone skinny-tie new wave, stick-twirling drummer Tommy Lee, and Mick Mars, advertising in the local weekly that he's a "loud, rude, and aggressive guitarist" though the others call him Cousin Itt. Nikki writes the songs and the set list—"Stick to Your Guns," "Toast of the Town," "Take Me to the Top" (it's not hard to figure what they're about)—and they cover the Raspberries' "Tonight." Sixx has the concept, pop tarts, and perdition, but the Crüe live it out and outer.

Base metal appeal: the speaker-shaking bombast of misspent

youth looking for a good time *all the time*, avowing the 1984 all-too-true mockumentary *Spinal Tap*. The Crüe's second album, *Shout at the Devil*, sets the reverb plate in stone: drums recorded as if in Carlsbad Caverns, the triple-*Shout* of the title song made for pump-fist holler. Tom Werman produces, emulating Roy Thomas Baker's sense of majesty perfected in Queen's "Another One Bites the Dust" (Baker had been called in to remix the group's homemade debut, *Too Fast for Love*), the soundscape designed to echo off arena rafters, wind-shear the retiring jerseys: REO Speedwagon, Aerosmith on the downslope, even KISS, who cancel Mötley's opening slot after five dates for "unprofessional behavior," though Nikki knows they're upstaging them. They're the new band in town, the town is Hollywood, and it's where bands want to be, regardless of where they're from.

To get in the movies. Or at least the videos.

IIIIII

THEY COME BEARING pointy-headstock guitars, rivulets of hair, bared and buffed skin, baskets of drugs, dissipation.

In September 1986, Hollywood sets out the litter box. Cornering La Cienega and San Vicente, the Cathouse opens its playpen for what will be known as hair metal, though whether the term is affectionate or scornful depends on a predilection for the well-tempered chorus, a squealing guitar solo, not too complicated in the sentiments; pop music's catnip.

It will be decreed throughout the Strip that each album contain within its bombast one track of bleeding heart. Romance metal. Mötley puts a soft-focus "Home Sweet Home" on *Theater of Pain* in the wake of Vince's car accident that kills Hanoi Rocks drummer Dazzle, made worse since Crüe have taken sartorial cues from Michael Monroe's glitzy pioneering Finnish hard rockers, happily welcoming them to party on their first US trek.

"Is This Love," David Coverdale of Whitesnake, a savvy English import to LA, wonders to Tawny Kitaen, the future Mrs. Coverdale, as she Salomes him in the bedroom. Guess it's yes. Stryper's 1985 "First Love" is you-know-who, since they are ambassadors from Christian rock, tossing Bibles to the audience, one-upping the Gideons. Tesla's "Love Song" sings for itself. The power ballad proves durable, possibly not reaching full maturity until the 1988–89 season, when Poison's "Every Rose Has Its Thorn," Mötley's "Without You," Giant's "I'll See You in My Dreams" (aimed at every tween in the audience), and the coupling of Ozzy and Lita in "Close My Eyes Forever" tingle tear ducts. Warrant's "Heaven" is all bended knee and double-neck guitars, pentatonics fully explored; Extreme's "More Than You" the most vulnerable, Nuno Bettencourt's meticulous acoustic plucking like a Renaissance gavotte, his voice and Gary Charonne's blending like the Everlys. The drummer sits by the side of the video, waving his lighter, just like in the arena.

Just like. Metallic guitars—the annunciation chord of Foreigner's "Juke Box Hero," Brian May's entrance in Queen's "We Will Rock You," Survivor's "Eye of the Tiger" *Rocky* theme—are the new bedrock of hits like Night Ranger's "Sister Christian," Heart's "Alone," Europe's "Final Countdown," Bon Jovi's "You Give Love a Bad Name" and "Livin' on a Prayer."

It is a fine time to be a guitar player, accomplished in the manner of Paganini: precise notation, Marshalls on fry, high-wire string bending, histrionics to match, nonetheless a challenge to warp speed and make it look easy. Each band has their shredding *guistar*: Ratt's Warren DeMartini and Winger's Reb Beach give their pinup singers gravitas, just like James Burton did with Ricky Nelson. George Lynch is an Orange County hotshot up-and-coming in the same late-seventies time zone as Van Halen and Quiet Riot's Randy Rhoads, who beats him out for Ozzy's guitar slot. He auditions again after Rhoads is killed stunt-flying, once again doesn't get the gig, and so enlists in Don Dokken's self-named band, the first of many animosities the two will share. *Tooth and Nail* in 1984 describes their fight-club relationship, not helped by Lynch writing Dokken's biggest crowd pleaser on the follow-up *Under Lock and Key*, "Unchain the Night," an old-school locomotion breech-delivered from Deep Purple and Judas Priest. They will end throwing punches in a limousine on the way to Wembley Arena.

Hair metal, surprisingly, doesn't travel well. It thrives in LA's desert night, lit by Kleigs. Which attract moths. Poison travel from Mechanicsburg, Pennsylvania, to get in on the action. Skid Row stay in Toms River, New Jersey, have their bad boy in Sebastian Bach. Cinderella from Philadelphia (the diabolic "Night Songs") is moodier than some, while KISS frantically tries to update, inversely removing their makeup. In California, the Bay Area flips its usual coin. The denim-ripped thrash emanating from the north is its own sound and fury, Exodus and Testament in the wake of Metallica, whose *Master of Puppets* doomsday scenarios will upend the headliners of the 1988 Monsters of Rock tour, letting Van Halen and the Scorpions and Dokken know they can't take the future for granted.

My hang is the Scrap Bar, on MacDougal Street in the Village, where once the folkies roamed. I start the night at Don Hill's Cat Club over on East Thirteenth, Cycle Sluts from Hell on stage, "I Wish You Were a Beer" their theme song, and end it after hours at the Lismar Lounge, Honey 1%er and She-Fire of Ice behind the bar. There's a couple of guys from Circus of Power, Greg and Elise from Raging Slab, Alice from Shag Motor Pony. Some girl whose eye I caught earlier, might see later, or not.

Back at the Cathouse, it's getting to the end of 1987. The club is let loose by Taime Downs of Faster Pussycat, and Riki Rachtman, soon host of MTV's Saturday night *Headbanger's Ball*, which disseminates bordello fantasias for girls and boys alike.

The females of Vixen, with a sheened "Edge of a Broken Heart" written by pop songwriter Richard Marx and Fee Waybill of the Tubes, match sass with Nitro, whose singer claims the bleachiest bouffant, whose guitarist, the adept Michael Angelo Batio, plays four necks simultaneously.

The Cathouse is where dissipation's torch is passed. Nikki straggles back from Mötley's international *Girls Girls Girls* tour, last stop Japan, strung out on heroin, freebasing cocaine, cowering in his closet from paranoia. "Drugs are killing me," he scrawls in his no-veins-spared diary in July, "or am I already dead?" He's taken a new band under his wing, Guns N' Roses, scheduled to open Mötley when they go back on the road after New Year's. Guitarist Slash first glimpses Nikki at the Starwood when he's fourteen. His group, with swivel-hipped rasper Axl Rose, now has a newly released debut, *Appetite for Destruction*. Feeding time.

Nikki's not off the plane six hours when he pours GNR's Steven Adler, Slash, and Ratt's Robbin Crosby into a limo and heads to the Cathouse. Three days to Christmas; every night is New Year's Eve. They get hammered, and Sixx has a nail of pure Persian awaiting in a bathroom stall. He will turn blue, hover out-of-body, soberize and survive, an unlikely paragon of redemption.

Guns N' Roses are post-hair, down and dirtier. They're the bastard child of two bands, L.A. Guns and Hollywood Rose, named for foundational members Tracii Guns and Axl Rose. After a first show in March 1985, Guns and Rose part unamicably; by June, when the reconstituted group sets off to tour the west coast—dubbed the Hell Tour when they have to hitchhike back to Los Angeles after their vans break down—the classic lineup is place-marked: Slash, drummer Adler, rhythm guitarist Izzy Stradlin, and bassist Duff McKagan. Amid the competitive swamp of bands posing and postering, clustered around the Roxy and the Troubadour (which after its singer-songwriter heyday has gone over to the dark side), the band's intensity swiftly sets them apart. "Welcome to the Jungle," the first survival-of-the-fittest challenge being major label interest. Axl tells the A&R person at Chrysalis that if she walks naked down Sunset Strip to Tower Records, they'll sign, but he's leery of their ideas on how to mold the band. Tom Zutaut at Geffen gives them half the advance but creative freedom, and doesn't have to take off his clothes. *Appetite for Destruction* will prove a slow burner, GNR relentlessly stoking it on the road. Their songs build in tiers, "Paradise City" revving climax after climax, Slash's cascading guitar licks in "Sweet Child of Mine," the allusion of "Mr. Brownstone" to the jonesing of *We go on stage at nine / Get on the bus at 11*. Distinguishing marks: Slash's top hat and Axl's head scarf. No makeup or spangles.

The Red Hot Chili Peppers have been around since 1983, funkifying a take on punk that foregrounds Joseph Bowie's De-Funkt, James White and the Blacks, the Contortions—art rock with a downbeat—and manifested by 1985's *Sleaky Freaky*, produced by George Clinton. In the same year, Jane's Addiction, with Perry Farrell's "Been Caught Stealing" as pickpocket, starts on the road to Lollapalooza. In the shadows some bands nurture drug habits, an autumnal glow that Anthony Kiedis of the Chili Peppers will nostalgically recall in "Under the Bridge" a few years later. It ain't pretty anymore.

But the glory hole of hair metal ever beckons. Steel Panther began as a fun-poke tribute band in the early 2000s and now is the solipsistic object of affection: "All I Wanna Do Is Fuck (Myself Tonight)." From the album *Heavy Metal Rules*, and happily ever after.

||||||

NEITHER NORWAY.

I was warned. "Watch out for the black metal," said muso friends when I told them I was off to the wilds of Bergen for a rock festival—as if I could be mortally wounded by shards of satanic shrapnel. But when I arrived in this bucolic fishing village (think Popeye's Sweet Haven) on the west coast of the country, supposedly the wettest place in Europe with over two hundred days of rain each year, the sun shone brightly and the air was clean, the whole town so benevolent and friendly that I wondered where the dreaded onslaught of Odineseque immolation might be hiding.

Little did I know, and would soon learn, that Bergen was the nexus of black metal's most notorious incidents, from the beaning of an audience member by a severed sheep's head flung into the crowd by Mayhem, to the 1992 burning of a twelfth-century Gothic church that the singer of Burzum, Varg Vikernes, claimed was at his instigation. That Vikernes, once bass player of Mayhem, later stabbed to death Mayhem's guitarist, Euronymous, who had supposedly boiled and eaten the brains of the group's vocalist, Dead, who'd committed suicide; that Faust, drummer of Emperor, had knifed a man to death in Lillehammer's Olympic Park with no provocation; that the music wallowed in apocalyptic and misbegotten confrontations between Norse mythology and Christian infidelity and demonic sacrifice and grade-B horror shlock played at mind-numbing volume and speed, beset by convoluted fantasies of racial purification and unrelenting retribution.

Scratch the Scandinavian surface and the gates of hell doth open. The music isn't confined to Norway—Sweden's Katatonia and Craft (*Total Soul Rape*) are among the most fecund purveyors of the music's extremities—but it is Norway that popularized the peculiar sword-and-sorcery that is black metal's uncompromising howl. *Skaol!* one is cheered in a country that lifts its glass to the Viking tradition—until you are reminded that it translates as "skull," which those Vikings used as flagons to toast their destroyed enemies. In this land of the midnight sun, Nobel laureate Knut Hamsun's 1890 novel, *Hunger*, describes a would-be writer wandering the streets of Oslo (then, tellingly, called Kristiania): "I remained a while looking into the dark, this dense substance of darkness that had no bottom . . . What if I myself became dissolved into the dark, turned into it?"

Like any subset, black metal has its ready-mades: massive sludges of distortioned guitars, twin bass drums machine-gunning under guttural Neanderthal vocals, corpse makeup, stage shows featuring mock cruci-fictions and smoke machines on overload, indecipherable band logos. Its bloodline is equal parts Metallica and Slayer, large swaths of Bathory and Celtic Frost, a dash of thrash mixed with pomp and circumstance that sometimes hearkens to prog rock; sometimes, even stranger to say, when the music descends to a maelstrom roar, the texture is akin to sonic-atmosphere bands like Flying Saucer Attack, My Bloody Valentine, Spaceman Three. Amid the rampant unintelligibility of growled syllables, words rise from the *malebolge* in snatches (most of the groups do sing in English) only to be dragged back into primordial swamp. It's pure Dr. Doom, threats against unmindful humanity, an embrace of the Dark Lord. Where would you like torment to begin? Perhaps by sitting in front of these speakers for eternity, pummeled by waves of jackhammer sound, until your very soul begins to shred and decay into that moment when the universe is made over into what it once was, when pagan gods ruled the fjords.

||||||

IN METALLIC GENEALOGY, black metal afterbirths from death metal, which renounces the mainstream embrace lofting once-controversial power-thrashers like Metallica, Anthrax, Megadeth, and Slayer to commercial communion as the eighties shudder to a close. It's a skateboard ollie from hardcore punk's fuel injection. Tampa—home to Morbid Angel and Deicide—becomes the go-to destination for bands willing to meet their maker, in this case producer-engineer Scott Burns of Morrisound Studios. He records Death (the band), Obituary, Napalm Death, Brazil's Sepultura, and ultimately Cannibal Corpse, whose exorcist roar penetrates the *Billboard* charts. Burns understands how to clear space in the entrails of the music, each double-bass drum paradiddle and guitar chug definitive, all this before ProTools made it easy.

Blasphemy, inverted crosses, pentagrams, and imprecations against Christianity had been carved in tombstone as far back as Black Sabbath's debut, released February 1970, Friday the thirteenth, following in the cloven-hooved footsteps of Robert Johnson's 1938 *Me and the Devil / Was walkin' side by side*. Venom, a British band from Newcastle, uncaged *Welcome to Hell* in 1981, hailing Satan like a cab. The following year their eponymous "Black Metal" commanded "Lay down your soul to the great gods rock and roll." The devil-you-know. Metal's extremities were exploited by Denmark's Mercyful Fate and Sweden's Bathory; the latter's 1987 *Under the Sign of the Black Mark* is the *black*print of what is to come, its enigmatic leader Quorthon unafraid to layer synthesizers in the permafrost of his bleak landscape. His group—though he plays all instruments and refuses to tour—is named after Elizabeth Bathory, a seventeenth-century baroness who bathed in virgins' blood before she was immured for her crimes. Black metal is the claustrophobia of being walled in, selling your soul to Beezlebub for the privilege of release, to do the bidding of a fallen angel.

But the question begs: when does black metal become its own damnation? Is it the kabuki makeup KISS slather on to assume their ghastly persona, the necromanticism plied by Slayer, the sacrilegious depravity that causes Deicide's singer Glen Benton to brand an upside-down cross on his forehead? With all this rampant devil-may-care—the initials of Blue Öyster Cult were meant to read Be O'Cult—it is still experience once removed, a work of art, a movie, a video game. It's not expected that Bosch personally wielded an instrument of torture in his *Last Judgment*, that the makers of *Texas Chainsaw Massacre* ever dismembered their actors. It's supposed to be entertainment, or so we expect, until we meet the Devil at the junction, sign in blood, and sell our souls for a hit record, a bargain at twice the price.

IIIIII

ON NOVEMBER 26, 1990, *die Norwegischen sensation* Mayhem come to the Eiskeller in Leipzig, East Germany. They need a back dressing room, Euronymous typewrites promoter Abo Alsleben in a chatty letter, "with mirrors and water (preferably hot water). It doesn't matter if it's a small, stinking toilette" so they can apply their "corpse paint" and "put together Dead if he cuts himself up." Their singer, Per Ohlin, doesn't want to be on this earth, he's told them many a time. He's been slashing himself onstage, breathing in noxious vapours of decomposing animals before he performs, burying his clothes in the earth so they begin to rot; they hope he'll stay alive until they make the album that Dead has already named: *De Mysteriis Dom Sathanas*.

"Are you dead?" the vocalist barks at the shell-shocked audience after "The Freezing Moon." The flip side of life's single. *Time to play b-sides* as Blue Öyster Cult yearns in "Burnin' for You." The set is the same as last February up in Sarpsborg, when Dead as well as new drummer Hellhammer were introduced to a live audience, opening with "Deathcrush," ending with "Pure Fucking Armageddon," settling in around "Funeral Fog" and the immersion of "Freezing Moon," "Carnage," "Buried by Time and Dust." All the hits, complete with pigs' heads flung at the audience. By Leipzig, nine months later, they've gained control of the twists and impels in the headlong rhythms, a certainty they've gained over the year. When Euronymous takes a rare solo, moving through notes into wig-out, he has militaristic Necro and Hell-hammer behind him, pummeling, a cyclotron of noise. Dead's monotone voice is out front, the serrated edge of a saw, not buried in the blur as it was a few months ago; it makes him uncomfortable, this human contact. He was the first in the band to paint himself like a corpse, foreshadowing his stage name. The month-long tour will take Mayhem as far as Izmir, Turkey, site of many massacres, where the electricity is shut off after four numbers. They're traveling by train, carting equipment, stopped by border officials, gigs canceled, *lost loads of money, tons of shit happened, but in general it was cool as fuck*. The roadeo.

Mayhem combines in 1984 when Øystein Aarseth and Jorn Stubberud—the future Euronymous and Necrobutcher—and drummer Kjerl Manheim take their name and page from Venom's "Mayhem with Mercy," losing the qualifier when singer Maniac (Sven Erik Kristiansen) completes the basic soup stock of a rock band. In 1986 a cassette demo, *Pure Fucking Armageddon*, is home-crafted in an edition of one hundred—side a: *Fuck*, side b: *Off*—and is seeded around the world by a connective of metal fans keeping in pre-internet touch by postal mail, tape-trading, duplicating, a word-of-mouth paper trail of fanzines like Norway's *Slayer*, whose editor, Jon "Metalion" Kristiansen, has set up the gig in Sarpsborg to pay for the last issue.

It's winter-dark in the north. Dead can feel the cryonic chill. When he was ten he fell through the ice, the waters enclosing. Dead once, he knows, and will be again. He's from Sweden, and sends Mayhem a cassette he made with his band, Morbid (it arrives with a putrefying mouse inside). When Maniac leaves Mayhem (still teenage, he is no longer able to ride two trains and a bus to rehearsal from his home in Rjukan), Øystein asks Per to take the blood oath. Now both live in an old house outside Oslo where Mayhem rehearse, in the forest town of Krakstad, and they goad each other on, daring Satan to reveal the preordained. When does your character become you? Let's see how far this game unfolds; they are not unfamiliar with Dungeons & Dragons.

De Mysteriis is hardly begun when Dead ends. On April 8, 1991, Euronymous returns home to find the door locked from the inside. When he gains entrance, he finds "Pelle" on the floor, knife nearby, a fired shotgun, a suicide note: *Excuse all the blood.* Øystein leaves and returns with a disposable camera to Instamatic Dead, artfully arranging rifle and blade for greater prominence. He takes bits of bone and fashions them into a necklace; he laces a stew with bits of frontal cortex. This is too much for even Nec-robutcher to take. He departs Mayhem in disgust, and his re-placement will be Varg Vikernes of Bergen, whose one-man band, Burzum, has come to the attention of Euronymous's newly formed record label, Deathlike Silence Productions.

In the wake of Dead's death, Euronymous has opened a record store named Helvete (Hell) in Oslo's Old Town, a corner shop on Schweigaards gate, twenty minutes' walk east from Central Station. He paints "Black Metal" on the basement walls, where members of local bands—they refer to themselves as the Inner Circle—congregate, sleep, party; a fraternity house. The shop's décor is early coven: candlelit, hooded mannequin and shrunken head, medieval weaponry, a surfeit of skulls, displayed albums on the walls from Venom to Voivod, which doesn't mean Eurony-mous won't sell a KISS picture disc if he has it in stock. Emperor guitarist "Samoth" Haugen lives in the dank cellar, as does Count Grishnackh, the *nom de ruin* (borrowed from *Lord of the Rings*) of Vikernes when he travels the three hundred miles from Bergen to see how Burzum is selling.

Euro (he hates when you call him that) is twenty-three, Varg five years younger. Of the shadow he casts, I find Øystein Aars-eth's time behind-the-counter the most touching, having enjoyed the camaraderie of record stores all my life. I wish I could've flicked through his bins, picking up a now-rare EP (only 1,000 made) of *Deathcrush*, Mayhem's first appearance on record in 1987, numbered and hand-signed by Euronymous. Though he feels black metal can only be made by true satanists, he admits to enjoying Kraftwerk, Silver Apples, the Residents, and asks Conrad Schnitzler of Tangerine Dream for an instrumental introduction to the EP. He may worship the pentagrammatical arts, but he's a music fan first.

Now, four years after *Deathcrush*, Mayhem is on the verge of a masterwork. Though they've lost two essential members, the brutal lockstep of Euronymous and Hellhammer work with producer Eirek "Pytten" Hundvine in Bergen's Grieghallen, place drums on the stage of a large concert hall with a reverb nine stories high, churn the guitars, and construct malevolent scenarios. Euronymous is familiar with Hundvine's working methods from visiting Vikernes when he makes his debut, *Burzum*, acknowledged as the second Norwegian black metal album after Darkthrone's breakthrough, 1992's *A Blaze in the Northern Sky*. Euronymous invites Varg to be temporary bassist and embellishes guitar riffs with Snorre Ruch of the Trondheim band Thorns (though he won't play on the record). Four songs—"Funeral Fog," "Freezing Moon," "Buried in Time and Dust" and "Pagan Fears"—remain from Dead's tenure in the band. The others, including "Cursed in Eternity," seem to have the currency of prophecy. To sing, Euronymous chooses someone not within the Helvete social whirl but Hungarian Attila Csihar, whose five-octave range will, between Mayhem incarnations, take him to a turn as Calaphas in *Jesus Christ Superstar* and collaboration with Sunn o))), a Seattle band whose specialty is metallic drone in dropped A.

The album is built within a backdrop of church burnings and desecrations throughout Norway. On June 6, 1992, the twelfth-century stave Fantoftkirke in Bergen is torched. Holmenkollen chapel in Oslo is lit on August 23. There is arson in Stavanger, Vindafjord, another two churches in Bergen: the 1795 Asane (ignited on Christmas eve) and Stortveit. Posited as retribution for the Christian invasion of northern Europe a millennium previous, a continuance of humankind's unceasing holy war in which conflicting mythologies claim God or the devil as their own, it is nonetheless viewed as opportunity for promotion by Varg and Euronymous. Vikernes puts out an EP called *Aske* (Ashes), recorded over the summer of 1992 and released in early 1993 with a cover photo of a smoldering Fantoftkirke; the first thousand copies come with a souvenir lighter picturing the ruins. To crown the upcoming release of Mayhem's long-awaited album, he and Euronymous plot to set fire to Nidaros Cathedral in Oslo, the cover church that will adorn *De Mysteriis Dom Sathanas.*

But when the album, whose title translates as "Lord Satan's Secret Rites," is finally released in 1994, Vikernes's bass is mixed into inaudability. Necrobutcher, asked to replace Varg's parts, refuses, thinking it "appropriate that the murderer and victim were on the same record." Ashes to ashes.

||||||

HARRY HOLE EMPTIES HIS MIND. Enters the crime scene.

He opens his senses to the room, feeling its composition like a song he will replay over and over, following insinuations and intuitions until he can detail its arrangement. To see how it fits together. A homicide detective has to be a musician.

Like the body lying on the stairs in his underwear, the door ajar, floor of the apartment littered with broken glass and a shattered lamp. Forensics tells him the dead man has been stabbed twenty-four times, in the back, in the chest, once through the rear of the head. Harry fingers the scar that runs from his ear to his rueful smile and wonders why he feels drawn to resolve depravities in human character, to find the murderer's why. Because it's what he needs to keep his own demons at bay.

Something is happening to Norway. Vampirists, church burnings, dread. And now this.

The victim is one Øystein Aarseth, known as Euronymous, guitarist of an underground rock band. Harry doesn't know too much about them, his tastes run more to classicism like Pink Floyd and Miles Davis's *Kind of Blue*, though his stepson, Oleg, will soon be into Slayer and Slipknot. The creator of this obsessive fictional sleuth, Norwegian writer Jo Nesbø, is a guitar player himself, and one night in Oslo he and I will share stage left as he sits in with Patti and the band. We cross and slash our fretboards together à la Blue Öyster Cult in "Cities on Flame (with Rock and Roll)." Music, pyromania, and murder.

On the night of August 10, 1993, Euronymous is visited by Varg, ostensibly to sign a contract for the next Burzum release, to inquire where his royalties are, or perhaps to make a preemptive strike on Øystein, who he has heard plans to kidnap and torture him to make a snuff film. The two have been antagonistic of late, Vikernes increasingly neofascist, claiming ancestry with Vidkun Quisling, the Nazi administrator of Norway's World War II occupation by Germany; and Øystein an eastern bloc communist supporter (his Deathlike Silence stationery features the Albanian crest). Varg thinks Euronymous is all bluff, his image more about impressing acolytes at the now-closed shop than conflagration. Or maybe there's practicalities to consider. Euronymous doesn't have the money to re-press Burzum's album, and Vikernes has gotten interest from the Candelight label, home of Emperor, for his newly recorded *Filosofem*. He wants out.

Varg is already under suspicion. In January 1993, he gives a supposedly anonymous interview to the *Bergens Tidende* newspaper in which he tells a journalist that he knows the arsonist's identity. "Show Odin to the people and Odin will be lit in their souls," he reasons, but when the front page (*"We lit the fires!"*) presents a full-length portrait of him, waist-length hair obscuring his features, holding a pair of long-bladed scimitars, the police knock at his door two days later.

Though he will eventually be released for lack of evidence, his arrest draws media attention to the black metal concentration around Helvete, and points the police toward the unsolved murder of a middle-aged homosexual man in Lillehammer the previous August. It is common knowledge within the Inner Circle that the perpetrator is Bard Eithun, Emperor's drummer, known as Faust, who had started working at the record store in July. Visiting his parents, he is importuned in Olympic Park, wilfully slashing the victim with a pocket knife. He returns to his family's home to sleep and wash off the blood. Back in Oslo, he tells Varg and Euronymous he is going to turn himself into the police; instead, they convince him to join them in the immolation of Holmkollen Chapel. So beckon the flames of hell.

An alibi has been prepared—a video rented to which Varg already knows the plot, his bank card to be used by a friend to withdraw money in Bergen on the night—before he and Snorre set out on the seven-hour drive. They arrive in Oslo at three in the morning, Vikernes huddling in the backseat of a Volkswagon Golf under a blanket so as not to be seen, Snorre behind the wheel with only a vague premonition of what is about to transpire. He waits downstairs while Varg rings the bell. Euronymous opens the door, half-asleep. In the frantic struggle that follows, each—though Euronymous must perforce testify from beyond the grave—claims self-defense. But which self? Over the past year their rivalry to outdo each other in heinous conception has pushed each further into diabolical character, immoral one-upsmanship. It's too late to turn back. "We are but slaves of The One With Horns," Euronymous boasts to *Kerrang!* magazine in their March 27, 1993, exposé on the satanic rituals of black metal. The Devil is about to take his due.

Despite protestations of innocence, Varg is careless. He

neglects to wear the gloves he's brought to the apartment, leaving his fingerprints in Euronymous's blood on the stairs. The bank card is the wrong one; the signed and dated contract is left on the floor. Vikernes calls the owner of Candelight Records to tell him of the murder before the news is released to the public.

On the way back to Bergen, he and Snorre blast Dead Can Dance. Varg does the driving.

||||||

TWENTY-ONE YEARS FOR VARG, the maximum, which includes three church burnings. Snorre gets seven for being an unwitting accessory. And for black metal, it's a lurid—pronounced *lou reed*—initiation into the world beyond Norway, flourishing on the world stage. The bands pass in ghostly processional— Enslaved, Gorgoroth, Immortal, Carpathian Forest—obscured by smoke machines and vomitous incantation, surviving damnation long enough to become regulars on the festival circuit, crossing borders like the plague. In neighboring Sweden, there is Entombed and Marduk (the demo of *Fuck Me Jesus* has a cover of a bare-breasted girl inserting a crucifix in her nether region) and Possessed; Finland offers Impaled Nazarene as ritual sacrifice; Austria's Abigor, Hungary's Ektomorf, the Grecian Rotting Christ, Nile from the biblical belt of South Carolina.

Dimmu Borgir's rhythm guitarist Silenoz (Sven Kopperud) begins visiting Helvete when he's fifteen, shortly before Euronymous's murder. The commercial breakthrough of 1997's *Enthrone Darkness Triumphant* will lead them to 2003's *Death Cult Armageddon*, accessorized by the Prague Philharmonic Orchestra. They're out-symphoniqued by Britain's Cradle of Filth, utilizing the Budapest Film Orchestra augmented by a forty-voice choir for *Damnation and a Day* in the same year. The Filth have already embraced horror cinema, a 1998 concept album about black metal centerfold Elizabeth Bathory, *Cruelty and the Beast*, narrated by Ingrid Pitt, who played the title character in the 1971 Hammer film *Countess Dracula*. Belief and role-play blur; black metal steps back from the precipice, back to b-movie entertainment.

Mayhem regroups with Necrobutcher and Hellhammer, adds a new guitarist (Blasphemer), and resurrects their vocalists, first Maniac, then Attila. They announce their return with the EP *Wolf's Lair Abyss* in 1997, part one of an exploration of Nietzschean-themed songs they expand with *Grand Declaration of War* in 2000. This is the Will to Power, how it corrupts, transcends, and creates its own bin in the record emporium, complete with box sets, multicolored vinyl, remixes, and collector-bait.

Even Norway seems to feel black metal has paid for their sins. There is a studious archive at the Litteraturhuset in Oslo, and Helvete has reopened, part record shop, part museum, with a steady stream of international pilgrims. Documentaries exhume footage and interviews, grainy video of Dead outside the Krakstad home in the sunshine, smiling, looking beatific; black-and-black VHS of Mayhem in Leipzig; interspersed with interviews of band members left behind, attempting to show how casually day-to-day it all was, even if it was madness, even it was deserved. In 2019 a feature film, *Lords of Chaos* (based on a minutely detailed book by Michael Moynihan and Didrik Soderlind), is directed by Jonas Akerlund, once drummer of Bathory, who has devised videos for Madonna ("Ray of Light"), Prodigy ("Smack That Bitch Up"), and Rammstein ("Pussy"). Its re-creation of the youthful shenanigans that begat the band and inexorable fatal denouement is prime-time prime-evil, of the metal that never says die, despite preaching it.

|||||

KAWAII!

Babymetal is onstage at the Tokyo Dome in 2016. They are three chirping adolescent girls dressed in PVC Lolita costumes, flashing devil's horns and choreographed head-banging while a masked skeleton-garbed band pummels the familiar breakneck tropes behind them: "Gimme Chocolate!" Metal meets J-pop idol. Yum.

The allure of alloy. Season to taste. The power chord plays well with other genres, a lingua franca that hyphenates progressive (Opeth, Queensrÿche, Voivod), industrial (Ministry, Nine Inch Nails), alt (Helmet, Type O Negative), funkish (Primus, Fishbone, Red Hot Chili Peppers), horror (White Zombie, F.K.U.), rap (Kid Rock, Limp Bizkit, System of a Down), airy-fairy (Nightwish), nu (Korn, Linkin Park), stoner (Sleep, Earth, Cathedral), politico (Rage Against the Machine), avant (John Zorn's Naked City, with guitarist Bill Frisell, keyboardist Wayne Horvitz, bassist Fred Frith, drummer Joey Baron), Japanoise, especially the Boredoms, and Masonna (Maso Yamazaki, who verges on the Captain Beefheart); in ever thinner slices of crossover and over. In 1997, Pat Boone releases *No More Mr. Nice Guy*, covering Metallica, Judas Priest, Ozzy. As for the renowned Blizzard of Ozz himself, in 2002 he is subjected to the televised all-too-reality of MTV's *The Osbournes*, a multi-generational Munsters sitcom that doesn't spare the dysfunction.

Despite its twisted family tree, there is something comforting about the decibel avalanche at metal's core, the layers of civilization it scrapes away. To unleash our subhuman roar, the primal animal.

SEATTLE
1991

THE LAND OF "LOUIE LOUIE" AND JIMI HENDRIX. WHERE the Ventures taught guitar. Where Harry Smith found the initial cache of scrapped 78s that would bed his *Anthology of American Folk Music*. The Sonics' "Psycho." The Space Needle. The enveloping damp.

Grunge. Suits the disheveled.

It backs away from flamboyance, the cockerels of Hollywood. It has more in common with the shambling drunkboat songcraft of the Minneapolis bands, the Replacements and Soul Asylum, and adopts their uni(n)formal thrift store flannel and jeans worn past the point of no return. Hüsker Dü gives a sense of purpose: "New Day Rising," and why not? The formulaic has moved northward through the hardcore of Black Flag and the lunge of Portland's Wipers, picking up Jello Biafra along the way, and then taking Sonic Youth's clamor to heart. One step up from the basement. Not much chance to be heard beyond the Cascades.

Everybody's in a band. For fun, mostly, your pals, your little brother, the girl down the street. "Friends playing music," as Van Conner from Screaming Trees reminisces in *Hype*, Doug Pray's 1996 film of how it was, five years after the dam broke, the town inundated. It's not an act, premeditated. The audience is in on the joke, bounding off each other and crowd-surfing and proscenium-diving without the aggressive shove of the hardcore pit. Anti-show. The players are the misfits you'd see at the record or comic shop on a Saturday, plowing through new releases, hoping to get their name on a flyer or seven-inch. Geekism once removed. About to find out what it means to be the new kid on the chopping block.

||||||

IN MARCH 1986 INTRODUCTIONS ARE MADE. The meet-and-greet is *Deep Six*, a sampler album put out by Chris Hanzsek and Tina Casale on their newly formed C/Z label, hearing unity as the bands sort themselves out: Green River, Melvins, Soundgarden, Skin Yard, Malfunkshun, U-Men.

It's a toss-up between Green River and the Melvins as to who downstrokes the opening chord. Green River's *Come On Down* EP might jump-start 1985, but the Melvins have been slowing tempo, adding humoresque, thickening the slurry from the amplifier since 1983. They share a song, "Leech," preserved on a 1984 Green River demo that the band thinks too repetitive, dropping it from their set as newer material adds parts and construed arrangements. The Melvins pick it up; they like the dumbed-down immersive. Guitarist Buzz Osborne and bassist Matt Lukin, originally from Montesano, become a band in drummer Dale Crover's parents' house in Aberdeen, a logging town just lumbering along, impressed with hardcore, punk, Sabbath and KISS. They're not afraid to be cartoonish, as long as they generate a roar that shows they're not fooling around.

Metal and hardcore seem to be speeding up; why not downshift? The Melvins take to the dropped-D tuning, Buzzo's guitar the weight of crush. Crover keeps the rumble aligned with a twenty-six-inch bass drum, and on *Deep Six* they seem the most confident of the assembled bands, aware that what they're doing will expand horizontally rather than upwardly mobile. Its modus operandi takes them well into the next half century, sludge over sluice, one of the last bands left standing.

Hanzsek and Casale have migrated from Boston to the Emerald City, opening a recording studio called Reciprocal in Interbay, where Chris engineers for ten dollars an hour, attracting locals like the Walkabouts, the Accused, and Green River, who tape six songs for an EP: *Come On Down*, like an engraved invitation from the then at-large serial killer that gives them their name. Green River has two tributaries, singer Mark Arm, who brings guitarist Steve Turner from their previous band, Mr. Epp and the Calculations (named after their high school math teacher); and bassist Jeff Ament, who finds common ground with second guitarist Stone Gossard, drafted when Arm gives up guitar to concentrate on singing. There will come a time when the halves cleave, but for now Green River are the catalyst behind *Deep Six*, vouching for Hanzsek and Casale, roping in the emerging cadres circulating between the Central Tavern in Pioneer Square, the Showbox on First Avenue, the Ditto on Fifth in Belltown, the Rainbow by U Dub.

Green River have punk and hard-core roots but *Come On Down* leans backward into more traditional hard rock, despite attempts to distance by turning up the feedback. The lead track's chant of *come on come on* strays dangerously close to Ted Nugent's "Stranglehold," and in fact, Turner quits the band when the *Come On Down* sessions are finished, uncomfortable with their metal leanings, replaced by Bruce Fairweather, an old bandmate (Deranged Diction) of Ament's. Arm's lyrics tend toward the paranoiac and the splatter—*born-again afterbirth* and *she turned out to be the woman of his screams* and *the ride of your life leads you down / speeding to a hole in the ground*, and he howls under-pitch at the massed guitars. You can overhear riffs from future bands within: Mudhoney, Mother Love Bone, Pearl Jam. This is just beginning.

The cast of *Deep Six* assembles in late summer 1985 at Iron-wood Studio, Hanzsek having lost his studio lease. He'd mixed *Come On Down* at Paul Scoles's uptown space and over two sessions, each band allotted four hours, the parameters of Seattle's coming-out carve into granite. Green River contributes two tracks, pack leader even though Homestead, their record label, hasn't enough money to release *Come On Down* by the time they ready to take it on the road. When they arrive at CBGB, they outnumber the audience; but at least they're out there in a van, sleeping on couches, like hundreds of other bands wandering the alt-circuit finding like-minded insularity.

For all *Deep Six*'s unity of purpose, the groups aren't mono-lithic. The metal undercurrent may be tongue-in-amp, split with punk's extremities, but everyone agrees on Motörhead and Led Sab. After the Melvins' forty seconds of bleating soup stock with "Blessing the Operation" and "She Waits," the bands split into separate practice rooms, come out with whatever they've been working on, ready for reveal. The Melvins one-take "Scared" and "Grinding Process," an untrammeled sonic boom leavened by Osborne's squall and wrenching changes in direction, the off-ramp taken. Green River have worked with Hanzsek on *Come On Down* and they're being professional. "10,000 Things" splits their divisive, and with Turner also about to take leave from the band's more-mainstream outlook, Arm does his best to keep things off-kilter, voice strangulating over guitars that, with dialed-down distortion, might be Jefferson Airplane, Grace Slick wailing over Jorma. Ament and Gossard aren't afraid of accessible, of being more than abrasive and confrontational. Jeff in particular has spent years getting up at 5 a.m. for a day job, and he wants to make this work.

Soundgarden are the sleeper of the bunch. The core of the

band, guitarist Kim Thayil and bassist Hiro Yamamoto, migrate from the Chicago area in the early eighties, hooking up with moody drummer Chris Cornell, a street-hardened kid who needs a place to live. Their second gig, in February 1985, is opening Hüsker Dü and the Melvins at Gorilla Gardens, an all-ages club on the edge of Chinatown that splits the tribal in Seattle's rock scene, soon to coalesce. The venue, officially known as Rock Theater, has two rooms: one devoted to punk, the other metal; the cover charge grants entrance to both. After warily eyeing each other in the lobby, respective hair lengths and amplifier settings entwine, variations on a theme. Thayil bypasses chomp with a gift for line and texture, throwing back to the seventies of Page and the eighties of the Cult's Billy Duffy, heavy on the phasing. Note choices land in unexpected places, his subcontinental Indian heritage leaning the way he hears melody. The Asiatic scale is enhanced by the Japanese Yamamoto, originally a mandolin player, which opens his bass approach beyond punk metal's root-note thrum while retaining its speed. Cornell can keep up the pace on drums—he likes Rush's Neil Peart—but his voice is meant to lead the band. He'll learn to remove his shirt, take singing lessons, dive lyrically into his depths of psyche, turn inner conflict into shrieking vowels. By the time they record their tracks on *Deep Six*—"Heretic," "Tears to Forget," "All Your Lies," onrushing time signatures impelling Cornell's rasp and Kim's dense riffage—Scott Sundquist has taken over drumming, Matt Cameron from Skin Yard waiting in the wings.

With future Seattle sound sculptor Jack Endino in the bass slot, Skin Yard is not surprisingly the most sonically adventurous, though, in Endino's recall, these "embryonic" songs are "slow, drony . . . semi-psychedelic and were pretty out of place on this record." Singer Ben McMillan conveys Bowiesque gravitas astride the pulsating bewail of "Throb," his saxophone—jarring in the midst of all the rampant guitars—introducing "Birds." As an engineer, Endino will do much to signature the blurred eight-track sound of grunge-to-come. Skin Yard prove too astute for such easy encapsulation, which renders them an acquired taste.

Andrew Wood's Malfunkshun have the hit single, or at least the catchiest number. In an alternate reality, the mantra of "With Yo' Heart Not Yo' Hands" would rival Queen for crowd-chant. Wood's stylized stage persona—"Landrew, the Love God from Mount Olympus"—even arrives for his *Deep Six* vocals bedecked in costumed character, brazenly outlandish, though it masks a vulnerability that will lead him to take refuge in hard drugs. The viscous noise stirred by his brother Kevin's guitar in "Stars-N-You" induces vertigo.

The U-Men have to be convinced. They are, after all, the top shelf of Seattle underground bands, around since 1981, avant-regarding Pere Ubu and Birthday Party, skewed by Tom Price's jazz guitar inversions, with an EP released in 1984 by future Sub Pop label co-conspirator Bruce Pavitt, then running a Capitol Hill record store. Their shows are known for wreaking havoc on venues, songs careening, no two performances alike. They stop at the studio and toss off "They," an apt descriptive of their distancing from the other bands, on their way ten minutes later to a scheduled gig in Idaho. Though now a footnote to future history, their 1985 Labor Day Bumbershoot Festival appearance when they pour lighter fluid into the water-filled moat separating them from the audience and set it alight, flames undermining the stage, will go down in local lore, a harbinger of the oncoming firestorm.

The U-Men headline the second night of the *Deep Six* premiere party March 22, 1986, at UCT Hall on Fifth at Aloha. Spring fling. The first night is front-loaded with Green River, the Melvins opening. "Since this is a record release party," announces Buzzo, "we're gonna play all our party songs tonight," one segue after another, quoting 21 tracks in 47 minutes, Sabbath's "Iron Man" nodding to Cher ("Bang Bang") to the Accused's "Reagan

War Puppets" and their own fecund catalog, "Over from Under the Excrement" and "Heaviness of the Load," sounding like a proper rock band (and they can be), with Soundgarden deep-throating in the middle. Two thousand copies make their way into the world, though nobody seems to care. The response is so tepid that Hanszek gets out of the label business. The bands want him to promote, wheedle, take ads, work the phones. There is a lot of clamoring to get into the alternative charts, college stations tabulated by CMJ (*College Music Journal*, founded in 1978), a parallel trade universe with its own Top 100. What will make these bands any different, that they might make a difference?

|||||

IT'S NOT ALL GODZILLA GUITARS and who can play the loudest; embracing proto-grunge isn't the only game in town. Seattle has many genomes in its lineage, from the Fleetwoods' sultry "Mr. Blue" to Heart (*Baaah-raahhh-cuuda!*) to an r&b circuit that chitlins the Central District, wavelengths on KYAC ("the Soul of the Northwest,"), funks-up groups like Black On White Affair or Cold Bold & Together, custom-made for a dance floor a half hour before closing time. There are mad billy-rockers, the Pacific Playboys and the Stripes and Butch Paulson with the Motations, and a tradition of instrumentals, as with many bands pre–English Invasion. The upper Pacific's remove from musical byways, Lewis and Clark meets Sacajawea, means most artists are never heard outside of town, resulting in 45s of trembling rarity: consult *Wheedle's Groove* (Light in the Attic) and Norton's trio of *Everybody's Boppin'*, *Chicken Session*, and *Shake Um Up Rock*.

White rock bands in the area get an unexpected national boost from the 1963 success of the Kingsmen, who cover Richard Berry's laconic 1957 "Louie Louie" as translated by Rockin' Robin Roberts and the Wailers (adding a beat per measure to Berry's original), itself derived from "El Loco Cha-Cha" by Ricky Rillera and the Rhythm Rockers, who in turn *barrio*-borrow from Cubano Rosendo Ruiz Jr. and his *"Amarren Al Loco."* Paul Revere and the Raiders record their version a week after the Kingsmen in the same studio, but their clean-edged approach can't compete with the Kingsmen's clatter of impending mess, a grunge touchstone and motivation to aspiring guitarists everywhere. Revere will have his own effect on garage (a word sharing meaningful letters with "grunge") when the Raiders become the house band for the televised *Where the Action Is*, Dick Clark's sixties' update of *Bandstand*, and everyone begins a band in their house.

There is no shortage of new wavers in the early eighties, the good-time punkish Fastbacks, the goth-glam Fags, many of the bands gathered in a 1981 sampler called *The Seattle Syndrome Vol. 1*: X-15 ("Vaporized"), the Blackouts (whose rhythm section, bassist Paul Barker and drummer Bill Rieflin, will impel Al Jourgensen's Ministry toward the industrial), *rama-lama-fa-fa-fa* from the Fartz, and other stepping-stones like the Pudz and the Refuzors. For many the *z* implies an end of alphabet; half the groups break up before the album is out.

The example of the college town of Athens, Georgia, with its B-52s' dance-a-thon and R.E.M. uplift soared by Peter Buck's *Ricken*-backing and Michael Stipe's saintly badinage, provides hope for pop-ist bands like the Young Fresh Fellows. Led by Scott McCaughey, they are hardly contrary, proper verse and chorus delivered with deprecating humor. Their homeschooled debut, *The Fabulous Sounds of the Pacific Northwest* (1984), and its follow-up, *Topsy Turvy*, gives their engineer Conrad Uno incentive to found PopLlama Records. Uno has jerry-rigged a recording facility in his garage, complete with egg cartons on the walls to absorb sound (hence Egg Studios) and he encourages bands willing to hatch on his label. "All it takes is magnetic tape and a microphone," he says, the "lo-fi" corroborated by Calvin Johnson and his K Records from the satellite town of Olympia, an hour's drive south of Seattle.

Johnson's credo was "demystifying the tools of media so access was not restricted due to fear," and puts his ideas into motion with his band Beat Happening and a cassette-friendly label that emphasizes the homemade and the unsullied. Olympia, with its freewheeling Evergreen State College and quirky bohemianism, provides get-out-the-word opportunity with *Op* magazine's championing of independent music, community-minded radio KAOS-FM, and a relaxation of gender role-play that helps inculcate the riot grrrl movement.

Connective tissue. For most, the confluence of record stores, fanzines, late night slots on radio, *what's happening-in-town* newsprints like the *Rocket*, and Dawn Anderson's *Backfire* will prove more labor of love than financial gain. But Bruce Pavitt and Jonathan Poneman of the gestating Sub Pop label see that Seattle is ripe for identity. Their model is Motown, and they don't want to confuse the issue by spreading their genre thin. Pavitt had trekked to Washington with Kim and Hiro, transplanting in Olympia where his KAOS radio show, *Subterranean Pop*, branches into a fanzine that sometimes appears as a cassette compilation of aspiration. He believes strongly in provincial identity, rails against the "bland sameness of the pop superstructure" and "the claustrophobic centralization of our culture. We need diverse, regionalized, localized approaches to all forms of art, music, politics." He shifts to Seattle, gets practical experience running a record store, and pens a column in the *Rocket* called "Sub Pop U.S.A." that stokes the native species. In 1986, his *Sub Pop 100* vinyl sampler showcases off-the-grid evangelism: Sonic Youth, the Wipers, Shonen Knife, Skinny Puppy, Steve Albini, alongside the indigenous U-Men and aspiring producer Steve Fisk. It's all one gene pool.

Bruce then decides to make Sub Pop a proper label, starting with a Green River EP, *Dry as a Bone*, recorded in June 1986 at the new Reciprocal that Hanzsek opens in Ballard with Endino behind the board. As a producer/engineer, Jack hones his philosophy on the job, "anti-perfection" as much necessity—time and equipment precious—as working within the confines of a triangular building with a control room that can't fit all members of a band. Eight tracks leave little room for error. "What sounded horrible back then," he told the *Rocket* in 1992, "is now a standard."

Green River are starting to crack. By the time their EP is finally released a year later (Pavitt hasn't the cash flow), the band's rift is about to go public. There is disconnect between synchronized guitars and Arm's caustic yap; both camps are wanting to go their own ways. Even though they separate in October 1987 after a show opening for Jane's Addiction in Los Angeles, Green River stays together for the sake of the kids, songs they've been assembling for *Rehab Doll*, a follow-up that comes out after they've remarried, maiden names replaced by Mudhoney (Mark reunited with original guitarist Turner), Ament/Gossard/Fairweather joining Andrew the Love God in Mother Love Bone.

Thayil go-betweens Pavitt and Poneman, who programs *Audio Oasis* on KCMU, has an itinerant band called the Treeclimbers, and books shows at Scoundrel's Lair and Rainbow Tavern. Jonathan perceives a developing "consciousness . . . A lot has to do with our geographic isolation," he writes in the *Rocket* at the end of 1986, predicting "Something's gonna happen." Or gotta. Sometimes you have to do it yourself. They make a good team, comedy/straight, Abbott and Costello, Martin Lawrence and Will Smith. Sub Pop might poke fun at itself (a perennially stoned Pavitt) as it promotes a business plan (Poneman is the occasional voice of reason); both want to make the label the focal point, a branding iron, like 4AD or Creation in England. A logo. On a

T-shirt. A Singles Club where subscribers collect monthly limited edition releases. Colored vinyl. Bands that fit the descriptive of "ultraloose GRUNGE that destroyed the morals of a generation," as Sub Pop describes *Dry as a Bone*. They know their market. Not that there is anything but outflow in the first months. The two quit day jobs (Pavitt works at Muzak as did Poneman at one time) to take a sky-top office in the Terminal Sales Building near Pike Market on April Fool's Day 1988. Early employees race to get to the bank before payroll runs out.

It will be a constant battle to stay ahead of mounting bills, but Sub Pop is a centrifugal force within Seattle. The first proper Sub Pop EP is Soundgarden's *Screaming Life* (the company can't afford albums yet), engineered by Endino at Reciprocal, with cover art of Cornell's pectorals by chiaroscuro photographer Charles Peterson, a sound-visual template that will become the company's calling card. Even at this early stage Soundgarden are fierce in attack, a remake of "Tears to Forget" showing how far they've progressed since *Deep Six*, tracks like "Hunted Down" and "Entering" teetering between metal screed and pure adrenaline. Cornell's voice has depth; "Nothing to Say" doesn't need to because he's learned to sing. When Endino samples discarded recordings of 1950s sermonizing for "Hand of God," Chris talks-in-tongues rock's newest testament, underdog salvation proffered.

Sub Pop slogans "Loser" on a T-shirt in 1988, anthems it on green vinyl by the corpulent TAD two years later: *Loss is what I gained*, portending Radiohead's 1992 "Creep" and Beck's 1993 "Loser." The label will host a Lamefest on June 9, 1989, at the Moore Theater, spotlighting the affront of Mudhoney, TAD, and a newer band who have been introduced around town by the Melvins, Nirvana. Sub Pop takes the long shot. In March they fly over English journalist Everett True to slug line *Seattle: Rock City* for *Melody Maker*, his heavy-breathing account ("trampling gleefully over the grave of punk rock and heavy metal . . . sheer physicality and sexiness") press-releasing the company and the town it distributes to the world. The bands fit well together on a tabloid page, nearly all on Sub Pop's roster, scruffy to match the music's mutation, and there's enough of them—Blood Circus and Cat Butt among the lesser known—to make an appealing crowd. "Sub Pop is a business set up to *encourage* freedom of thought," Bruce tells Everett, even if everyone's thinking alike.

|||||

SOUNDGARDEN ARE THE FIRST TO break out of Seattle and go major. They've been on a steady ascent, though wary of outrunning themselves. In 1988 Sub Pop releases another EP, *FOPP*, featuring their metal-funk cover of the Ohio Players complete with separate dub remix, a "Kingdom of Come" original with Kim in full flail, and a revision of Green River's "Swallow My Pride" that seems retro amid the stylish experimentation. They're ready to record a full-length album, though sympathetic to Sub Pop's encouragement of regional identity. "Soundgarden's pockets were empty, as were Sub Pop's coffers," Kim explains thirty years later when *Ultramega OK* is lovingly remixed (and imprinted on Sub Pop). Courted by SST, the label founded by Black Flag's Greg Ginn with an impeccable pedigree of the Minutemen, Hüsker Dü, Bad Brains, and Sonic Youth, Soundgarden is excited by the company they will keep, signing a one-album handshake deal. They've been working on songs with Endino at Reciprocal, but SST suggests they move up to a sixteen-track mobile truck run by engineer Drew Canulette with an adjacent studio outside Portland. They're familiar with Drew's working method because he recorded them at the Moore Theater with Steve Fisk producing for *FOPP*. Sessions start in spring of 1988, "Flower" opening with Thayil breathing across his strings before the crunch, the mortar and pestle of the rhythm section and bulked-up heft of the guitars in "All Your Lies" and the frantic "Circle of Power" giving Cornell wailing room. *Ultramega OK* will surprisingly be nominated for Best Metal Performance when Grammys are awarded the following year. They're beaten by Jethro Tull.

Soundgarden is already in talks with A&M, and other corporate labels are eavesdropping with interest. *Ultramega OK* is meant to bridge the band between independent and major, a delicate balance when graduating to the outsize expectations that come with investment and capital, SST a way to build their fan base and preserve street credibility. Steve Ralbovsky is the new head of A&R at A&M, familiar with independent labels ready for the stepping-stone; he brokered Def Jam's partnership with Columbia. Even before he formally assumes the A&M job, he has tucked Twin-Tone's Soul Asylum into his portfolio, another band whose songwriting and volatile romp seem ready for mass appeal. He goes to see Soundgarden in Vancouver with savvy George Drakoulias (who has discovered both the Beastie Boys and the Black Crowes) and A&R associates Aaron Jacoves and Brian Huttenhower, who have championed them at A&M, playing to a tiny audience. When Chris skyrockets his voice to the top of its range, the band oblique in dark intimation, metal subsumed by Bauhaus and Killing Joke, Ralbovsky is convinced. It's mutually agreed they need the bona fides and experimental room of SST before moving forward. Soon enough Soundgarden will be made aware of the financial shortcomings of an independent label. The rushed mix of *Ultramega OK* lacks depth and warmth, and they've already progressed beyond its boundary testing and sense of humor—"665" and "667" poke fun at metal's coven inclinations, and they "cover" John Lennon's "One Moment of Silence."

Louder Than Love, their major label debut, finished in early 1989, math-majors Cameron's lopsided time signatures with Thayil's sedimental layering. Cornell bends producer Terry Date's metal lean (Metal Church and Chastain) into an invocation of portent, given sonic breadth by hired-gun mixers Steve Thompson and Mike Barbiero, a new tier of production added to record making in the 1980s. Their task is not to tame but compress, delineate, specify frequencies for the radio and the up-and-coming digital formats. *Louder Than Love* sounds great. But as the old Chet Atkins joke goes (sorry if you've heard it before), someone says "Chet, your guitar sounds great tonight." And Chet puts it on the stand and says "how does it sound now?"

They're ready but A&M isn't. Sheened metallic, the album doesn't hew to predilection. Cornell's voice is a sinewy flexi-disc instrument whose wrenched phrasings parse Thayil's *sturm-und-drang*, ominous lyrics—*you're gonna kill your mother and I love her*—not much concerned with afterparty. "Loud Love" shadows Stooges' chords to the downward-dog of its leviathan refrains; the inexorable accelerant of "Gun" ascends like an elevator stopping at all the rhythmic floors of metal, subwoofer hump to punkish flight. Despite the truism that will eventually demarcate Seattle, they won't sound like everyone else.

Soundgarden's breakthrough struggles uphill due to a cultural divide between A&R and field promotion at A&M, the crux of the music business in a one-stop. The chorus of "Big Dumb Sex"—*I'm gonna fuck fuck fuck fuck you / Fuck you*—makes president Gil Friesen wonder if, ah, the album might be a bit more acceptable to distributors if it bears an *Explicit Lyrics / Parental Advisory* sticker. More problematic is Hiro's discomfort with the band being lumpened as "metal," that they're becoming a "product," coupled with his desire to not spend his life on the endless road. He leaves for pharmacy school, temporarily replaced by Jason Everman, newly let go from Nirvana. Everyone's still trading cards.

Mark Arm decides to stay home. In the wake of Green River's demise, he goes on a bender at the OK Hotel, reunites with Steve Turner, who has been marking time in the Thrown-Ups along with drummer Dan Peters of Bundle of Hiss, recruits bassist Matt Lukin from the Melvins, who have decamped for San Francisco, and sends Sub Pop a mangled rehearsal tape that intrigues Pavitt enough to pass them over to Reciprocal and Endino. Arm and Turner share an anti–rock star dogma, but that doesn't mean they don't want to make it. The name Mudhoney comes from a Russ Meyer film, and their debut "Touch Me I'm Sick" hit-singles in all the alt-markets that matter, mainly Sonic Youth, who take them on a west coast tour and later mentor them in England. Great minds run in the same gutters. "I'm a creep, yeah, I'm a jerk," Arm caterwauls in the sweet spot of Sub Pop's peers when the 45 is released in August 1988. He's back on guitar, playing slide on a Hagstrom II, distortion pedals maxed, leaping and lurching into Turner, the crowd, the amplifiers. It's a mess, cacophony its own reward. Nineteen eighty-nine belongs to Mudhoney in Seattle, lines around the block, and a growing reputation in Europe that ping-pongs back to America.

Their EP *Superfuzz Bigmuff* adds to the clamor. Its wilful ethos of *drag it through the mud* ("Mudride") backstrokes *doll-stooges* and headlongs into Dinosaur Jr., J. Mascis and his emphasis on the din. Like Sonic Youth, Mudhoney don't want to be careful. Songs are less important than attack. "Making a record" is not the same as the frenetic slapdash of live. Seattle's paradox of how to harness raw without losing thrust keeps Mudhoney unruly. Their debut album for Sub Pop, the formal introduction of *Mudhoney*, "Flat Out Fucked" to "Here Comes Sickness," tries to catch bedlam on the fly, dutifully sloppy. They'll resist assimilation as long as they can.

||||||

ANDREW WOOD HAS NO SUCH misgivings. He wants the flair of rock stardom, and from the moment he joins with Ament, Gossard, and Fairweather, Mother Love Bone seems preordained. In Malfunkshun he'd masked in whiteface like his hero Paul Stanley, proud to poseur. Now, leaving older brother Kevin behind, the sibling foil whose agitated guitar solos outrun Andrew's voice in Malfunkshun's "Make Sweet Love," he begins to take his calling seriously, though he's quick to smile and can be disarming. All who know him speak of his humor, his ability to make people laugh, though he finds it difficult to turn the joke back on himself. It's too close to home, where he sits in the living room with his family on his twenty-third birthday, January 8, 1989, blond mane tied back, dressed down in purple sweatpants, football in the background, looking very much like the slightly pudgy alien who left Bellingham to take the ferry to Seattle. "I made it," he says wonderingly, out of another spell in rehab, not only marveling at being alive but the imminence and excitement surrounding Mother Love Bone.

He and his exotic girlfriend Xana have moved in with Chris Cornell, a *Three's Company* sitcom in the making, while Mother Love Bone rehearses in the Pioneer Square space Malfunkshun once shared with Green River. They're called Lords of the Wasteland at first, but Wood wants to emphasize Love, because he wants you to love him. Puts the *L* in Landrew. At first it seems the two groups might coexist, but their aims are incompatible. Stone and Jeff want solidity instead of ruckus, and after a few rehearsals, Malfunkshun drummer Regan Hagar comes to practice to find Andrew rehearsing with Greg Gilmore from 10 Minute Warning on the traps, writing and future record deal on the wall. There is already interest from Geffen Records' Anna Statman, who was fond of Green River, and gives the new band a demo deal, though Geffen already has their Guns N' Roses. The smell of chum attracts record companies. When Mother Love Bone showcases at Central Tavern, there's an A&R auction in the street outside the club. Polydor's Michael Goldstone doesn't offer the most money (though he dangles a quarter-million-dollar advance), but his belief in the band's integrity lets them know they have a benevolent home.

They get right to work. The EP *Shine* presents Landrew a-prance, heavy on the *sho' nuf*, the naughty-naught of *half ass monkey boy* testing limits of camp but for the tightrope of guitars that Fairweather and Gossard plait with Ament. It's when Andrew sits at the piano for the ballad "Chloe, Dancer," underlining *A dream like this must die*, prologue to "Crown of Thorns" with its *he who rides the pony must someday fall* that he looks past Mother Love Bone. To Elton John. Or the craving, which has its own song, the refrain that gets under your skin, that you need to hear again and again. The addiction of a hit.

"Crown of Thorns" is refashioned as an epic for *Apple*, the album that is to be their ceremonial unveiling; forbidden fruit as drug of choice. Wood has been on and off heroin, and though it fuels his stage charisma, he wonders if he can be who he aspires to be without its encouragement. The album is set for release in late March 1990, the result of three months' hard labor over the winter, having gone through pre-production (Davitt Sigerson), production (Terry Date and the band), and mixage (Tim Palmer). In the rear taillight of thirty years, it has swagger, boast, balls-to-the-wall (a phrase I was advised to emphasize when producing syndicated radio shows for FM formats in the eighties, don't spare the rod), ready for an arena road test. "Captain Hi-Top" and "Stardog Champion": cue the flashpots and fleshpots.

"This is Shangri-La," Andrew exults as *Apple* (a word yet to assume global dominion) gets under way. But the mythical mountains of Shang conceal their idyll behind purposeful detachment from this world. Hither or yon; Landrew can't decide. He sings the song as if he's already past his sell date, *been around the world . . . a million songs . . . it's all a bore to me.* He says he doesn't *believe in smack / So don't you die on me.* It's the strut of the stage he comes alive for, though he cloaks himself in the raiment of sacrificial: *bread body, wine blood,* die cast.

He's been clean throughout the making of the album, but in the interim he must be anxious, aware of the awaiting exposé. Downtime. There is a grand tour in the works, videos, promotion, the prospect of living up to an idealized vision of who and what he's wanted all his life. On the verge. Of an urge. On March 16, 1990, he relapses for the last time. Xana is delayed at work, returning home to find Andrew oxygen-starved, approaching coma. He spends his last three days on life support while friends gather, before the respirator is turned off, before his legend has a chance to prove itself.

The vigil at the hospital waits until Cornell returns from tour to say farewell. Devastated at the loss of a close friend straddling the same rocket of ascent, his grief spills into two songs, "Say Hello 2 Heaven" and "Reach Down," dreaming of Andrew garbed *in a long white leather coat / Purple glasses and glitter in your hair.* He continues writing while on the road with Soundgarden, though some of what pours from him doesn't fit his band; Andy's spirit haunts him. It seems only right to ask Stone and Jeff to be part of what by December will have grown into an album titled from Mother Love Bone's "Man of Golden Words," *Temple of the Dog.* Gossard and Ament have their own bereavement to share. They've been attempting to raise themselves from the dead with guitarist Mike McCready in the attic of Stone's family home, determined not to let devastation take them down as well.

The album only partially marks Andy's grave site. With Matt Cameron's pistol-shot snare cracking the whip, the focus is on the purged rush of continuance, made in a flurry of weekends, spit out quickly, even joyously. Stone supplies a riff from an unfinished Mother Love Bone song that Chris visualizes as "Times of Trouble"—*When the spoon is hot and the needle's sharp / And you drift away . . .*—but the album isn't about what went wrong. In the several-minute coda of "Reach Down," McCready leaps to faith with a guitar solo that bursts like a fireworks display, Cornell embracing canine virtues of loyalty and pack, and you can feel Ament-Gossard's relief at being able to remember who they were before tragedy struck. In the words of Allen Ginsberg: *light the candle and continue the dance.*

Watching from a corner of the studio is a singer who's just come to town from San Diego, to see if he might hit it off with the band rising from the broken bones of Mother Love. Asked to counterpart *I'm getting hungry* on "Hunger Strike," Eddie Vedder finds himself invited to family dinner, to join hands, say grace.

|||||

INSIDE THE PERFECT CIRCLE, sun glinting and sparkling through the wave as it curls over him. He has been listening to the tape from the Seattle band all night, working graveyard hours at Chevron, over and over, until the instrumentals become part of him. When he goes to the beach in the early morning and takes to the water, he can feel their songs emerge. Surfing the birth canal.

It was Stone who wanted, needed, to keep going over the summer, obsessively sectioning riffs, writing chords on sheets of paper and shuffling them around until they cohere. He collaborates with guitarist Mike McCready after seeing him play Stevie Ray Vaughn's "Couldn't Stand the Weather," and then convinces Jeff to join in. Matt Cameron assists on drums, and they demo the nascent songs at Reciprocal. They need a drummer and singer, and the one thing they know is that it can't be a reincarnation of Mother Love Bone. It wasn't going to be about bombast. They tell *Rolling Stone* in September that "to go out and find another singer who looked like Andy and maybe sang a little bit like Andy would just be prostitution." They want the freedom to play anything that comes to mind.

Jack Irons is the conduit, a drummer temping with Joe Strummer on his 1989 *Earthquake Weather* tour when it stops at San Diego's Bacchanal Club. One of the original Red Hot Chili Peppers, he's still recovering from the 1988 blindside of that band's tragic overdose, guitarist Hillel Slovak. He meets Eddie backstage helping out, forms a friendship based on weekly basketball gaming, and soon Vedder finds himself on the periphery of the Peppers, visiting Yosemite with their coterie, singing in bands that have their funk-rock flavor such as the short-lived Indian Style. When Jeff and Stone visit Los Angeles in September to halfheartedly promote the postponed Mother Love Bone album, they bring their new demos with them to track down Irons, telling him they're also looking for a singer. Jack is in a new band, has a child on the way, and can't move to Seattle, but he bounce-passes the tape to Eddie.

As Vedder surfs, lyrics form; he hastens back to dry land to write them down before they're lost at sea. He draws psychological inspiration from his tangled past, a father he'd met only briefly, who he didn't know was his father until too late, imagining his mother drawn to the father figure within him, and then fictionally embroidering the tale by creating a serial killer to go with intimations of incest, culminating in the murderer's execution. He records this mini-operetta—the seedlings of "Alive," "Once," and "Footsteps"—over a Merle Haggard cassette, adds the date, September 13, and puts it in the mail to Stone and Jeff. The name of the trilogy, *Momma-Son*, subliminally acknowledges lineage from Mother Love Bone though, as Eddie reveals to Jessica Letkemann, he's more inspired by the plot line of the Clash's "Straight to Hell." Vedder's emotional intensity and raw-nerved impassion hurries the band to invite him to Seattle a week later.

Another week and they have more songs at the ready, celebrating team spirit by a show at the Off-Ramp, calling themselves Mookie Blaylock after the Nets basketball star. They tip off, game face on.

Mookie's number *Ten* titles the group's first album, but they become Pearl Jam in the forge of its making. Michael Goldstone has extricated Ament and Gossard from their previous contract, moving the band to his new posting at Epic, and they've scaled back expectation and budget. Almost a day to the year after Andrew Wood's death, they reenter London Bridge Studio with Rick Parashar (with whom and where they made *Temple of the Dog*) to record the catharsis of *Alive*. Dislocation and psychic storm scar Vedder's vocals, desperation's character studies—"Jeremy" and the deflower of "Once"—giving ground to the hoot of affirmation that is "Black" and *Ten*'s closing hymn, "Release." Jeff and Stone are studio savvy; Mike and Eddie, with deputy drummer Dave Krusen, have to keep up, especially Vedder, who is undergoing the bends, the pressure drop of finding himself in a strange town, on a major label, learning to lead a band. They open tracks for him to experiment, leave him on his own in the studio overnight. By the time he dangles from the lighting rig in the video for "Alive," he has daredevil to spare.

While still Mookie Blaylock, the group takes their new material for a West Coast shake-out opening for Alice in Chains, a neighboring band (managed by Susan Silver and Pearl Jam's caretaker Kelly Curtis; it's all in the family) that has leaned left from suburban metal. There is suspicion about their glam origins from the alterna-police, but they've bonded inside the free-for-all of a multi-band rehearsal building called the Music Bank under the Ballard bridge. With a newly pressed debut album, *Facelift*, and claustrophobic hit, "Man in a Box," singer Layne Staley and guitarist Jerry Cantrell slip sideways into Seattle's foreboding cloud cover. They twin vocals, Cantrell on talk box (ventriloquism that gimcracks Pete Drake's "Forever" to *Frampton Comes Alive* and

Richie Sambora), Layne bewailing Jesus, imminent burial, and a premonition of the drug confinement that increasingly isolates him from the rest of the band. Producer Dave Jerden is fresh from capturing Jane's Addiction, drummer Sean Kinney basic-tracks with a broken hand, and its barnyard MTV video takes them to the heartland.

Alice in Chains bridges the bands they open for after *Facelift* comes out in August 1990—Van Halen, Poison, Extreme, a sacrificial slot on the 1991 *Clash of the Titans* tour where they battle Slayer, Anthrax, and Megadeth—with the downer miasma of Seattle. They detour for an acoustic EP, *Sap*, with guesting from "Alice Mudgarden" and Heart's Ann Wilson. By the time they roll in the muck of 1992's *Dirt*—"Junkhead," "God Smack," the skin-pop "Down in the Hole"—even Jerry's baleful storm of guitars can't save his singer from the scourge of overdose and oblivion. *I think it's gonna Rain When I Die* sings Layne, but it's always raining in Seattle.

Vedder conversely seeks sun, surfs riptide and undertow, maintains balance as Pearl Jam hangs *Ten* on August 27. Six weeks later Soundgarden's third album, *Badmotorfinger*, joins the fray, songs united by elephant-tusk riffs dredged out of the lower end of the guitar neck by Chris and Kim, new bassist Ben Shepard a full songwriting partner, adjoining Cameron's lockdown of the rhythm section: denominator 4, nominator any. "Slaves and Bulldozers" displays the astonishing range of Cornell's octavian vocal, Thayil matching with a solo bastinado. "Jesus Christ Pose" both exalts and mocks the rock star tableaux that Chris, bare sternum, flinging hair, enacts onstage nightly. Stripped of askew time signatures and stompbox guitars, "Rusty Cage"—so much Seattle music about breaking out of prison—is bare bones, a plaintive country rocker that Johnny Cash gnarls on his 1996 *Unchained*, bringing out the unbowed and unvanquished. Cash preaches the second half, *raining ice picks on your steel shore*. It would've been great to hear him do it at San Quentin.

There's more accessible song construction with 1994's *Super-unknown* and the sixties Brit psychedelia of "Black Hole Sun," but in this fall all Seattle, *Badmotorfinger* is the trailblazer. Listening just five minutes ago, three decades into the album's future, its sleek segues, Cthulhu lyrics, drop-D*ead* tuning and knife-blade execution, make it the most aspirational of their graduating class, their own magnificent beast.

Both Pearl Jam and Soundgarden multiply platinum, but on September 28 another group splits the infinitive. Enter phenomenon.

||||||

NIRVANA IS THE RUNT OF THE LITTER.

They contain all the bands of Seattle within them, which is why they're picked from the pack. They offer Melvins' heft, the sprawl and chaos of Mudhoney, Soundgarden's angst and power hooks, Posies' chorus and pop hooks, Alice in Chains' bottomless pit, Pearl Jam's reckless uplift, and the in-betweens: Screaming Trees, TAD, Gas Huffer, the Gits, and your favorite underdog whom I've left out.

In some ways they're more of an Olympia band, at least in lo-fi ideal and anti-star attitude, though Kurt Cobain doesn't want to admit that he yearns to be the center of attention. He moves to the Evergreen College–correct town in the summer of 1987, a bohemian bastion that is Washington's go-to outsider destination, after growing up in a schism'd family situation that bisects him, a spell of homelessness and an attraction to graffiti, drugs, and turtles. He takes refuge in obsessive notebook scribbling, painting, and practicing his guitar in a room illustrated with role-play ripped from local gig flyers, like many inclined in his generation, attracted to all the usual suspects: Sex Pistols, AC/DC, Alice

Cooper, MC5, Minor Threat, Bad Brains, Scratch Acid, Pixies, and yes, the Beatles. Meeting an older classmate at Aberdeen High School, Buzz Osborne and his nascent version of the Melvins, he curves toward a punk rock that suits his alienation, an alien himself. When he travels to Seattle in August 1984 to see Henry Rollins and Black Flag agitate "Damaged II," he finds his "godsend," as he tells Michael Azerrad. Now he's ready for a band.

Krist Novoselic is another Aberdeen High student of Cobain's acquaintance, a gangling misfit with a penchant for drunken hijinx who frequents the Melvins' practice space. Though initially reticent, he takes a liking to a home-baked tape called *Illiteracy Will Prevail* that Kurt makes in the spring of 1986 on his Aunt Mary's four-track, with Dale Crover banging drums and bass. The "band" was called Fecal Matter, sometimes augmented by other Melvins over its six months of existence before dissolving, with titles like "Class of '86," where Cobain takes on the persona of a jock who beats up "punk rock faggots," the cross-gendered "Laminated Effect" about a lesbian's affair with a male AIDS victim who was raped by his father, and "Spank Thru," an ode to masturbation that piques Krist's interest and will be handed down through Cobain-Novoselic to Nirvana's early repertoire. One song not recorded at the "session" is "Suicide Samurai." He's already spelling his name Kurdt, "guitar/mouth," trying on guises. In between songs are audio snatches of *Reefer Madness* and Cobain coughing; prescience as aspiration.

The Melvins relocated to San Francisco later that year, leaving Crover behind, and Novoselic returns from Phoenix where he'd gone to look for steady employment. By March 1987 Kurt and Krist start playing out with the first of several drummers that will pass through early Nirvana, though they haven't yet come up with the name. They call themselves Ted Ed Fred on the night of January 23, 1988, when they perform to twenty people at the Community World Theater in Tacoma. That afternoon they've traveled to Seattle to Reciprocal studios, where Jack Endino records nine and a half songs (they run out of tape and can't afford the thirty dollars for another reel) with Crover, who's paved the way for the session; his involvement provides credibility. Endino is intrigued enough to mix down a cassette for himself, taken with Kurt's "rock scream," the way his melodies don't just replicate guitar riffs, and passes it to Jonathan Poneman at Sub Pop.

Can you see into the future? In the rearview mirror, what has become known as *Dale Demo* is Nirvana closer-than-they-appear, glimpsing destiny; Kurt's word spray in "Downer," down/up verse/chorus in "Floyd the Barber," a manic "Spank Thru" solo, the *Exorcist* vocals of "Hairspray Queen," his overloaded amplifier squeal and struggle to be heard. Sub Pop plays safe, making Nirvana's cover of "Love Buzz" the lead-off 45 of their subscription Singles Club in November 1988, first one thousand numbered, another couple hundred unnumbered, black vinyl, a Shocking Blue surefire: more pop than sub.

He's not like the other guys in town. Kurt courts vulnerability, the raw wound, just shy of the dreaded *cute* despite the bravado it takes to bend these songs to his will. He tries to camouflage into his surroundings, a shapeless sweater, favored band T-shirt, tattered jeans and dirty-blond hair curtaining his closed eyes, searing blue when opened. He plays guitar lefty, like Jimi, which makes it hard to glimpse how unadorned his chords are. Early on he finds it difficult to sing and play at the same time, so he simplifies to do both.

Their first proper show in Seattle is at the Vogue on April 24, 1988, in the 2000 block of First Avenue, opening band in front of twenty people, sure they'd blown it. I know the view from that stage myself, having played there in the summer of 1981 when it was called WREX, a former gay bar turned New Wave, the front window viewing First Avenue when it was still the seedy destination for merchant seamen on the prowl, littered with signposts of ill repute: tattoo parlors, x-rated book shops, bars below dive. I miss the milieu.

They may be learning to play, at the mercy of battered equipment and recalcitrant PA systems, despite Kurt's emphasis on intensive practice, but new drummer Chad Channing tightens them over the spring. When they showcase for Sub Pop at Central Tavern on June 5 they're ready to record "Love Buzz." This time the Endino session is more painstaking, thirteen hours over three days, with another stab at "Spank Thru" and a pair of Cobain originals vying for the b-side: "Big Cheese" and "Blandest." Though Kurt is frustrated with Sub Pop's money glitches and the limited edition of their debut, he's realizing the band is not just a figment of his overactive imagination. He smashes his first guitar onstage at a Halloween party in Olympia, a Fender Mustang, as the single is about to come out, his coming out celebrated like the shattered bottle of champagne that christens a seafaring vessel.

They score a coveted third-track slot on *Sub Pop 200*'s labelware sampler with "Spank Thru" in December, placing them on a par with TAD, Soundgarden ("Sub Pop Rock City"), Blood Circus, the Walkabouts, Mudhoney, and doomed Burroughsesque performance-poet Steven "Jesse" Bernstein. On Christmas Eve Nirvana begin a proper album, Endino again at Reciprocal, finishing in the first breaths of 1989. They bring Jason Everman along, debating a second guitarist, but his only contribution is good-humoredly paying for the session. Despite Kurt's slouch and mischievous glimmer, he is untangling how to streamline his out-of-control. For all their onstage havoc, he runs a tight ship. Channing's fiberglass futurama kit initially attracts him, and on *Bleach* Chad ably pinpoints Cobain's arithmetic, though he can't match Kurt's aggression; the perfect isosceles for their triangle is yet to show. For now Nirvana readies to tour up and down the coast, sleep on floors, scrounge for gas money, eat crap food, listen to the Smithereens and Celtic Frost and the Sugarcubes in the van, see if Everman fits (he doesn't), and hone their set list for the album's release.

Bleach adheres to Sub Pop's blueprint more than Cobain wants, but he's not in a position to bargain. He needs the record out, and there's something to be said for the album's clarity of purpose. There are holdovers from the demos with Crover, "Paper Cuts" and "Floyd the Barber," but Cobain (or is it Kurdt Kobain, as he names himself in the credits) is outgrowing his Melvins fixation. They drop even lower than D, to C where strings flop against the neck, for "Blew," Novoselic's bass growling, and "School" is *reductio ad absurdum*, fifteen words complaining about the *no recess* of Seattle's band cliques: *You're in High School Again.* Class clown. The album's surprise is "About a Girl," slow enough in comparison to the other tracks to be considered a ballad, timbre and b-section straight off *Meet the Beatles.* Paced within the album, "Love Buzz" seems even more trance-like, and "Swap Meet" perfectly describes the *what-will-I-find?* anticipation of entering a flea market, foraging in society's leavings now yours for the taking. Kurt sloughs off *Bleach*'s lyrics, says he didn't spend much time on them, last minute on the way to the studio, but his phrases and word associations work like cutups, snatches of mood-swing and unerring slogan: *You could do anything* from "Blew" to the obverse *I'm a Negative Creep and I'm stoned.*

It's a motto that could be a T-shirt for Sub Pop's Lame Fest on June 9, 1989, at the Moore, capacity 1,100, a quasi-release party for *Bleach* as well as pin-in-the-map for Seattle. The sold-out show culminates in a bouncer-band free-for-all with headliners Mudhoney. It may seem odd to see Nirvana with Kurt center stage, flanked by Krist and Jason's long hair-whipping, but when all hell breaks loose at the end of "Blew," Kurt racing back and forth swinging his guitar by the strap like a lasso, leaping headfirst into the drums, his exhilaration is a joy to behold.

Roadside America, then to Europe for six weeks in the fall, again as a trio, thirty-six shows with TAD, nine musicians and crew packed in a Fiat minivan (including three hundred pounds of Tad Doyle and Novoselic's six feet, seven inches), eyewitnessing the collapse of the Berlin Wall, a Kurt meltdown in Rome where he climbs the PA speakers and attempts to jump, winding up December 3 at the Lame Festival, London Astoria, Mudhoney atop the bill as they are on the British alternative charts. The rock weeklies' incendiary coverage and John Peel's championing of Sub Pop's miscreants have given provenance to the Seattle sound. Nirvana's set ends with Kurt and Krist playing baseball, Cobain pitching his guitar at Novoselic, who wields his bass as a bat. Home run.

They return, perhaps not as conquering heroes, but able to think of themselves as professionals, to wonder whether Sub Pop, verging on perennial bankruptcy, has the wherewithal to do more than haphazardly release and promote their records. Kurt doesn't like being portrayed by the label as "illiterate redneck cousin-fucking kids that have no idea what's going on at all," as he tells the *Rocket*, and is also having doubts about Chad, who hoped to have more creative input into Nirvana than just be their "drum machine," the designated object of percussive destruction at the end of a show.

The group leaves Seattle for a tour east in the wake of Andrew Wood's death, and in early April arrives at Butch Vig's Smart Studios in Madison, Wisconsin, to record songs for a proposed second album. Vig is referred to Nirvana by TAD, who worked with him on *8 Way Santa*, which introduces complementary melodic elements to TAD's blunt force, enhanced by Butch's empathy with Killdozer, the Laughing Hyenas, Die Kruzen. Kurt too is looking for the right meld, somewhere between Flipper and the Knack. We contain multitudes. Seven songs are recorded, and Kurt sees them as his ticket out of Sub Pop.

Bleach filters through the alt-rock grapevine over the next year, giving Nirvana name-to-drop recognition. *From Seattle!* is emblazoned on a flyer when they visit the Pyramid Club on April 26 in the East Village, on a bill with local noise merchants Rat At Rat R and Cop Shoot Cop, Iggy Pop witnessing along-side Sonic Youth's Thurston Moore and Kim Gordon, who have brought Gary Gersh, A&R head of Geffen's DGC alternative imprint, major label awareness that what was once independent and marginal is now cutting-edge mainstream. Ill at ease, Kurt gets into sound hassles with the club's tech staff, though mid-set songs from the Vig sessions—"Immodium" (later titled "Breed") and "In Bloom"—catch the attention of the chattering crowd. The guitar smashed that night is an Epiphone ET-270 for those who care, as I do. Nirvana feels their show is so dire that Krist shaves his head in penance by the time they get to Maxwell's across the river; they've already crossed the Rubicon with Sub Pop, new recordings now a demo tape. Chad is let go after a last show in Boise, Idaho, at the end of the two-month tour, resigned and diplomatic about leaving.

Sonic Youth takes Nirvana under their wing, up and down the coast with Dale Crover subbing, opening in prestige venues like the Hollywood Palladium, the Warfield in San Francisco, their hometown Moore. Susan Silver introduces them to a do-the-deal music attorney in Los Angeles, and Sonic Youth recommends their management firm, Gold Mountain, run by Danny Goldberg, a rock scribe and former *Circus* editor who has parlayed his taste and savoir-faire to the executive suites of record companies. Danny's progressive politics and understanding of Nirvana's need to honor "their values and the culture that formed them" along with Sonic Youth's vouchsafe does much to allay Kurt's fear of selling his soul. Sign here.

As a working record producer of the time, I'm a grateful recipient of demo possibilities, artists looking for someone to shepherd them through the recording process, especially in the rite of passage that is independent-moving-to-major. Most are looking for what I've already done, as opposed to what I might do, but I've learned what not to do. Somewhere around Thanksgiving 1990 Arista A&R sends me a cassette, one side Smashing Pumpkins, the other Nirvana. Ready for the big time. Clive Davis doesn't bite—he's in another kingdom of the music business with Whitney Houston—though I'm taken with Nirvana, especially "Polly," its sudden acoustic empathy amid bawling Stooges lineage. My only thought is that they sound perfect as is. And will be.

||||||

IT'S BEEN LESS THAN two years since they were crashing three to a mattress while on the road, Kurt and Krist scheming about starting a cleaning service in Olympia (Pine Tree Janitorial, though there are no takers) to make ends meet. Now they're the biggest band in the world.

In the short span of fall 1991 making way for winter, *Nevermind* leapfrogs to top the *Billboard* album charts in early January, displacing Michael Jackson's *Dangerous*, which cost ten million dollars and is the most genre-encompassing release of the world's reigning superstar (the first single is a biracial duet with Paul McCartney). Yes, *Nevermind* has been primed by the flash point of "Smells Like Teen Spirit" (not on the demo) with its kissin'-cousin chorus chords reminiscent of Boston's "More Than a Feeling" and Pixies-ish dynamics; MTV-demographic video set in an apocalyptic school gym, complete with sexily deadpan cheerleaders wearing anarchy symbols, a riotous student uprising, and the furor surrounding Seattle as rock and roll's newest mecca. But this "palace coup," as *Billboard*'s Paul Grein puts it, is not only on the charts, but off the charts, unprecedented in ascendance for an underground band.

The recording of *Nevermind* takes place over six weeks in May and June at Sound City, a venerable Van Nuys studio with RIAA-certified credentials framed on its walls from the likes of Fleetwood Mac and Neil Young, known for its Rupert Neve recording console and drum-friendly acoustics. This last will highlight Nirvana's missing link. Butch Vig's proven working relationship with the band has retained him as engineer/producer; his experience as a drummer gives him something to engage with newest member Dave Grohl, who hits as hard as his hero John Bonham, but with the urgency and frontal push-comes-to-shove of the Washington, D.C., hardcore community from which his band Scream has emerged.

There is immediate connection between Kurt and Dave when they get together in September 1990. Once again, the Melvins provide matchmaking, taking Kurt and Krist to see Scream at the I-Beam in San Francisco, Buzz passing along Dave's phone number. He soon moves in with Kurt in Olympia; in the fall Nirvana tour England, returning home to practice incessantly, awaiting fate's writing on the wall, which turns out to be Kathleen Hanna of Bikini Kill, Grohl's girlfriend, scrawling *Kurt smells like teen spirit* in his bedroom, the spoor of pubescent female and runaway success.

Expectations are modest at DGC, which would be pleased to move half Sonic Youth's 200,000 units for *Goo*, maybe more so with the undeniable "Teen Spirit" that Nirvana premieres on April 17 at the OK Hotel, where Kurt abashedly tells the crowd "Hello, we're major-label corporate rock sell-outs." But the company knows to leave well enough alone. If anything, Kurt has planned for this all his life, a vessel of disparate conflictions and influences and razor-sharp instinct for dredging the perfect phrase from his demonology. What is most remarkable about *Nevermind* is that his songs leave nothing to chance. They are his way out of himself, his pain and self-hatred, his physical suffering, his mental misbegotten. Has inner rage ever been more sing-a-long?

For an album to mean more than the sum of its hits, it has to anticipate cultural need, articulate disembodied undercurrents and unfulfilled longings for a communal voice that offers solution, if not absolution. *A denial* Kurt crows at the end of "Teen Spirit," but there has to be more to negation than annihilation. At least for now. *Nevermind* arrives on the cusp of change—the profligate 1980s of indulgence, flaunted wealth, and the last gaspings of boomer hero worship betrayed in Reaganomics and backstages full of wanton misogyny and machismo—a harbinger of transformation coded in fragments of estrangement. Kurt's lyrics enact less linear than splintered dichotomy, *mosquito/libido*, both with their rush of blood.

Rock noir. Dissecting Alan Ladd's "cinematic cool" in 1942's *This Gun for Hire*, Joel Dinerstein close-ups "'the sympathetic rebel' and his sexual charisma; the combination of toughness and vulnerability; the allure of violence as metaphorical revolt; the self-absorption of teenagers and their need for cinematic icons to dream on." It's a ritual that moves through youth as growth spurt, *Nevermind*'s Elvis and James Dean, Mick/Keith and Johnny Rotten, run aground in the bleak dystopias of Metallica and metal's increasing fascination with death.

There is something ascetic about Kurt, as well as his Seattle compatriots. Soundgarden are referred to as "Frowngarden" when they open for Guns N' Roses and don't participate in the buffet of debauchery; Pearl Jam as well keep distance, emphasizing moral elevation (Alice in Chains splits the difference). This isn't to say that things are staid on the festival circuit where alternative bands go to frolic at the end of the summer. In *1991: The Year Punk Broke*, a home movie compered by Sonic Youth's Thurston

Moore of a sojourn through northern Europe with Nirvana, Dinosaur Jr., Mudhoney, Babes in Toyland, cameos of the Pixies and the Ramones, food fights and guzzled wine and abrasive noise-on-overload pop the cork on the ascendance of rock's newest revolutionary guard. There is innocence to the movie's embrace of destiny, a giddy joy in feeling that the battle is being won, even if the war is over. "God knows what it's gonna be like in the future and the future to us is a dare," Thurston proclaims, taking up the cudgel. "Fuck 'em all."

||||||

IN SPRING OF 1991 director Cameron Crowe scripts a rom-com around Seattle's mating dance, alerted to the local music scene by his then-wife, Heart's Nancy Wilson. *Singles* only uses bands as window dressing—there are bit parts for Eddie Vedder and Jeff Ament, Alice in Chains playing to a crowd as interested in picking each other up as the music onstage, and Matt Damon as a lovable lunk who sweetens the grunge image with his Abelard to Bridget Fonda's Heloise. Kind of like Kurt meeting Courtney Love. And as ménage à trois adds dramatic frisson, there will be a third party to their introduction: narcotics, with their beckon of seduction.

Yet they're made for each other, in a moon-june-spoon kind of way. She's aggressive; he's passive-regressive. *How-did-you-meet?* They love-at-first-sight when she and Cobain exchange interested glances at Portland's Satyricon in early 1989 (he reminds her of Soul Asylum's Dave Pirner), but their attraction is sealed when she punches him in the stomach at a Butthole Surfers concert in Los Angeles in May 1991 while Nirvana is embarking on *Nevermind*. Kid stuff. She's friendly with Dave Grohl and is a fellow traveler in the alterna-world, having passed through Faith No More on her way to forming her band Hole in late 1989 with guitarist Eric

Erlandsen. Their debut album, *Pretty on the Inside*, produced by Kim Gordon, is about to come out on Caroline and Love is dating the lead singer on the other side of my demo cassette, Billy Corgan of Smashing Pumpkins. She and Kurt exchange phone numbers. Courtney gifts him a heart-shaped box. He opens it.

They play tag on the Sonic Youth tour ("Kurt Cobain makes my heart stop. But he's a shit," she tells the camera), and first kiss at Chicago's Metro club in October when she leaves Corgan, the same month *Nevermind* goes gold. By November they're in Europe together on separate itineraries, connected by telephone and a mutual attraction to heroin. In December they decide to get married, not yet knowing Courtney is pregnant. She has become part of the Nirvana entourage, as has their drug of choice. When Nirvana play *Saturday Night Live* on January 11, the same week *Nevermind* tops the charts, Kurt overdoses in his hotel room after. These events are not unrelated.

||||||

NOW IT'S THE WORLD'S TURN to overdose on Seattle.

Grunge packages easily, like china white in a glassine envelope. Alternative bands—even those who hardly resemble Nirvana— are pulled along in its wake, the rush of promised riches and an audience baying for fresh fish. Labels like Amphetamine Reptile, Touch-and-Go, Wax Trax!, and Sub Pop itself not only find their rosters raided, but themselves up for corporate merger, negotiating distribution deals. It's full-fad fashion, shorts and timberland plaids, mess of hair, clunk of boots. It's a lingo, though invented on the spot when Sub Pop's Megan Jasper answers a call from the *New York Times* Style section. Her colloquialisms are priceless: an "uncool person" is a *lamestain*, "hanging out" is *swingin' on the flippity-flop*, staying home over the weekend is *bound-and-hagged*. I wish she would've written lyrics for a band.

Mudhoney sticks with Sub Pop for *Every Good Boy Deserves Fudge*, released July 1991, tidal-waved unfairly by Seattle's fall schedule. Recorded in Conrad Uno's basement studio, its controlled grip on disarray shows why Nirvana was once considered, in the words of Thrown-Ups bassist John Beezer, the "next best Mudhoney." They stay close to home, garaging punk, which amounts to Steve Turner's new Farfisa organ alongside ramrod guitars. Prolegomenon "Generation Genocide" hearkens toward Iron Butterfly before "Let It Slide" foretells *Everybody's got a price* and *shoulda seen it coming* in "Something So Clear." They would be happy to stay with Sub Pop, but label finances seem beyond recoup (this before overrides on *Nevermind* kick in). Mudhoney won't change working methods for 1992's *Piece of Cake* when Reprise considerably upgrades their budget (they stay at Uno's and keep the change), because they're happy where they are, their circuit, their fans, their freedom to fuck up and have fun. Put a down payment on a house you can afford. Keep playing. Their contribution to the *Singles* soundtrack, "Overblown," gets it all-too-right: *Everybody loves us / Everybody loves our town / That's why I'm thinking lately / The time for leaving is now.*

Grunge's governance threatens to overwhelm bands outside its castle keep. Popster Posies Jon Auer and Ken Stringfellow have been working from their basement in the style of XTC and Squeeze since 1988, and are one of the first groups picked up by Geffen subdivision DGC in August 1990. Their prime number *Dear 23* is lyrically darker than Hollies' harmonies and pealing guitars might suggest. Like Big Star, they never get the hit they deserve (Auer and Stringfellow actually join the Chilton-Stevens reunion edition of Big Star in 1993), though "Golden Blunders" is covered by Ringo. "Apology" and "I May Hate You Sometimes" (from their PopLlama debut *Failure*) will feature on Rhino's *Children of Nuggets*; kids coming home for the holidays.

As expected there are sound-alikes, but grunge aspirants are often unjustly tarred despite fan approval that cares little for geo-graphic origin. Stone Temple Pilots, led by Scott Weiland, may have Pearl Jam in their veins ("Plush") and a song called "Creep" on their 1992 debut *Core*, but this San Diego band did meet at a Black Flag concert. By the time they get to 1994's *Purple* and its stand-out "Interstate Love Song," an Eagles-ish twilight suf-fuses their northwest cloud cover. Gavin Rossdale's Bush, from the United Kingdom, are unapologetic about Nirvana's influence, though by 1994 and *Sixteen Stone* the sound of grunge must be as attractive as the British Invasion was to every American garage band. Even Seattleites aren't immune to charges of "flying the flannel." Candlebox signs with Madonna's Maverick label amid grumblings though they've been a local undercard since the late eighties; and Courtney Love finds her star ascendant to where her million-dollar deal with DGC eclipses her husband's.

Both TAD and Screaming Trees predate the furor, long in tooth when the majors start trawling. Led by magisterial Tad Doyle, TAD have been on Sub Pop since 1988, produced by En-dino; their introductory album, *God's Balls*, cements industrial-strength din with horrorcore bludgeon, drive-in ripe: "Cyanide Bath" and "Sex God Missy (Lumberjack Mix)." It makes sense to up the rasp with Chicago's Steve Albini of Big Black for an EP, *Salt Lick*, adding shrill and surgical diligence, while *8-Way Santa*, produced by Butch Vig, grounds their roar melodically (a pro-ducer path Nirvana will reverse engineer). Sub Pop imagine TAD as bong-hitting, chain-saw-carving backwoods primitives, and Tad (an affable guy, by all accounts) goes along with the hillbilly humor (Haystacks Calhoun wrestling Antonino Rocca at Madi-son Square Garden), leading off *God's Balls* with "Behemoth." *8-Way Santa*'s tunefulness comes out in January 1991, set to her-ald a year of breakthrough, but fate puts coal in their stocking. Pepsi sues for a drunk-driving song called "Jack Pepsi" (though it's more Jack Coke), as does the stoned couple on the cover, now born-again Christians, the album yanked from stores as it arrives. Warners subsidiary Giant sponsors them in-studio with Dinosaur Jr.'s J. Mascis for 1993's *Inhaler*, good job all around, pups on the cover, but grunge is refining past gruff into a sleeker mongrel.

Screaming Trees have already gone through several bust-ups as a band, three albums on SST, two brothers that are, well, two brothers, and a lead singer who hates everything they do. "Our records were a shitty mishmash of half-baked ideas and catchy tunes derailed by the stupidest of lyrics," Mark Lanegan memoirs in *Sing Backwards and Weep*, finding himself constantly at war with "lunatic Falstaffian" guitarist Gary Lee Conner. "Lee had been solely responsible for generating our music and always acted as if he were . . . the center of our universe." His brother Van helps keep the peace, but Lanegan's blackout drinking and mounting heroin habit adds to the Trees' dysfunction, though Susan Silver manages to secure them one of the first major label contracts with Epic's Bob Pfeifer in 1990. *Uncle Anesthesia*, released in January 1991, produced by Terry Date and Chris Cornell, might be enough to keep them going, with its minor hit "Bed of Roses," but for Mark it's "more of the same shit we'd always done, it just sounded better." In his mind, Lee is a "controlling, obsessive, savant-like brother residing somewhere . . . in fantasyland," who demo'd three to four songs a day and hogged the spotlight wind-milling his guitar. For his part Lee refuses to hit below the belt. "The sum total of us was a gestalt called Screaming Trees. We did not ever get along like friends and sometimes it felt like we were enemies, but we did work together . . . to create a musical legacy that I am very proud of." Band shit, as Memphian producer Jim Dickinson would say.

Lanegan makes a solo album for Sub Pop in 1990, during one of the Trees' dissolutions, the dirge-like *The Winding Sheet*, and finds someone he can respect when Nirvana visits the Trees' hometown of Ellensburg two years before. Kurt is a Trees fan, and though the show only lasts a couple of songs before an imposed curfew ends in fistfights and Krist swinging his bass like a battle axe, it's enough for Mark to see Nirvana as "fully developed," what he would like his band to be. He begins listening to Nick Cave and Drake, and when Kurt visits Seattle from Olympia, the two plan an album of Leadbelly songs, never realized, though "Where Did You Sleep Last Night" so resonates with Cobain that he will use it to close Nirvana's MTV *Unplugged*, a performance sculpted by *The Winding Sheet* where it first appears as finale, Krist on bass and Kurt harmonizing.

Cajoled back into the band by an offer of lyric writing and mutual cooperation, heartened by new drummer Barrett Martin from Skin Yard, 1992's *Sweet Oblivion*—buoyed by "Nearly Lost You" on the *Singles* soundtrack—gives new life to Screaming Trees, though a November tour with Alice in Chains finds two frontmen enabling each other's drug vortex. Despite the warning of Andrew Wood's demise, heroin has dug its claws into Seattle. Mark Arm nurtures a habit. In June 1992, 7 Year Bitch guitarist Stefanie Sargent succumbs to a lethal cocktail of alcohol and heroin. And then there's Kurt, whose enticement to what he calls *heroine* in his journal has pulled Nirvana off the road at their moment of triumph.

Perversely, Alice in Chains thrives. *Dirt* takes them from clubs to theaters and beyond, a confessional cycle of a dozen songs backsliding the twelve steps of Anonymous. It's not just Layne's attrition, *What's my drug of choice / well, what have you got?* to the cold sweats of "Hate to Feel," but Jerry Cantrell's need to make peace with his father, a Vietnam vet who brought the war home to his family. In "Rooster," producer Dave Jerden snakes his guitar through a thirty-one-inch bass drum into a woofer, an ordnance exploding in jungle combat, the imminence of death courted like a lover. Charlie Parker's Dial sessions. Any album by Chet Baker.

Tim Hardin, Tim Buckley. Neil Young's *Tonight's the Night. Dirt* follows down the hole the needle opens, vein to pleasure center of the brain where it enfolds pain. Opposites attract.

Can music unlock sobriety? In 1994, Mike McCready finishes a stay in a Minnesota rehab where he befriends bassist John Baker Saunders. They side-project together as mutual reinforcement, add Barrett Martin on drums, and in an attempt to encourage Layne in a similar direction, place him center stage. Staley's lyrics are fit for a therapist's couch, an agree-to-disagree inner dialogue that shows he's aware but unwilling to take his own advice. *Slow suicide is no way to go-oh* he croons in "Wake Up," but that's exactly the path in store for him, Saunders as well. Mad Season's *Above* paces like a sustained nod, long bluesworthy meditations interspersed with guitar solos that hint at redemption. When Mark Lanegan stops by, he and Staley write "Long Gone Day," lyrics passed between them like a straw over chopped crystal, one more, then one more, and then another.

||||||

HE WEARS A BALL-GOWN WHEN Nirvana visits MTV'S *Headbanger's Ball*. Cinderella. Host Rikki Rachtman doesn't get Kurt's sense of humor, but then few do.

Has he become what he set himself against? His attempts to undermine—on the cover of *Rolling Stone* wearing a T-shirt that protests *corporate magazines still suck*, videos for MTV that pisstake videos, brought onstage at the Reading Festival in a wheelchair to laugh off rumors that he's ill—only accelerate Nirvana's impact.e He may resist his crown as the ragged *voiceofhisgeneration*, but he has no choice. The omega has spoken.

Cobain is torn between Olympian ideals that caused him to have Calvin Johnson's K Records logo tattooed on his left forearm, and the corporate stardom that has taken him to unimaginable heights. Johnson—whose acolytes refer to themselves as Calvinists—is staunchly anti-rock, his motto "learn not to play." There is a new breed of take-charge feminist energy emanating from Olympia, the riot grrrrl movement sparked by Bikini Kill (whose drummer, Tobi Vail, was Cobain's girlfriend pre-*Nevermind*) and Sleater-Kinney. He is aware his audience now includes the macho meatheads who once scorned him, and warns on the compilation *Insecticide* that "if any of you hate homosexuals, people of color, or women . . . leave us the fuck alone."

The July 1993 murder of Mia Zapata of the Gits while walking home from the Comet Tavern only underscores danger. *It hurts me to be angry / Kills me to be kind*, she sings in "Bob (Cousin O.)," her stage presence devoid of artifice, an exemplar of empowerment for gender that knows no boundaries, providence foreshortened. The crime sends shock waves throughout the Seattle band community, and it will be ten long years before her random killer is brought to justice.

In choosing Steve Albini to subtract slick, *In Utero* recoils against *Nevermind*'s supposed radio-friendly sheen, though except for a starker vocal-band balance and a need to up the treble control, its state-of-mind teeters on disavowal. *Teenage angst has paid off well* is the opening salvo of the album ("Serve the Servants") and "Radio Friendly Unit Shifter" repetitions *what is wrong with me?* like a record skipping, Kurt's guitar an unearthly shriek. It's recorded quickly, in less than two weeks, almost as if they were back at Reciprocal. Though Geffen is hoping for a do-over, not only for Albini's production but *Nevermind*'s success, a dismissive Albini, who thinks Nirvana has "R.E.M. with a fuzz-box" tendencies, is adamant that this was the record the group asked him to make. Avoiding obvious sing-a-longs, *In Utero* is in his view "a powerful personal punk rock record." Kurt see-saws, and the two most accessible tracks—"Heart Shaped Box" and "All Apologies"—are remixed by Scott Litt, who works with R.E.M. Small world.

Pearl Jam is also reactive in their follow-up to *Ten*, an album whose slow burn up the charts—it finally breaks into the Top Ten in May 1992 and tops *Nevermind*'s sales early the following year—is no less discomfiting for their lead singer. The group relentlessly tours, videos for "Alive" and "Jeremy" transforming their fan base, and Seattle's hoopla has boosted their deserved fortunes. The press, always ripe for a schoolyard brawl, replays a Beatles-Stones rivalry with Nirvana. Cobain takes the bait—he calls Pearl Jam "careerist," "only in it for the money," "a safe rock band." He who is without sin. Pearl Jam have punk bona fides of their own, and when Eddie and Kurt slow dance in September at the MTV video awards while watching Eric Clapton's "Tears in Heaven," a nation sighs in relief.

Pressure weighs heavily on Pearl Jam when they embark on what will be *Vs.* Producer Brendan O'Brien loosens the band by starting each workday with a softball game, but when he refers to a prospective song, "Better Days," as a hit, it's promptly shelved until the group's next album, *Vitalogy*. Unlike Nirvana's recidivism, Pearl Jam take on the challenge presented by mass acceptance and, like Soundgarden, use it to push themselves over the cliff edge of what they are capable. *Vs.* bolts out the gate with the hyperventilating "Go," and in a dizzying fury—"Animal," "Daughter," "Dissident"—offers no apologia, even if Eddie has to drive from the well-appointed studio in Marin County to San Francisco's skid row, spending nights in his truck to reclaim desolation. The topics are lethal, covering child abuse, police racism, the *fuckin' circus* that is the media vampire of "Blood." Like the angora on the cover, Pearl Jam are ready for a cage match.

In Utero tees off first on September 21, two years to the week after *Nevermind*; Pearl Jam follows on October 19. The opening tallies show which band has beguiled the mainstream. Both albums debut at number one. Nirvana SoundScans 180,000; Pearl Jam nearly a million. *Time* juggles which of Kurt/Eddie to put on the cover of their October 25 issue. To Vedder's dismay, it's him, titled "All the Rage." It only makes Pearl Jam more wary of outside interference.

But for me, it's another band whose album also releases September 21 that captures the truest resonance of Seattle, there at the beginning and ever after. Kurt has used his cachet to get Atlantic to sign the Melvins with him as ostensible producer. *Houdini*, with its Darger-esque cover, followed by *Stoner Witch* in 1994, and much later by *Stag* (1996), has Buzz and Dale doing pretty much the same thing they always have, clumps of opaque chords, absurdist lyrics, depth-charge riffings, strangely hummable. They know they're in it for the long haul, no chance of sellout because they're not for sale. They take a side trip to *Prick*, a noisy little fucker that actually comes out on Boner to complement *Stoner Witch*, and cause Atlantic to release them into the wild with *Stag*, an album (sitar!, horn section!) calculated to weed out unbelievers, or just reach for the weed. They waste no time, *Honky* in the can when they are released from servitude. At last count, they have over forty albums, not including compilations. Lord love 'em.

Nirvana dutifully sets out to promote *In Utero* in America, but Cobain is uneasy with the band lineup, distancing himself from Krist and Dave. He adds Pat Smear from the Germs on second guitar, brings along a cellist, and when the band does *MTV Unplugged* in November, finds a path to reevaluation in a more austere ensemble. Ex–Screaming Trees drummer Mark Pickerel sends him a copy of Talk Talk's *Spirit of Eden*, an album about the quietude of space between sound. He talks of keyboards and strings with John Robinson of the Fluid, of collaborating with Mark Lanegan, of working with Michael Stipe of R.E.M., of getting off the road.

Though things at home are hardly serene. Despite the safe haven the Cobains have moved into overlooking Lake Washington, Kurt's increasing drug immersion, Courtney's attempts to stay clean and her frequent absences to record Hole's new album, results in police calls, overdoses, confiscated guns, "domestic violence." When Frances Bean enters the world in August 1992, Mom and Dad's beaming joy playing with her in the bathtub gives hope that they might prove a paranormal family, something like the Addams.

He can't get out of an upcoming European tour that opens in Portugal on February 6, 1994. By the time they arrive in Paris only eight days a week in, Kurt takes refuge at photographer Youri Lenquette's studio, refusing to answer calls. Showtime at the Zenith draws near. He doesn't want to go. They talk of visiting Cambodia, and Youri, who has befriended the band since their first French visit, takes a few pictures. In one Kurt picks up a prop pistol, mimes putting it to his temple, snaps his head back in recoil. Finally Youri convinces him to get on the back of his motorbike and drops him at the Zenith as the first song begins. He remembers it as the best Nirvana he ever saw.

The Melvins' arrival to open Italian and German dates doesn't lighten Kurt's mood; it makes him miss who he thought he'd be when he first saw them eleven years ago. And he misses her. Courtney's in London, overseeing details for Hole's upcoming album, *Live Through This*, scheduled for early spring. Ever the romantic, aware they need reconciliation, Kurt plans a hearts-and-flowers reunion in Rome when the tour takes a break. But when she flies in on March 3, they have no time to even get used to each other. There is champagne, roses, gifts of a chunk of the Colosseum, a rosary from the Vatican, and the date-rape drug Rohypnol, of which more than fifty doses find their way into Kurt's aching stomach by early morning. Downhill from there.

Even as his demise is trumpeted on CNN, he rises from the

dead, requesting a strawberry milk shake, corroborating the official explanation that it's accidental. On purpose. Those within Nirvana's inner circle know otherwise. The expected intervention is staged, where all participants blame each other, not untrue, which only hardens Kurt's resolve to get more fucked up, to feel manipulated, persecuted, to take refuge in annihilation. He spends long nights on the nod in cheap north-side Seattle motels, avoiding decisions about keeping Nirvana together, fulfilling commitments like the upcoming Lollapalooza of which he will be trophy-headliner, of the realization that his band's name has resulted in the opposite afterlife. He's in hell.

Courtney, though dealing with her own drug inducements and scattershot sound bites, the tawdry headlines, judgmental naysayers, the perception of her as Lucy to Desi (or worse, Nancy to Sid), proves of sterner resolve. Hole's *Live Through This* is ruthless in its expiation of female anger, Medea with an electric guitar, screed through Nirvana's melodic aggrieved pop-ism. As a woman she wants to be viewed *whole*, not a collection of "Doll Parts." She wants "the most cake," and why not? She wants male privilege, retaining the freedom to wear a baby doll dress and not be pawed over, even though she truth-or-dares when she leaps into the audience and returns to the stage in tatters. Want: and you shall get. "Asking for It," but *did she ask you twice?*

It's an album made for blasting in the car for women on the way to the grind of daily work, readying for confrontation. *You should learn how to say no!* Courtney enrages, the vitriol of "Violet," birthright claimed much as she birthed Frances Bean, because "I wanted his beautiful genes in there, in that child." She's not Kurt, who is weakening, *a denial,* and won't live to see *Live Through This* released in the second week of April.

||||||

TRAPPED. HIS ADDICTION, MARRIAGE DISINTEGRATING, pain radiating from his belly, responsibilities of fatherhood, enormous global infamy. He wants out.

Kurt knows far too well how his broken childhood family stranded him between warring parents. Now he's about to replay asunder. He has taken Nirvana as far as he is able, pro forma guitar destruction at show's end, the carnal love of the audience, their ravenous need so like dope-sick. Now it's his turn to enact sacrifice, a shattered instrument against the amplifier, feedback piercing his torso like St. Sebastian's arrows. The love bite of the syringe, shotgun at the ready. "All Apologies": *I wish I was like you / Easily amused . . .*

Would he really want that? To not go as far as ordained, unable to separate from the character you invent to entertain? Artists try to balance expression and corrosive need. Others run out of psychic room. On April 5, 1994, Kurt obliterates his self-creation, surrendering to the torments with which he began.

Layne follows him eight years later to the day, a wraith holed up in his apartment, a hollow shell unrecognizable to his friends. Chris Cornell hangs himself in 2017 after a Soundgarden show in Detroit, the farewell song Led Zeppelin's "In My Time of Dying" still echoing in the Fox Theater. Even Scott Weiland of Stone Temple Pilots does the grunge-ish thing, succumbing on his tour bus in 2014. It hardly shocks. What isn't all too clear in *Superunknown*'s "Like Suicide," in Alice in Chains' *I want you to kill me . . . I wanna live no more*, in Nirvana's funerary florals decorating the set of *Unplugged*?

It doesn't have to be that way. Pearl Jam soldiers on, Eddie Vedder always up to lend support for a righteous cause, a succession of albums that heighten the human condition, taking on Ticketmaster, reaching out to fans, their own channel on the Sirius satellite, choosing life. May it be long and fruitful.

||||||

OUR SHOW CANCELED, the night suddenly free. Portent in the air, seasoned with dread. I'm in Seattle, near Pike Market with its glow-in-the-dark Ferris wheel, on First Avenue, in a dive down the street and down the stairs called Screwdriver. It used to be a recording studio, the owner Chris tells me. I ask for red beer—*Mt. Rainier* with a shot of tomato juice—and he shows me a back room where there's a stage. Sometimes you like to bang a guitar for the hell of it, the enhancement of drinks on the house. Never know what will happen. So random anything can.

I've reached the point in the chapter where Pearl Jam begins work on *Ten*, Eddie sleeping on the floor of the studio to comprehend his voice, that summer when it all becomes entangled. Halfway there. Afterward the successful bands detach from Seattle on their way to world renown; for many, a tale edged in tragedy. They leave behind locals, this should-be star, this fallen angel, this musician holding on because that's what he or she does. There is writ self-destruction to come, but at the moment all is awash in hope, as the incoming meteor approaches.

The streets are quiet, in this wary time. Occasional car, wind spitting up from the Sound, a city tucked in for the night. Entertainment, increasingly streaming, hives the virtual world. Sports events, live concerts, political demonstrations acclimate to television's slo-mo replay, the crowd a studio prop, applause on cue, camera-ready. Soon we'll each be hooked into the world teleprompter, isolated, confined to quarters. That's why tonight seems the right place to be. Out in a crowd. The pestilence not yet fully arrived, though advancing. Might as well turn up.

I know how the story reveals, though I haven't yet written the finale. I'd wanted to play "With Yo' Heart Not Yo' Hands" for closure at our Paramount show, to salute Andrew Wood and those who come after, and before, the Paramount the first place we played in Seattle back in 1978. The world in free fall, out of our hands but not our hearts.

The band learned the Malfunkshun song in soundcheck at the Fillmore two days ago, and it sounded massive, as Andrew might've appreciated, ready for the rafters. If I can't launch it at the Paramount, well, there's a rock den somewhere. This one's within walking distance, jukebox, 45 inserts in the bar top, room enough to keep intimate, framed pictures of Chris Cornell and Johnny Ramone, kind of like what Squid Row must have been like on an accidental Wednesday. Which this is. I was leaning on the bar the night before when news that Seattle had been shut down was made real. Past the witching hour when I join two or three bands, dance to "White Wedding," open to suggestion. A place to play. One more night as a musician. Sure.

I'm wearing an H-bar-C shirt embroidered with guitars, gifted to me an hour before by our tour manager whose name is also Andrew, *Nuggets* spun by the deejays before I hit the stage, and El Vez opens up. El perfecto. Start with "Love of the Common People," end with "Gloria," everything in between. I think of Landrew in this moment when elbows replace handshakes: the uncanny prophecy of "With Yo' Heart Not Yo' Hands." Nobody knows where it's going. Let's live in the now. The present, how we experience music, played or received.

This moment, this place. It's all we have.

AFTERMATH

Rock 'n roll will always be
It'll go down in history

—DANNY AND THE JUNIORS

A MUSICAL LIFETIME.

At this fifth of century, the rock and the roll that granted me revelation has now become classic, vintage, a golden oldie (but goodie). New sounds abound, and though *it will never die*, there is that moment when innovation makes way for interpretation, when a music outlives itself.

This doesn't mean rock is dead. Far from it. It now assumes its hallowed place among the many ways musical invention can be subdivided and explored, be it romantic piano music of the nineteenth century, dixieland *jass* of the early twentieth, big band swing or doo-wop vocal harmony, blues of every shade, any of the endless permutations that slice EDM into its component bpm's. In this moment of rock's twilight gleaming, we still reside in the *saeculum*, the time span invented by the Etruscans to demarcate those who experience events firsthand, bearing ear- and eyewitness. When the last rocker has gone to Valhalla, all we'll have left is hearsay, a guitar left leaning against the amplifier shrieking as the band leaves the stage, the recorded hieroglyphic, the memory motel. Today we can see the Rolling Stones in a stadium, Bob Dylan at the Beacon, Mötley and Def, the Cure and Polly Harvey and My Bloody Valentine, or any number of survivors at Doc Ike's Ponderosa Stomp (Irma Thomas I love you). The Hall of Fame holds their artifacts, as befits a museum; but there's nothing like the provenance of history in the making, living to tell the tale.

I was in the audience for Little Anthony and the Imperials, Jimi Hendrix, Big Brother and the Holding Company with Janis, my homegrown New York Dolls and Ramones, along with some nondescript band who broke up as soon as their first show was over, never to be heard from again. I time-traveled back and forth as a record collector, the joy of tangent and obscurity, filling interstices in my musical acumen. What I didn't bank on is that this immersion would prove endlessly fascinating; that no matter how much I absorbed and investigated, there was evermore.

In part this tour guide charts my personal journey of discovery, by its nature hardly inclusive, filtered through inclinations and the musician I was able to become within my shortcomings and strengths, the role models I emulated, the guitar-bass-drums combo that was my chosen mode of presentation. Or did it choose me as a teenager in the 1960s when I learned my first chord and had a ready-made music to try it out on? Even at this juncture when the guitar itself seems a reliquary, when it doesn't appear as if there's anything left that hasn't already been done twice, the instrument's versatility, portability, and ten-minute learning curve to play three chords will ensure its entry-level immediacy and longevity. And then you have a lifetime to figure yourself out. Just like rock and roll.

||||||

CAN THERE BE SUCH A thing as time-bound geography when cyber-technology erases national borders and enables algorithmic (and algomelodic) ease of listening? It is no coincidence that *Lightning Striking* ends on the cusp of a web-o-net (thank you Phast Phreddie) rewiring neural connectives, our circuit board of reception. If one of the pleasures investigating *scenius* is how they spring unbidden, taking their sweet time to find how to unfold before presenting breakthrough to an awaiting universe-at-large, does this still hold true in a world of immediate gratuity, replacing regional with global hegemony? Piped into cafes, pumped on dance floors, caught as snippets from passing cars and underscoring commercials, available with a whisk of a finger on a computer key, the present-tense pop mart seems monocultural, a soupçon of synthesized hooks and beats grazing a buffet of hip-hop, Latin trap, country, K-pop and emo and something called poprock, auto-tuned and designed for spectacle, crossbreeding despite niches that define format. Rock-based music might own a portion of the bandwidth, sometimes utilized more as a ringtone of "rock" as lifestyle than actual foundation, but increasingly we tune our dial to the same space station revolving around a planetary orb. Wherever you travel, the soundtrack familiarizes, modern pop's revenge and glory.

Don't get me wrong. I love pop music, happily stream my favorite anthem-of-the-moment, the chorus I can't stop singing. Today I've Shazamed Tove Lo's "Habits (Stay High)." It got me. Tomorrow my wandering will alight somewhere else. Means of dissemination escalate, the Tikking Tok that now renders the methodology of chronicling an artist through album release increasingly outmoded, the ubiquity of streaming and endless remixes altering and fragmenting the concept of a standalone hit. I have no wish to turn the clock back, little nostalgia for when guitars ruled the world, though I've learned how to play one. Each generation chooses their channeling, the instruments to express it, what they look for in a song, which is, despite sea changes in style, remarkably similar from era to era, addressing basic human needs and joys and moral crises up for grabs. I experience the future's greatest hits, maybe even grab a stray lick and figure how to make it mine. But I know where I live, how to find my way home.

Rock—that "dark, sexy, dangerous, radical music," as Amanda Petrusich depicts in her *New Yorker* profile of Iggy Pop, the perfect Pan—might domesticate (*I wanna be your dog . . . lay right down in my favorite place*), but its cornerstone remains constant. "People say rock 'n' roll changes," *philosophe* Todd Snider notes, "but it does not. It is antihatred, antiwar, prolove, and profreedom—not democracy, necessarily," he adds, "but freedom."

|||||

I NEVER THOUGHT IT WOULD turn out like this.

Traversing the world with my one-pickup Stratocaster (the middle), unlocking how records are made, and unmade, seeing tendrils of influence flow from work I've done as I was guided by those who pointed me in a right or wrong direction, then left me to figure it out on my own: I couldn't ask for more.

If I'd have known that more than five decades later I'd still be playing, a too-perfect word capturing the quality time spent translating an instrument's second language, I'd have learned to read music. Applied myself more diligently to scales and modes. Theorized, memorized, gotten my shit together. Not be lazy, or shy, or full of myself, wary of stepping too close to the edge or not far enough.

You learn what you need to know. There's no tougher sensei than yourself. It's like reading backward in a mirror, understanding in reverse, so by the time you get to the end of the song or the show you've unraveled the music, not just as performer, but listener and appreciator, *back atcha*. Hand in hand. *It takes two to tangle*, as Patti sings.

I have my rituals, sound-check fiddling with dials, how the guitar meets the stage, pretending I'm rehearsing the set though I usually wind up playing anything but what I'm supposed to. It helps to know where you're going, but too well and there's no out-on-a-limb sway, ominous cracking, what happens when it breaks. I was shown the bent knee as a record producer, rife with big ideas, and then realized the speakers were telling me what the artist needs. Mostly faith, understanding, a sense of humor. You never know where curiosity leads, but each song has its own motivation of who it wills itself to be, as does the audience.

People think it's reveling in the crowd's pleasure, the hand-claps and catcalls for a favored b-side, as well as getting paid at the end of the night. I do like to get paid because I am a professional, a third-generation member of Local 802 AFM, though my motto is *if I play for free I play for me*. When the crowd yells enough that I don't feel alone, when we're having a wild togetherness, when *it's the late show always the great show*, that's where the *when* kicks in.

It's easy to unbalance. Space and time, sex and drugs; rock and roll squared. I can't say I'm immune to temptation, around since the seductive lure of the Sirens. But to steer clear of ship-wreck, lashed to the mast like Odysseus, is a reminder to keep my eyes on destination, to turn their song into a repeat chorus, to realize that no matter how long the party goes on and on, you have to head home and do your work. My motivational speech.

To be there, not admire there. That's the trickster of music.

Before 100,000 festival goers at Glastonbury when the Dalai Lama comes onstage to be sung happy birthday and drapes a white silk scarf around my neck; looking out at Carnegie Hall or Central Park or the mountains of Fuji Rock; or twenty hardy late-nighters at Tom Clark's Treehouse on Avenue A, making it up as we go along. It doesn't matter. To send one's song into the cosmos, to experience music in the instant it is made. That's why I do it.

It is my blessing to wake each morning with music on my mind. To listen to the last record I bought, follow a tributary to its source, to sit at the *qwertyuiop* and fold that experience into words. To turn on the radio and spin the dial until something strikes my fancy, tune my guitar to see what magically appears 'neath my fingers, to imagine the song that has wiggled into my subconscious and bring it to the surface, one chord at a time.

To be music. What I do. Do be do be do.

ACKNOWLEDGMENTS

TO TRY AND SUM DEBTS OWED, ENCOURAGEMENTS AND guiding lights and the guitar-of-plenty that music has granted me over a lifeline, would prove a living diary of who I've listened to, who I talked about it with, who pointed me in a direction or showed me insight, a new chord, a key to find the root note of a song.

When I'm on the road I gravitate to the local record or book shop. I learned behind-the-counter lingo (*these records ain't getting younger!*) apprenticing at Village Oldies on Bleecker Street in the West Village in the early seventies, under the demanding and discerning ears of Bleecker Bob and Broadway Al. These days, when I need a record, I stop by my local, the Main Street Jukebox, and have Tom LeFevre and Charley Pishnick extricate it from the stacks, along with accompanying backstory. I have my favorite haunts—in Brussels, Amsterdam, Los Angeles (let's hear it for Amoeba), and whatever I randomly unearth at a neighborhood garage sale. You never know.

This book grew from an idea that my agent, Betsy Lerner, agreed upon one winter lunch about seven years ago. Publisher Daniel Halpern overheard a conversation I was having with someone who asked what I was up to, and brought it to Ecco, an act of faith that sustained me over many deadlines. There is no wine before its time, as Orson Welles once said. In England, Lee Brackstone contributed his voluminous and caring musical acumen to shepherd the book in both minutiae and expanse for his imprint White Rabbit. Gabriella Doob guided the manuscript through its transformation into an actual volume. Karen Pals unknotted the half-hitches of lyric permissions. Steven Sebring and Dawn Linden visualized my respective covers, capturing that moment of psychic transformation when a guitar takes on a life of its own. Alec Paleo helped curate an off-the-beaten-path double-CD soundtrack, now available on Ace Records. Tony Shanahan produced the audiobook, and has been my band brother for over thirty years. Those I have shared musical moments with—Joe Garthe in the Vandals; Jon "Bug" Eilenberg in the Zoo; The Connection (Dave Donen, C.P. Roth, Paul Dugan); the Jim Carroll Band; and of course Jay Dee and Jackson and always Patti, not to mention that random grouping whom I join for a song anywhere in the world—all have made me a "friend to music," as an astrologer once told me.

David Brendel introduced me to Brian Eno's concept of *Scenius* in a casual conversation about Lou Reed. Ned Sublette guided me through the birth pangs of New Orleans rhythm and blues, elaborating on its kinship with the Caribbean; Doc Ike Padnos brought me to the Ponderosa Stomp to wander through the Crescent City, arranging for Link Cromwell to appear at his revue of cult figures resurrected from rock and roll's primeval swamp, of which I am pleased to be a denizen. Jerry Blavat escorted me around Philadelphia's finest Italian restaurants, making me an honorary *yon teenager.* Terry Stewart—social chairman of a Rutgers fraternity I played in college days, paying my band an extra twenty-five dollars if we didn't take a break for four hours because they were going on probation, later to head the Rock and Roll Hall of Fame—lent his expertise and have-you-heard-this guidance; Andy Leach of the Rock and Roll Hall of Fame Library provided access to their collection of *Mersey Beat* and the opportunity to wander within their serendipitous archives.

Family is forever: Anna, Frank III, Stephanie, Jude, and Linda. And the musician-friends who inspire me to write a song each time I see them perform: Tom Clark, Kevn Kinney, Alejandro Escovedo, Dave Pirner. So I will.

LYRIC PERMISSIONS

Inc. and Kusada Music. All Rights Reserved. Used by Permission. All rights for Trio Music Company administered by BMG Rights Management (US) LLC. Reprinted by permission of Hal Leonard LLC. All rights on behalf of itself and Little Guy Music administered by Fort Knox Music, Inc. Used by Permission of Alfred Music.

"1969"

Written by Dave Alexander, Scott Asheton, Ronald Asheton, and James Osterberg © 1969 (Renewed) BMG Bumblebee, Warner-Tamerlane Publishing Corp. and Stooge-Staffel. All Rights Reserved. Used by Permission.

All rights for BMG Bumblebee administered by BMG Rights Management (US) LLC. Reprinted by permission of Hal Leonard LLC. All rights on behalf of itself and Stooge-Staffel administered by Warner-Tamerlane Publishing Corp. Used by Permission of Alfred Music.

"(WHITE MAN) IN HAMMERSMITH PALAIS"

Words and Music by Joe Strummer, Mick Jones, Paul Simonon, and Topper Headon © 1979 Nineden Ltd. All Rights Reserved. Used by Permission. All rights in the U.S. and Canada controlled and administered by Universal-PolyGram International Publishing, Inc. Reprinted by permission of Hal Leonard LLC

"OVERBLOWN"

Written by Steven Turner, Matthew Lukin, Daniel Peters, and Mark Arm © 1992 Better Than Your Music.

"ROCK AND ROLL IS HERE TO STAY"

Words and Music by David White © 1957 One Song Publishing © 1958 (Renewed 1986) One Song Publishing, and Sandra White. All Rights Reserved. Used by Permission. All rights administered by BMG Rights Management (US) LLC. Reprinted by permission of Hal Leonard LLC

SELECTED BIBLIO-DISCOGRAPHY

THERE WAS A TIME WHEN INFORMATION ABOUT ROCK and its many varietals was hard to come by, the province of dedicated archeologists and keepers of the flame, unearthed in yellowing trade magazines and fan journals, word-of-mouth discoveries passed among collectors like a secret handshake, records excavated and discographies enumerated, each puzzle piece revealing musical fixation and fascination. No longer: anyone with an inclination to slide down the rabbit hole of serendipity, amuse ad infinitum, is now a particle of global cyber-community that connects our obsessions, frames the music we listen to wherever our fancy takes us, overwhelms us with tangent and obscurity.

The immersion of *Lightning Striking*, spending time in each city as if I'd moved into an unfurnished room a block or two from where it was all ongoing, where I could hear the echo of crowd noise and bass drum in the night, the reverberation of song, reflects these sources. Eyewitness accounts, interviews, snapshots, moving images, the almighty recorded artifact; all guided me in navigating the inner circles of these legendary scenes.

Yeah, I had a good tour. Can't wait to get out on the road again.

MEMPHIS 1954

Bonomo, Joe. *Jerry Lee Lewis Lost and Found* (Continuum, New York, 2009).

Bragg, Rick. *Jerry Lee Lewis: His Own Story* (Harper, New York, 2014).

Broven, John. *Record Makers and Breakers: Voices of the Independent Rock 'n' Roll Pioneers* (University of Illinois Press, Urbana, 2009).

Cohen, Rich. *The Record Men: The Chess Brothers and the Birth of Rock & Roll* (W. W. Norton, New York, 2004).

Escott, Colin, and Martin Hawkins. *Catalyst: The Sun Records Story* (Aquarius, London, 1975).

———. *The Complete Sun Label Session Files (Revised)* (Martin Hawkins, 1975).

———. *Good Rockin' Tonight: Sun Records and The Birth of Rock 'n' Roll* (St. Martin's Press, New York, 1991).

Guralnick, Peter. *Last Train to Memphis: The Rise of Elvis Presley* (Little, Brown and Company, Boston, 1994).

———. *Sam Phillips: The Man Who Invented Rock 'n' Roll* (Little, Brown and Company, New York, 2015).

Heatley, Michael. "Solar Power." *Vintage Rock*, Summer 2013.

Hopkins, Jerry. *Elvis: A Biography* (Simon & Schuster, New York, 1971).

Kaye, Lenny. "The Very Large Legend of Carl Perkins." *Guitar World*, July 1982.

Kienzle, Rich. "The Electric Guitar in Country Music: Its Evolution and Development." *Guitar Player*, November 1979.

Lauterbach, Frank. *The Chitlin' Circuit and the Road to Rock 'n' Roll* (W. W. Norton, New York, 2011).

———. *Beale Street Dynasty: Sex, Song, and the Struggle for the Soul of Memphis* (W. W. Norton, New York, 2015).

Marcus, Greil. *Mystery Train: Images of America in Rock 'n' Roll Music* (E. P. Dutton, New York, 1976).

Menand, Louis. "The Elphic Oracle." *New Yorker*, August 27, 2016.

Moore, Scotty, and James L. Dickerson. *Scotty & Elvis: Aboard the Mystery Train* (University Press of Mississippi, Jackson, 2013).

Nash, Alanna. *The Colonel: The Extraordinary Story of Colonel Tom Parker and Elvis Presley* (Simon & Schuster, New York, 2003).

Olsson, Bengt. *Memphis Blues* (Studio Vista, London, 1970).

Palmer, Robert. *Deep Blues* (Viking Press, New York, 1981).

———. *Jerry Lee Lewis ROCKS!* (Delilah, New York, 1981).

Penman, Ian. "Shapeshifter." *London Review of Books*, September 25, 2014.

Russell, Tony. *Blacks, Whites and Blues* (Stein & Day, New York, 1970).

Strausbaugh, John. *Reflections on the Birth of the Elvis Faith* (Blast Books, New York, 1995).

Tolinski, Brad, and Alan Di Perna. *Play It Loud: An Epic History of the Style, Sound, and Evolution of the Electric Guitar* (Doubleday, New York, 2016).

Tosches, Nick. *Hellfire: The Jerry Lee Lewis Story* (Penguin, New York, 1982).

———. *Unsung Heroes of Rock 'n' Roll: The Birth of Rock in the Wild Years Before Elvis* (Harmony, New York, 1991).

Vernon, Paul. *The Sun Legend* (London, 1969).

|||||

Cash, Johnny. *Now Here's Johnny Cash* (Sun 1255; LP).

Lewis, Jerry Lee. *I Am What I Am*, directed by Mark Hall (White Star, 1987; DVD).

———. *Jerry Lee's Greatest!* (Sun 1265; LP).

Orbison, Roy. *At the Rock House* (Sun 1260; LP).

Perkins, Carl. *Teen Beat* (Sun 1225, LP).

Presley, Elvis. *Elvis at Sun* (RCA/BMG 82876 61205; 2 CD).

———. *Prince from Another Planet (As Recorded at Madison Square Garden)* (RCA/Legacy, 88691953882; 2 CDs, 1 DVD).

———. *Way Down in the Jungle Room* (RCA/Legacy 88985318102; 2 CD).

Prisonaires. *Five Beats Behind Bars* (Charly CR30176; LP).

Various Artists. *Sun Records: The 50th Anniversary Collection* (BMG/Heritage 74465 99000; 2 CD).

———. *Sun Rockabillys Vols. 1–3* (Sun 6467 025, 027, 028; LP).

———. *The Sun Story 1952–1968* (Sun 6641–180; 2 LP).

———. *The Sun Blues Box: Blues, R&B And Gospel Music in Memphis 1950–1958* (Bear Family, ECD 17310 JK; 10 CD).

———. *Memphis Blues at Sunshine* (Redita 105; LP).

————. *Good Rockin' Tonight* (Bopcat 100; LP).

————. *Meteor: Hillbilly Bop Memphis Style* (Meteor M5000; LP).

NEW ORLEANS 1957

Asbury, Herbert. *The French Quarter* (Pocket Books, New York, 1949).

Aswell, Tom. *Louisiana Rocks! The True Genesis of Rock & Roll* (Pelican, Gretna, La., 2010)

Brothers, Thomas. *Louis Armstrong's New Orleans* (W. W. Norton, New York, 2006).

Broven, John. *Walking to New Orleans: The Story of New Orleans Rhythm & Blues* (Blues Unlimited, Bexhill-on-Sea, Essex, England, 1974).

Celestin, Ray. *The Axeman's Jazz* (Pan, London, 2014).

Charters, Samuel B. *Jazz: New Orleans 1885–1957* (Walter C. Allen, Belleville, N.J., 1958).

Coleman, Rick. *Blue Monday: Fats Domino and the Lost Dawn of Rock 'n' Roll* (Da Capo, Cambridge, Mass., 2006).

Crane, Larry. "Deke Dickerson Interview." *Tape Op* #110, November/December 2015.

Gaines, Grady, and Rod Evans. *I've Been Out There: On the Road with Legends of Rock 'n' Roll* (A&M University Press, College Station, Texas, 2015).

Gaul, Emily. "Cosimo Matassa: New Orleans R&B Recording Guru." *Goldmine* #489, April 23, 1999.

Gillespie, Dizzy, and Al Fraser. *To Be or Not to Bop* (Doubleday, New York, 1979).

Hadlock, Richard. *Jazz Masters of the 20's* (Macmillan, New York, 1965).

Hamm, Charles. *Music in the New World* (W. W. Norton, New York, 1983).

————. *Yesterdays: Popular Song in America* (W. W. Norton, New York, 1979).

Hitchcock, H. Wiley. *Music in the United States: A Historical Introduction* (Prentice-Hall, Englewood Cliffs, N.J., 1988).

Krist, Gary. *Empire of Sin* (Crown, New York, 2014).

Lauterbach, Preston. *The Chitlin' Circuit and the Road to Rock 'n' Roll* (W. W. Norton, 2011).

Lawrence, Vera Brodsky. *Strong on Music: The New York Music Scene in the Days of George Templeton Strong.* Vol. 2 *(Reverberations 1850–1856)*; Vol. 3 *(Repercussions 1857–1862)* (University of Chicago Press, 1995, 1999)

Lomax, Alan. *Mister Jelly Roll* (Cassell, 1950).

Mass, Dominic. *New Orleans Radio* (Arcadia, Charleston, S.C., 2014).

Palmer, Robert. *Deep Blues* (Viking, New York, 1981).

Rotante, Anthony et al. "Imperial Discography." *Record Research* 215/16–253/54 (July 1985–January 1995).

Scherman, Tony. *Backbeat: Earl Palmer's Story* (Da Capo, Cambridge, Mass., 2000).

Schumacher, Craig, and Roger King. "Cosimo Matassa Interview." *Tape Op* #40, March/April 2004.

Spera, Keith. "Frankie Ford, New Orleans Singer of 'Sea Cruise' Fame, dies At 76." *Times-Picayune*, September 30, 2015.

Sublette, Ned. *The World That Made New Orleans* (Lawrence Hill, Chicago, 2009).

White, Charles. *The Life and Times of Little Richard* (Da Capo, Cambridge, MA, 1994).

Williams, Martin. *Jazz Masters of New Orleans* (Macmillan, New York, 1967).

Wirt, John. *Huey "Piano" Smith and the Rocking Pneumonia Blues* (Louisiana State University Press, Baton Rouge, 2014).

Zolten, Jerry. "Interview with Art Rupe." October 11, 2011.

||||||

Archibald. *The Complete New Orleans Sessions 1950–1952* (Krazy Kat KK7409; LP).

Brown, Roy. *Good Rocking Tonight* (Route 66 KIX-6; LP).

DeVille, Willy. *In New Orleans* (Big Beat CDWIKD 295; CD).

Domino, Fats. *Legendary Masters Series* (United Artists S-9958; 2 LP).

Little Richard. *Every Hour with Little Richard* (RCA Camden 2430(e); LP)

———. *His Biggest Hits* (Specialty SP 2111; LP).

Professor Longhair. *Singles 1949–1957* (Floating World M6174; CD).

———. *New Orleans Piano* (Atlantic Jazz 7225-2; CD)

Smith, Huey "Piano," and the Clowns. *Having a Good Time* (Ace 1004; LP).

———. *'Twas the Night Before Christmas* (Ace 1027; LP)

Various Artists. *Clap Your Hands and Stomp Your Feet* (Imperial Records 1949–1957; EMI-America ST-17200; LP).

———. *Cosimo Matassa Story* (Proper 129; 4 CD).

———. *Cosimo Matassa Story: Gumbo Ya-Ya Vol. 2* (Proper 174; 2 CD).

———. *Crescent City Bounce* (JSP 7792; 4 CD).

———. *Hitsville, U.S.A.* (Imperial 9084; LP).

———. *Hitsville,* Vol. 2 (Imperial 9099; LP).

———. *New Orleans Rhythm & Blues 1955–1962* (Rhythm and Blues RANDB032; 6 CD).

———. *New Orleans Rock & Roll & R & B* (Rarin'; LP).

———. *Rhythm 'n' Blues: The End of an Era* (Imperial LM-940 03; LP).

———. *Rhythm 'n' Blues: Sweet and Greasy,* Vol. 2 (Imperial LM-94005; LP).

———. *The New Orleans Sessions 1950* (Bear Family BFD 15308; 2 LP).

———. *Urban Blues: New Orleans Bounce,* Vol. 2 (Imperial LM-94004; LP).

———. *Walking to New Orleans: A History of the Crescent City Piano Pioneers* (Proper 185; 4 CD).

||||||

Hannusch, Jeff. "The South's Swankiest Night Spot: The Legend of the Dew Drop Inn," Louisiana Music Archive, http://www.satchmo.com/ikoiko/dewdropinn.html.

Mabry, Donald J. "Rock 'n Roll: An Interview with Johnny Vincent of Ace Records," http://historicaltextarchive.com/sections.php?action=read&artid=174.

www.cosimocode.com.

www.offbeat.com/articles/jm-studio-house-of-rock/.

www.knowla.org/entry/1096.

www.motherjones.com/mixed-media/2011/04/stack-o-lee-stagolee-blues-murder-ballads.

PHILADELPHIA 1959

Blavat, Jerry. *You Only Rock Once* (Running Press, Philadelphia/London, 2011).

Blitz, Stanley J., and John Pritchard. *Bandstand: The Untold Story* (Cornucopia, Phoenix, Ariz., 1997).

Clark, Dick, and Richard Robinson. *Rock, Roll & Remember* (Thomas Y. Crowell, New York, 1976).

Cole, Clay. *Sh-Boom: The Explosion of Rock 'N' Roll 1953–1968* (Morgan James, New York, 2009).

Delmont, Matthew F. *The Nicest Kids in Town: American Bandstand, Rock 'n' Roll, and the Struggle for Civil Rights in 1950s Philadelphia* (University of California Press, Berkeley, 2012).

"Dick Clark Denies Receiving Payola; Panel Skeptical." *New York Times*, April 30, 1960.

Jackson, John A. *American Bandstand: Dick Clark and the Making of a Rock 'n' Roll Empire* (Oxford University Press, New York 1997).

|||||

Avalon, Frankie. *Swingin' on a Rainbow* (Chancellor CHLX 5004; LP).

Blavat, Jerry. *TV Song Storybook* (C-101; LP).

Cannon, Freddy. *Solid Gold Hits* (Swan 505; LP).

The Castelles. *The Best of . . . Featuring George Grant* (Grand 1000; LP).

Fabian. *The Fabulous* (Chancellor CHLX 5005; LP).

Various Artists. *The Best of Grand Records* (Collectables 6004; LP).

———. *Dick Clark 20 Years of Rock N' Roll* (Buddah 5133–2; 2 LP).

———. *The American Dream: The Cameo-Parkway Story 1957–1962* (London DA-161/162: 2 LP).

|||||

http://flavorwire.com/421925/controversial-teen-dance-crazes-that-pissed-off-parents-throughout-history.

http://whenwordsmatter.typepad.com/bandstand_beat/.

https://www.youtube.com/watch?v=im9XuJJXylw.

The Twist/Chubby Checker, https://www.youtube.com/watch?v=Ij JJQW0vK_c

Fabian wedding video, https://www.youtube.com/watch?v=mQLT my3YYC8.

Fabian live 1959, https://www.youtube.com/watch?v=fDFHvoEaziE.

Fabian manufactured idol, https://www.youtube.com/watch?v=35D QZgLUYJk.

Bobby Rydell on *Philly Factor.* https://www.youtube.com/watch?v =35DQZgLUYJk

LIVERPOOL 1962

Burns, Julie. "Rocking Up a Storm." *Vintage Rock: The Beatles: The Early Years* (Anthem, London, 2017).

Clews, Frank. *Teenage Idols* (Brown, Watson, London, 1962).

Cohn, Nik. *Rock from the Beginning* (Pocket Books, New York, 1970).

Davies, Hunter. *The Beatles* (Dell, New York, 1969).

Epstein, Brian. *A Cellarful of Noise* (Doubleday, New York, 1964).

Harry, Bill, ed. *Mersey Beat: The Beginnings of the Beatles* (Quick Fox, New York, 1977).

———. *Mersey Beat*, various issues, 1961–64.

Kozinn, Allan. *The Beatles* (Phaidon, London, 1995).

Leigh, Spencer. *The Cavern Club: Rise of the Beatles and Merseybeat* (McNidder & Grace, Carmarthen, UK, 2016).

Mankowitz, Wolf. *Expresso Bongo: A Wolf Mankowitz Reader* (Thomas Yoseloff, London, 1961).

Miles, Barry. *The Beatles Diary,* Volume 1: *The Beatles Years* (Omnibus, London, 2001).

Pop Weekly, various issues (first and second series 1962–64).

Repsch, John, *The Legendary Joe Meek* (Woodford House, London, 1989)

Shepherd, Billy, *The True Story of the Beatles* (Bantam, New York, 1964)

||||||

Beatles, *The Decca Tapes* (DOL 930HG, LP).

———. *Live! At the Star Club in Hamburg, Germany*, 1962 (Bellaphon BLS 5560; 2 LP).

———. *Please Please Me* (Parlophone PMC 1202; LP).

———. *With the Beatles* (Parlophone PMC 1206; LP).

———. *The Savage Young Beatles* (Savage BM 69; LP).

Big Three. *At the Cavern* (Decca DFE 8552, EP).

Honeycombs. *The Honeycombs* (Repertoire RR 4098 WZ; CD).

Meek, Joe. *I Hear a New World* (RPM 103; CD).

Various Artists. *Britain Learns to Rock*, compiled by Bob Stanley (Ace FVC0005; CD).

———. *The Beat Merchants: British Beat Groups 1963–1964* (UA UDM 101/2; 2 LP).

———. *Mersey Beat* (E.M.I. PCSP 1783293; 2 LP).

———. *Mersey Beat '62–'64: The Sound of Liverpool* (United Artists USD305/6; 2 LP).

———. *The Joe Meek Story*, Vol. 1: *1960* (Triumph TRCD 9.01081; CD).

———. *The Joe Meek Story: The Pye Years* (Sequel NED CD 171; 2 CD).

———. *Recorded Live at the Cavern* (Decca BLK 16294-P; LP).

———. *The Weekend Starts Here* (Big Beat WIKA 48; LP).

———. *The Exciting New Liverpool Sound* (Columbia CL 2172; LP).

||||||

Kaye, Lenny. "Joe Meek: The Meek Shall Inherit the Stars." http://www.emusic.com/features/spotlight/277_200609.html.

http://www.triumphpc.com/mersey-beat/birth/.

http://www.merseybeatnostalgia.co.uk.

http://www.rockhistory.co.uk/cd-parnes-shillings-pence/.

Wilde, Marty. *Juke Box Heroes BBC Television*, https://www.youtube.com/watch?v=ebl5tWv796g.

Rory Storm and the Hurricanes, a documentary, ttps://www.youtube.com/watch?v=1iuvv828F5I

Donegan, Lonnie. "Cumberland Gap." https://www.youtube.com /watch?v=GynnhBUOHkg

SAN FRANCISCO 1967

Anthony, Gene. *The Summer of Love: Haight-Ashbury at Its Highest* (Celestial Arts, Millbrae, CA, 1980).

Bernstein, David W. ed. *The San Francisco Tape Center: 1960s Counterculture and the Avant-Garde* (University of California Press, Berkeley, 2008).

Braunstein, Peter and Michael Doyle, eds. *Imagine Nation: The American Counterculture of the 1960s & 70s* (Routledge, New York, 2002).

Chapman, Rob. *Psychedelia And Other Colours* (Faber & Faber, London, 2015).

Cohen, Allen. *The San Francisco Oracle*, Facsimile Edition 1966–68 (Regent Press, Berkeley, 1991).

Dalton, David. *Piece of My Heart: The Life, Times and Legend of Janis Joplin* (St. Martin's Press, New York, 1985).

DeRogatis, Jim. *Kaleidoscope Eyes: Psychedelic Rock from the '60s to the '90s* (Citadel Press, Secaucus, N.J., 1996).

Doukas, James N. *Electric Tibet* (Dominion, North Hollywood, 1969).

Drummond, Paul. *Eye Mind: Roky Erickson and the 13th Floor Elevators* (Process Media, Los Angeles, 2007).

Echols, Alice. *Scars of Sweet Paradise: The Life and Times of Janis Joplin* (Holt, New York, 1999).

Glatt, John. *Live at the Fillmore East & West* (Lyons Press, Guilford, Conn., 2016).

Gleason, Ralph J. *The Jefferson Airplane and the San Francisco Sound* (Ballantine, New York, 1969).

Jarnow, Jesse. *Heads: A Biography of Psychedelic America* (Da Capo, New York, 2016).

Kauppila, Paul. "The Sound of the Suburbs: A Case Study of Three Garage Bands in San Jose, California, during the 1960s." *Popular Music and Society* (2006): 391–405.

Kesey, Ken. *The Further Inquiry* (Viking, New York, 1990).

Mason, Lisa. *Summer of Love* (Bantam Spectra, New York, 1994).

Metzner, Ralph, ed. *Psychedelic Review*: issues 5 through 8 (New York, 1965–66).

McNally, Dennis, *A Long Strange Trip: The Inside History of the Grateful Dead* (Broadway, New York, 2002).

Richardson, Peter. *No Simple Highway: A Cultural History of the Grateful Dead* (St. Martin's Griffin, New York 2014).

Selvin, Joel. *Summer of Love* (Plume/Penguin, New York, 1994).

Shaw, Greg, ed. *Mojo Navigator*: issues 6 through 13 (San Francisco, 1966–67).

Walker, Cummings G. *The Great Poster Trip: Art Eureka* (Coyne and Blanchard, Palo Alto, Calif., 1969).

Wolfe, Tom. *The Electric Kool-Aid Acid Test* (Bantam, New York, 1968).

||||||

Big Brother and the Holding Company. *Big Brother and the Holding Company* (Mainstream S/6099; LP).

———. *Cheap Thrills* (Columbia KCS 9700; LP).

———. *Live California Hall 1966* (Rhino RNLP 121; LP).

———. *Ball and Chain: Live in Studio San Francisco '67* (Rhino 1411; VHS).

Charlatans. *The Amazing Charlatans* (Big Beat CDWIKD 138; CD).

Grateful Dead. *The Golden Road, Volumes 1 & 2* (Bedrock Records; 8 CD).

———. *The Golden Road* (1965–1973 (Rhino R2–74401; 10 CD).

Great Society with Grace Slick. *Conspicuous Only in Its Absence* (Columbia CS 9624; LP).

Jefferson Airplane. *Loves You* (RCA/BMG-61110–2; 3 CD).

Magic Trip. Directed by Alex Gibney & Allison Ellwood (Magnolia Home Entertainment, 2011; DVD).

Moby Grape. *Moby Grape* (Columbia CS 9498; LP).

Quicksilver Messenger Service. *Quicksilver Messenger Service* (Capitol ST 2904; LP).

———. *Happy Trails* (Capitol ST-120; LP).

Santana. *Santana* (Columbia CS 9781; LP).

Steve Miller Band. *Children of the Future* (Capitol SKAO 2920; LP).

Subotnick, Morton. *Silver Apples of the Moon* (Nonesuch H-71174; LP).

Various Artists. *Love Is the Song We Sing: San Francisco Nuggets 1965–1970* (Rhino R2 165564; 4 CD).

———. *Revolution Original Motion Picture Score* (United Artists S5185; LP).

|||||

Corry 342. "North to San Francisco: The Warlocks in the South Bay, 1965," http://lostlivedead.blogspot.com/2009/09/north-to-san-francisco-warlocks-in.html.

DETROIT 1969

|||||

Danny Says. Directed by Brendan Toller (Magnolia Home Entertainment, 2016, DVD).

Demolition Doll Rods. *Live at Fortune Records* (ProA.S.S. Records, 2005; DVD).

Frost. *Rock and Roll Music* (Vanguard VSD 6541; LP).

———. *Through the Eyes of Love* (Vanguard VSD 6556; LP).

Grand Funk Railroad. *Mark, Don & Mel 1969–71* (Capitol SABB 11042; 2 LP).

Laughing Hyenas. *Life of Crime* (Touch And Go T6061; LP).

MC5, *MC5* (Elektra EKS 74042; LP).

———. *Back in the USA* (Atlantic SD 8247; LP).

———. *High Time* (Atlantic SD 8285; LP).

———. *A True Testimonial*, directed by Dave Thomas (Avatar, unreleased).

Rationals. *The Rationals* (CGC CR 1334; LP).

Savage Grace. *Savage Grace* (Reprise 6399; LP).

SRC. *SRC* (Capitol ST2991; LP).

Stooges. *The Stooges* (Elektra EKS 74051; LP).

————. *Funhouse* (Elektra EKS-74017; LP).

————. *Live at Ungano's* (Rhino RHM2 525148; CD).

Third Power. *Believe* (Vanguard VSD 6554; LP).

Various Artists. *The Fortune Records Story* (One Day DAY3CD058; 3 CD).

————. *Michigan Rocks* (Seeds and Stems 77001; LP).

||||||

https://marshamusic.wordpress.com/page-joe-von-battle-requiem-for
-a-record-shop-man/#comment-83385.

http://www.bluffton.edu/homepages/facstaff/sullivanm/michigan
/detroit/riveramurals/north2.html.

http://www.crainsdetroit.com/article/20170618/news03/631696
/hastings-street-blues-the-economic-roots-that-contributed-to-
detroits.

http://www.thedetroiter.com/JUN03/DIGGINGMAY.html.

http://www.motorcitymusicarchives.com.

NEW YORK 1975

Antonia, Nina. *The New York Dolls: Too Much Too Soon* (Omnibus Press, London, 1998).

Blush, Steven. *New York Rock: From the Rise of the Velvet Underground to the Fall of CBGB* (St. Martin's Griffin, New York, 2016).

Bockris, Victor, and Gerard Malanga. *Up-Tight: The Velvet Underground Story* (Omnibus Press, London, 1983).

Fletcher, Tony. *All Hopped Up and Ready to Go: Music from the Streets of New York 1927–77* (W. W. Norton, New York, 2009).

Hermes, Will. *Love Goes to Buildings on Fire: Music Made New in New York City in the '70s* (Faber & Faber, New York, 2011).

Heylin, Clinton. *From the Velvets to the Voidoids: A Pre-Punk History for a Post-Punk World* (Penguin, New York, 1993).

Kasher, Steven, ed. *Max's Kansas City: Art, Glamour, Rock and Roll* (Abrams Image, New York, 2010).

Kaye, Lenny. Liner notes for *New York Dolls: Rock 'n Roll* (Polygram, 1994).

Koch, Stephen. *Star-Gazer: Andy Warhol's World and His Films* (Praeger, New York, 1973).

Kozak, Roman. *This Ain't No Disco: The Story of CBGB* (Faber & Faber, Boston, 1988).

Lloyd, Richard. *Everything Is Combustible: Television, CBGB's and Five Decades of Rock and Roll* (Beech Hill, Mount Desert Island, Maine, 2018).

Reynolds, Simon. *Shock and Awe: Glam Rock and Its Legacy* (Faber & Faber, London, 2016).

Scherman, Tony, and David Dalton. *POP: The Genius of Andy Warhol* (Harper, New York, 2009).

Smith, Patti. *Just Kids* (Ecco, New York, 2010).

———. *Witt* (Gotham Book Mart, 1973).

Stein, Seymour, and Gareth Murphy. *Siren Song: The Autobiography of America's Greatest Living Record Man* (St. Martin's Press, New York, 2018).

Waterman, Bryan. *Marquee Moon* (33 1/3 Omnibus Press, New York, 2011).

||||||

Blank Generation, directed by Ivan Kral and Amos Poe (Visual DR 4323; DVD)

Blondie. *Blondie* (Private Stock PS 2023; LP).

———. *Parallel Lines* (Chrysalis CHR 1192; LP).

Heartbreakers, *L.A.M.F.* (Track 2409–218; LP).

Richard Hell and the Voidoids. *Blank Generation* (Sire SR 6037; LP).

New York Dolls. *New York Dolls* (Mercury SRM 1–675; LP).

———. *In Too Much Too Soon* (Mercury SRM-1–1001; LP).

Ramones, *Ramones* (Sire SASD-7520).

———. *Leave Home* (Sire SA7528; LP).

Patti Smith Group. *Horses* (Arista AL 4066; LP).

———. *Radio Ethiopia* (Arista AL 4097; LP).

———. *Easter* (Arista AB4171; LP).

————. *Wave* (Arista AB 4221).

————. *Free Music Store (live WBAI, May 28,1975)* (bootleg; LP).

————. *Teenage Perversity and Ships in the Night: The Roxy, L.A., January 30, 1976* (Ze Anonym Plattenspieler ZAP 7854, bootleg; LP).

————. *Live at Max's 9/8/74*, directed by Bob Gruen (video, unreleased).

Talking Heads. *77* (Sire SR 3066; LP).

Television. *Marquee Moon* (Elektra 7E-1098; LP).

————. *Double Exposure* (Scorpio, DE-92-SC, bootleg; CD).

————. *Arrow: My Father's Place, March 20, 1978* (bootleg; LP).

Various Artists. *Blank Generation: The New York Scene 1975–78* (Rhino R2 71175; CD).

————. *Live at CBGB's* (CBGB/OMFUG 315; 2 LP).

————. *Punk Nuggets 1974–1982; Not Good for Your Health* (Rhino R1–566957; 2 LP).

————. *Max's Kansas City 1976* (Ram 1213; LP).

Velvet Underground. *Velvet Underground and Nico* (Verve V6–5008; LP).

————. *White Light White Heat* (Verve V6–5046; LP).

————. *The Velvet Underground* (Verve SE-4617; LP).

————. *Loaded* (Cotillion SD 99034).

————. *Live at Max's Kansas City* (Cotillion SD 9500; LP).

||||||

Krystal, Hilly. *History by Hilly!* http://www.cbgb.com/history-by -hilly.

LONDON 1977

Black, Johnny. "Destination Nowhere." *Mojo*, December 1996.

Coon, Caroline. *1988: The New Wave Punk Rock Explosion* (Orbach and Chambers, London, 1977).

Czezowski, Andrew, and Susan Carrington. *The Roxy: London 1976– 77: The Club That Forged Punk* (Carrczez, London, 2016).

Dalton, David. *El Sid: Saint Vicious* (St. Martin's Press, New York, 1997).

Egan, Sean, ed. *The Clash on the Clash: Interviews and Encounters* (Chicago Review Press, Chicago, 2018).

Goldman, Vivien. "Lasses of the Mohicans." *New Statesman*, October 31, 2011.

Hebdige, Dick. *Subculture: The Meaning of Style* (Methuen, London, 1979).

Heylin, Clinton. *Anarchy in the Year Zero: The Sex Pistols, the Clash, and the Class of '76* (Route, Pontefract, England, 2016).

Hibbert, Tom. "Malcolm McLaren: Pernicious? Moi?," *Q*, August 1989.

Jones, Steve. *Lonely Boy: Tales from a Sex Pistol* (Da Capo, Boston, 2017).

Murray, Charles Shaar. "The Sex Pistols, the Clash, the Buzzcocks. Screen on the Green, Islington, London," *New Musical Express*, September 11, 1976.

Nolan, David. *I Swear I Was There: Sex Pistols, Manchester and the Gig That Changed the World* (Music Press, London, 2016).

Rambali, Paul. "Clash Credibility Rule!" *New Musical Express*, October 10, 1981.

Savage, Jon. *England's Dreaming: Anarchy, Sex Pistols, Punk Rock and Beyond* (St. Martin's Press, New York, 1992).

———. "Punk Five Years On." *The Face*, November 1981.

Strongman, Phil. *Pretty Vacant: A History of UK Punk* (Chicago Review Press, Chicago, 2008).

Vermorel, Fred, and Judy Vermorel. *The Sex Pistols* (Universal, London, 1978).

Wood, Lee. *The Sex Pistols Diary: Sex Pistols Day by Day* (Omnibus, London, 1988).

||||||

Adverts. *Crossing the Red Sea with the Adverts* (Bright 201, LP).

Buzzcocks. *Singles Going Steady* (IRS SP 001; LP).

Clash. *The Clash* (Epic JE 36060; LP).

———. *Give 'Em Enough Rope* (CBS 82431; LP).

———. *London Calling* (Epic E236328; 2 LP).

————. *The Future Is Unwritten*—Joe Strummer, directed by Julien Temple (Sony Legacy; DVD).

Damned. *Damned Damned Damned* (Stiff Seez 1; LP).

Dr. Feelgood. *Down by the Jetty* (United Artists 29727; LP).

Generation X. *Generation X* (Chrysalis 1169; LP).

Jam. *In the City* (Polydor PD-1–6110; LP).

Punk Rock Movie, directed by Don Letts (Star Classics L1401; DVD).

Roots, Rock, Reggae: Inside the Jamaican Music Scene (Shanachie 1202; DVD).

Sex Pistols. *Anarchy in Sweden '77* (Gun 001, bootleg; LP).

————. *Gun Control Live at Winterland January 14, 1978* (Ruthless Rhymes Sp2900, bootleg; LP).

————. *Never Mind the Bollocks, Here's the Sex Pistols* (Virgin V2086; LP).

————. *Spunk* (Blank BLA 169, bootleg; LP).

————. *The Great Rock 'n' Roll Swindle* (Virgin 2510; 2 LP).

————. *The Filth and the Fury*, directed by Julien Temple (New Line Home Video; DVD).

————. *The Great Rock 'n' Roll Swindle*, directed by Julien Temple (Shout Factory 826663001–792; DVD).

————. *Never Mind the Bollocks, Here's the Sex Pistols*, directed by Julien Temple (Classic Albums EV300209; DVD).

Slits. *Cut* (Island ILPS 9573; LP).

Siouxsie and the Banshees. *The Scream* (Polydor 5009; LP).

————. *Once Upon a Time* (Polydor 1056; LP).

Various Artists. *The Roxy London WC2 (Jan–Apr 77)* (Harvest SHSP 4069; LP).

————. *Punky Reggae Party* (Trojan TJDDD 040; 2 CD).

Wire. *Pink Flag* (Harvest SHSP 4076; LP).

X-Ray Spex. *Germ Free Adolescents* (EMI International INBS 3023; LP).

Zukie, Tapper. *Man Ah Warrior* (Mer 101; LP).

LOS ANGELES 1984 / NORWAY 1993

Bienstock, Richard, and Joseph Bosso. "The Last Days of Hair Metal." *Guitar World*, February 2019.

Blush, Steven. *American Hair Metal* (Feral House, Los Angeles, 2006).

Campion, Chris. "In the Face of Death." *Guardian*, February 20, 2005.

Christie, Ian. *Sound of the Beast: The Complete Headbanging History of Heavy Metal* (HarperCollins, New York, 2003).

Danville, Eric. *The Official Heavy Metal Book of Lists* (Backbeat, New York, 2009).

Elliott, Paul. "Dokken: The Band That Tore Itself Apart." *Classic Rock*, November 2015.

Grow, Kory. "Mayhem's Long, Dark Road to Reviving a Black-Metal Classic." *Rolling Stone*, February 9, 2017.

Moynihan, Michael, and Didrik Soderlind. *Lords of Chaos: The Bloody Rise of the Satanic Metal Underground* (Feral House, Venice Beach, CA, 1998).

Mötley Crüe and Neil Strauss. *The Dirt: Confessions of the World's Most Notorious Rock Band* (HarperCollins, New York, 2001).

Oien, Tore. "Black Murderer Gets 14 Years!" *Kerrang!*, April 9, 1994.

Patterson, Dayal. *Black Metal: Evolution of the Cult* (Feral House, Venice Beach, CA, 2013).

Popoff, Martin. *Hair Metal: The Illustrated Oral History of Heavy Metal's Debauched Decade* (Voyageur Press, Minneapolis, 2014).

Sixx, Nikki, and Ian Gihins. *The Heroin Diaries: A Year in the Life of a Shattered Rock Star* (Gallery Books, New York, 2007).

Walser, Robert. *Running with the Devil: Power, Gender, and Madness in Heavy Metal Music* (Wesleyan University Press, Middletown, CT, 2014).

Wells, Steven. "Varg Vikernes: This Is the Most Evil Man in Rock." *New Musical Express*, September 5, 1998.

||||||

Babymetal. *Babymetal* (BMD Fox TFCC 89405; CD).

Bathory. *Under the Sign of the Black Mark* (New Renaissance 33; LP).

Burzum. *Burzum* (Deathlike Silence ANT-MOSH 002; LP).

Darkthrone. *A Blaze in the Northern Sky* (Peaceville VILE 28; LP).

Decline of Western Civilization Part II: The Metal Years, directed by Penelope Spheeris (Shout Factory 826663165555; DVD).

Dokken. *Tooth and Nail* (Elektra 60376–1; LP).

Emperor. *In the Nightside Eclipse* (Candlelight 008; CD).

Lords of Chaos. Directed by Jonas Akerlund (Gunpowder and Sky; DVD).

Mayhem. *Cursed in Eternity* (Peaceville, 4 LP).

———. *De Mysteriis Dom Sathanas* (Deathlike Silence ANTI-MOSH 006; LP).

———. *De Mysteriis Dom Sathanas Alive* (The True Mayhem MOR 001; 2 LP).

———. *Grand Declaration of War* (Season of Mist 459; LP).

———. *Pure Fucking Mayhem*, directed by Stefan Rydehed (Prophecy 0887813; DVD).

Metallica. *Master of Puppets* (Elektra 60439–1; LP).

Mötley Crüe. *Shout at the Devil* (Elektra 60289–1; LP).

———. *Theater of Pain* (Elektra 60418–1; LP).

Once Upon a Time in Norway. Directed by Martin Ledang and Pal Aasdal (Anotherworldent B001GLHS6G; DVD).

Slayer. *Reign in Blood* (Def Jam GHS 24131; LP).

Steel Panther. *Heavy Metal Rules* (Steel Panther SP002VL2; LP).

Until the Light Takes Us. Directed by Aaron Aites and Audrey Ewell (Factory 25; DVD).

Van Halen. *Van Halen* (Warner Bros. BSK 3075; LP).

Venom. *Black Metal* (NEAT 1005; LP).

SEATTLE 1991

Anderson, Kyle. *Accidental Revolution: The Story of Grunge* (St. Martin's, New York, 2007).

Azerrad, Michael. *Come as You Are: The Story of Nirvana* (Doubleday, New York, 1994).

Borzillo-Vrenna, Carrie. *Nirvana: The Day to Day Illustrated Journals* (Barnes & Noble, New York, 2000).

Cross, Charles R. *Heavier Than Heaven: A Biography of Kurt Cobain* (Hyperion, New York, 2001).

Henderson, Justin. *Grunge Seattle* (Roaring Forties, Berkeley, 2016).

Humphrey, Clark. *Loser: The Real Seattle Music Story* (MISC Media, Seattle, 2016).

Lanegan, Mark. *Sing Backwards and Weep* (White Rabbit, London, 2020).

Marin, Rick. "Lexicon of Grunge, Breaking the Code," *New York Times*, November 15, 1992.

Moran, Caitlin. "Courtney Love: Hole in One." *Melody Maker*, February 19, 1994.

Pavitt, Bruce. *Sub Pop USA: The Subterranean Pop Music Anthology 1980–1988* (Bazillion Points, 2014).

Prato, Greg. *Grunge Is Dead: The Oral History of Seattle Rock Music* (ECW, Toronto, 2009).

Segal, Dave. "Patti Smith Guitarist Lenny Kaye's Semi-Secret Gig at Belltown Yacht Club Cured the COVID-19 Blues." *Stranger*, March 13, 2020.

Thompson, Dave. *Never Fade Away: The Kurt Cobain Story* (St. Martin's Press, New York, 1994).

Tow, Stephen. *The Strangest Tribe: How a Group of Seattle Rock Bands Invented Grunge* (Sasquatch, Seattle, 2011).

True, Everett. "Sub-Pop, Seattle: Rock City." *Melody Maker*, March 18, 1989.

Yarm, Mark. *Everybody Loves Our Town: A History of Grunge* (Crown, New York, 2011).

||||||

Alice in Chains. *Dirt* (Columbia CK 52475; CD).

———. *SAP* (Columbia CK 67059; CD).

Green River. *Come On Down* (Jackpot, JPR048; LP).

Hype! Directed by Doug Pray (Shout Factory 826663178517; DVD).

Hole. *Live Through This* (DGC 24631; CD).

Mad Season. *Above* (Columbia/Legacy 88765441701S1; LP).

Malfunkshun. *Return to Olympus* (Loosegroove/Sony BK 66657; CD).

Melvins. *The Bootlicker/The Maggot* (Ipecac 213; LP).

———. *Eggnog* (Boner BR28–2; CD).

———. *Houdini* (Third Man TMR 295; LP).

———. *Stoner Witch* (Third Man TMR 296).

Mother Love Bone. *Apple* (Polydor 843 191; LP).

Nirvana. *Bleach* (Sub Pop 34; LP).

———. *In Utero* (DGC 0720642453612; LP).

———. *Insecticide* (DGC 21125; LP).

———. *Nevermind* (DGC/Sub Pop 24425; CD).

Pearl Jam. *Ten* (Epic ZK 47857; CD).

———. *Vs.* (Epic/Legacy 88697843131-jkl; LP).

———. *No Code* (Epic EK67500; CD).

Screaming Trees. *Sweet Oblivion* (Epic EK 48996; CD).

Soundgarden. *Badmotorfinger* (A&M 75021 5374 2; CD).

———. *Louder Than Love* (A&M 5252; CD).

———. *Superunknown* (A&M D102515; CD).

———. *Ultramega OK* (SST/Sub Pop 1172; LP).

TAD. *8-Way Santa* (Sub Pop SP89; LP).

———. *Busted Circuits and Ringing Ears*, directed by Adam Pease/ Ryan Short (King of Hearts; DVD).

Temple of the Dog. *Temple of the Dog* (A&M 75021; CD).

Various Artists. *Deep Six* (C/Z 01; LP).

———. *1991: The Year Punk Broke*, directed by Dave Markey (Sonic Youth SONR35; DVD).

||||||

https://www.revolutioncomeandgone.com Northwest Passage: "Deep Sixed: The Making of the First Grunge Compilation," "Reciprocal Recording: The Story of a Recording Studio."

https://www.youtube.com/watch?v=pkHu7Jec4qs; the Melvins live at Deep Six Release party March 21, 1986.

https://www.youtube.com/watch?v=3WLsMQHMfO0; Nirvana manager Danny Goldberg reflects on Kurt Cobain.

INDEX